DEVELOPMENT AND DIPLOMACY

DEVELOPMENT AND DIPLOMACY

Resetting Caribbean Policy Analysis in the Aftermath of the COVID-19 Pandemic

EDITED BY

Winston Dookeran

M. Raymond Izarali

Foreword by Sir Hilary Beckles

The University of the West Indies Press

Jamaica • Barbados • Trinidad and Tobago

The University of the West Indies Press
7A Gibraltar Hall Road, Mona
Kingston 7, Jamaica
www.uwipress.com

A catalogue record of this book is available from the National
Library of Jamaica.

ISBN: 978-976-640-935-7 (print)
978-976-640-936-4 (ePub)

Cover design by David McCartney

Printed in the United States of America

Contents

Figures

Tables

Message from The Development Bank of Latin America and the Caribbean

In November 2002, the Development Bank of Latin America and the Caribbean (CAF) presented its flagship Report on Economic Development (RED), in Port of Spain, Trinidad and Tobago, which explored key challenges related to international and intra-regional trade. I was delighted to participate in this auspicious event and to pay homage to Winston Dookeran for his vision and for guiding the then government toward taking the step to become a full member of CAF in 2012. The CAF was also proud to launch its Regional Hub for the Caribbean in Port of Spain, which is intended to strengthen our relations with current member countries and to also expand our support to all CARICOM nations, as we invite them to join our organization.

This publication, *Development and Diplomacy: Resetting Caribbean Policy Analysis in the Aftermath of the COVID-19 Pandemic*, edited by Winston Dookeran and M. Raymond Izarali is both timely and relevant, given this moment in history where countries are actively pursuing diverse strategies to recover from the myriad effects of the pandemic.

In the Preface, Winston Dookeran begins by noting that "*the COVID-19 pandemic is 'forcing a rethink in macroeconomics' and generating 'geostrategic shifts' in the world of diplomacy.*" Some of the chapters examine the underlying logic of the Lewis model of growth and point out key policy concepts such as linearity and convergence, circular economy, frontier development, competitiveness, and complexity analysis to which growth models must respond.

This publication is a bold attempt to close the gap between theory and practice, by including chapters from a wide group of scholars and practitioners, rising above the orthodoxy of development thinking, and striving to meet the challenge of relevance in development performance. The nineteen chapters explore sustainability in health security, strategies in Small Island Development States (SIDS), boosting resilience in the Caribbean, and ask questions about what drives economic complexity, whether the model of convergence will fit the post-pandemic recovery, and whether the trends in external financing flows are in the right direction. The final part is titled "Resetting Diplomacy: Regionalism and Geo-Strategic Shifts."

Boxes

This work of scholarship will certainly add to the rich discourse in the literature on development and diplomacy in small states while, at the same time, providing a clear focus on the pathways ahead for the Caribbean. It is an invaluable addition to the reading list of students of Caribbean studies. Moreover, this publication also helps to advance the CAF's commitment to deepening its relations with academia through research on crucial development issues to inform policy and decision-making in the Caribbean.

As executive president of the CAF, I am pleased to support the work of the University of the West Indies Press within the framework of our Memorandum of Understanding with the University of the West Indies. Like the regional university, the CAF recognizes the critical role of knowledge in advancing sustainable development. We, therefore, look forward with anticipation to the meaningful and enduring contribution that this publication will make to policy discussions and decisions on boosting the economic recovery of the Caribbean.

Sergio Díaz-Granados
Executive President
Development Bank of Latin America and the Caribbean (CAF)

Foreword

In 2015, when I presented on the theme Rekindling the Revolution at the Forum on the Future of the Caribbean in Trinidad and Tobago, to over six hundred participants, mostly young persons, I urged then that "the future now calls for a deliberate detachment from the many…reactionary aspects of our tradition . . . the assumption is that the Caribbean is fixed to inhibiting structures while the world is rapidly evolving and moving on" (Beckles 2016, 20).

Little did I anticipate that, five years later, what was peculiar to the Caribbean became characteristically valid to the whole world, as the COVID-19 pandemic exposed the fixed inhibiting structures on a global scale. The World Economic Forum acknowledged this in its COVID-19 *The Great RESET*, which sets the conceptual framework – interdependence, velocity, and complexity – as the three defining characteristics of today's world (Schwab and Malleret 2020). There is no time to wait, said the managing director Dominic Waughray of the World Economic Forum Centre for Global Public Goods, noting that "We're in a very, very unique moment in human history . . . sustainability is a cresting mainstreaming issue working across all horizontals of the economy" (Waughray 2021).

Then the onslaught of the Russian–Ukraine violent confrontation arose in 2022 which unleashed new tremors in the world's commodity and energy markets, adding new stresses to a world order and with forces of fragmentation in the monetary and financial structures. These layers of shocks and ripples inevitably affect the regional economy. Policy options and research priorities for Caribbean advancement must now open up to new approaches and possibilities. Since I spoke in 2015 on calls for deliberate detachment, rekindling the revolution has now taken on a more urgent imperative and with deeper clarity on the tools of analysis for sustaining progress in the region.

Development and Diplomacy: Resetting Caribbean Policy Analysis in the Aftermath of the COVID-19 Pandemic fills an increasingly growing gap across all horizons in research and policy analysis in Caribbean development and diplomacy. It is diagnostic and probing, craving and searching, and conducts an intense discourse on rising above the orthodoxy of traditional thinking with deliberate detachment. It strives for a new synthesis between theory

Adding the Pandemic to Caribbean Economic Thought

Caribbean thought since independence saw the influence of the New World Group in the 1960s, the structuralist of the 1970s, and the rise of the market power of the 1980s. By the turn of the twenty-first century, politics became a crucial variable in models of development, creating a new focus on issues of political economy. For each period, we saw a distinct set of policy directions. In the early period, harnessing more economic and institutional space was led by the role of the state. Policies aimed at control of the main pillars of the economy and building institutions with developmental mandates became a center piece. Soon, the structuralists' thinking came to the fore as the structure of the economy to build resilience and export potential led to the strategy of industrialization by invitation. By the 1980s, the Washington Consensus and its reliance on the power of the markets took the main stage as the region sought to insert itself into the global economy. By the turn of the twenty-first century, political discontent and rising expectations of society saw a new meshing between the political and economic forces at work, and a greater focus on the workings and relevance of political behavior. The quest for sustainability in the political economy became critical.

Closing the Gap between Theory and Practice

Linking theory and practice has become a most critical challenge in public policy. The university's test of relevance is increasingly being measured by this challenge. Closing the gap between theory and practice is itself an act of scholarship, to converge knowledge creation with real benefits to society in the present and the future. It is a complex relationship, and like so many complexities, universities are a starting point for this discovery. Sir Hilary Beckles, Vice Chancellor of the University of the West Indies, in his search for a "broader and more diverse university system" formulated the Triple A strategy – Access, Alignment, Agility – aimed at shifting the key performance pillars of the institution – dedicated to revitalizing Caribbean development.

The Sequel to Synchronize the Logics of Politics with the Logics of Economics

I have always been fascinated by linking politics with economics. It became not only my research preoccupation over the years but has also informed my career choices in my long journey of policy action. My earlier edited book, *Choices and Change: Reflections on the Caribbean* (Dookeran 1996), took stock of the issues that must be confronted in the Caribbean by noted scholars.

and practice, thus enhancing the university's commitment for deepening its relevance to the shaping of Caribbean societies.

This publication is in keeping with the vision and value of the university in appointing Professors of Practice to forge that synthesis between theoretical constructs and practical policy outcomes. This brings an intellectual agility and analytical rigor to the study of Caribbean societies. In an historical context, the Caribbean has a legacy of persistent poverty, and as it reckons with the historical conflicts of human justice, but likewise emerging is a rich heritage of scholarship, firmly embedded, that rises above these obstacles and creates better societies for current and future generations. This publication is in keeping with that endeavor.

I commend the editors, Winston Dookeran and M. Raymond Izarali, and the contributing authors for this most timely publication. I am sure it will add significantly to scholarly discourse, policy dialogue, and public action, which are integral to the mission of the University of the West Indies.

Professor Sir Hilary Beckles
Vice Chancellor, The University of the West Indies

References

Beckles, Hilary. 2016. "Rekindling the Revolution." In *Shifting the Frontier*, edited by Winston Dookeran and Carlos Elias, 20–32. Kingston, Jamaica: Ian Randle Publishers.

Schwab, Klaus, and Thierry Malleret. 2020. *Covid19: The Great Reset*. Geneva, Switzerland: World Economic Forum.

Waughray, Dominic. 2021. "How WEF Converts Blue-sky Thinking into Real-World Action." *Sustainable Business*, 26 January 2021. https://www.reutersevents.com/sustainability/interview-how-wef-converts-blue-sky-thinking-real-world-action.

Preface

Development and Diplomacy: Resetting Caribbean Policy Analysis in the Aftermath of the COVID-19 Pandemic

WINSTON DOOKERAN

The COVID-19 pandemic – the ability to survive in its aftermath, the rethinking of development strategies, and the geostrategic shifts in diplomacy – created challenges and opportunities for the world and even more so for the small developing states. The "loop-type" cycle of shocks experienced during the pandemic and continuing, and the disruption shock anticipated by sanctions and economic warfare, along with climate change risks and structural interruptions in supply change management are testing the old paradigms at the limit. These challenges have added complexities to our analysis and policy dictates. This has forced a rethink of how we cope with economic shocks and shifts in politics. Small states face huge challenges in the formulation of growth strategies in the "loop-type" shock cycles. At the same time, the global order is in flux, and the changing geopolitics has opened up strategic shifts in diplomacy.

In this book, some chapters examine the underlying logic of models of growth, as it discusses the concepts – linearity and convergence, circular economy, frontier development, complexity analysis – to which such models must respond. Other chapters look at the forces at play in the changing global political order – hegemonic struggles, dialectics of *realpolitik*, multilateralism and regionalism, new forms of integration, and dialogue space for small countries. In the years ahead, research priorities and policy actions will face both technical and political challenges in global security and health diplomacy, One-World-Information-Space and political stress in public policy management.

This book is a conversation on policy solutions in the aftermath of COVID-19. It places the Caribbean at the center but may have wider applicability to small countries elsewhere, as it attempts to shape the contours of a general theory in a fragile global politics. It is located in the history of economic thought, digs deep into the economic challenges of today, and explores a synthesis between the logics of economics and politics. It is a study on development economics and small states diplomacy.

Some years later, during my stint in government, I began to see the issues in a political framework, as published in *Power, Politics and Performance: A Partnership Approach to Development* (Dookeran 2012). In the foreword of the book, P.J. Patterson (2012, xi), the distinguished former prime minister of Jamaica, referred to that work as "a fascinating collection of Essays of ideas which span the gamut from Thomas Hobbes to Mahatma Gandhi and against the background of writing from Machiavelli to Marx." While affirming that it is high time that the perception of politics as an obstacle to the advancement of the Caribbean be removed, Patterson noted that the insights and prescriptions in the book are, in a large measure, also valid for universal application and that the ideas serve as an intellectual bridge to fill the gap between expectations and performance. It is partially to address this gap that *Crisis and Promise in the Caribbean: Politics and Convergence* (Dookeran 2017) was written. Arguing that the ideas in the book chart new development spaces, Paula Morgan (2017, viiii) in her foreword to the book described that work as "A comprehensive offering . . . that combines bedrock pragmatism with a fierce insistence on the higher ground of transcendent aspirations and ideals."

In this sequel of writings, and with time to reflect, I put together *The Caribbean on the Edge: Political Stress of Stability, Equality and Diplomacy* (Dookeran 2022) which traces my ideas on the Caribbean as developed over the years. In a time of persistent uncertainty, fragile eco-structures, the politics of "populism," and the limits in institutional leadership that publication sets the baseline for the road map into new shifts in globalization and regionalism for the countries on the edge of history in the Caribbean Sea.

Then, an event titled "Forum on the Future of the Caribbean in Trinidad and Tobago," attended by nearly 600 Caribbean scholars (mostly young) and practitioners, resulted in *Shifting the Frontiers* (Dookeran & Elias 2016) with contributions from a wide cross-section of persons from within and outside the Caribbean region. It was that Forum, and the pandemic that followed, that prompted the work presented now in this edition.

My sequel ends with this co-edited volume with M. Raymond Izarali, *Development and Diplomacy: Resetting Caribbean Policy Analysis in the Aftermath of the COVID-19 Pandemic.* It forges a rethink of development in the geostrategic shifts, as the world and the Caribbean navigated a COVID-19 pandemic reset to reignite Caribbean progress in the years yet to be travelled.

References

Dookeran, Winston, ed. 1996. Choices and Change: Reflections on the Caribbean. Washington, D.C.: Inter-American Development Bank.

_____. 2012. Power, Politics and Performance: A Partnership Approach to Development. Kingston, Jamaica: Ian Randle Publishers.

_____. 2017. Crisis and Promise in the Caribbean: Politics and Convergence. New York: Taylor and Francis.

———. 2022. The Caribbean on the Edge: The Political Stress of Stability, Equality, and Diplomacy. Toronto, ON: University of Toronto Press.

Dookeran, Winston, and Carlos Elias G., eds. 2016. Shifting the Frontiers: An Action Framework for the Future of the Caribbean. Kingston: Ian Randle Press.

Morgan, Paula. 2017. Foreword to Crisis and Promise in the Caribbean: Politics and Convergence. New York: Taylor and Francis.

Patterson, P.J. 2012. Foreword to Power, Politics and Performance: A Partnership Approach to Development, by Winston Dookeran. Kingston, Jamaica: Ian Randle Publishers.

Acknowledgments

This book has emerged from a period of stress faced by just about everyone in every part of the world, as it was put together during the period of the COVID-19 pandemic. The commitment on the part of the contributors to share their energies and wisdom during such trying times to help give a sense of how to understand the pandemic's ordeal, how to plan beyond it, and to provide insight to policy makers and researchers alike is commendable and appreciated.

It need hardly be said that producing such a large volume on a pandemic context that was new and that had caught the world off-guard required considerable effort and has had enormous pains in light of lockdowns, social limitations, remote engagement, and simply struggling to adjust to a new way of life. A number of persons were instrumental in helping to meet the demands required for its production, notably: Michelle Seeraj of the Institute of International Relations, UWI, whose support and outreach were present from the inception of this endeavor to its completion; David McCartney, who did the art work for the cover design; Rayne Alfonso, Ria Chaitram, and Kumaree Ramtahal who provided kind editorial support to Winston Dookeran on several of his chapters; Eshan Ali, who had served as Winston Dookeran's former Personal Assistant at the Ministry of Foreign Affairs and who sourced relevant material for his research for this volume; and Caron Asgarali, who worked tirelessly and committedly as the editorial assistant for this project throughout its development.

The editors gratefully acknowledge the funding and research assistant supports provided through the Laurier Work Study Program (LWSP) and the office of the Dean of the Faculty of Human and Social Sciences at Wilfrid Laurier University (Brantford Campus), Canada. We also acknowledge the kind assistance of Señor Gianpiero Leoncini of the Development Bank of Latin America (CAF) and Professor Laurent Cleenewerck of EUCLID University in the early stages of the preparation of this publication.

We extend gratitude as well to the anonymous reviewers of the manuscript for their insightful and thoughtful feedback that have helped to enrich this book, and for their reassurance of the book's epistemic significance to this period in human history across the Caribbean and the world. Finally, we also acknowledge the support of the late Joseph Powell of the University of the West Indies Press and his endorsement of the scholarly value of this publication.

Acronyms

9/11	September 11, 2001
AAAA	Addis Ababa Action Agenda
ACP	African Caribbean and Pacific group of states
ACS	Association of Caribbean States
ADB	Asian Development Bank
AFCFTA	African Continental Free Trade Area
ALBA	Bolivarian Alliance for the Peoples of Our America
AMSP	African Medical Supplies Platform
ASEAN	Association of Southeast Asian Nations
BMC	Borrowing Member Country
BPO	Business Process Outsourcing
BREXIT	British exit from the European Union
BRI RMB	Renminbi (Official currency of the People's Republic of China)
BRI	Belt Road Initiative
BRICS	Brazil, Russia, India, China, and South Africa
BSAs	Bilateral Swap Agreements
CARDI	Caribbean Agricultural Research and Development Institute
CAREC	Caribbean Epidemiology Center
CARICOM IMPACS	CARICOM Implementing Agency for Crime and Security
CARICOM	Caribbean Community
CARIFORUM	Caribbean Forum of the African, Caribbean, and Pacific Group of States (ACP)
CARIFTA	Caribbean Free Trade Association
CARPHA	Caribbean Public Health Agency
CAS	Complex Adaptive Systems
CCJ	Caribbean Court of Justice
CCRIF	Caribbean Catastrophic Risk Insurance Facility
CDB	Caribbean Development Bank
CDC	Centre for Disease Control
CDEMA	Caribbean Disaster Emergency Management Agency

CEHI	Caribbean Environmental Health Institute
CELAC	The Community of Latin American and Caribbean States
CEPI	Coalition for Epidemic Preparedness Innovations
CFNI	Caribbean Food and Nutrition Institute
CHRC	Caribbean Health Research Council
CMML	CARPHA Medical Microbiology Laboratory
CoCos	Contingent Convertible Bonds
COFA	Compact of Free Association
COFCOR	Council for Foreign and Community Relations
CONSLE	Council for National Security and Law Enforcement
COP 21	The 21st Conference of the Parties
COP26	26th United Nations Climate Change Conference of the Parties
COTED	Council for Trade and Economic Development
COVAX	CEPI and GAVI collectively/ COVID-19 Vaccines Global Access
COVID-19	Coronavirus disease 2019
CPTPP	Comprehensive and Progressive Agreement for Trans-Pacific Partnership
CRDLT	Caribbean Regional Drug Testing Laboratory
CRF	Caribbean Resilience Fund
CRNM	Caribbean Regional Negotiating Machinery
CROP	Council of Regional Organizations in the Pacific
CSAs	Currency Swap Agreements
CSME	CARICOM Single Market and Economy
CT	Complexity Theory/Thinking
CTO	Caribbean Tourism Organization
CUSMA	Canada-United States-Mexico Agreement
DFAT	Department of Foreign Affairs and Trade
DFC	Development Finance Corporation
DFI	Development Finance Institution
DOLS	Dynamic Ordinary Least Squares
EC	European Commission
ECB	European Central Bank
ECCB	Eastern Caribbean Central Bank
ECi,t	economic complexity
ECLAC	Economic Commission for Latin America and the Caribbean
EDF	European Development Fund
EIU	Economist Intelligence Unit

EM	Emerging Market
EMBI	JPMorgan Emerging Markets Bond Index
EMBIG	JPMorgan Emerging Markets Bond Index – Global
EME	Emerging Market Economy
EPA	Economic Partnership Agreement
EPA	Environmental Protection Agency
ESG	Environmental, Social and Governance
EU	European Union
FDI	Foreign Direct Investment
FEALAC	Forum of East Asia Latin Asia-African Cooperation
FEMM	Forum Economic Ministers Meeting
FFA	Forum Fisheries Agency
FIMA	Foreign and International Monetary Authority
FMOLS	Fully Modified Ordinary Least Square
FTA	Free Trade Agreements
FTAA	Free Trade of the Americas
FX	Foreign Exchange/Forex
G20	Group of Twenty
G7	Group of Seven
GAVI	The Vaccine Alliance
GDP	Gross Domestic Product
GEF	Global Environment Fund
GEPU	Global Economic Policy Uncertainty Index
GFCF	Gross Fixed Capital Formation
GHSI	Global Health Security Initiative
GNI	Gross National Income
HDI	Human Development Index
HIV/AIDS	Human Immunodeficiency Virus
HKD	Hong Kong Dollar
ICES	Index of COVID-19 Economic Stimulus
ICMA	International Capital Markets Association
ICT	Information and Communications Technology
IDB	Inter-American Development Bank
IHR	International Health Regulations
IIF	Institute of International Finance
IMF	International Monetary Fund
IR	International Relations
JRCC	Joint Regional Communications Centre
KPI	Key Performance Indicators
LAC	Latin America and the Caribbean

LIAT	Leeward Island Airline Transportation
MDBs	Multilateral Development Banks
MDGs	Millennium Development Goals
MENA	Middle East and North Africa
MERCOSUR	Common Market of the South
MFAT	Ministry of Foreign Affairs and Trade
MSG	Melanesian Spearhead Group
MW	Mega Watts
NAFTA	North American Free Trade Agreement
NCDs	Non-communicable diseases
NDICI	Neighborhood Development and International Cooperation Instrument
NEMO	National Emergency Management Organisation
NGO	Non-Governmental Organization
OACP	Organization of the African, Caribbean and Pacific states
OAS	Organization of American States
ODA	Official Development Assistance
OECD	Organisation for Economic Cooperation and Development
OECS	Organization of Eastern Caribbean States
OLS	Ordinary Least Square
OTN	Office of Trade Negotiations
PACER	Pacific Agreement on Closer Economic Relations
PAHO	Pan American Health Organization
PCR	Polymerase Chain Reaction
PHEIC	Public Health Emergency of International Concern
PICTA	Pacific Island Countries Trade Agreement
PIFS	Pacific Islands Forum Secretariat
PPE	Personal Protective Equipment
PPE	Personal Protective Equipment
PTA	Preferential Trade Agreements
RCEP	Regional Comprehensive Economic Partnership
RHIs	Regional Health Institutes
RMB	Ren Min Bi
RRM	Regional Response Mechanism
RSE	Recognized Seasonal Employment
RSS	Regional Security System
SARS	Severe Acute Respiratory Syndrome
SDGs	Sustainable Development Goals
SDR's	Special Drawing Rights
SICA	Central American Integration System
SIDS	Small Island Developing States

SLB	Sustainability-linked Bond
SLBP	Sustainability-Linked Bond Principles
SMEs	Small- and Medium-sized Enterprises
SPARTECA	South Pacific Regional Trade and Economic Cooperation Agreement
SPC	Secretariat of the Pacific Community
SPEC	South Pacific Bureau for Economic Cooperation
SRC	Seismic Research Centre
SSMECI	Small State Manufactured Export Competitiveness Index
SVG	St. Vincent and the Grenadines
SWP	Seasonal Worker Program
T20	Think 20
TCX	The Currency Exchange Fund
TGU	Trinidad Generation Unlimited
The UWI	The University of the West Indies
TNC	The Nature Conservancy
TPSEP	Transpacific Strategic Economic Partnership Agreement
TSTT	Telecommunications Services of Trinidad and Tobago
UAE	United Arab Emirates
UK	United Kingdom
UN	United Nations
UNAIDS	United Nations Programme on HIV/AIDS
UNASUR	Union of South American Nations
UNCTAD	United Nations Conference on Trade and Development
UNDP	United Nations Development Programme
UNECLAC	United Nations Economic Commission for Latin America and the Caribbean
UNEP	United Nations Environmental Programme
UNFPA	United Nations Population Fund
UNICEF	United Nations Children Fund
UNIFEM	United Nations Development Fund for Women
US	United States
USP	University of the South Pacific
UWI	University of the West Indies
WB	World Bank
WEF	World Economic Forum
WHA	World Health Assembly
WHO	World Health Organization
WTO	World Trade Organization
WTTC	World Travel and Tourism Council

Part 1

Conceptual Thought and Framework of
Analysis

1

Setting Caribbean Development Rethink in the Aftermath of the COVID-19 Pandemic

M. RAYMOND IZARALI

The Caribbean encompasses a wide heterogeneity of peoples and cultures, with different languages and roots. In varied ways, commentators and writers allude to this heterogeneity by talking about the English Caribbean, the Dutch Caribbean, the Spanish Caribbean, and the French Caribbean (UNDP 2012; Izarali 2018). As implied in this linguistic demography and geography, the Caribbean embodies historical lineages from other parts of the world.

The linguistic distinction of the geography in reference to the English, the French, the Spanish, and the Dutch Caribbeans depicts the history of colonial control and not the cultural roots and histories of the people. As Andy Knight (2019, 407) notes: "The Caribbean's original inhabitants (Caribs and Arawaks), along with blacks from Africa and Indians from India, were all victims of direct violent crimes committed by the European colonial masters (the British, the French, the Spanish, the Portuguese and the Dutch)." Thus, the region is home to people of a multitude of origins – for example, Africa, India, and to a much lesser extent China and Europe (Nathan 2022; Premdass 2011; Long 2020; Khan 2020; Ramsaran and Lewis 2018). It is also home to people of the world's major religions – Hinduism, Christianity, and Islam – where people of the various faiths coexist respectfully and peacefully in countries like Trinidad and Tobago, Guyana, and Suriname (Izarali 2018; Nathan 2022; Khan 2020; Ramsaran and Lewis 2018; Persaud 2022). There are therefore cultural pluralities of peoples in the region. Given this backdrop of coloniality in accounting for the region's demographic plurality, it is perhaps no small wonder that the historian Alvin Thompson (1997, 11) remarked that: "We have contributed much to the development of the international economy through agriculture and mineral resources, but only very little to our own economic development" in addressing what he saw as underdevelopment of the region.

The Caribbean is comprised mostly of island states which make up an archipelago stretching from the Greater Antilles (south of the Gulf of Mexico) across to the Lesser Antilles in the south and encompass some of the mainland

South American countries (Knight 2019, 405). Thus, not all the states in the region are "island" states or "micro" states, as there are countries that are situated "on the mainland of the northern portion of the South American continent," notably Belize, Suriname, Guyana, and French Guyana (Knight 2018, 220). According to Baldacchino (2020, 278), "The Caribbean is the basin with the largest concentration of small states and territories in the world. In a relatively small area – about the same size as the Mediterranean Sea – we find today thirteen sovereign states (and an almost equal amount of subnational jurisdictions) all of which are islands or archipelagos." The largest population is held by Cuba, which has 11.5 million people, followed by Haiti at 10.7 million, and Dominican Republic at 10.2 million (Knight 2019; Baldacchino 2020). The population of most states is below 1.5 million people (Knight 2019). For example, St. Kitts and Nevis has a population of 53,090, Dominica 74,020, and St. Vincent and the Grenadines 101,840 (Baldacchino 2020).

Moreover, there are subgroupings in the region that are differently categorized (UNDP 2012). Identification with the Caribbean may be in reference to geographical features, to regional and subregional organizational membership, to linguistic groups, or to shared ethno-cultural and political history (UNDP 2012; Singh 2013; Izarali 2018). Major organizations in the region include the Caribbean Community (CARICOM), the Organization of Eastern Caribbean States, and the Association of Caribbean States (ACS). The countries of the Greater Caribbean are those said to be "washed up" by the Caribbean Sea (Knight 2019). The demographic features, levels of development, and capacities of the state also vary greatly (UNDP 2012). Per capita Gross National Income across the region ranges from US$ 800 to US$ 30,000, much of which relies on tourism and others on various commodity exports such as rice, sugar, vegetables, fruits, fisheries, and extractive resources (World Bank 2021).

There have been growing and developmental hardships which have been exacerbated over the years by issues relating to governance, corruption, and crime (Knight 2019). The impact of these issues can strain public confidence, stunt growth over time, and weaken access to needed capital in international settings, let alone handling hegemonic behaviors by big and powerful actors and volatilities in the global economy. Globalization, the process of integrating the economies of the world through the liberalization of the trade markets to create one global union of commerce (Izarali 2019), emerged as a route of promised benefits to make everyone's lot better. But it actually came with a good bit of hardship as well for some states and private industries in the region, including fiscal fragility (Knight 2019; Barker, Dodman, and McGregor 2009). Some states in the global arena fared better than others, especially rich developed ones. Small states struggled to adjust and survive on an uneven playing field in the global arena. While it paved the way for some new markets in the Caribbean, some of the existing local industries and markets were painfully impacted. As Knight (2019, 410) puts it: "We have clearly witnessed across the Caribbean region over the past few decades: stagnation and decline in manufacturing in, for example, Barbados, Trinidad and Tobago, Jamaica, St. Vincent and the Grenadines (SVG), and Dominica; a decline in the region's competitiveness; chronic balance-of-payment deficits due to low elasticity of international demand for exports and high elasticity of demand for imports; and widening trade and current account deficits." Barker, Dodman, and McGregor (2009) suggest that the field of agriculture in the Caribbean was particularly made vulnerable by trade liberalization. It may be said, therefore, that Caribbean societies and economies have had their struggles to rise above and survive through the years. Issues with capital flows, access to markets, currency exchange volatility, and inequitable international trade regimes all bear heavily on Caribbean societies.

Tourism revenues have come from land-based tourism, yachting, and cruise ship and have been vital for the small islands' sustainability and development, ranging from hotel infrastructure to the various service sectors (ECLAC 2005). According to the Caribbean Tourism Organization (CTO) (2020), in 2018 there were 32.2 million tourist arrivals to the Caribbean. Given this industry, the many small islands' dependence factor is significant. Of the fifty-eight small island developing states (SIDS) that have been recognized by the United Nation, twenty-nine of them are said to be in the Caribbean (Hambleton, Jeyalseelan, and Murphy 2020). While the tourism industry highlights the extent to which a segment of the region depends on tourism revenues, it also highlights the extent to which tourism connects the region to the world through air travel and ocean liners and, as such, is the bridge for the small islands and others to the international economy. But as Peterson and DiPietro (2021) note, the tourism and hospitality industries were among the hardest struck by the effects of COVID-19 as a consequence of nationwide lockdowns, restrictions on travel, closure of businesses, and how people's lives and livelihoods were impacted as a result. Byron et al. (2021, 101) capture the issue succinctly in noting that "the negative economic impacts associated with COVID-19 for CC [Commonwealth Caribbean] territories are linked to the region's high dependence on tourism and remittances, economic openness and limited resources."

In 2019, the direct contribution to GDP from tourism was 11.8 percent across the Caribbean and the combined total of direct and indirect contribution was 28.5 percent, according to ECLAC (2020). However, there are variations across economies in the region, as there are some states that are naturally more dependent on tourism revenues such as Aruba where the direct contribution to GDP is 30.4 percent and the combined total of direct and indirect contribution is 73.6 percent. Statistics from the Caribbean Development Bank (2020) show that by June 28, 2020, there were 53,006 cases of COVID-19 in the Caribbean, which means the region was already feeling the impact at the level of health and revenue by that time. The World Travel and Tourism Council's (WTTC) Global Economic Impact and Trends report of 2021 indicates that the Caribbean had a disproportionate travel tourism GDP fall of 58 percent in 2020 due to the COVID-19 proliferation and restriction measures (WTTC 2021, 9). St. Kitts and Nevis suffered a travel tourism GDP fall of 72.3 percent and St. Lucia 71.7 percent, compared to 2019 (WTTC 2021, 9). The fall in the Bahamas, the UK Virgin Islands, and St. Vincent and the Grenades were 68 percent, 67.6 percent, and 67 percent, respectively (WTTC 2021, 9). In other words, the economic losses were significant and would have permeated other aspects of people's lives and stymied development.

As such, the region needs to be connected to international platforms for exports and imports. It needs to have space and place in global markets for revenue generation through exports, for the acquisition of goods it does not produce, and for access to capital and finance. The region has not been without hurdles, however. Most of the countries in the region are relatively young, with the exception of Haiti, the Dominican Republic, and Cuba, which got independence in 1804, 1821, and 1902, respectively (UNDP 2012).

The COVID-19 pandemic, while being a global health crisis from the rapid and pervasive transmissibility of the disease across the world's populations, also became a point of economic despair and crisis for the world and the region in ways other than tourism (Knight and Reddy 2020; Meighoo 2020; Byron et al. 2021). The COVID-19 global pandemic was immensely disruptive to the routine functionality of national economies, people's ways of life, and livelihood itself for most of the world, as Wendy Grenade has so aptly noted in chapter 2 of this volume. It caused fears and disruptions not just across civil society but for professionals as well such as dentists, doctors, and other frontline workers who were exposed to its elements in caring for patients, and resulted in the decline of the subjective well-being of people across the population at large (Garces-Elias et al. 2022). Small states in the Caribbean had to straddle with the major disruptions of the pandemic, in the effects it has had on trade, employment, air travel, industrial production, public health infrastructure and emergency response, and the states' ability to keep their respective economy afloat (Byron et al. 2021; Peterson and DiPietro 2021; Sobers et al. 2021). While the impact may have been largely readily observed in macroeconomic terms, there were also more acute impacts at the level of mental health with increased anxieties and depression, substance abuse, and post-traumatic stress disorder (Llibre-Guerra et al. 2020; Garces-Elias et al. 2022). Llibre-Guerra et al. (2020) noted in the early period of the pandemic that the effects of the COVID-19 virus on the countries of the Caribbean may have been particularly disproportionate owing to factors such as income insecurity, vulnerable economies stemming from their reliance on tourism, chronic levels of poverty, and having a large proportion of older persons. As we look back retrospectively at the havoc of the pandemic, it is a good time to revisit their forecast.

The need and resources required to put in place intensive care bed capacity, infection control and prevention, healthcare equipment, testing for the COVID-19 virus, and social distancing measures, while at the same time conducting effective border management, were not without financial implications for what were already struggling economies in the region (Resiere, Resiere, and Kallel 2020; Byron et al. 2021). The shocks imposed by the pandemic have thus had ripple effects.

Consequently, major lockdowns of the society – of industries, schools, public offices, and so on – have had major effects on GDP and the states' ability to adequately respond to the pandemic climate. Providing income subsidies to affected persons and families may have been affordable for wealthier countries but was a luxury for many in the Caribbean region, as a number of the contributors in this volume have made clear. In these ways, the effects on the societies were and are multiple, and on many levels.

Lockdowns required pedagogical transitions in the schools and universities in the region and elsewhere in the world because schools are especially sites of large gathering which are themselves congenial to the transmission of contagious disease. But here too perhaps the economic underdevelopment of many Caribbean societies especially stands out. While the use of computer technology is imperative in the times in which we live, in the Caribbean there was an associated array of issues in transitioning to online learning – among them, the availability of computer technology, availability of electricity, internet affordability and availability, teachers' and students' competence in computer technology for pedagogy, and affordability to purchase computers in light of very limited incomes (UN 2021; Jaramillo 2020). As a UN (2021, 4) policy brief noted, "In Barbados, British Virgin Islands and Guyana, where online learning capacity was inchoate or non-existent, school closures required emergency deployment of new technologies and educator training." University libraries such as those at the University of the West Indies had to transition to a significantly larger scale of online delivery than ever before, with all the concomitant strains and challenges for library staffing, resources, and budgets to meet the demands (Nelson and Tugwell 2022). Indeed, it ought to be noted, as Harris' (2021) study points out in the case of the Jamaican academic libraries, that support staff dedication and outreach beyond what was required of them were major strengths during those times.

This array of issues highlights ethical concerns for development and state management planning. These concerns include equitable access to resources needed for educational success and care for teachers' and students' well-being in light of the amount of time that was required of them to spend online and the stress they endured from teaching and learning at home amid distractions (Leacock and Warrican 2020; Byron et al. 2021). While some studies by Caribbean researchers were carried out in the education sector on the effects shaped by COVID-19, there appeared to have been none in the early childhood education sector (Abdul-Majied, Kinkead-Clark, and Burns 2022). This is regrettable considering the enormity of stress and demands that would have been endured by early childhood teachers in light of the age group they teach, availing themselves to parents beyond normal time frames, and having to reach out to parents and students in varied ways in light of the challenges posed by issues relating to internet accessibility, availability, affordability, and connectivity. But this gap may itself be a consequence of the pandemic.

Looked at from this perspective, the COVID-19 pandemic's disruption has had health, social, economic, and educational dimensions, among others, and any careful developmental rethink must consider ways to ameliorate such conditions in both moving ahead and planning for a more resilient future in times of pandemics and other crises (Knight and Reddy 2020; Leacock and Warrican 2020; Meighoo 2020; Resiere, Resiere, and Kallel 2020; Byron et al. 2021). The disruptive lockdowns had deleterious economic impacts, but they also brought to light the gaps and deficits in Caribbean societies from not having the resources and adequate preparedness to adapt sufficiently to an era of technology.

States are limited in their abilities, as they are constrained by a narrow stream and small size of revenues and resources. At the same time, civil society has high expectations of them, especially so in times of adversity. When leaders and states appear not to deliver on these expectations, discontent and apathy naturally ensue. It is reasonable to expect that the populations at large will look upon the state for solutions to navigate through difficult times when incomes are strained, if not lost; when children and families have to be fed; and when citizens' security at a broader level is challenged by abrupt interventions in their lives and a return to normality becomes a daily wonder. The COVID-19 milieu imposed public health and public safety struggles in the larger context of citizens' security and in the need for swift adaptation by the states of the Caribbean to respond with effective leadership and a shift in focus and resources.

It is useful to bear in mind that some Caribbean states were already familiar with major disruptions to their economies and livelihoods from having endured the wrath of major tropical storms and, in the case of Haiti, major earthquakes (Abdul-Majied, Kinkead-Clark, and Burns 2022; Knight 2019). These storms disrupted livelihoods, displaced people, resulted in electricity supply outage, and punctuated schooling. There is an average of twelve storms that traverse the Caribbean annually (Knight 2019). The effects of climate change are likely to intensify this situation, causing damage to critical infrastructure, food security, homes, tourism revenue, and trade – all of which would put inhabitants in small states in a perilous plight (Knight 2019; Barker, Dodman, and McGregor 2009). There are countries in the region that had already seen their economies ravaged by seasonal hurricanes while for some people in countries elsewhere in the region, these incidents appeared as remote and delinked from them. Thus, some were already painfully aware of what crisis disruptions can entail for the society whereas others were not.

In this sense, the global pandemic spawned by the COVID-19 disease has perhaps made people in the larger Caribbean community of nations more aware of the abruptness in which disruptive interventions to lives and economies can take place. They may have become more sensitive and receptive to the need for a robust reexamination of macroeconomic management and strategies, diplomatic engagement and prioritization, and regional collaboration. In the case of Guyana, there was a double sadness and struggle, as massive floods from unusually heavy rainfalls in parts of the country submerged many homes and damaged the livelihoods of many people during the pandemic, including large-scale agricultural crops, expensive farming machineries, and personal automobiles. The Irfaan Ali government carried out a commendably massive outreach undertaking in those communities to help provide the means of life to those affected and to help rebuild their livelihoods. Members of civil society, Youtubers, the private sector, and the Guyanese diaspora as well as elements in Caribbean regional systems also played strong roles.

Extolling the efforts and erudition of Barbados prime minister Mia Motley through these times, Knight and Reddy (2020, 464) pointed out that "individual Caribbean states acting on their own cannot adequately address such transnational and trans-regional global pandemics." The chapters throughout this book overwhelmingly point to regional cooperation as a vital need and a vital lesson from the COVID-19 pandemic experience; they also focus on the broader Caribbean. June Soomer's discussion on the premise of the ACS, for example, is a clarion call for the community of nations in the region to develop regional systems of cooperation and frameworks that embed resilience for human protection and well-being in addition to economic survival.

The times in which we live and the lessons learned from a global pandemic that carried on for over two years oblige us to consider different ways of doing things that extend beyond our comfort zones of the past so as to avoid the pitfalls and blind spots to which we were awakened. It is an opportunity to rethink how to embed resilience for the survival and prosperity of economies, and the kind of leadership and vision required in the modern age to effectively lead societies through levels of transformation that can augment the public good. Such transformations must give the young and the old alike a strong sense of preparedness and a strong sense of confidence that the well-being of the people is always a foremost priority in the management of public affairs.

Certainly this is easier said than done, but being idle would not get us there or anywhere close. Already, as a result of external factors, the island economies of the Caribbean have experienced major disruptions from which we can learn – notably the catastrophic impact the 9/11 tragedy in the United States had on tourism and related hotel and service sectors as Griffith (2004) had documented, as well as seasonal storms like hurricanes and health epidemics. As Hambleton, Jeyaseelan, and Murphy (2020, 1114) note, "Three of the 10 countries most affected by extreme weather events over the past 20 years are in the Caribbean (Puerto Rico, Haiti, Dominica)." Similarly, Llibre-Guerra et al. (2020) remind us that the region has faced many epidemics over the last decade including Dengue, Zika, and Chikungunya, and the experience from those epidemics could inform ways to move. As they had suggested, a multilevel well-coordinated response was required to manage and mitigate the COVID-19 pandemic.

We have endured the pandemic period and have emerged with the rollout of vaccines across the world despite vaccine hesitancy by some people, but the economic impact will still be present in the years to come. At the level of optics, Guyana may appear asymmetric in some ways because of the major growth in economic activity in the construction sector and its multiplier effects, but this has to be understood in the context of the projected growth of a new-born oil economy. However, this new-born oil economy does not mean that the economic impact of the pandemic was absent. CARICOM, the ACS, the Caribbean Disaster Emergency Management Agency, and the Caribbean Public Health Agency have played vital roles during the pandemic. So have institutions like the Caribbean Development Bank and universities across the region. As Knight and Reddy (2020, 465) had point out in the first year of the pandemic: "The Caribbean needs to find a way, regionally, to build resilience into its operating system intersecting health, social, and economic sectors to deal effectively with manifold vulnerabilities. Building that resilience to external shocks requires intersectoral collaboration, strong regional institutions, and strengthened regional efforts." That insight continues to have relevance.

The Caribbean needs to engage in a critical rethink and visioning of what its future should look like and how to be resilient in the face of other possible pandemics and the like. Greater medical and scientific cooperation is vital (Resierre, Resiere, and Kallel 2020), and health diplomacy needs to be prioritized as noted by Vijay Kumar Chattu in chapter 16. The COVID-19 pandemic has highlighted that there are considerable gaps between where the societies of the Caribbean are and where they need to be, and thus it may be said that the COVID-19 global pandemic presented an inadvertent opportunity to carefully reexamine what the priorities are, what the action plans need to be, what guiding paradigms no longer have yields, and what paradigm shifts and innovation need to take place to transcend the pitfalls of pandemics and to generate human flourishing and well-being. The dynamics between the strains from Delta to Omicron have certainly shown how quickly things can change.

The region has to find ways to soldier through the adversities of the global economy and the vicissitudes in international relations. It needs to have access to markets and finance in the international arena, and it needs to be robust in the approach it takes in moving forward. But it also needs to be creative in generating investments and financing, and adamant in spearheading and preserving vital components for an environment of economic success and human well-being such as transparency, equity, opportunity, safety, fairness, accountability, good governance, sound public policy, and compliance with the rule of law – all things that are discussed across the chapters in this volume.

Caribbean development is paramount, and there is a need to recognize from the challenges of the COVID-19 global pandemic crisis the urgency to revisit, to reconceptualize, and to reorganize the approaches to public management, to diplomacy, and to macroeconomic planning and strategies. This book is conceived in response to that, but it is also an extension of a series of other works by Winston Dookeran in focusing on the plight of small states more generally and the Caribbean states more specifically in exhorting the imminent need to rethink the paradigms employed in theorizing and managing social and economic life.

The book is divided into five parts. Part 1, comprised of this chapter (1), provides a sketch of contexts in the Caribbean in the age of the pandemic. Part 2 addresses COVID-19, health security, and future resilience with a focus on sustainability analysis. Part 3 addresses the gap between theory and practice with a focus on development frontiers. Part 4 takes up issues of flows and frameworks in a discussion on the recovery process in moving the Caribbean forward. Part 5 addresses regionalism and geostrategic shifts focusing on resetting diplomacy. Together, these parts help to crystallize the issues, sharpen the conceptual lens, and navigate toward solutions for better outcomes and a better future. They map out the frontiers, flows, and frameworks of the issues and challenges in the Caribbean and the policy responses needed to address them.

Miriam L. Campanella and Winston Dookeran, in chapter 2, acknowledge the period of policy uncertainties spawned by the COVID-19 pandemic, noting the critical economic and financial variables presented, the high levels of joblessness, the major drop in fixed-asset investment, and the stark outflow of capital from emerging economies. In light of weak buffers and shock absorbers in many emerging and developing countries, they claim that there must be an equivalent fiscal injection to the size of the fall in GDP to prevent a worst-case scenario, a long L-shaped recession. They address the economics of the lockdowns and take up ways for the full impact of the COVID-19 pandemic to be mitigated among Caribbean countries.

In chapter 3, Wendy C. Grenade brings readers to a grip with the defining nature of the year 2020 in modern history. She points to three major crises that require simultaneous attention from the global community: the enormity of the health crises from the COVID-19 pandemic, its extension into crisis in the global political economy, and these two taking place against the backdrop of a climate change crisis. Grenade claims that both human lives and livelihoods and the natural environment are at stake, which together give rise to a situation of exacerbated development challenges especially for SIDS because of their limitations to mitigate those struggles on their own. Undertaking to reconceptualize the regional security for CARICOM SIDS, Grenade looks at the issues through a Critical Security Studies lens. Aside from the pitfalls of the pandemic, she suggests that it has also made available an opportunity in real time, as part of a larger regional security framework, to (re)imagine the direction for regionalism in the future through mainstreaming regional health security.

In chapter 4, Helvia Velloso takes a closer look at new opportunities in external financing mobilization by Caribbean countries. The author believes that the key challenge of mobilizing and directing such resources as sustainable development is posed by the increasing importance of private flows to the region. Feasible alternatives in resource mobilization may be had in financial instruments that have promise in bolstering resilience and transferring risks in cost-effective ways, according to Velloso. Green, social, and sustainability bonds along with state-contingent debt instruments and hurricane clauses can be designed to fortify against regional vulnerabilities such as natural disasters, negative economic shocks, and restricted capital access on the international level. Likewise, intra-Caribbean and international cooperation would play a vital role.

Winston Dookeran, in chapter 5, examines development and growth strategies in the Caribbean. Dookeran states that a rethink of strategies such as the loop-type shock cycle has been obliged by the COVID-19 pandemic, which has also shown the obsolescence of some of the older paradigms. In this chapter, however, it is observed that this trend of analysis was already predated by Arthur Lewis' growth theory and thus is not wholly owing to the pandemic of the present time. Dookeran thus undertakes to trace the growth theory of Lewis and to test the linearity assumption in the development pathway in an effort to delineate ideas on the frontiers of a nonlinear growth path.

In chapter 6, Winston Dookeran and Preeya Mohan outline that competitiveness is as much a foreign policy issue as it is an economic one. According to the authors, there is already a global dialogue on competitiveness and economic development, and there is a vested interest in small economies in this dialogue. Dookeran and Mohan claim that the limitations faced by small states in facilitating resources to diplomacy and valuable interaction can be mitigated through networks and alliances in light of a significant number of small states that have similar interests.

In chapter 7, Winston Dookeran and Preeya Mohan take up a discussion in setting the agenda for the "circular economy" for small Caribbean economies, pointing out that the concept of the circular economy is not an abstract one but one whose principles can help to cope with the post-pandemic period of the current times. In the authors' view, the circular economy has promise in materializing an inclusive and economically social, and environmentally resilient, path ahead for Caribbean societies. They state that the concept reflects a new line of thought in development strategy, where environmental growth is pursued and social and environmental impacts are mitigated.

Vaalmiki Arjoon, in chapter 8, looks at what drives economic complexity and notes that such complexity is reflective of the ability of a country to export a wide range of complex commodity mix that would have otherwise been produced only by a small number of economies. Such export, Arjoon claims, can benefit export competitiveness, income sources, and economic growth. Thus, Arjoon looks at a sample of nineteen Latin American and Caribbean countries with a view to examining their determinants of economic complexity, using co-integration econometric methods. The results ascertained led the author to conclude that public policy plays an important role in improving economic complexity for Latin America and the Caribbean.

In chapter 9, Shane Justin Pantin claims that the COVID-19 pandemic transformed much of the world in ways not seen since World War II but that the situation is especially tender for the Caribbean in light of the nature of its economies. In Pantin's view, governments have to move with the times by being adaptive with decisive action through a reconfiguration of the macroeconomic responses instead of through response to shocks and booms. This approach, however, requires good governance that is characterized by transparency, fairness, accountability, consistency, and responsiveness to society's needs. In this regard, Pantin carries out a survey of the macroeconomic challenges and the significance good governance has for tackling the pandemic.

In chapter 10, David Anyanwu inquires as to whether the model of convergence is suitably fit for a post-pandemic recovery period. Anyanwu underscores the point that the impact of the pandemic on Caribbean economies is especially a consequence of their small size and heavy dependence on elsewhere beyond the region. The author argues that there may be more benefits for Caribbean economies through an alternative development approach that is grounded in convenience and that harnesses the wider economies of the region as part of a partnership. For Anyanwu, good leadership capacity is vital in the state having a pivotal role so as to foster and preserve a process of convergence through economic diplomacy.

In chapter 11, in underscoring the decline in development assistance to the Caribbean and the importance of private flows, Helvia Velloso examines the trends in capital flows from the 1980s onward. Velloso closely examines the region's access to private international debt markets from 2000 to 2020 and points out that they have been typically more limited and more costly than those of larger countries in Latin America.

In chapter 12, Miriam L. Campanella and Winston Dookeran explore venues for fresher sources of finance for a quality investment. The authors claim investment in quality infrastructure and its value chain is the basis for an economic opportunity because it plays a vital role in helping emerging economies to navigate past the weary export-led model. Looked at in this way, Campanella and Dookeran regard quality infrastructure development as an immediate priority and a major responsibility in order for emerging economies to avoid the "middle-income trap." Rising trade tariffs and protectionist measures have impact on global finance and result in increased volatility in foreign exchange rates and difficulties in capital flows. Thus, the authors look for initiatives that governments in the Caribbean can take to cope with liquidity drought when infrastructure investments are greatly needed.

In chapter 13, Khushbu Rai takes up the issue of resetting Caribbean and Pacific policies in a discussion on frontiers, flows, and frameworks. Rai fleshes out parallels between the Caribbean and the Pacific on account of distance from major markets, smallness in production scale and a limited export base, institutional weakness, restraining infrastructure, digital divide, and homogeneity. In Rai's view, there are enough shared economic characteristics among small islands such that the economic policy prescriptions that are applied could be similar, despite the fact that in the Oceania Pacific the islands are widely spread whereas in the Caribbean they are quite close. Rai features a comparative analysis of the two regions in the context of regional integration in the resetting of their agendas.

In chapter 14, Annita Montoute focuses on CARICOM's external engagements in addressing the strengths and limits of regional integration for the future and the implications they have for regional integration and development in the post-pandemic period. According to Montoute, the external relations of CARICOM have shifted away from North America and European transatlantic partners to more varied relationships with new partners, and these have both pros and cons. In her view, development efforts and regional integration can be affected in contexts where agendas overlap.

In chapter 15, June Soomer gives a lucid background of the outlook that gave rise to the creation of the ACS and what the ACS represented. In the author's view, it was emblematic of a strategic opportunity for new forms of regional cooperation in recognition of the human, social, and cultural attributes of the region that can proliferate regional integration. Soomer explores elements for redesigning its future, seeing leadership as playing a pivotal role. Soomer also addresses ways through which the ACS may consider building frameworks of resilience and recovery that prioritize citizens.

In chapter 16, Vijay Kumar Chattu looks at the impact on health diplomacy in the Caribbean from geopolitical shifts. Chattu sees the COVID-19 pandemic as having been both a source of major challenges and of opportunities to respond to inequities in health, gender, and various components of socioeconomic development. Taking note of the challenges faced by the region due to natural disasters, chronic and infectious disease, and economic crisis, Chattu claims that small island development states have to find ways to resuscitate so that they may properly respond to health service delivery in a way that equitable access and gender-responsive policies are ensured. In the author's view, the COVID-19 pandemic featured opportunities for peace, health, and well-being to be promoted through global health diplomacy, and it is vital for the CARICOM's systems to be modernized.

In chapter 17, Faies Jafar provides a framework for international relations (IR) studies to engage complexity theory. Jafar employs an inductive reasoning strategy to do so, as guided by the prevailing literature. According to the author, there is a need to explicate the relevance of complexity theory and the instrumental role it can play in advancing IR scholarship, particularly given the COVID-19 pandemic experience and beyond. Jafar undertakes this task in the chapter with a focus on small Caribbean states, and he outlines some potential challenges in integrating complexity theory with IR studies.

In chapter 18, Winston Dookeran claims the geostrategic choices that confront small states are not clear-cut. In the author's view, the COVID-19 pandemic especially affected the development and political landscapes of small states. Dookeran believes that small states' experience with the pandemic is akin to undergoing a stress test of a political nature wherein the ones to survive would be the ones who had the capability of resetting.

Finally, in chapter 19, Winston Dookeran and Manfred Jantzen look at the new directions and political stress tests in the frontiers of the global pandemic and beyond. The authors claim that the global pandemic has brought to light disturbing issues that have been ignored in the past in the development trajectory of many societies and their sovereign nation-states. In the authors' view, the pandemic may have actually served to usher in a new global frontier that requires resetting, reconceptualizing, and redirecting priorities at the societal and global level.

The COVID-19 pandemic period in which we lived was not easy. It urges new ways of planning and better levels of preparedness. It has shown in reality what might have only been previously assumed to take place in movies and works of fiction, namely, that the entire world more or less can come under a cloud of despair stemming from a common source. The experience impels the world community to recognize our global connectiveness in which incidents that affect distant strangers in remote parts of the world can affect the entire world. It obliges regional and global cooperation, and it has defined more reasons why there is a need to rethink, reconceptualize, reset, and reorganize the approach taken to navigate through such times. The guiding paradigms for social and economic development must be fit to respond to the challenges of the time, must be sound and effective to yield growth, and must be resilient to fortify us in future pandemics. Diplomacy has a significant role to play, but its focus must be prioritized and its tasks must be allocated the needed resources.

The chapters in this volume have made earnest efforts to address the multitude of issues raised by the global pandemic for development consideration and reconceptualization, and for diplomacy prioritization. At their core, they endeavor to furnish frameworks and frontiers through which economic progress and human well-being may flow. While the volume may not be without imperfections, it is hoped that it elucidates epistemic value that may inspire interests among students, researchers, and policymakers alike to more deeply explore the ideas presented, in the hope of spearheading better trajectories of development and diplomacy at the level of theory and at the level of practice, now and much beyond.

References

Abdul Majied, Sabeerah, Zoyah Kinkead-Clark, and Sheron C. Burns. 2022. "Understanding Caribbean Early Childhood Teachers' Professional Experiences during the COVID-19 School Disruption." *Early Childhood Education Journal*. doi: https://doi.org/10.1007/s10643-022-01320-7.

Baldacchino, Godfrey. 2020. "Island versus Region: The Politics of Small States in the Caribbean." In *Handbook of Politics and Small States*, edited by Godfrey Baldacchino and Anders Wivel, 278–93. Cheltenham: Edward Elgar Publishing.

Barker, David, David Dodman, and Duncan McGregor. 2009. "Caribbean Vulnerability and Global Change: Contemporary Perspectives." In *Global Change and Caribbean Vulnerability: Environment, Economy and Society at Risk*, edited by Duncan McGregor, David Dodman, and David Marker, 3–21. Kingston, Jamaica: University of the West Indies Press.

Byron, Jessica, Jacqueline Laguardia Martinez, Annita Montoute, and Keron Niles. 2021. "Impacts of COVID-19 in the Commonwealth Caribbean: Key Lessons." *The Round Table*, 110 (1): 99–119.

Caribbean Development Bank. 2020. "COVID-19 Pandemic in the Caribbean." file:/// Users/researcher/Downloads/COVID-19%20daily%20new%20cases%20June%2028 .pdf.

CTO (Caribbean Tourism Organization). 2020. "Barbados." https://www.onecaribbean .org/buy-cto-tourism-statistics/annual-statistical-report/.

ECLAC (Economic Commission for Latin America and the Caribbean). 2005. "Issues and Challenges in Caribbean Cruise Ship Tourism." Port of Spain. https:// repositorio.cepal.org/bitstream/handle/11362/38788/1/LCCARL075_en.pdf.

———. 2020. "The Case for Financing: Caribbean Resilience Building in the Face of the COVID-19 Pandemic." Studies and Perspectives Series 97. https://repositorio .cepal.org/bitstream/handle/11362/46629/4/S2000887_en.pdf.

Garces-Elias, Maria-Claudia, Roberto A. Leon-Manco, Ana Armas-Vega, Andres Viteri-Garcia, and Andres A. Agudelo-Suarez. 2022. "Impact of Mandatory Social Measures due to the COVID-19 Pandemic on the Subjective Well-Being of Latin American and Caribbean Dentists." *Journal of Clinical and Experimental Dentistry*, 14 (1): e40–7.

Griffith, Ivelaw. 2004. *The Caribbean in an Age of Terror*. Kingston, Jamaica: Ian Randle Publisher.

Hambleton, Ian R., Selvi M. Jeyaseelan, and Madhuvanti M. Murphy. 2020. "COVID-19 in the Caribbean Small Island Developing States: Lessons Learnt from Extreme Weather Events." *The Lancet*, 8 (September): e1114–15.

Harris, Sasekea Yoneka. 2021. "The Coronavirus Pandemic in the Caribbean Academic Library: Jamaica's Initial Interpretation of Strengths, Biggest Impact, Lessons and Plans." *Library Management*, 42 (6/7): 362–75.

Izarali, M. Raymond. 2018. "Issues of Crime, Violence and in/Security in the Contemporary Caribbean." In *Crime, Violence, and Security in the Caribbean*, edited by M. Raymond Izarali, 1–15. New York: Routledge.

————. 2019. "Towards an Inclusive Approach to Human Rights in Africa in an Age of Globalization." In *Expanding Perspectives on Human Rights in Africa*, edited by M. R. Izarali, Oliver Masakure, and Bonny Ibhawoh, 268–84. New York: Routledge.

Jaramillo, Sandra Garcia. 2020. "COVID-19 and Primary and Secondary Education: The Impact of the Crisis and Public Policy Implications for Latin America and the Caribbean." UNDP Latin America and the Caribbean #COVID19, Policy Documents Series. file:///Users/researcher/Downloads/undp-rblac-CD19-PDS-Number20-UNICEF-Educacion-EN.pdf.

Khan, Aliyah. 2020. *Far from Mecca. Globalizing the Muslim Caribbean*. New Brunswick: Rutgers University Press.

Knight, Andy. 2018. "Vulnerabilities and Security Threats in the Caribbean." In *Crime, Violence and Security in the Caribbean*, edited by M. Raymond Izarali, 220–39. New York: Routledge.

————. 2019. "The Nexus between Vulnerabilities and Violence in the Caribbean." *Third World Quarterly*, 40 (2): 405–24.

Knight, W. Andy, and K. Srikanth Reddy. 2020. "Caribbean Response to COVID-19: A Regional Approach to Pandemic Preparedness and Resilience." *The Round Table*, 109 (4): 464–65.

Leacock, Coreen J., and Joel Warrican. 2020. "Helping Teachers to Respond to COVID-19 in the Eastern Caribbean: Issues of Readiness, Equity and Care." *Journal of Education for Teaching (International Research and Pedagogy)*, 46 (4): 576–84.

Llibre-Guerra, Jorge J., Ivonne Z. Jimenez-Velazquez, Juan J. Llibre-Rodriguez, and Daisy Acosta. 2020. "The Impact of COVID-19 on Mental Health in the Hispanic Caribbean Region." *International Psychogeriatrics*, 32 (10): 1143–46.

Long, Tom. 2020. "Small States in Central America." In *Handbook of Politics and Small States*, edited by Godfrey Baldacchino and Anders Wivel, 242–58. Cheltenham: Edward Elgar Publishing.

Meighoo, Kirk. 2020. "The Caribbean and Covid-19: Not a Health Crisis, But a Looming Economic One." *The Round Table*, 109 (3): 340–41.

Nathan, Ronald A. 2022. "Caribbean Churches, Capacities, and Responses to the COVID-19 Pandemic." In *Racialized Health, COVID-19, and Religious Experience*, edited by R. Drew Smith, Stephanie C. Boddie, and Berts D. English, 148–57. New York: Routledge.

Nelson, Karlene Saundria, and Yolanda V. Tugwell. 2022. "Information-Seeking Behaviour of Students at a Caribbean University during the COVID-19 Pandemic." *Library Management*, 43 (3/4): 257–79.

Persaud, Seelall. 2022. *Stepping Out of the Herd: My Life in the Guyana Police Force*. Altona, Manitoba: Friesen Press.

Peterson, Ryan R., and Robin B. DiPietro. 2021. "Exploring the Impact of the COVID-19 Pandemic on the Perceptions and Sentiments of Tourism Employees: Evidence from a Small Island Tourism Economy in the Caribbean." *International Hospitality Review*, 35 (2): 156–70.

Premdass, Ralph. 2011. "Identity, Ethnicity, and the Caribbean Homeland in an Era of Globalization." *Social Identities*, 17 (6): 811–32.

Ramsaran, Dave, and Linden Lewis. 2018. *Caribbean Masala: Indian Identity in Guyana and Trinidad*. Jackson: University Press of Mississippi.

Resiere, Dabor, Dajour Resiere, and Hatem Kallel. 2020. "Implementation of Medical and Scientific Cooperation in the Caribbean Using Blockchain Technology in Coronavirus (Covid-19) Pandemics." *Journal of Medical Systems*, 44: 122–23.

Singh, Priti. 2013. "Introduction." In *The Contemporary Caribbean: Issues and Challenges*, edited by Priti Singh and M. Raymond Izarali, 1–15. New Delhi: Shipra Publications.

Sobers, N.P., C.H. Howitt, S.M. Jeyaseelan, N.S. Greaves, H. Harewood, M.M. Murphy, K. Quimby, and I.R. Hambleton. 2021. "Impact of COVID-19 Contract Tracing on Human Resources for Health – A Caribbean Perspective." *Preventive Medicine Reports*, 22: 1–5.

Thompson, Alvin. 1997. *The Haunting Past: Politics, Economics and Race in Caribbean Life*. Kingston, Jamaica: Ian Randle Publishers.

UN. 2021. "Selected Online Learning Experiences in the Caribbean during COVID-19." Policy Brief, LC/CAR/2021/3, 19 May.

UNDP. 2012. *Caribbean Human Development Report 2012*. New York: United Nations Human Development Programme.

World Bank. 2021. "Caribbean Overview." https://www.worldbank.org/en/country/caribbean/overview#1.

WTTC (World Travel and Tourism Council). 2021. "Global Economic Impact and Trends." https://wttc.org/Portals/0/Documents/Reports/2021/Global%20Economic%20Impact%20and%20Trends%202021.pdf?ver=2021-07-01-114957-177.

Part 2

Sustainability Analysis

COVID-19, Health Security, and Future Resilience

2

COVID-19 Symmetric Shock and Its Asymmetric Consequences

MIRIAM L. CAMPANELLA AND WINSTON DOOKERAN

Introduction

The outbreak of the COVID-19 pandemic has opened a period of policy uncertainty for all of us. Infection fighting, a fundamental responsibility of governments, and measures to contain the virus – quarantine, social distancing, and shutdowns of non-essential businesses – are bringing the economy into a "loop-type" cycle of shocks – between demand and supply. In growth models, shock absorbers would mitigate the effects on growth. But buffers and shock absorbers are weak in several emerging and developing countries, and to prevent an immediate collapse, the size of the fiscal injection must be equivalent to the fall in the gross domestic product (GDP). This is a tall order under any circumstances but has dire complications to debt, credit, incomes, and poverty levels, and above all the cost implications of the financing modes used and the prospect of recovery that is in a "loop-type" cycle.

The upcoming massive recession presents critical economic and financial variables, a steep rise of jobless claims, fixed-asset investment falling by 45 percent year-on-year, and capital outflows from emerging markets by USD $83 billion (Dimitrijevic and Williams 2020). Yet, the key determinant factor of the COVID-19 economic shock is its ability to damage an economy's supply side and, more specifically, capital formation. With the credit intermediation disrupted and the capital stock contracted, the shock becomes structural. Depending upon the intensity of the damage inflicted on the economy's supply side, the shape of the shock could be V, U, or L. This "shock geometry" will be the structural legacy of the infection crisis on the economy.

What, then, can Caribbean countries do to mitigate the full impact of the pandemic tsunami? With weak public health infrastructures and the limited fiscal space to ramp up such infrastructures, and to keep afloat their economies, several developing economies cannot afford to run higher debt issuance for the risk of rating. The chapter suggests a two-pronged strategy: First, calling on multilateral development banks (MDBs) to repurpose climate change investment plans to fight the COVID-19 pandemic crisis, as this shift would be meaningful and coherent with the climate change rationale of "public good"; second, teaming up and drawing on their joint political capital to urge G20 core nations to abide by their public commitments to the ten principles of the Pandemic Response Protocol signed in 2005.

Exiting from the Lockdown

Emerging Economies' Financing Gaps, a Major Threat of the COVID-19

The outbreak of the COVID-19 pandemic has opened a period of policy uncertainty for all of us. As Gopinath (2020) argues, infection fighting, a fundamental responsibility of governments, and measures to contain the virus such as quarantine, social distancing, and shutdowns of non-essential businesses are exceeding all previous human pain and economic metrics. This, she adds, can be viewed as a truly global crisis as no country is spared. For the first time since the Great Depression, both advanced economies and emerging markets and developing economies are in recession. Figure 2.1 illustrates this point.

Equally to climate change, the COVID-19 pandemic shares the features of a global catastrophic event, or external shock, that calls for collective action. Each country's contagion has the potential to spread the infection exponentially, and each country's abatement of the disease entails higher cost than benefit unless effective, concerted collective actions take place.

Extensive roles in fighting the infection and keeping the whole economy afloat need to put at work extensive monetary and fiscal policies. The measures needed for stepping up financial provisions to manage the health situation, avoiding a dramatic human death toll from COVID-19 and supporting the population and companies through a period of quasi-suspended economic activity remain uncertain, as nobody can know how long the crisis will last, how bad it will be, or how it will play out. While there is some expectation that the pandemic is on the ebb, the 2022 Ukraine-Russian war has a further complication to the analysis in the "loop-type" shock model. Eminent economist Nouriel Roubini (2022), in addressing this issue, said that "the war in Ukraine will trigger a massive negative supply shock in a global economy that is still reeling from COVID-19 and a year-long build-up of inflationary pressures." A typical charactertistic of a pandemic crisis is that it opens a period of the economy into a "loop-type" cycle of shocks – between demand and supply. In growth models, shock absorbers would mitigate the effects on growth. But buffers and shock absorbers are weak in several emerging and developing countries and to prevent an immediate collapse, the size of the fiscal injection must be

Global crisis
Both advanced economies and emerging market and developing economies are in recession. Major economies have also been significantly downgraded.

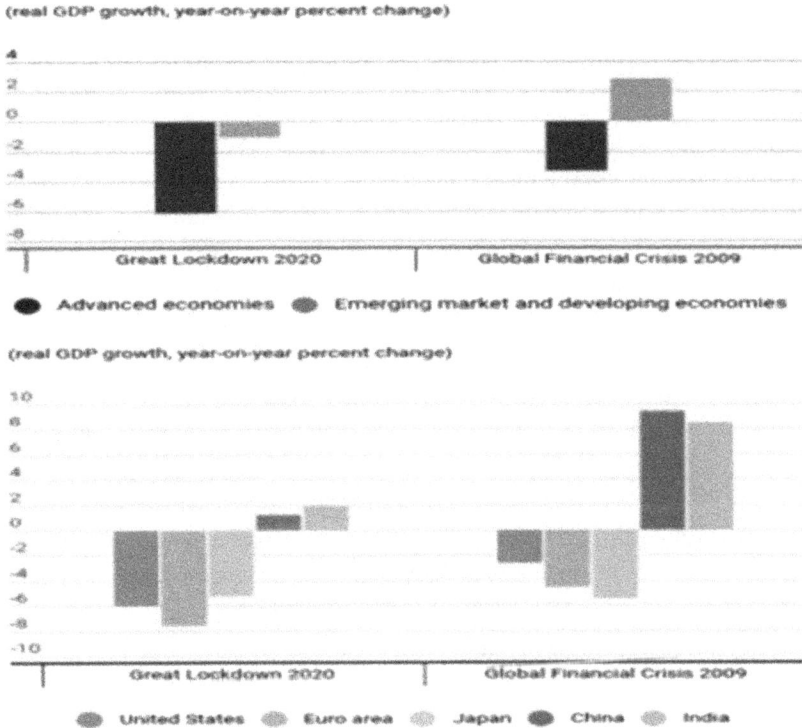

(real GDP growth, year-on-year percent change)

Advanced economies ● Emerging market and developing economies

(real GDP growth, year-on-year percent change)

United States ● Euro area ● Japan ● China ● India

Figure 2.1 Advanced and emerging and developing economies in 2009, 2020.
Source: Werner (2020).

equivalent to the fall in the GDP. This is a tall order in any circumstances. But it has dire complications to debt, credit, incomes, poverty levels, and above all, the cost implications of financing modes used and the prospect of recovery that is in a "loop-like" cycle (Dookeran 2020). He adds that as the economy enters into a "loop-type" cycle of shocks – between demand and supply – old policy prescriptions for recessionary times may no longer work. The coronavirus crisis has induced a supply shock – reducing wages and production – which in turn fuels a demand shock – a fall in purchasing power.

For now, the metric measures vary according to the fiscal space of each country. Advanced economies have enough fiscal space to manage the health situation. Issuing sovereign bonds denominated in their own currency to keep afloat the whole economy, and stepping in with massive financial instruments have given them munitions to relaunch the post-COVID-19 crisis. The US Federal Reserve and the Bank of England have put up extraordinary financial operations to avoid triggering down rating pressures and currency devaluations (Smialek 2020; Elliott 2020). The Ukraine shock may trigger "a negative supply shock in a global economy that is still reeling from COVID-19" according to Roubini (2022), which may usher a sustained trade-off between growth and inflation.

A different story is read when looking at emerging and developing economies. The Institute of International Finance (IIF) (2020) considers developing economies' fiscal policy space and finds that a significant number of emerging markets (EMs) on balance have room for fiscal easing despite elevated global debt levels, including many countries in Europe and Asia. Several ASEAN countries have already announced fiscal packages, and Turkey will likely try to offset negative growth effects from lower tourism revenues – (Figure 2.2).

In Latin America, Chile has ample policy space and will tap into its stabilization fund, while Colombia has space on the margin. The Middle East and North Africa countries, including Kuwait, Qatar, the United Arab Emirates, and possibly Saudi Arabia, have room for fiscal measures but are likely to stay neutral given widening deficits and lower oil prices. Most importantly, however, the IIF finds that a number of key EMs will not be able to use fiscal policy to a significant extent due to high debt levels and/or large deficits, including Argentina, Brazil, India, and South Africa (IIF 2020).

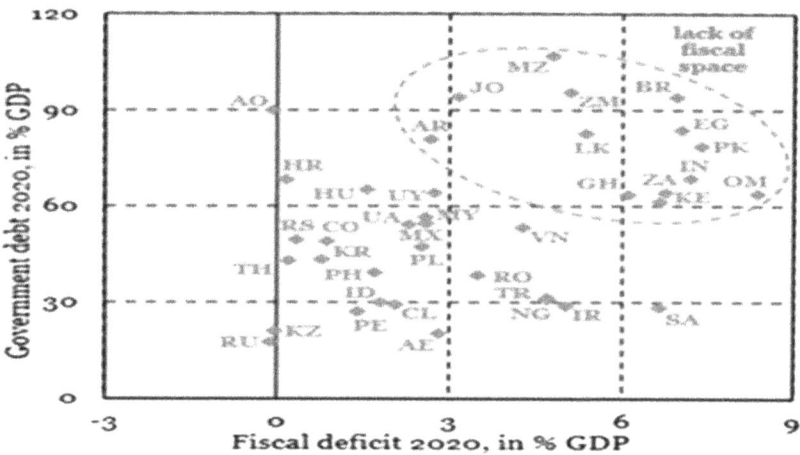

Figure 2.2 Fiscal space is unevenly distributed.
Source: IIF (2020).

Caribbean countries are facing the pandemic disease with weak public health infrastructures, limited fiscal space to ramp up public health services, and affected economic sectors and households. Even more threatening, they are vulnerable to the dollar financial shock. With a large share of credit, trade, and debt priced in dollars, the smallest countries would barely afford expansionary debt measures, and fatally, they could fall under more rating pressures on sovereign debts. In March alone, there was a capital outflow from EMs of USD $83 billion, a sum larger than in the previous financial crisis, which is a signal of increasing pressures on sovereign ratings (Lanau and Fortun 2020). Figure 2.3 highlights this point on capital outflows.

The economic impact of the pandemic in Latin American countries is likely to vary due to regional and country-specific characteristics and would run through three channels: sovereigns, commodities, and tourism (Figures 2.4, 2.5, and 2.6). Unequal distribution is also the fallout of the crisis. The sharp fall in the oil price is expected to benefit the oil-importing countries in the region, and at the same time will dampen investment and economic activity in countries that are heavily dependent on oil exports (Figure 2.5). In the event of a local outbreak, service sector activity will likely be hit the hardest as a result of containment efforts and social distancing, with sectors such as tourism and hospitality, and transportation particularly affected –(Figure 2.6). Yet, the worst-case scenario would be an increase in risk aversion with capital outflows from the region and the worsening of global financial conditions. In those awful circumstances, the whole region will be equally hit with the consequences of currency devaluations and financial crisis.

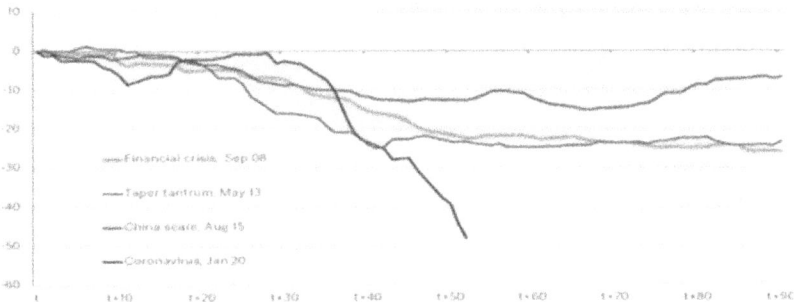

Figure 2.3 Cumulative non-resident portfolio flows to EMEs in times of global shocks, time in number of days, in US$ billions.

Source: Lanau and Fortun (2020).

(Sovereign spreads, emerging-market bond index; basis points)

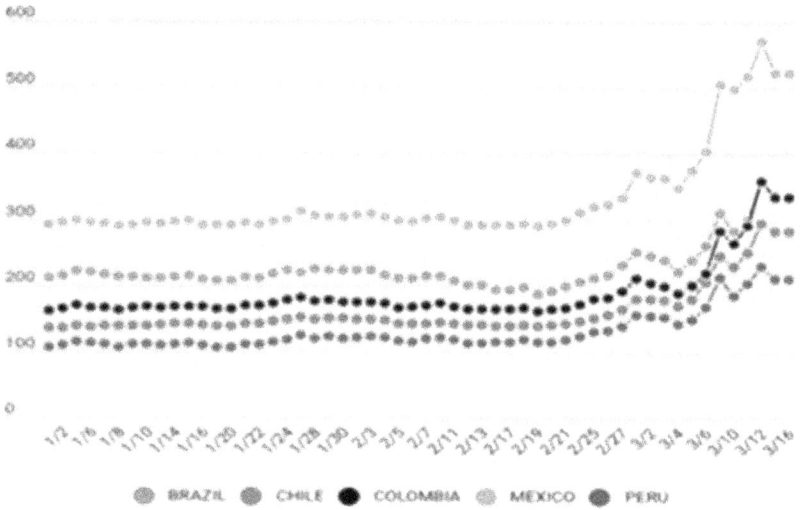

Figure 2.4 Tightening financial conditions. Sovereign spreads.
Source: Werner (2020).

(Commodity exports, percent of GDP)

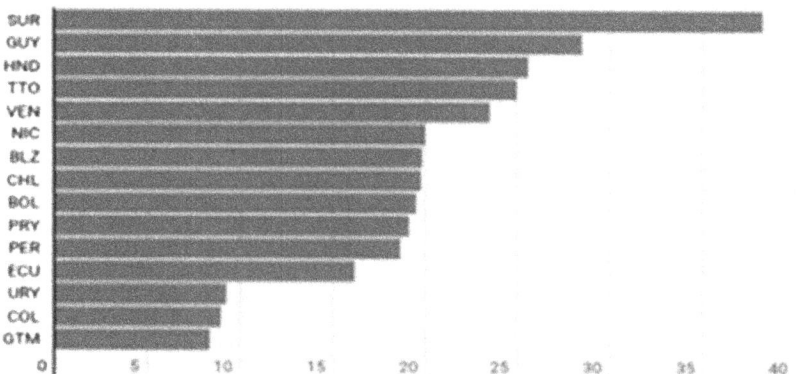

Figure 2.5 Commodities.
Source: Werner (2020).

(International tourism receipts, percent of GDP)

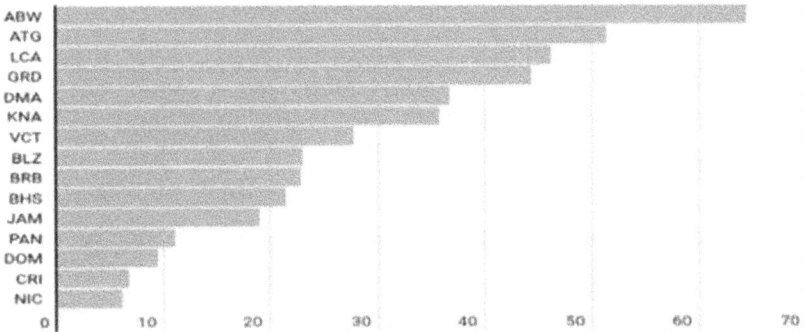

Source: World Bank. World Development Indicators database and IMF staff calculations
Note: Latest available data. Country abbreviations refer to the International Organization for Standardization code

Figure 2.6 Tourism.
Source: Werner (2020).

The Geometry of the Crisis and Its Legacy

The recovery from the COVID-19 pandemic could take many forms depending on initial conditions, yet the size of the stimulus and financing modes will mostly contribute to the shape of the shock. In a recent paper, Carlsson-Szlezak, Reeves, and Swartz (2020) have reconstructed along these lines the variable geometry of the shock (Figure 2.7), the classical V, U, and L shapes from the 2008 financial crisis. An interesting feature of the paper consists of taking three countries – Canada, the United States, and Greece – equally hit by the 2008 financial crisis to model three different shapes of the ensuing recession.

- *V-shape.*

In 2008, Canada avoided a banking crisis, credit continued to flow, and capital formation was not as significantly disrupted. Avoiding a deeper collapse helped keep labor in place and prevented skill atrophy. GDP dropped but substantially climbed back to its pre-crisis path. Canada typically developed a classic "V-shape" recession, where output is displaced but growth eventually rebounds to its old path (Figure 2.8).

- *U-shape.*

In 2008, the United States, due to a serious banking crisis and disruption of debt intermediation, growth dropped and never rebounded to its pre-crisis path, and the recession took a lengthy U (Figure 2.9).

The financial turmoil of Covid-19 smacks substantially emerging economies, as global investment portfolios move to safer asset classes. This means, Cavallo explains "that the COVID-19 shock is creating a "sudden stop" in capital flows for emerging markets", yet the consequent exchange rate devaluation will not benefit the region's exports. Unlike past sudden stops, "the covid-19 crisis affects global supply and demand. All countries are hit at practically the same time. Who, then, will buy our region's exports? Real exchange rates will need to depreciate greatly, and even such depreciation may fail to stimulate demand among potential importers with plenty of problems of their own" (Cavallo 2020).

The damage on the real exchange rate depreciations is highly disruptive in the short run, and the most important reason is referred to as "balance sheet effects". In "Latin America and the Caribbean, a large portion of countries' debts are denominated in foreign currency, often US dollars. "This means that the balance sheets of indebted agents in those economies are hit in proportion to the real depreciation, increasing their debt burden which is going up exactly when their ability to pay is declining". The result is a vicious cycle that leads to ever increasing borrowing costs (also known as country risk, as reflected in Emerging Market Bond Index—EMBI—spreads). Moreover, experience with previous episodes (all too abundant in Latin America) shows that large real exchange rate depreciations can lead to major losses in output." (Cavallo 2020).

To the picture, Cavallo adds the initial weak conditions in Latin America and the Caribbean (LAC) countries notably weaker than in 2008 at the outset of the Global Financial Crisis because fiscal and external deficits, as well as levels of liability dollarization, are on average higher than in 2008. International reserves are also higher—a positive development—but IDB calculations suggest that they are not enough to offset the increased risk from deterioration in other fundamentals" (Cavallo 2020).

Figure 2.7 COVID-19 external shock shifting to financial crisis.
Source: Cavallo (2020).

- *L-shape.*

Greece, by far in the worst shape, never recovered from its prior output path, and a structurally low economic growth rate has declined. The crisis has left lasting structural damage to the economy's supply side. Greece is a textbook example of an L-shape, by far the most pernicious shape (Figure 2.10).

Additionally, they note that depending upon what shape the shock will take, and what intensity each of them will have, the shape of the shock will leave a structural legacy on the economy.

The dynamics of the crisis, though, depend on the initial state of selected countries. Emerging economies will be the hardest beaten on the borrowing costs, a most serious factor of financial vulnerability owing to debt sprees accumulated over years of low interest rates.

Incapacitated to ramp up public health services and support for economic sectors and households, there remain significant challenges for rapid and

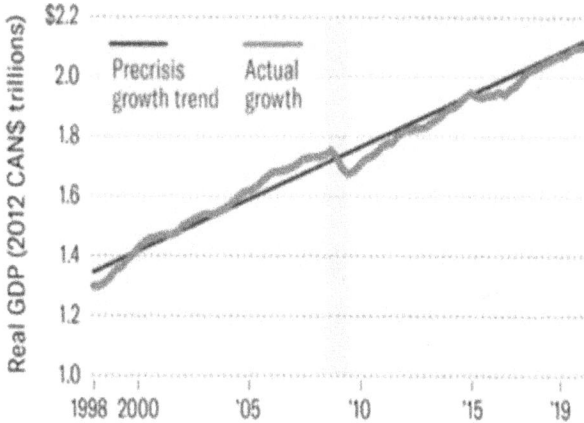

Figure 2.8 V-shaped Canada 2020.

Source: Carlsson-Szlezak, Reeves, and Swartz (2020).

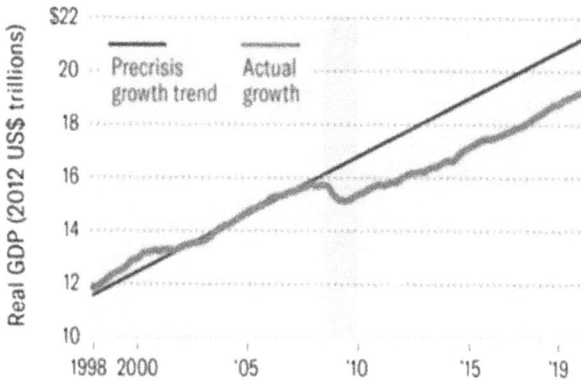

Figure 2.9 U-shaped United States.

Source: Carlsson-Szlezak, Reeves, and Swartz (2020).

sizeable financial interventions to keep afloat the economy. Fiscal incapacities would likely extend the duration of the crisis and further worsen their financial ratings. The length of the crisis, the resilience of the country's economic and political base, and the speed and adequacy of policy response will be key for the trajectory of sovereign ratings (Dimitrijevic and Williams 2020).

Will Caribbean Countries Avoid the L-Shaped Recession?

Weak public health infrastructures, limited fiscal space to keep economies afloat, and low debt ratings call for exceptional policy actions. What can

L-shaped (Greece)

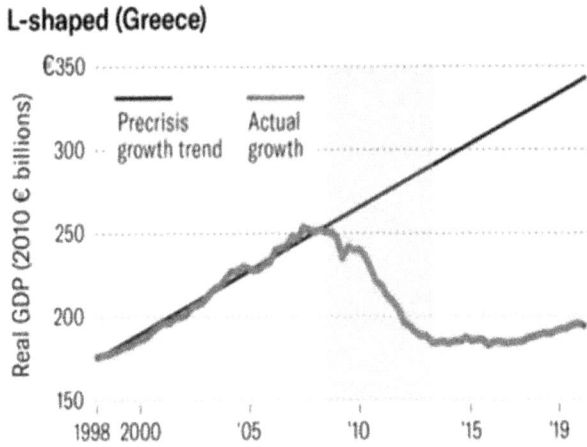

Figure 2.10 L-shaped Greece.
Source: Carlsson-Szlezak, Reeves, and Swartz (2020).

Caribbean countries do to avoid the worst-case scenario? Advanced economies and China have put together massive government packages that will extend a USD $5 trillion lifeline to their economies. The rapid financial response will mitigate the extent of the shock in people's lives and the economy; and will translate to a USD $1 trillion to USD $2 trillion injection of demand into the major G20 economies, and a two-percentage-point turnaround in global output. Nevertheless, the world economy is expected to go into recession with a predicted loss of global income in trillions of dollars and will do little for developing countries, with the likely exception of China.

Owing to fiscal and foreign exchange constraints, which are bound to tighten further over the course of the year, developing economies, according to the United Nations Conference on Trade and Development (UNCTAD) estimates, will endure a USD $2 trillion to USD $3 trillion financing gap over the next two years. These numbers suggest that "lacking the monetary, fiscal administrative capacity to respond to this crisis, the consequences of a combined health pandemic and a global recession will be catastrophic for many developing countries and halt their progress towards the Sustainable Development Goals" (UNCTAD 2020).

In a likely L-shaped scenario, the external shock is amplified by endogenous shocks that cascade through the economy. A financial crisis emerges as a result of an unprecedented drop in corporate profits and household incomes, which governments cannot plumb without endangering debt sustainability. Credit and mortgage spreads blow out further, and the ensuing bankruptcies are followed by a prolonged deleveraging cycle. However, this can be avoided if the fiscal stimulus is enough to prevent an L recession from becoming a permanent slowdown (Figure 2.10).

At the moment, most "climate change" finance flows are allocated to the MDBs. Many MDBs have established specific funds to address climate change, but these account for a relatively small share of the overall MDB energy-related lending. For example, donor countries have committed a total of USD $6.1 billion to capitalize on the World Bank's Climate Investment Fund (World Bank 2008) (Figure 2.11).

As the COVID-19 pandemic brutally hits developing economies, the G20 should invite the MDBs to boost crisis lending by USD $100 billion to USD $200 billion, in a measure comparable to 2009 commitments. From this standpoint, Morris and Glassman (2020) argue that:

> It was no coincidence that the statement of G20 leaders in April 2009 committed the MDBs to an additional USD $100 billion in financing, almost exactly the amount achieved in the following year. G20 governments proved instrumental in setting a counter-cyclical lending target for the MDBs. This was part of a broader package of measures – monetary, fiscal, and regulatory – that was adopted by the G20 countries in their response to the crisis.

According to Frankel (2021), the G20 Summit held in Rome in October 2021 took place at a time of heightened uncertainty about public health and

Climate financing by the world's largest multilateral development banks (MDBs) in developing countries and emerging economies rose to an all-time high of $43.1 bn in 2018, boosting projects that help developing countries cut emissions and address climate risks.

This represents an increase of more than 22 percent from the previous year, where climate finance totaled $35.2 bn. This is also a 60 percent increase since the adoption of the Paris agreement in response to the ever more pressing challenge of climate change, which disproportionately affects the poorest and most vulnerable.

The latest MDB climate finance figures are detailed in the 2018 Joint Report on Multilateral Development Banks' Climate Finance, show that $30.2 bn, or 70 percent, of the total financing for 2018 was devoted to climate change mitigation investments.

MDBs report another $68.1 bn in net climate co-finance – investments from the public and private sector - adding up to total climate finance for the year of $111.2 bn.

"In 2018, the World Bank Group announced it will invest and mobilize $200 billion over 2021-2025 to support countries in addressing climate adaptation and resilience, doubling its commitments from the previous five years."

Figure 2.11 Repurposing "climate change finance" to the COVID-19 crisis.
Source: World Bank (2019).

the global economy. International coordination, the new allocation of the International Monetary Fund's (IMF) special drawing rights, and its proposed plan of action on vaccines were high on the agenda for the leaders.

The chapter also explores donors providing resources to a trust fund to pay World Bank debt service, with the objective of freeing up resources of International Development Association (IDA) countries for them to finance urgent expenditures (World Bank 2020, 12).

The lack of a clear target, which sends an important signal to markets that developing economies will be supported during a global downturn, perhaps explains the tentative signals coming from the World Bank so far. To the Bank's credit, it has sought to reassure its client countries that support for COVID-19 efforts will be forthcoming. But these reassurances have mostly been targeted directly at health sector responses, and the USD $12 billion headline number reflects this. If we are to expect anything bolder from the World Bank, including a coordinated announcement with other MDBs, then the MDBs' leading shareholders will almost surely need to drive it, with the G20 as the most likely coordinating body, and so free up IDA countries to finance other priority expenditures in the pandemic.

What Can Caribbean Small Islands Do That They Didn't before the Crisis?

The Caribbean Coronavirus Tracker helps to provide insight on what is happening in the region, and these government figures, while constantly changing, are very tiny compared to other regions. The data on the infection do not talk about the devastating impact on the economy. Travel and tourism, the main sources of foreign currency revenue and the engine of Caribbean economies, are the most exposed to take the hit. In 2019, the travel and tourism industry contributed more than 15 percent to Caribbean GDP, covering 18 percent of the employment. The pandemic has inevitably hit the whole industry, and with traditional and informal jobs prevailing, the sector is unlikely to return to pre-crisis numbers. The travel and tourism sectors, "the lynch pin of the Caribbean economies and societies" (ILO 2020), sustain several economic activities, including agriculture, manufacturing, transport, and construction. (Figure 2.12).

The COVID-19 crisis will further exacerbate pitfalls in Caribbean economies, notably in health and the environment. As ECLAC (2018, 64) pointed out:

> Critical sectors in the Caribbean have lost talent. Professional workers, especially in
> critical sectors such as nursing, allied health, teaching, and engineering professions,

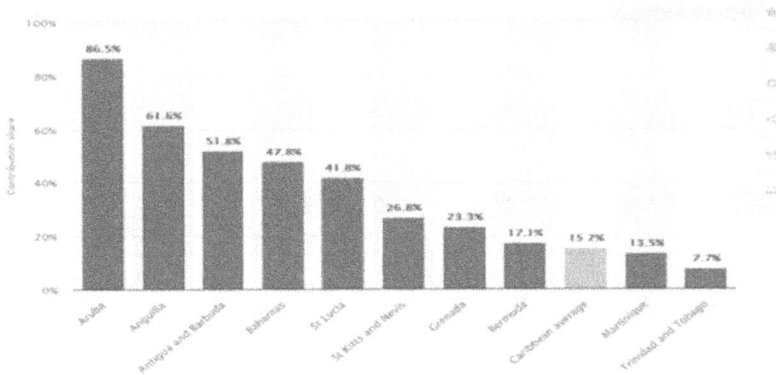

Figure 2.12 Total contribution of travel and tourism to GDP in selected countries in the Caribbean in 2017.

Source: Statista (2020).

have more mobility. The departure of such professionals to more developed nations has resulted in a shortage of qualified labor. They leave the Caribbean for many reasons, including poor working conditions; remuneration and benefits that are not commensurate with qualifications; underuse of skills; and insufficient training and opportunities for career progression.

The most critical failure involves environmental policy. Caribbean countries are counted as "the most environmentally hazard-prone region in the world. Natural disasters are the main environmental challenges, along with concerns about climate change, loss of biodiversity, anthropogenic stressors on freshwater and land-based sources of pollution" (ECLAC 2018, 81). On another side, travel and tourism, the main export sectors of Caribbean economies, have also put pressure on the Caribbean region's natural ecosystems. The complex environmental challenges require countries in the whole region to put up coherent governance frameworks to address economic, social, and environmental policies. Some of these challenges are related to climate change – adaptation, water resources and solid waste management, energy transition, and sustainable transportation – the core infrastructure of the United Nations Conference on Sustainable Development (Rio+20), all of which the COVID-19 crisis has intensified.

Shock scenarios via the tourism sector reveal the significance of the sector and the impact on the Country Department Caribbean (CCB) economies (Bahamas, Barbados, Guyana, Jamaica, Suriname, and Trinidad and Tobago). Figure 2.13 identifies GDP projections in LAC tourism sectors.

Latin America and the Caribbean: Real GDP Growth

(Year-over-year percent change)

	2017	2018	2019	Projections		
				2020	2021	2022–25
Latin America and the Caribbean	1.3	1.1	0.1	-5.2	3.4	2.7
LAC excluding Venezuela	2.0	1.7	0.8	-5.0	3.6	2.7
South America	0.7	0.4	-0.1	-5.1	3.4	2.6
Argentina	2.7	-2.5	-2.2	-5.7	4.4	2.5
Brazil	1.3	1.3	1.1	-5.3	2.9	2.4
Chile	1.2	3.9	1.1	-4.5	5.3	2.7
Colombia	1.4	2.5	3.3	-2.4	3.7	3.9
Peru	2.5	4.0	2.2	-4.5	5.2	3.9
Mexico	2.1	2.1	-0.1	-6.6	3.0	2.3
CAPDR	4.2	3.8	3.2	-2.4	4.0	4.1
Caribbean						
Tourism dependent	0.9	1.9	1.4	-7.5	5.9	2.2
Commodity exporters	-1.2	0.7	0.9	-4.6	3.6	5.1

Figure 2.13 Projections GDP in LAC economies and Caribbean tourism dependent.
Source: IMF (2020).

CCB governments are likely to face increased financing needs driven by both the direct costs of crisis mitigation and the revenue implications of the economic shock. Policymakers should work toward developing contingencies and identifying low-cost supplemental financing options over the near term, including those available from international financial institutions (Mooney and Zegarra 2020).

The size of fiscal stimulus packages in 2020 to cope with the pandemic crisis ranged from one percent to 15 percent of GDP in Africa, three percent in Asia, and over ten percent in the United States and Europe. An Index of COVID-19 Economic Stimulus (ICES index), developed to measure policy response across countries, looked at 168 countries and classified their responses from high to low (Siddik 2020, 7–10). Caribbean countries were among the lowest responses. These disparities in responses give rise to an asymmeteric economy-wide impact on wealth inequalities, social stress, and political tensions.

In this developing crisis, no government is able to finance with its own resources the COVID-19 health crisis and its economic fallout. Advanced central banks, the US Federal Reserve, the European Central Bank, the Bank of England, and the Bank of Japan, are all deeply involved in financing respective governments. Differently, the central banks in emerging market economies (EMEs), however, cannot afford to do the same. Large USD debt exposure and weak foreign exchange reserves hinder efforts to adopt large stimulus packages. Marek Dabrowski noted in 2020 in a blog article entitled "Is Covid-19 Triggering a New Emerging-Market Crisis?" that emerging and developing countries should be "extremely careful with their own monetary and fiscal measures. Their macroeconomic room for maneuver is more limited compared to advanced economies because of the limited credibility of emerging-market currencies" (Dabrowski and Dominguez-Jimenez 2020).

Countries that overlooked activating a policy of insurance for their currencies, endowing central banks with foreign exchange reserves and sovereign funds, become the most vulnerable in accessing financial markets. Following the Asian financial crisis of 1998–1999 and the great financial crisis of 2008–2009, the collective sovereign fund and central bank reserves raised up to USD $22.1 trillion in 2018 from USD $19.8 trillion in 2015, with more than half of these held in Asia and the Middle East. While others did little to ensure their currencies' safety net by increasing debt exposure in the US dollar (Kyriakopoulou 2020), LAC countries, as indicated in Figure 2.14, are a case in point where countries did little to mitigate against the financial fallout.

Lacking reserve back-ups, those countries are almost cut off from capital markets and could suffer capital flight and currency substitution. Consequently,

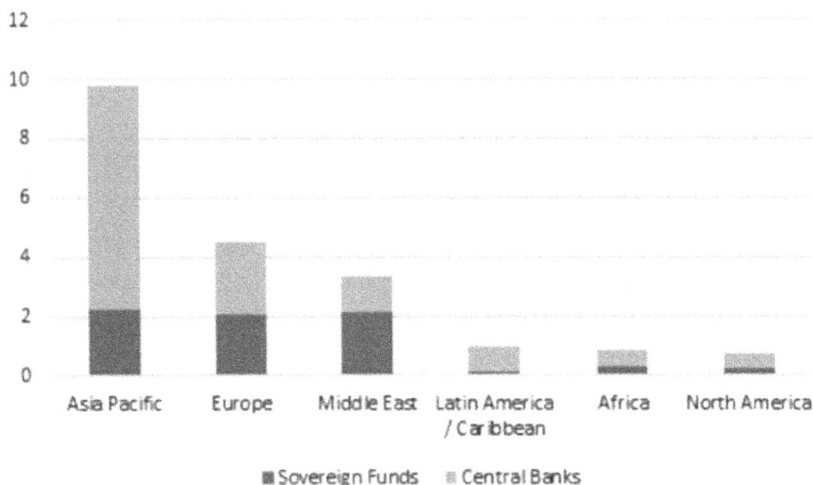

Figure 2.14 Reserves by region and type of institution, $trillion.

Source: Kyriakopoulou (2020).

the financial relief from the COVID-19 "should come, at least partly, from outside" (Dabrowski and Domínguez-Jiménez 2020).

Policy Suggestions and Concluding Thoughts

Along this short investigation, we see a historic opportunity for policymakers and for all of us to do what we did not do before the crisis. Caribbean countries deserve a special consideration for this endeavor. Physical dispersion and the fragile beauty of their small islands would make them extremely vulnerable to asymmetric upshots. For this purpose, the platform of international institutions is primarily called to take action. The IMF should provide immediate financial assistance to emerging and developing economies as it did from 2008 to 2010. This time, the IMF seems to be sufficiently funded (having around USD $1 trillion at its disposal), although nearly 80 countries have already asked for its support.

The G20 also has a role to play. It can provide a coordinated policy response to the crisis and fight protectionism and other "beggar-thy-neighbor" policies, as it did from 2008 to 2010 (Bery, Biondi, and Brekelmans 2019). So far, G20 countries are still a way from a coordinated global economic response to the uphill tasks ahead. The Working Group of the Caribbean, established as a doorway to the G20, could be revived to provide a Caribbean voice to the global financial demands. To provide effective representation, there will be a need for an innovative form of diplomacy.

UNCTAD Proposal to G20

UNCTAD proposed to G20 members a realistic action plan to address the COVID-19 fallout, which seems to be fitting well with Caribbean countries' financing needs. UNCTAD made several recommendations to G20 on the issue.

The first is a USD $1 trillion liquidity injection; it is a kind of helicopter money drop for those being left behind through reallocating existing special drawing rights at the IMF and adding a new allocation that will need to go considerably beyond the 2009 allocation made in response to the global financial crisis.

The second recommendation is a debt jubilee for distressed economies. An immediate debt standstill on sovereign debt payments should be followed by significant debt relief. A benchmark could be the German debt relief administered after World War II, which canceled half of its outstanding debt. On that measure, around USD $1 trillion should be canceled this year and should be overseen by an independently created body.

The third recommendation is for a Marshall Plan for a healthy recovery. It was suggested that the plan could be funded from some of the missing official development assistance (ODA) which was long promised but not delivered by development partners. UNCTAD estimates that an additional USD $500 billion – a quarter of the last decade's missing ODA – largely in the form of grants should be earmarked for emergency health services and related social relief programs.

And finally, capital controls should be given their legitimate place in any policy regime to curtail the surge in capital outflows, to reduce illiquidity driven by sell-offs in developing country markets, and to arrest declines in the currency and asset prices (UNCTAD 2020).

The proposed packages amount to the size of assistance that would have been delivered to emerging and developing countries over the last decade if countries in the Development Assistance Committee of the Organization for Economic Co-operation and Development had met their 0.7 per ODA target. The measures required to act against the recession should also come from MDBs, which have better insights by being closer to the communities, have a better understanding of the needs, and can provide swiftly the necessary means. Repurposing MDBs that are earmarked as "climate change" funds for the fallout of the COVID-19 crisis could help to set off digital infrastructures as a central part in reshaping health care to meet the needs of communities and of the challenges of the virus.

In a concluding note, governments of advanced countries should carefully consider that "if the supply disruption caused by COVID-19 will be severe and persistent, the spread of the virus might cause a demand-driven slump, giving rise to a supply-demand doom loop, and open the door to stagnation traps induced by pessimistic animal spirits" (Fornaro and Wolf 2020, 8). In the aftermath of the COVID-19 pandemic, Caribbean economies must cope with the *"stagflation effects"* of the global economy, which in light of the *"Ukraine shock effect"* may see more economic ripples surfacing on the shores of the Caribbean economy.

In lay words, if the EMEs sink deeper into macroeconomic and financial stress, the COVID-19 and the Ukraine shocks will hit the entire world economy, including advanced economies and their financial sectors. These factors, along with the geopolitical shifts between major powers, will undermine global confidence. As such, the fragile recovery from the pandemic, even in the small economies of the Caribbean, will face new uncertainties, due to rising inflationary pressures and the knock-out effects of the Ukraine-Russian crisis. Core G20 countries should sooner come together and think seriously about the implications and vast damage that may be due to the lack of effective action on the part of the global coordinating bodies.

References

Bery, Suman, Filippo Biondi, and Sybrand Brekelmans. 2019. "Twenty Years of the G20: Has It Changed Global Economic Governance?" *Russian Journal of Economics*, 5 (4): 412–40. doi: 10.32609/j.ruje.5.49435.

Carlsson-Szlezak, Philipp, Martin Reeves, and Paul Swartz. 2020. "Understanding the Economic Shock of Coronavirus." *Harvard Business Review*, 27 March. https://hbr .org/2020/03/understanding-the-economic-shock-of-coronavirus.

Cavallo, Eduardo. 2020. "Latin America Has Experienced Sudden Stops in the Past. The Coronavirus Takes the Challenge to a New Level." *Ideas Matter* (blog) IADB, Washington, DC, 24 March. https://blogs.iadb.org/ideas-matter/en/latin-america -has-experienced-sudden-stops-in-capital-flows-in-the-past-the-coronavirus-takes -the-challenge-to-a-new-level/.

Dabrowski Mark, and Marta Domínguez-Jiménez. 2020. "Is COVID-19 Triggering a New Emerging-Market Crisis?" *Bruegel Newsletter* (blog), 30 March. https://www .bruegel.org/2020/03/is-covid-19-triggering-a-new-emerging-market-crisis/.

Dimitrijevic, Alexandra, and Gareth Williams. 2020. "COVID-19 Credit Update: The Sudden Economic Stop Will Bring Intense Credit Pressure." *S&P Global Ratings*, 17 May. https://www.spglobal.com/ratings/en/research/articles/200317-covid-19 -credit-update-the-sudden-economic-stop-will-bring-intense-credit-pressure -11392437.

Dookeran, Winston. 2020. "Reflections on the COVID-19 Pandemic and the Caribbean." *Elucid Global Health* (blog), 30 March. https://globalhealth.euclid.int/ reflections-on-the-covid-19-pandemic-and-the-caribbean/.

ECLAC (Economic Commission for Latin America and the Caribbean). 2018. "The Caribbean Outlook 2018." https://repositorio.cepal.org/bitstream/handle/11362/43581 /4/S1800607_en.pdf.

Elliott, Larry. 2020. "Bank of England to Finance UK Government Covid-19 Crisis Spending." *The Guardian*, 9 April. https://www.theguardian.com/business/2020/apr /09/bank--england-to-finance-uk-government-covid-19-crisis-spending.

Fornaro, Luca, and Martin Wolf. 2020. "Covid-19 Coronavirus and Macroeconomic Policy." BSE Working Paper: 1290. Barcelona, Spain: Graduate School of Economics. https://www.barcelonagse.eu/research/working-papers/covid-19-coronavirus-and -macroeconomic-policy.

Frankel, Jeffrey. 2021. "The G20's COVID Agenda." *Project Syndicate*, 23 August. https://www.project-syndicate.org/commentary/g20-rome-summit-covid-agenda -by-jeffrey-frankel-2021-08.

Gopinath, Gita. 2020. "The Great Lockdown: Worst Economic Downturn Since the Great Depression." *IMF Blog* (blog), 21 April. https://blogs.imf.org/2020/04/14/the -great-lockdown-worst-economic-downturn-since-the-great-depression/.

IIF (Institute of International Finance). 2020. "Macro Notes–COVID-19: Uneven Policy Space among EM." https://www.iif.com/Publications/articleType/ ArchiveView/Year/2020/currentpage/40.

ILO (International Labour Organization). 2020. "COVID-19 Leads to Massive Labour Income Losses Worldwide." *ILO News,* 23 September. https://www.ilo.org/global/ about-the-ilo/newsroom/news/WCMS_755875/lang--/index.htm.

IMF (International Monetary Fund). 2020. *World Economic Outlook 2020.* Washington, DC: International Monetary Fund.

Kyriakopoulou, Danae. 2020. "Beyond Swap Lines." *OMFIF,* 26 March. https://www .omfif.org/2020/03/beyond-swap-lines/.

Lanau, Sergi, and Jonathan Fortun. 2020. "The Covid-19 Shock to EM Flows." *Economic Views,* Institute of International Finance, 17 March. https://www.iif.com/ Publications/ID/3802/Economic-Views-TheCOVID-19-Shock-to-EM-Flows.

Mooney, Henry, and María Alejandra Zegarra. 2020. *Extreme Outlier: The Pandemic's Unprecedented Shock to Tourism in Latin America and the Caribbean.* https:// publications.iadb.org/publications/english/document/Extreme-Outlier-The -Pandemics-Unprecedented-Shock-to-Tourism-in-Latin-America-and-the -Caribbean.pdf.

Morris, Scott and Amanda Glassman. 2020. "The G20 Should Tell the MDBs to Boost Crisis Lending by $100 to $200 Billion." *Center for Global Development* (blog), 10 March. https://www.cgdev.org/blog/g20-should-tell-mdbs-boost-crisis-lending -100-200-billion.

Roubini, Nouriel Roubini. 2022. "Russia's War and the Global Economy." *Project Syndicate Newsletter,* 25 February. https://prosyn.org/8tnqDd6.

Siddik, Md Nur Alam. 2020. "Economic Stimulus for COVID-19 Pandemic and its Determinants: Evidence from Cross-country Analysis." *Heliyon,* 6: 1–10. https://doi .org/10.1016/j.heliyon.2020.e05634.

Smialek, Jeanna. 2020. "How the Fed's Magic Money Machine Will Turn $454 Billion into $4 Trillion." *The New York Times,* 26 March. https://www.nytimes.com/2020/03 /26/business/economy/fed-coronavirus-stimulus.html.

Statista. 2020. "Caribbean: Total Contribution of Travel and Tourism to GDP 2017." https://www.statista.com/statistics/814155/caribbean-total-contribution-travel -tourism-gdp-country/.

UNCTAD. 2020. "UN Calls for $2.5 Trillion Coronavirus Crisis Package for Developing Countries." https://unctad.org/news/un-calls-25-trillion-coronavirus -crisis-package-developing-countries.

Werner, Alejandro. 2020. "COVID-19 Pandemic and Latin America and the Caribbean: Time for Strong Policy Actions." *IMF Blog* (blog), 19 March. https://blogs .imf.org/2020/03/19/covid-19-pandemic-and-latin-america-and-the-caribbean-time -for-strong-policy-actions.

World Bank. 2008. "Donor Nations Pledge over $6.1 Billion to Climate Investment Funds." https://www.environmental-expert.com/news/donor-nations-pledge-over -us-6-1bn-to-climate-investment-funds-37783.

———. 2019. "MDB Climate Finance Hit Record High of $43.1 Billion in 2018." https://www.worldbank.org/en/news/press-release/2019/06/13/mdb-climate-finance-hit-record-high-of-us431-billion-in-2018.

———. 2020. "Protecting the Poorest Countries Role of the Multilateral Development Banks: Explanatory Notes." https://thedocs.worldbank.org/en/doc/976541595021399817-.

3

Regional Health Security

An Antidote for COVID-19 within Caribbean SIDS

WENDY C. GRENADE

Introduction

The contemporary moment is by far the most defining in modern history. On March 11, 2020, the World Health Organisation (WHO) declared COVID-19 a pandemic. COVID-19 is nearing its two-year mark and has intensified, as new waves surge and more infectious and deadly variants emerge. At the time of writing (December 3, 2021), there have been 263,563,622 confirmed cases of COVID-19, including 5,232,562 deaths reported to the WHO (World Health Organisation 2021) with the Omicron variant declared a cause for concern. The COVID-19 pandemic is a health crisis that transcends the health sector with grave implications for economies, societies, and human security.

In 2020, the World Bank (WB) predicted that the economic impact of the COVID-19 pandemic will plunge most countries into recession in 2020, with per capita income contracting in the largest fraction of countries globally since 1870 (World Bank 2020). Over the longer horizon, the deep recessions triggered by the pandemic are expected to leave lasting scars through lower investment, an erosion of human capital through lost work and schooling, and fragmentation of global trade and supply linkages (World Bank 2020). The WB confirmed that despite the unprecedented global effort, the pandemic has reversed gains in global poverty reduction for the first time in a generation, pushing nearly 100 million people into extreme poverty in 2020 (World Bank 2021). The WB also reported that as new waves emerged, the pandemic "continued to affect countries around the world causing a global health and economic crisis unprecedented in scale and impact, with overstretched health systems, widespread lockdowns, school closures, disruptions to food supply and income losses that disproportionately affect the poor, women, the elderly, informal workers and other vulnerable groups" (World Bank 2021, 3).

The COVID-19 pandemic and its negative impact on the world economy are ongoing against the existential climate crisis. This cascade of crises undermines security and development, particularly for small island developing states (SIDS). There is a large body of work that analyzes SIDS in the context of vulnerability and resilience (Commonwealth Secretariat and World Bank 2000; Thomas 2003; Commonwealth Secretariat 2011; Brigugilo 2014).

Although COVID-19 is a relatively new phenomenon, there is emerging literature which seeks to analyze its impact on the Caribbean (Jhinkoo-Ramdass 2020; Knight 2020; Murphy et al. 2020; Bryon et al. 2021; Campbell and Connell 2021). This chapter assesses the Caribbean Community's (CARICOM)[1] experience with COVID-19 utilizing a regional health security framework. Given their shared vulnerabilities and common threats, Caribbean SIDS have had a history of regional cooperation to promote collective resilience. For the Caribbean, regionalism is a necessary imperative to achieve sustainable development. Established in 1973, CARICOM can be characterized as a regional security complex. This refers to "regional sub-systems consisting of a set of states whose major security perceptions and concerns are so inter-linked that their national security problems cannot reasonably be analysed or resolved apart from one another" (Buzan, Wæver, Wilde 1998, 198).

CARICOM is, for the most part (except for the Caribbean Court of Justice),[2] an intergovernmental arrangement that rests on four pillars: functional cooperation, foreign policy coordination, economic integration, and security cooperation. An assessment of CARICOM reveals a mixed scorecard (West Indian Commission 1992; Gilbert-Roberts 2013; Grenade and Skeete 2015; Lewis, Gilbert-Roberts, and Byron 2017; Grenade 2018). In the area of functional cooperation, CARICOM has achieved relative successes, particularly in health, education, and disaster management (Thomas 2008). There have

---

[1] The Caribbean Community consists of fifteen full member states: Antigua and Barbuda, Barbados; Belize, Commonwealth of The Bahamas, Commonwealth of Dominica, Grenada, Guyana, Haiti, Jamaica, Montserrat, St. Kitts and Nevis, St. Lucia, Saint Vincent and the Grenadines, Suriname and Trinidad, and Tobago. Most CARICOM member states are part of the island chain, while Guyana and Suriname are located in South America and Belize in Central America, while Haiti shares with the Dominican Republic the land and marine space of Hispaniola. CARICOM also consists of five full or associate members which are British Overseas Territories.

[2] The Caribbean Court of Justice (CCJ) was established in 2005 with two jurisdictions: an original jurisdiction to adjudicate matters arising from the Revised Treaty of Chaguaramas and an Appellate jurisdiction to replace the British Privy Council as the highest Court of Appeal. To date four CARICOM member states are members of the CCJ in its Appellate jurisdiction: Barbados, Belize, Commonwealth of Dominica and Guyana.

been moderate achievements in the realm of foreign policy coordination.[3] Economic integration is problematic, but there is much promise within the economic union of the subregional grouping of the Organisation of Eastern Caribbean States (OECS), which has an economic and monetary union. Security cooperation is CARICOM's newest pillar, and it has the potential to deepen regionalism among CARICOM SIDS. Using the case of CARICOM, the central question is: how has CARICOM utilized regional health security in confronting COVID-19 and what may be some of the impediments to its effectiveness?

The chapter, consisting of three sections, is framed within discourses of Critical Security Studies as a subfield of International Relations (IR). Following this introduction, the first section conceptualizes security in general and health security in particular. The second section explores the case of CARICOM SIDS in the context of the COVID-19 pandemic. It discusses ways in which CARICOM member states utilized various dimensions of regional health security and some of the impediments to its effectiveness. The final section offers conclusions.

Rethinking Security as a Multidimensional Phenomenon

This chapter departs from the narrow realist conceptualization of security, which has constructed states as the referent object of security, in a Hobbesian world of anarchy. In that context, security refers to "the study of the threat, use and control of military force, especially of specific policies that states adopt in order to prepare for, prevent or engage in war" (Walt 1991, 212). The neorealist discourse has, at its core, the concept of the security dilemma. This refers to a

---

3 CARICOM member states have collectively supported global efforts to scale up global health initiatives. During the last two decades, all the member states of CARICOM unanimously endorsed a series of resolutions on global health. They actively participated in discussions on major UN conferences and summits which have contributed to the advancement of the global health agenda, including formulating the Millennium Development Goals (MDGs), the Rio Political Declaration on Social Determinants of Health adopted at the 2011 World Conference on Social Determinants of Health, the 2011 Political Declaration on HIV and AIDS: Intensifying Our Efforts to Eliminate HIV and AIDS, the 2011 political declaration of the high-level meeting of the General Assembly on the prevention and control of noncommunicable diseases, World Health Assembly resolution 66.11 of May 27, 2013, on health in the post-2015 development agenda, and adoption of Economic and Social Council resolution 2013/12 of July 22, 2013, on the UN Inter-Agency Task Force on the Prevention and Control of Non-communicable Diseases among others.

situation when the military preparations of one state create an unresolvable uncertainty in the mind of another as to whether those preparations are for "defensive" purposes only (to enhance its security in an uncertain world) or whether they are for offensive purposes (to change the status quo to its advantage) (Booth and Wheeler 2007). Therefore, realism is concerned primarily with the struggle for power among self-interested states to guarantee national security.

However, realism pays insufficient attention to non-state actors, non-military issues, domestic politics, and small and relatively weaker states such as those in the developing world. In essence, while realism still has relevance in the post-Cold War and post-9/11 worlds, it is ill-suited, on its own, to analyze the interwoven complexities thrown up by the COVID-19 pandemic. On the other side of the debate, for neoliberal institutionalists, rules and institutions can mitigate the security dilemma through collective security. This refers to a principle where the security of one is the concern of all. Here the role of the United Nations (UN) becomes paramount, although the UN Security Council is predominantly concerned with great power politics.

Since the end of the Cold War, there has been an ongoing debate that is reshaping the security discourse. It is argued that the traditional focus on military security is no longer adequate on its own to explain non-military threats. Realists ignored fundamentally the fact that the lives and livelihoods of the overwhelming majority of people on this planet are at greater risk from diseases than from wars, terrorism, or other forms of violent conflict (McInnis 2013). These debates have three roots: a discontent among some scholars with the neorealist foundations that have characterized the field, a need to respond to the challenges posed by the emergence of a post-Cold War security order, and a continuing desire to make the discipline relevant to contemporary concerns (Krause and Williams 1996, 229–30). Scholars who attempt to go beyond the neorealist conceptualization of security interrogate a diverse range of potential threats, ranging from economic and environmental issues to human rights and migration (Ullman 1983; Mathews 1989, Buzan and Waever 2003). As Paris (2001) argues, these efforts to reconceptualize security have been prompted in part by contributions of critical theorists including feminists, postmodernists, and constructivists (Williams and McDonald 2018).

However, attempts to broaden and deepen the neorealist notion of security have been met with intense criticism. Critics argue that the broadening and deepening of security make the field intellectually incoherent and practically irrelevant (Dorff 1994; Mearsheimer 1995). A major contention is that "alternative approaches have provided neither a clear explanatory framework for analysing security nor demonstrated their value in concrete research"

(Mearsheimer 1995, 92). Walt observes that the adoption of alternative conceptions is not only analytically mistaken but also politically irresponsible (Walt 1991, 213).

Nonetheless, there is a case to be made for broadening the conceptualization of security to include health threats. For instance, following the Severe Acute Respiratory Syndrome (SARS) outbreak in Asia in 2002, many security analysts made a case for infectious diseases to be treated as national security threats. For example, with fewer than 10,000 cases, SARS cost Asian countries US$ 60 billion in gross expenditure and business losses in the second quarter of 2003 alone. As Caballero-Anthony (2005) argues, given the multidimensional threats to national security posed by infectious diseases such as SARS, it is imperative that states treat these diseases within a security framework. He posits that SARS should be seen as a wake-up call for how security should be reconceptualized to account for new and serious threats. In Caballero-Anthony's view, by framing infectious diseases as a matter of national security, governments and their people would be better prepared to handle sudden outbreaks that endanger human lives and threaten the existence and survival of nation-states (Caballero-Anthony 2005, 476).

Health Security

Historically in the West, disease was often seen as an impediment to exploration and a challenge to winning a war. Cholera and other diseases killed at least three times more soldiers in the Crimean War than did the actual conflict. Malaria, measles, mumps, smallpox and typhoid felled more combatants than did bullets in the American civil war. (Brundtland 2003, 417)

Concerns about global health and security are not new. In 1946, the principles set out in the preamble of the constitution of the WHO included the declaration that the health of all peoples is fundamental to the attainment of peace and security and is dependent on the fullest cooperation of individuals and states (World Health Organisation 1946). Yet, despite that declaration, the praxis of Western-centric IR relegated health to the realm of "low politics." However, in the post-Cold War era, as globalization intensified, the concept of health security became prominent. Importantly, in May 2001, the World Health Assembly (WHA) passed a resolution on "Global Health Security: Epidemic Alert and Response." A background report to the meeting warned that:

The globalisation of infectious disease is not a new phenomenon. However increased population movements, whether through tourism or migration or as a result of disasters; growth in international trade in food and biological products; social and environmental changes linked with urbanisation, deforestation and alterations in climate; and changes in methods of food processing, distribution and consumer habits have affirmed that infectious disease events in one country are potentially a concern for the entire world. (World Health Assembly 2001, 1 cited in Elbe 2010, 3)

Since the turn of the twenty-first century, global health issues increasingly gained prominence. For example, under their initiative on Global Health and Foreign Policy, launched in September 2006, the Ministers of Foreign Affairs of Brazil, France, Indonesia, Norway, Senegal, South Africa, and Thailand issued the Oslo Ministerial Declaration on March 20, 2007. The Oslo Ministerial Declaration statement affirmed in part that in today's era of globalization and interdependence, there is an urgent need to broaden the scope of foreign policy. The statement advocated that health is one of the most important, yet still broadly neglected, long-term foreign policy issues of our time. It asserted that life and health are our most precious assets, and there is a growing awareness that investment in health is fundamental to economic growth and development. Importantly, the statement affirmed that it is generally acknowledged that threats to health may compromise a country's stability and security. Additionally, the Global Health Security Initiative (GHSI) was established to institutionalize the idea of health security in response to the 9/11 attacks. The focus of the GHSI was "to better prepare for and respond to acts of biological, chemical and radio-nuclear terrorism" (Elbe 2010, 4).

What makes a health issue a human security risk? Several factors can be identified: The scale of the disease burden now and in the future; the urgency for action; the depth and extent of the impact on society; the interdependence of "externalities" that can exert ripple effects beyond particular diseases, persons, or locations (Ogata and Sen 2003, 97). Hence, there is a body of work that concentrates on public health security. This refers to the activities required, both proactive and reactive, to minimize vulnerability to acute public health events that endanger the collective health of national populations. Global public health "widens the definition to include acute public health events that endanger the collective health of populations living across geographical regions and international boundaries . . . Global health security, or lack of it, may also have an impact on economic or political stability, trade, tourism, access to goods and services and, if they occur repeatedly, on demographic stability" (World Health Organisation 2007, 1).

It is argued that the levels of ill health in countries constituting a majority of the world's population pose a direct threat to their own national economic and political viability, and therefore to the global economic and political interests of all countries. Therefore, investing in global health is investing in national security (Brundtland 2002). There are some distinct approaches to the health security nexus. Global health security is concerned with health promotion on a global scale – risks have been globalized beyond what individual states are capable of managing. With respect to national security, health issues are part of the security agenda if they are seen as a potential threat to the internal security of the state, have an impact on international stability, or cause exceptional levels of morbidity and or mortality (McInnes and Lee 2012; Elbe 2010).

There is no universal definition of health security, and its meaning is "quite fluid, imprecise and ambiguous" (Elbe 2010, 4). Generally, health security is viewed as part of a larger human security agenda, which focuses on freedom from want and freedom from fear. As globalization intensified, the notion of human security gradually acquired greater resonance. Human security refers to "security with a human face" (Peoples and Vaughn-Williams 2010, 120). The UNDP Human Development Report (UNDP 1994) identified seven elements of human security: economic, food, health, environmental, personal, community, and political security. Although a slippery concept, human security is a useful analytical tool to interrogate the impact of COVID-19, particularly among SIDS.

Caribbean Security

For the CARICOM region, security is multidimensional and has never been viewed merely as protection from military threats. Environmental, economic, and health crises bring to the fore the crosscutting and complex nature of security threats. Griffith (2003) defines security as "protection and preservation of a people's freedom from external military attack and coercion, from internal subversion and from the erosion of cherished political, economic and social values. Within this framework, security becomes critical to survival, not only for the viability of the state but also for socio-economic development" (Griffith 2003, 386).

Following the terrorist attacks on the United States on 9/11, Griffith (2004) edited a volume that assessed security in the age of terrorism. Significant contributions to that volume were analyses of the nontraditional security scenario in the Caribbean. The focus was placed on "the menace of drugs," "globalization and economic vulnerability," "the environmental security challenge," and "the Caribbean, HIV/AIDS, and security." Byron (2011, 136) examined the role of CARICOM as a "security provider" in the region and observed that "CARICOM is a group of small developing states with limited defense capabilities located in an area dominated by the security interests of the United States." On the policy front, the CARICOM Crime and Security

Strategy seeks to significantly improve citizen security by creating a safe, just, and free community, while simultaneously improving the economic viability of the Region (CARICOM Community IMPACS 2013, 4). The risks and threats identified in the strategy are prioritized into four tiers. Importantly, climate change and pandemics were then classified as "Future Risks," with unknown probabilities and consequences. This is no longer the reality, and the COVID-19 pandemic presents an opportunity to further probe the multidimensionality of Caribbean security.

Conceptualizing Regional Health Security: The Case of CARICOM

Regionalism is imperative for small developing states as they seek to confront crosscutting global threats to their security and development. CARICOM is a regional security complex, and, as such, regional health security is an antidote for COVID-19. I define regional health security as an integrative approach to regional governance that routinely prioritizes public health concerns as an indispensable necessity for regional security and development. This approach locates people as the referent object of security. It involves collective efforts by the global community, sovereign states, regional institutions, and non-state actors to mainstream public health as part of a comprehensive strategy to prepare for, prevent, and collectively respond to the multidimensionality of global health threats. At its core, regional health security must be buttressed by regional strategic leadership; an integrative institutional network; regional and global partnerships; solidarity; and shared sovereignty, gender justice, economic viability, and democratic governance. This is, in turn, aimed to build resilience and balance the imperatives of human, economic, and national security.

The COVID-19 pandemic is a severe threat to health security globally. As table 3.1 shows, the Americas is the region most affected by the pandemic.

CARICOM is one of the regions in the world with the highest incidences of non-communicable diseases and relatively weak health infrastructure. As such, prior to COVID-19 the region was already grappling with risks and threats to its health security. The first confirmed case of COVID-19 was reported in Jamaica on March 10, 2020. During the first wave of the pandemic, the region was relatively successful in containing disease spread and fatalities, despite limited resources and relatively weak health systems. As of June 2020, there were 8,327 confirmed cases and 185 deaths among 20 Caribbean countries (see table 3.2). As the pandemic intensified and as Caribbean countries opened their borders in July/August 2020, confirmed cases in the Caribbean began to

Table 3.1 Comparison of COVID-19 global situation June 2020–November 2021

Region	Confirmed Cases				Deaths			
	June 2020	Nov 2020	June 2021	Nov 2021	June 2020	Nov 2020	June 2021	Nov 2021
Americas	5,950,570	287,546	73,007	95,089	30,950	8,360	1,920	2,320
Europe	2,788,500	211,384	56,297	80,935	19,780	4,550	1,190	1,480
South-East Asia	923,266	11,082,209	35,219,144	44,273,117	24,613	169,507	495,939	699,920
Eastern Mediterranean	1,153,238	4,288,875	11,133,262	16,564,274	27,077	107,258	218,804	305,396
Africa	356,666	154,756	41,727	61,852	6,746	3,448	9,766	1,516
West Pacific	223,913	914,734	36,341	97,723	7,481	1,772	5,576	1,346
Total	11,396,153	16,939,504	46,559,779	61,198,271	116,647	294,895	733,195	1,011,978

Source: WHO 2021; Our World in Data. Available at ⟨ourworldindata.org⟩.

Table 3.2 COVID-19 in select Caribbean countries 2020–2021

Country	Population	Confirmed Cases				Deaths				Recoveries	Vaccinations
		June 2020	Nov 2020	June 2021	Nov 2021	June 2020	Nov 2020	June 2021	Nov 2021	Nov 2021	
Anguilla	15,205	3	6	109	1,137	0	0	0	4	1,053	18,782
Antigua and Barbuda	98,064	68	141	1,263	4,118	3	4	42	107	3,916	114,309
The Bahamas	393,873	104	7,541	12,586	22,601	11	163	254	665	21,525	263,795
Barbados	287,432	97	276	4,081	22,316	7	7	47	194	13,639	284,659
Belize	398,746	24	5,743	13,251	29,105	2	147	329	544	26,741	398,131
Bermuda	62,240	146	260	2,514	5,704	9	9	33	106	5,558	101,341
British Virgin Islands	30,265	8	71	313	2,725	1	1	1	37	2,649	34,608
Cayman Islands	65,851	200	274	614	4,203	1	2	2	2	1,352	119,435
Dominica	72,016	18	85	193	5,336	0	0	0	35	4,973	53,955
Grenada	112,610	23	41	161	5,863	0	0	1	200	5,602	72,282
Guyana	787,183	245	5,406	20,055	36,872	12	151	469	959	33,598	652,332
Haiti	11,425,866	5,933	9,294	18,658	24,635	105	233	436	708	20,703	153,182
Jamaica	2,961,314	698	10,763	50,124	90,209	10	257	1,075	2,329	61,024	1.06 mil
Montserrat	4,992	11	13	20	41	1	1	1	1	40	2,949
St. Lucia	183,766	19	259	5,296	12,837	0	2	84	270	12,328	96,913

St. Kitts and Nevis	53,262	15	22	446	2,749	0	0	3	27	2,661	50,872
St. Vincent and the Grenadines	110,998	29	85	2,225	5,326	0	0	12	72	3,981	49,816
Suriname	587,511	515	5,312	21,732	50,078	13	117	522	1,139	29,530	467,553
Trinidad and Tobago	1,400,240	130	6,669	32,793	62,670	8	120	847	1,870	53,829	1.27 mil
Turks and Caicos Islands	38,805	41	748	2,425	3,045	2	6	18	23	2,966	56,343
Total	**19,092,239**	**8,327**	**53,009**	**183,859**	**391,570**	**185**	**1,220**	**4,176**	**9,292**	**307,668**	**5,321,257**

Source: World Meters.info. Available at (www.worldometers.info) Our World in Data. Available at (www.ourworldindata.org).

increase, although marginally in most countries. By November 30, there were 53,009 confirmed cases, and 1,220 COVID-19-related deaths were recorded. Despite the comparative rise in confirmed cases from August to November 2020, the Caribbean region had not experienced the devastating effects of the health crisis relative to other regions of the world.

In 2021, as the pandemic intensified and new variants emerged, the Caribbean followed the global trend of increased cases and deaths (see figure 3.1).

How did CARICOM utilize regional health security as an antidote against COVID-19? A key dimension of regional health security is regional strategic leadership. During the first wave, in the first two quarters of 2020, CARICOM governments took several proactive measures to mitigate the severity of the health crisis itself. Effective regional leadership and governance were critical. For the period January to June 2020, Prime Minister Mia Amor Mottley of Barbados was the chairperson of CARICOM. Prime Minister Mottley demonstrated decisive leadership of the regional grouping. At an emergency meeting of CARICOM Heads via video conferencing on April 15, 2020, CARICOM Heads received presentations from the Caribbean Public Health Agency (CARPHA), the University of the West Indies (UWI), the Caribbean Development Bank (CDB), and Archbishop Jason Gordon. The Press Release reported that:

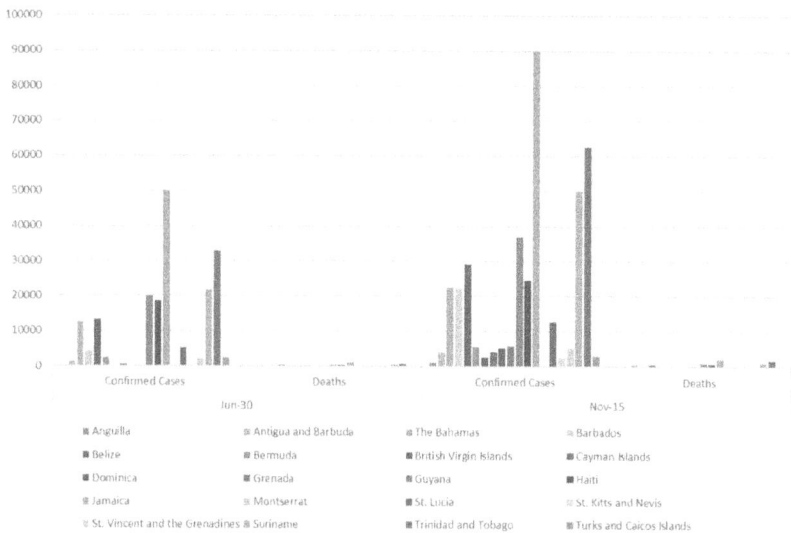

Figure 3.1 Confirmed cases and deaths in CARICOM member states and associate member states from June to November 2021.

Source: World Meters.info. Available at (www.worldometers.info) Our World in Data. Available at (www.ourworldindata.org)

Heads of Government agreed on a collective approach to the International Financial Institutions in accessing assistance to meet the fiscal financial challenges arising from the crisis. They urged that the criterion of GDP per capita should not be the sole consideration in assessing the needs of the Community and that an understanding of each country's vulnerability is a far better measurement to determine need, especially in light of multiple challenges. (CARICOM Secretariat 2020)

Other critical decisions from that meeting included: Proposals on a Common Public Health Policy to include proposals for joint procurement – including pharmaceuticals and personal protective equipment (PPE) and sourcing of additional medical personnel. It was also agreed that there would be a protocol on reopening borders, which all member states would adhere to at the same time when such a decision was taken. Other issues such as food security, Caribbean transport, and a robust digital architecture were discussed. It was also reported that the Council for National Security and Law Enforcement was considering the threats to security during the pandemic and was preparing recommendations for the way forward. At that summit, Heads of Government also called for the lifting of sanctions on Cuba and Venezuela on humanitarian grounds as, in the view of Heads of Government, all countries must be part of the global effort to combat the COVID-19 pandemic (CARICOM Secretariat 2020).

Another dimension of regional health security is an integrative institutional network. A major strength of CARICOM is its achievements in the realm of functional cooperation through a web of institutions and associate institutions. Thus, a network of regional institutions played a significant role in combatting COVID-19 in the initial stages in the Caribbean. In fact, CARICOM's model of integration is based predominantly on the efficacy of its institutions. One of the institutions that continues to play a critical role in the fight against COVID-19 is the CARPHA, which was designated an Institution of CARICOM pursuant to Article 21 of the Revised Treaty of Chaguaramas. CARPHA is the single regional public health agency for the Caribbean. It was legally established in July 2011 by an Inter-Governmental Agreement signed by CARICOM member states and began operation in January 2013. The agency rationalizes public health arrangements in the region by combining the functions of five Caribbean Regional Health Institutes into a single agency.[4]

---

[4] CARPHA consists of the Caribbean Environmental Health Institute (CEHI), the Caribbean Epidemiology Centre (CAREC), the Caribbean Food and Nutrition Institute (CFNI), the Caribbean Health Research Council (CHRC), and the Caribbean Regional Drug Testing Laboratory (CRDTL).

The objectives of CARPHA are to: (a) promote the physical and mental health and wellness of people within the Caribbean; (b) provide strategic direction, in analyzing, defining, and responding to public health priorities of the Caribbean Community; (c) promote and develop measures for the prevention of disease in the Caribbean; (d) support the Caribbean Community in preparing for and responding to public health emergencies; (e) support solidarity in health, as one of the principal pillars of functional cooperation in the Caribbean Community; and (f) support the relevant objectives of the Caribbean Cooperation in Health (CCH) as approved by the Council. CARPHA's Medical Microbiology Laboratory (CMML) has been actively involved in the regional response to COVID-19. As the regional reference laboratory, the CMML conducts tests for suspected COVID-19 cases in member states using the WHO's recommended testing protocol. Other institutions at the frontline in the fight against the coronavirus are the CARICOM IMPACS[5] and the Regional Security System (RSS).[6]

The Caribbean Disaster Emergency Management Agency (CDEMA) also played a significant role. As chair of the UWI's COVID-19 Task Force, Landis (2021) provides a comprehensive account of the role of regional institutions in the COVID-19 response. He observes that CDEMA engaged in coordination of national, regional, and international entities through the Regional Response Mechanism. It also activated and coordinated the regional emergency response plan, including the facilitation of regional surveillance and the establishment of an Integrated Regional Logistics Mechanism comprising a hub with air and sea bridge. CDEMA was also instrumental in the dissemination of information

---

[5] CARICOM's Implementation Agency for Crime and Security (IMPACS) was established in 2006 to implement the regional agenda on combating crime and security. Its key functions include research on evaluation and monitoring of security trends in the region, security-related project development and implementation, and information centralization and dissemination. IMPACS now has two sub-agencies, the Joint Regional Communications Centre which is the clearing house for advanced passenger information and the Regional Intelligence Fusion Centre, which gives regional intelligence support. The advanced passenger information systems supplied by the JRCC allows for better management at the ports of entries across the region fostering collaboration between that entity and port health authorities. This entity allowed for better screening and better management across island borders in the midst of the COVID-19 pandemic.

[6] The RSS consists of Barbados and the independent members of the OECS. It was created in 1982 out of a need for collective security in the Eastern Caribbean after the Union Island Uprising in Saint Vincent and the Grenadines. Although initially a US-led military initiative, the RSS has evolved into a Caribbean institution with a multidimensional security agenda.

including COVID-19 research products to member states and coordinating emergency airlift capacity with the RSS for the transport of medical supplies and patient samples between islands while commercial airlift was suspended. Landis (2021) argued that the role of the RSS was crucial: "flying up and down the island chain to maintain the flow of patient samples from smaller islands to the CARPHA reference laboratory in Trinidad and maintaining inter-island supplies of medical products and equipment at a time of major transport disruptions" (Landis 2021, 87).

As a regional public good, the UWI played a significant role in monitoring and ensuring a coherent pandemic response. The UWI was invited by CARICOM to provide its research expertise to help synthesize the evidence based upon which informed decisions could be taken. The UWI used open-access data to contextualize the evolving outbreak within CARICOM with modeling studies and daily surveillance outputs, supplemented with peer-reviewed publications (Landis 2021, 87–88). As a regional university, the role of the UWI was critically important to the pandemic response.

Regional health security also includes regional and global partnerships. For more than a century, the Pan American Health Organisation (PAHO) has served its member countries in the Americas and has been instrumental in the eradication of smallpox and polio and the elimination of endemic transmission of measles and rubella. PAHO is at the forefront in the fight against COVID-19. Landis (2021) explains that PAHO took the lead in: "Procurement of COVID-19 test kits; Funding of training of CARICOM laboratories on WHO approved COVID-19 PCR kits; and assessment of likely resource needs (human and physical plant infrastructure, such as estimation of intensive care unit beds, ventilator capacity and personal protective equipment regarding hospital readiness)" (Landis 2021, 87–88).

Global advocacy and partnerships must also be a catalyst for regional health security, given unequal power relations and unfair trade. The global public health emergency created by COVID-19 led to a scarcity of medical resources and a drastic reduction in government revenues. In keeping with the Trump administration's "America First" policy, the then US president invoked the Korean war-era Law, referred to as the Defense Protection Act of 1950. The Act authorizes the president to use loans, direct purchases, and other incentives to boost the production of critical goods and essential materials. Multiple countries accused the Trump administration of unfairly acquiring the equipment necessary for fighting COVID-19. Three Caribbean countries – Barbados, The Bahamas, and the Cayman Islands – had container loads of PPE purchased from US vendors in April 2020 blocked from leaving the United States by US Customs and Border Protection (Knight and Reddy 2020). Caribbean countries also experienced a shortfall of medical staff. Consequently, they sought medical support from Cuba, which is a long-standing partner. Over the course of two months, Cuba sent more than 500 medical professionals to assist various CARICOM countries (Mowla 2020, 1–2). Cuban medical diplomacy has continued into the second year of the pandemic.

In the initial wave of COVID-19, global advocacy was a critical component of CARICOM's response. As chairperson of the regional grouping, Prime Minister Mottley appeared in several international fora to advocate globally for CARICOM member states. In an address to the WHA, Mottley indicated that the CARICOM region is characterized by developing health systems that suffer from the same vulnerabilities as many of its member states. Prime Minister Mottley referred to low numbers of ICU beds per capita, few intensivist doctors and critical care nurses, and few ventilators per capita. She indicated further that Caribbean people have a higher rate of non-communicable diseases and obesity than is desired. The then CARICOM chair reported that CARICOM mobilized all its regional agencies such as its public health agency, CARPHA, the UWI, and CDEMA. Mottley stated that CARICOM states adopted a "whole of government" and "whole of society" approach. The then chair of CARICOM referred to the first wave as "long and treacherous" but indicated that CARICOM banded together to ride out that wave (Mottley 2020). Prime Minister Mottley also gave interviews to the BBC and CNN on CARICOM's regional response to the pandemic and discussed some of the global inequalities that exacerbate the development challenges of Caribbean SIDS.

Access to vaccines is a major issue for SIDS as they seek to manage the pandemic. The WHO established the COVAX facility to facilitate the global distribution of vaccines. However, there is vaccine nationalism, where the richest and most powerful countries have secured billions of doses of COVID-19 vaccines, while developing countries struggle to access supplies.

CARICOM countries displayed a high degree of cooperation and solidarity in the procurement and distribution of vaccines among themselves, given the unequal access to vaccines globally. Barbados and Dominica received a gift of 10,000 and 70,000 Oxford AstraZeneca from the Government of India, and both countries shared vaccines with other Eastern Caribbean countries, Guyana, and Trinidad and Tobago. Barbados' prime minister Mottley remarked: "I hope that Barbados, Dominica and the rest of the Caribbean can be an example to the rest of the world about how you cooperate. And even when you have a little, you share and you work together because we know that is the only thing missing in the world today" (*Jamaica Observer* 2021). As CARICOM countries experienced spikes and vaccine shortages, other member states showed solidarity. For instance, Trinidad and Tobago received donations of 2,000 Oxford Astra-Zeneca vaccines from Barbados, 1,600 doses from Saint Vincent and the Grenadines, 9,000 from Bermuda, 10,000 from Grenada, and 5,000 doses of Sinopharm vaccines from Antigua and Barbuda (Media Institute of the Caribbean 2021). Similarly, Trinidad and Tobago donated 10,000 doses of Oxford AstraZeneca to The Bahamas, St. Kitts and Nevis, and Dominica (*Trinidad Express* 2021).

Regional cooperation in disaster management is one of CARICOM's strengths, given the severe threats to its environmental security. Even as the region continued to grapple with COVID-19 and economic shocks, environmental disasters compounded the problem. In early April 2021, the La Soufriere volcano in Saint Vincent and the Grenadines violently erupted. The scientific team from the UWI Seismic Research Centre (SRC) was instrumental in constantly monitoring the volcano and rendering scientific advice to the Government of Saint Vincent and the Grenadines. CDEMA worked alongside the Saint Vincent and the Grenadines National Emergency Management Organisation, the SRC, and the RSS. Additionally, in August 2021, a magnitude 7.2 earthquake struck Haiti. Those two major natural disasters had implications for regional cooperation efforts during the pandemic. Based on the evidence, there is no doubt that climate change is a clear and present danger that requires urgent action at multiple levels, and CARICOM has demonstrated collective resolve in the global fight against climate change.

Impediments to Regional Health Security

There are several impediments to regional health security which include sovereignty constraints, economic (in)security, and democratic deficits within member states.

CARICOM is a community of sovereign independent states that operates within a predominantly intergovernmental framework. Consequently, there is often tension between national imperatives and the common regional "good," which impedes greater efforts at institutionalizing regional health security. A promising development was the creation of a "Bubble," which was intended to allow citizens from several identified states within CARICOM to travel within the region without the requirement of the fourteen-day quarantine. However, CARICOM member states were affected differently by COVID-19 and national security, and border controls took precedence over a common regional health security approach. The problem was compounded by severe disruptions to regional transportation. The economic fallout from COVID-19 had dire consequences for the regional airline carrier Leeward Island Airline Transportation (LIAT). Given the economic impact, three shareholder governments – Barbados, Dominica and Saint Vincent, and the Grenadines – decided to withdraw their contributions to LIAT, and the airline went into liquidation. This was catastrophic for the region on multiple fronts. The lesson is, regional health security requires sovereignty bargains and trade-offs, strategic diplomacy, and the maximization of shared regional sovereignty. The paradoxical community of sovereign independent states often limits regional health security.

Economic resilience (Brigugilo 2014) is a cornerstone to building regional health security. Yet, the COVID-19 pandemic has exacerbated the economic vulnerability inherent in the economies of CARICOM SIDS. Most CARICOM countries are generally categorized as medium to high on the Human Development Index (HDI). In the 2019 HDI Report, of the 189 countries classified, Barbados ranked 56, Bahamas 60, Trinidad and Tobago 63, St. Kitts and Nevis 73, Antigua and Barbuda 74, Grenada 78, St. Lucia 89, Saint Vincent and the Grenadines 94, Jamaica 96, and The Commonwealth of Dominica and Suriname 98. Three CARICOM countries ranked low: Belize 103, Guyana 123, and Haiti 169 (UNDP 2019). Despite the fact that the WB has graduated most CARICOM countries as middle- or high-income countries, there is persistent and severe economic (in)security among CARICOM SIDS as they face constraints to growth, which can impede efforts to build resilience. Within CARICOM economies, there is evidence of dependence on external trade, limited private-sector capacity, narrow production base, lack of diversification, diseconomies of scale, inadequate human resource, insufficient institutional capacity, and limited infrastructural development, among other constraints. In fact, the majority of Caribbean countries depend on a few sectors to drive economic growth. Apart from energy-based Trinidad and Tobago, for most CARICOM countries, the services sector is the main economic pillar, especially tourism and financial services. Therefore, macroeconomic volatility is a distinct feature of Caribbean economies, a testament to their vulnerability to external shocks (Grenade and Skeete 2015).

The CDB reported that in 2019, economic performance in the Caribbean was set against a background of decelerating global activity, such as the ongoing trade tensions between the United States and China, continued uncertainty surrounding BREXIT, growing geopolitical uncertainty, particularly in the Middle East, and significant political and environmental protests in many parts of the world. Consistent with the global slowdown, most of CDB's Borrowing Member Countries (BMCs) experienced slower economic expansion than in the previous year. Regional Gross Domestic Product (GDP) increased by 1.0 percent, following 1.6 percent growth in 2018 (CDB 2019, 16). Importantly, unemployment rates remained higher for women than for men.

At the start of 2020, CDB was projecting regional economic growth, consistent with forecasts of increased global economic activity. Since then, there has been the rapid global spread of the novel coronavirus, with significant adverse impact on developed and developing countries. With many countries going into lockdown to contain the spread of the virus and to ease pressure on health services, economic activity collapsed. Closure of borders led to a rapid decline in international travel, putting pressure on transport providers, particularly airlines. Governments and central banks announced fiscal and monetary policies in an effort to protect businesses and workers (CDB 2019, 21).

The CARICOM region is over-dependent on tourism; however, the global travel and tourism industry is one of the major vehicles for the spread of infectious diseases such as COVID-19. The impact on the Caribbean region was significant. Many tourism-dependent economies reported mass cancellations. Hotels had become virtually empty by March, and cruise ships ceased to operate (CDB 2019, 21). As at the end of April 2020, the International Monetary Fund predicted that due to the "sudden stop" in tourism, the Caribbean would experience negative growth of 6.2 percent (Mowla 2020, 1). Regarding the subregional grouping of the OECS, the Governor of the Eastern Caribbean Central Bank reported that:

> As countries around the world and in the region moved to shut their borders and economies to safeguard lives, livelihoods became the second round casualties of the pandemic. Tourism ground to a halt, with devastating spill-over effects and our economies have been in free fall ever since. Unemployment is estimated to be as high as 50.0 per cent in some member countries. Revenues have plummeted by at least 50.0 per cent. At all levels of society, some of our best-laid plans have been confounded as we have all had to adjust to new ways of doing things and to embrace a new normal in this COVID-19 world. (Antoine 2020, xi)

Therefore, there is a security dilemma: the travel and tourism sector is one of the main *root* causes for the spread of infectious diseases, such as COVID-19. Yet, CARICOM SIDS depend heavily on that very sector as the *route* to a post-COVID-19 recovery. This dilemma is a major impediment to regional health security.

Additionally, regional health security requires resources, and CARICOM SIDS had to reallocate scarce resources to manage the pandemic. In the initial phase of the pandemic, Caribbean economies spent between 1 percent and 4 percent of GDP to mitigate the immediate effects of COVID-19 on their economies (Bárcena 2020 cited in Jhinkoo-Ramdass 2020). As Jhinkoo-

Ramdass asserts further, Caribbean economies were forced to implement health and safety, fiscal, and social measures. In terms of health and safety measures, all CARICOM countries enforced lockdown measures, although to different degrees. All had to allocate additional and scarce resources to the health sector. With respect to fiscal measures, most CARICOM countries instituted tax relief for affected sectors and sought financing from international financial institutions. Murphy et al. (2020) document the variety of government measures introduced across the Caribbean and explore their impact on aspects of outbreak control.

Regional health security also requires social protection. All Caribbean governments had targeted an increase in social spending such as unemployment grant cards and hampers to children affected by school closures. Also, many of them have given support to businesses, which include loan deferrals and liquidity support for Small- and Medium-sized Enterprises, individuals, and corporations. The increased expenditure for healthcare consists of the testing and treatment of confirmed COVID-19 cases and the need for equipment for enhanced public health surveillance (See Jhinkoo-Ramdass 2020). A positive development was that healthcare finance was delivered through a grand coalition of grants and loans from the regional and international donor community and development banks, notably the CDB to supplement the national treasuries of CARICOM member states (Landis 2021, 87–88). Yet, the economic constraints are an impediment to regional health security, given limited resources and high levels of poverty and inequality.

The region of the Americas is one of the most inequitable in the world, and COVID-19 has highlighted and worsened that unfortunate reality (PAHO 2021). As the pandemic intensified, within the Latin America and the Caribbean (LAC) region, developmental challenges such as poverty, inequality, unemployment, and high levels of debt persist. As Economic Commission for Latin America and the Caribbean confirms, the sharp contraction in economic activity eroded public revenues. Thus, in 2021 the economic context of LAC remained complex and uncertain, given the persistence of the pandemic, the slow rollout of vaccination campaigns, and questions over the capacity to sustain the expansionary fiscal and monetary policies (ECLAC 2021). Within that broad context, as the pandemic persisted, in June 2021, the CDB reported that thirteen of CDB's nineteen BMC recorded double-digit declines in the GDP, with an average downturn of 7.2 percent in 2020. Regional exports fell by 26 percent while imports decreased by 27 percent in 2020. BMCs that had debt-to-GDB ratios above 60 percent had increased to 13 percent in 2020, compared to 9 percent in 2019 (CDB 2021). Therefore, economic constraints can impede efforts to promote regional health security.

Democratic deficits can also undermine regional health security. From a public health perspective, the cross-border nature of the health crisis warrants the protection of lives and livelihoods. This requires legislation and policy interventions to protect borders and limit people-to-people connectivity within states. However, the COVID-19 "lockdowns" brought into sharp focus the perennial tension between order and freedom. As countries engaged in "lockdowns," individual freedoms were curtailed for public health safety. National security became an interlocking force between health security and economic security. Yet despite the imperative of national security, in some cases there have been concerns about excessive use of executive power through a prolonged state of emergencies, violation of civil rights and liberties, lack of consultation and participation, and insufficient inclusion of opposition parties and civil society organizations in decision-making. Democratic deficits were evident in the campaigns for vaccination. PAHO (2021) confirms that there is a high level of vaccine hesitancy in the Americas. As of December 1, 2021, only 54 percent of people in LAC had been fully vaccinated against COVID-19. In several CARICOM countries, mistrust of the government stymied efforts to mount successful vaccination campaigns. This has dire implications for a resilient recovery.

Conclusion

CARICOM countries have shown some level of resilience in addressing the health crisis by adopting a regional health security approach. This was manifested in strong regional leadership during the initial phase of the pandemic, a network of regional institutions, regional partnerships, solidarity, and global advocacy. The region's relative success to date is a testament to its history of resistance, the realities of small size, an instinct to survive, and a long tradition of regional collaboration. Despite the gains, there are impediments to regional health security which include sovereignty constraints, economic (in)security, and democratic deficits within member states. Finally, post-COVID-19 recovery presents an opportunity for CARICOM states to deepen regionalism by formalizing a comprehensive regional health security framework.

Acknowledgment

I wish to thank Ms. April Louis, Research Assistant, The University of the West Indies, Cave Hill Campus, Department of Government, Sociology, Social Work and Psychology; and Ms. Karyl Pivot for their assistance with data gathering.

References

Antoine, Timothy. 2020. "Governor's Foreword: Navigating an Unprecedented Crisis Toward a Transformed and Resilient Region." In *Eastern Caribbean Central Bank Annual Report 2019-20*. St. Kitts and Nevis: Eastern Caribbean Central Bank.

Booth, Ken, and Nicholas Wheeler (eds.). 2007. *The Security Dilemma Fear, Cooperation and Trust in World Politics*. New York: Palgrave.

Brigugilo, Lino. 2014. "A Vulnerability and Resilience Framework for Small States." In *Building the Resilience of Small States a Revised Framework*, edited by Denny Lewis-Bynoe, 10–76. London: The Commonwealth.

Brundtland, Gro Harlem. 2002. "AIDS and Global Security." Speech to the Nobel Centenary Roundtable, 25 January. http://www.who.iny/director-general/speeches/2002/english/20020125_nobelroundtable.html.

———. 2003. "Global Health and International Security." *Global Governance*, 9 (4): 417–23. http://www.who.iny/director-general/speeches/2002/english/2002125_nobelroundtable.html.

Buzan, Barry, and Ole Wæver (eds.). 2003. *Regions and Powers: The Structure of International Security*. Cambridge Studies in International Relations. Cambridge: Cambridge University Press. doi: 10.1017/CBO9780511491252.

Buzan, Barry, Ole Wæver, and Jaap de Wilde (eds.). 1998. *Security: A New Framework for Analysis*. Boulder: Lynne Rienner Publishers.

Byron, Jessica. 2011. "The Caribbean Community's 'Fourth Pillar': The Evolution of Regional Security Governance." In *The Security Governance of Regional Organizations*, edited by Roberto Dominguez and Emil J. Kirchner, 417–23. London: Routledge.

Byron, Jessica, Jacqueline Laguardia Martinez, Annita Montoute, and Keron Niles. 2021. "Impacts of COVID-19 in the Commonwealth Caribbean." *The Round Table: The Commonwealth Journal of International Affairs*, 110 (1): 99–119. doi: 10.1080/00358533.2021.1875694.

Caballero-Anthony, Mely. 2005. "SARS in Asia: Crisis, Vulnerabilities, and Regional Responses." *Asian Survey*, 45 (3): 475–95. doi: 10.1525/as.2005.45.3.475.

Campbell, Yonique, and John Connell (eds.). 2021. *COVID in the Islands: A Comparative Perspective on the Caribbean and the Pacific*. 1st ed. New York: Palgrave MacMillan.

Caribbean Community IMPACS. 2013. *Caricom Crime and Security Strategy-Securing the Region*. Port-au-Prince, Haiti: IMPACS/CARICOM.

Caribbean Community Secretariat. 2020. "Press Release Re: Ninth Special Emergency Meeting of the Conference of Heads of Government of the Caribbean Community, via Videoconference, 15 April 2020." https://caricom.org/press-release-re-ninth-special-emergency-meeting-of-the-conference-of-heads-of-government-of-the-caribbean-community-via-videoconference-15-april-2020/.

Caribbean Development Bank. 2019. "Annual Report." Wildey, St. Michael Barbados.

———. 2021. "CDB Calls for Improving Competitiveness for Strong, Inclusive Growth after COVID-19." *News Release*, 17 June 2021. Wildey, St. Michael Barbados. https://www.caribank.org/newsroom/news-and-events/cdb-calls-improving-competitiveness-strong-inclusive-growth-after-covid-19.

Commonwealth Secretariat. 2011. "Meeting of Experts on Growth and Development in Small States," 17–18 November 2011, Malta, Commonwealth Secretariat, London.

Commonwealth Secretariat and World Bank. 2000. "Small States: Meeting Challenges in the Global Economy. Report of the Commonwealth Secretariat and World Bank Joint Task Force on Small States." Commonwealth Secretariat and the World Bank.

Dorff, Robert H. 1994. "A Commentary on 'Security Studies for the 1990s' as a Model Curriculum Core." *International Studies Notes*, 19 (3): 23–31.

ECLAC. 2021. "Fiscal Panorama of Latin America and the Caribbean 2021" (LC/PUB2021/5-P). Santiago.

Elbe, Stefen. 2010. "Security and Global Health: Towards the Medicalization of Insecurity." *International Sociology*, 27 (5): 690–92. doi: https://doi.org/10.1177/0268580912452378.

Gilbert-Roberts, Terri-Ann P. 2013. *The Politics of Integration Caribbean Sovereignty Revisited*. Kingston, Jamaica: Ian Randle Publishers.

Grenade, Wendy C. 2018. "New Dimensions of Regionalism in the Caribbean: An Analysis of the Shanique Myrie Case." In *Caribbean Realities and Endogenous Realities*, edited by Debbie A. Mohammed and Nikolaos Karagiannis, 203–20. Kingston, Jamaica: The University of the West Indies Press.

Grenade, Wendy C., and Kai-Ann Skeete. 2015. "Regionalism among Small States - Challenges and Prospects: The Case of the Caribbean Community (CARICOM)." *The Commonwealth Secretariat*, The Small States Digest, no. 1 (January).

Griffith, Ivelaw. 2003. "Security and Sovereignty in the Contemporary Caribbean: Probing Elements of the Local – Global Nexus." In *Living at the Borderlines: Issues in Caribbean Sovereignty and Development*, edited by Cynthia Barrow Giles and Don D. Marshall, 209–25. Kingston, Jamaica: Ian Randle Publishers.

———. 2004. *Caribbean Security in the Age of Terror*. Kingston, Jamaica: Ian Randle Publishers.

Jamaica Observer. 2021. "Bd'os, Dominica to Share Donated COVID-19 Vaccines with Regional Neighbours," 10 February 2021.

Jhinkoo-Ramdass, Julia. 2020. "A Summary of Caribbean Economies' Policy Responses to the Covid-19 Pandemic." DeLisle Worrell & Associates. http://delisleworrell.com/A%20Summary%20of%20Caribbean%20Economies%E2%80%99%20Policy%20Responses%20to%20the%20Covid-19%20Pandemic.

Knight, W. Andy, and K. Srikanth Reddy. 2020. "Caribbean Response to COVID-19: A Regional Approach to Pandemic Preparedness and Resilience." *The Round Table*, 109 (4): 464–65. doi: 10.1080/00358533.2020.1790759.

Krause, Keith, and Michael C. Williams. 1996. "Broadening the Agenda of Security Studies: Politics and Methods." *Mershon International Studies Review*, 40 (2): 229–54. doi: 10.2307/222776.

Landis, R. Clive. 2021. "Coronavirus and CARICOM the Benefit of a Regional University in a Coherent Pandemic Response." In *COVID in the Islands: A Comparative Perspective on the Caribbean and the Pacific*, edited by Yonique Campbell and John Connell, 1st ed., 71–91. New York: Palgrave MacMillan.

Lewis, Patsy, Terri-Ann Gilbert-Roberts, and Jessica Byron. 2017. *Pan Caribbean Integration: Beyond CARICOM*. New York: Routledge.

Mathews, Jessica Tuchman. 1989. "Redefining Security." *Foreign Affairs*, 68 (2): 162–77. doi: 10.2307/20043906.

McInnis, Colin. 2013. "Health." In *Security Studies: An Introduction*, edited by Paul D. Williams, 2nd ed., 324–36. New York: Routledge.

McInnes, Colin, and Kelley Lee. 2012. *Global Health and International Relations*, 324–36. Cambridge: Polity Press.

Mearsheimer, John J. 1995. "A Realist Reply." *International Security*, 20 (1): 82–93. doi: 10.2307/2539218.

Media Institute of the Caribbean. "Trinidad and Tobago Country Report." Port of Spain, 16 December 2021. https://www.mediainstituteofthecaribbean.com/trinidad-and-tobago.

Mottley, Mia A. "Speech to the 73rd World Health Assembly." Virtually, 18 May 2020. https://www.who.int/about/governance/world-health-assembly/seventy-third-world-health-assembly.

Mowla, Wazim. 2020. "A Cuban Lifeline to CARICOM." *Global Americans*. https://theglobalamericans.org/2020/05/a-cuban-lifeline-to-caricom/.

Murphy, Madhuvanti, Selvi M. Jeyaseelan, Christina Howitt, Natalie Greaves, Heather Harewood, Kim, R. Quimby, Natasha Sobers, R. Clive Landis, Kern D. Rocke, and Ian R. Hambleton. 2020 December. "COVID-19 Containment in the Caribbean: The Experience of Small Island Developing States." *Research in Globalization*, 2: 100019.

Ogata, Sadako, and Amartya Sen. 2003. "Human Security Now." New York: Commission on Human Security.

Pan American Health Organisation. Annual Report of the Director of the Pan American Sanitary Bureau "Working through the COVID-19 Pandemic." (Official Document: 364) Washington, DC: Pan American Health Organisation, 2021.

Paris, Roland. 2001. "Human Security: Paradigm Shift or Hot Air?" *International Security*, 26 (2): 87–102.

Peoples, Columba, and Nick Vaughan-Williams. 2010. *Critical Security Studies: An Introduction*. London: Routledge.

Thomas, Clive. 2008. "The Urgency of Functional Cooperation: Priority Interventions in Selected Areas (Disaster Preparedness, Health, Education and Security)." In *The Caribbean Community in Transition Functional Cooperation as a Catalyst for Change*, edited by Kenneth O. Hall and Myrtle Chuck-A-Sang, 359–82. Kingston, Jamaica: Ian Randle Publisher.

Thomas, Clive Y. 2003. *Making Global Trade Work for People: The Concerns of Small States' in the Global Trade Regime*. Resilience Series, vol. 6. New York: UNDP.

Trinidad Express. "Trinidad and Tobago has Begun Donating AstraZeneca Vaccines," 8 October 2021.

Ullman, Richard H. 1983. "Redefining Security." *International Security*, 8 (1): 129–53. doi: 10.2307/2538489.

United Nations Development Programme. 1994. "New Dimensions of Human Security." In *Human Development Report*. New York: United Nations Development Programme.

United Nations Development Programme. 2019. "Beyond Income Beyond Averages Beyond Today: Inequalities in Human Development in the Twenty-First Century." In *Human Development Report*. New York: United Nations Development Programme.

Walt, Stephen M. 1991. "The Renaissance of Security Studies." *International Studies Quarterly*, 35 (2): 211–39. doi: 10.2307/2600471.

West Indian Commission. 1992. *Time for Action - The Report of the West Indian Commission*. Black Rock, Barbados: West Indian Commission.

Williams, Paul D., and Matt McDonald (eds.). 2018. *Security Studies: An Introduction*. 3rd ed. New York: Routledge.

World Bank. 2020. "The Global Economic Outlook during the COVID-19 Pandemic: A Changed World." https://www.worldbank.org/en/news/feature/2020/06/08/the -global-economic-outlook-during-the-covid-19-pandemic-a-changed-world.

World Bank. Annual Report 2021. "From Crisis to Green, Resilient and Inclusive Recovery." Washington, DC. https://openknowledge.worldbank.org/handle/10986 /36067.

World Health Assembly. 2001. "Global Health Security – Epidemic Alert and Response." Report by the Secretariat prepared for the Fifty-Fourth World Health Assembly. A54/9. Geneva: World Health Assembly.

World Health Organisation. 1946. *Constitution of the World Health Organisation*. Geneva: World Health Organisation.

———. 2007. *The World Health Report 2007 – A Safer Future: Global Public Health Security in the 21st Century*. Geneva: World Health Organisation.

———. 2021. "Corona Disease Dashboard." Updated at 3 December. https://covid19 .who.int/.

World Meters.info. http://www.worldmeters.info/.

4

Boosting Resilience in the Caribbean

New Strategies for a Sustainable Future

HELVIA VELLOSO[1]

Introduction

The economic challenges in the Caribbean can be linked in significant measure to the region's external vulnerability. Vulnerability to economic shocks and small size – implying a narrow range of economic activities, limited economies of scale, and constrained competitiveness – adversely affects access to international capital. This is particularly relevant in the context of the 2030 Agenda and the Sustainable Development Goals (SDGs), which have underscored the need to find new ways of mobilizing resources to support long-term solutions to development challenges (ECLAC 2017d).

The Caribbean region is once again facing a severe global shock: the COVID-19 pandemic, one of the most urgent health, economic, and social crises the world has faced in decades. The pandemic and the policy response it has elicited have dealt a devastating blow to the tourism and service sectors across the Caribbean region. The sharp decline in economic activity and the expansion of public spending toward emergency relief have put pressure on an already difficult fiscal situation for many countries of the region. In this scenario, the

[1] Economic Affairs Officer of the United Nations Economic Commission for Latin America and the Caribbean (ECLAC), Office in Washington, D.C. The views and opinions expressed are my own and do not necessarily reflect the views of ECLAC or the countries it represents.

Acknowledgments: I would like to thank Winston Dookeran for generously sharing his deep knowledge of the Caribbean region with me during his year-long stay in Washington, D.C. It was through the work we did together then that the main concepts and ideas for this chapter were developed. I am also thankful to Inés Bustillo for her comments on the topics discussed in this chapter.

need to mobilize resources for economic reactivation and development has become even greater.

Historic trends clearly show the adverse impact that crises, the 2008 global crisis in particular, had on the region's ability to mobilize resources. If the region was already constrained in its access to external financing, the situation will likely worsen as a result of the pandemic. In the context of (1) a decline in official development assistance and the increasing importance of private flows in the global external environment, (2) the Caribbean region's vulnerability and need to strengthen its resilience, and (3) the need to channel resources toward the 2030 Agenda and to "build back better" after the pandemic, this chapter examines new opportunities in the mobilization of external financing.

New and innovative debt instruments have emerged in the context of the 2030 Agenda and the Paris Climate Agreement, such as blue, green, social and sustainability bonds. Financial instruments that can bolster resilience and help transfer risk in cost-effective ways may complement traditional international resource flows and offer a viable alternative for the mobilization of resources toward sustainable development. From a sovereign perspective, these include countercyclical instruments, such as hurricane clauses and sovereign contingent convertible bonds. However, these instruments and mechanisms will be successful only to the extent that there is a broad collaborative effort – among the public sector, multilateral institutions, the private sector, and international development partners – to design and mobilize resources for regional projects that address the Caribbean's long-term challenges and potential.

The Caribbean Economy: Vulnerability, Fragility, and the Need to Strengthen Resilience

Caribbean economies have serious development challenges. They have shown slow and volatile economic growth and high levels of unemployment (see figure 4.1), especially among young people; significant incidence of poverty; inequality of income and wealth; underachievement of the Millennium Development Goals in the areas of health, access of basic services, gender equality, and environmental sustainability (Mendoza and Stuart 2011); acute vulnerability to natural disasters and substantial risks ensuing from climate change and rising sea levels; and a very high debt burden, which, in turn, has a pernicious effect on growth (McLean, Sheldon, and Don Charles 2018). In addition, fiscal challenges limit governments' ability to respond to external shocks and to enhance social protection programs.

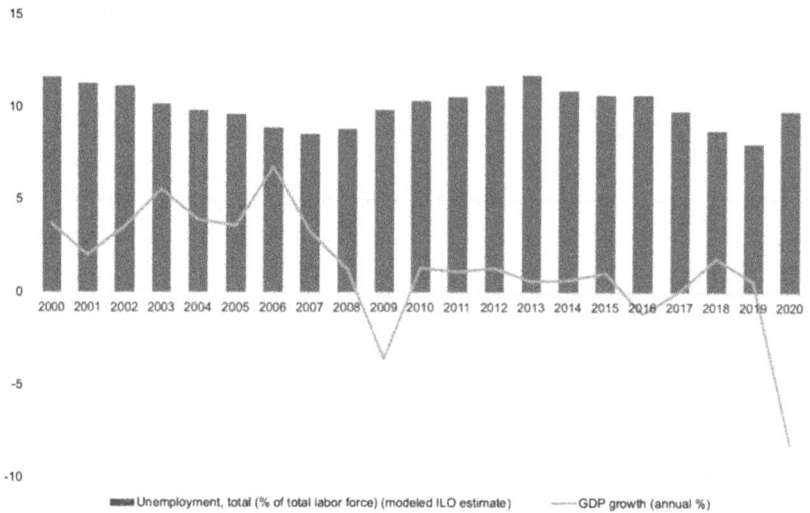

Figure 4.1 Caribbean: low growth and high unemployment (Average GDP growth and unemployment rate in percentage).

Source: World Development Indicators – World Bank Database, Caribbean Small States.

Vulnerability as a Structural Variable

The geography of the Caribbean renders it vulnerable. The uniqueness of these vulnerabilities is that they are of a structural nature. Vulnerability is dictated by geology and geography, reinforced by economic forces and flows, and defined by history and politics.

The Caribbean region is one of the most disaster-prone regions in the world, and natural disasters have severe economic consequences for the countries of the region, which include contraction in economic output, worsening of external balances, deteriorating fiscal conditions, increasing debt, and increasing poverty, as natural disasters affect poorer segments of the population disproportionately. Given the recurrence of these natural disasters in the region, their macroeconomic impacts, which would be transitory in nature, linger over time and turn into a long-term feature. These economic consequences compound as every new disaster takes place before the region can fully recover from the previous one.

In the context of the Caribbean, there are inherent permanent or quasi-permanent features that translate into vulnerability and susceptibility to external economic shocks. These features include geographic size, remoteness, and insularity; economic openness; and lack of economic and export diversification due to limited natural resources. The heavy reliance on few activities and few source markets for exports leaves the Caribbean extremely vulnerable to external shocks. The relative stagnation of its exports reflects the Caribbean region's difficulty in overcoming an export structure with limited diversification, in which more than half of the value of its total exports is concentrated in commodities and natural resource-based manufactures.

Fragility as a Process Variable

Fragility is largely the result of process variables, including conflict situations, inertia in institutions, and exposure to shocks and violence. Fragility in the process of development has often been cited as a recurring feature of the workings of the institutions – always stuck in transition mode (from colonial times), with a persistent shortage of resources, and missing systems for accountability and effectiveness in delivery. Institutional inertia is a process outcome that is endemic, yet in a sense it is "curable" when institutions are strengthened and firmly anchored in democratic values and the rule of law. Fragility is deeply embedded in the advancement and success of development itself, which largely depends on a reduction in the region's fragility, as one feeds the other (Dookeran 2017).

Resilience as a Strategy Variable

External shocks are often seen as temporary in nature, but given the recurrence of these shocks, the vulnerability of the region, and the fragility of Caribbean institutional frameworks, their effects tend to linger and never fully disappear, thus building resilience becomes an imperative. Building resilience in Caribbean economies is the most challenging strategy variable – to generate a net inflow of funds, sustain competitive enterprises, and grow the well-being of its citizens on a persistent path.

Briguglio's pioneering work on a measurement matrix of resilience calculates the gaps in resilience variables and points toward policies – domestic and international – that are required to close them (Briguglio 2014). Building economic resilience relies on macroeconomic stability, market efficiency, political governance, social development, and environmental governance. It is measured by the ability of an economy to absorb a shock, as well as to implement counteraction policies. Steps to build financial buffers for resilience are a key approach to economic survival and placing equality at the center of sustainable development. Survivability today is a key requisite to sustainability tomorrow and is at the heart of a viable strategy for economic resilience in Caribbean economies.

There is a nexus between economic and environmental resilience. The geographic location of Caribbean economies makes them highly susceptible to hurricanes, storms, and floods. The effects of these are further compounded by the impacts of climate change, which manifest as prolonged periods of drought, rising sea levels, and higher temperatures. The main economic sectors of small state economies in the Caribbean are particularly vulnerable to climate change impacts. The catastrophic storms that have ravaged the Caribbean brought devastation to fisheries and agriculture sectors, as well as to critical tourism-related infrastructure (hotels, restaurants, and air and seaports). These disasters often lead to deterioration in government fiscal balances as the decline in economic activity decreases tax revenues and increases government expenditure due to emergency relief and reconstruction efforts.

Caribbean countries therefore must rely on international financing to expand their limited fiscal capacity to respond to these persistent shocks. Nonetheless, some official sources of financing have been on a downward trend. The counterpart of this decline has been an increase in private sources of financing, including foreign direct investment, remittances, and private portfolio flows, which so far have not been enough to offset the loss of official assistance.

The capacity to access international capital markets and use private portfolio flows in an effective manner varies widely among the countries of Latin America and the Caribbean, with access being more limited and borrowing costs higher for Caribbean countries. Efforts to expand the mobilization of resources need to consider this heterogeneity when looking for ways to channel private resources toward SDGs, building Caribbean resilience, and meeting the challenges of the new development agenda. Resilience is more than an issue of financing, however. It also involves opening new spaces for development within the Caribbean economies and outside.

Strategies for Building Caribbean Resilience

The constraints and disadvantages that small states face in pursuit of development have been well discussed in the literature over the past several decades, including small size and lack of diversification. Moreover, with the 2030 Agenda and the SDGs bringing global attention to the environment and the need for sustainable development, the geographic and environmental vulnerability of small island and low-lying coastal countries, such as the ones found in the Caribbean region, has come to the fore. The Caribbean countries are exposed and susceptible to exogenous economic and environmental shocks, and a major drive of economic vulnerability is the region's exposure to natural disasters. While resilience may be viewed as the ability to adjust and to cope with such shocks, in the context of the 2030 Agenda for sustainable development and the recent United Nations climate conference COP26, a more expansive perspective is warranted, one in that building resilience requires efforts that also address the long-term consequences of these recurring shocks to find sustainable solutions.

There are several possible strategies for building resilience and finding long-term solutions for long-term development challenges. One such strategy would be to *link debt solutions to resilience measures*. The premise is that the current high level of debt in the Caribbean is rooted in external shocks and compounded by inherent structural weakness and vulnerabilities, particularly extreme weather events. Moreover, the upper- and middle-income classification of most Caribbean countries poses a number of challenges, such as limited access to concessional external finance and a decline in official development assistance. Addressing structural vulnerabilities, such as debt sustainability, is thus key to building resilience in the Caribbean economies.

The United Nations Economic Commission for Latin America and the Caribbean (ECLAC) has proposed channeling pledged climate funds to write down Caribbean debt through "debt for climate adaptation swaps" and the creation of a Caribbean Resilience Fund (CRF) to help ease the region's debt burden and provide financing for investment in climate resilience, green growth, and structural transformation in the economies of the region (ECLAC 2016, 2017a,b). The CRF would be supported by writing off multilateral debts of the Caribbean countries, and those economies benefitting from the debt relief would make annual payments in local currency to the CRF (other bodies would also be able to donate to it).[2]

Another strategy would be *deepening the link between domestic savings in the economy and the external flow of funds*, which is critical to fostering capital formation. Strategic measures to deepen this relationship would add to the resilience of the economy. As such, the question of building partnerships with councils and bodies fostering business incubators and innovative capital will unearth new space for the integration of the small business sector with the world industry. Here, the banking sector, along with the Chambers of Commerce and trade union movement, may take the lead in setting up institutions to achieve these goals.[3]

---

[2] The ECLAC proposal was discussed at the 36th CARICOM Heads of Governments meeting in July 2015 and at ECLAC's Caribbean Development Roundtable held in Saint Kitts and Nevis in April 2016. Heads of Government in their report to the 37th CARICOM Conference agreed that ECLAC should pursue the "initiative to the extent feasible, on behalf of the region."

[3] Tennant (2007, 75) argues that the region's commercial banks are important to the mobilization of resources for development, "as, if they maintain high standards of performance, banks can maximize the mobilization of domestic funds, maintain efficiency in the transferral of savings to the real sector, minimize financial costs and interest rate spreads, and efficiently allocate funds to growth-enhancing investments."

Addressing the limitations of the Caribbean economies in accessing *concessional financing* would also contribute to strengthening resilience in these countries. The Caribbean economies face great vulnerabilities to external shocks and a fragile fiscal situation. Despite these vulnerabilities, the Caribbean countries are categorized as middle-income countries by international financial institutions, complicating their ability to access concessional financing (UNDP 2015). It is imperative that the conditions for accessing concessional funding be altered, to assist in reconstruction efforts in the aftermath of external shocks that are beyond their control. Gross Domestic Product per capita criteria fail to take into account threats from natural disasters, and/or global shocks such as the COVID-19 pandemic. This problem must be collectively addressed by the international community and remain a top priority in the regional and global landscapes.

Another important strategy would be to *build up new financial buffers for small economies through instruments that build resilience*. Finance and liquidity are the lifeblood of any economic system. The 2030 Agenda, Paris Climate Agreement, and COP26 commitments have underscored the urgent need to scale up public and private financing for sustainable development. New and innovative debt instruments, as well as countercyclical sovereign instruments, have emerged as mechanisms that could play a role in the mobilization of resources by the Caribbean countries. However, the success of these strategies for building Caribbean resilience will require two necessary ingredients: a competitiveness agenda and improved coordination.

Innovative Debt Instruments to Boost Resilience

The growing importance of private external financing offers an opportunity to mobilize and channel private resources toward development objectives. However, flows of private capital are driven mostly by the search for yield rather than concerns about economic development. Therefore, investment may be insufficient in areas that are crucial for sustainable development if the anticipated economic returns are unsatisfactory relative to other investment opportunities. In this context, cooperation between the public sector, the international community, and the private sector should be encouraged, so that a cost-benefit analysis of investment projects includes social and environmental criteria.

Meeting developing countries' challenges following the devastating socioeconomic impact of the COVID-19 pandemic, as well as the growing demand for quality public services and infrastructure, which are sustainable and climate-friendly, will require a considerable fiscal effort and an increase in the participation of the private sector. Capital markets can play an important role in boosting sustainable investments. Some promising new debt instruments that could contribute to the mobilization of resources toward sustainable development include green, social, sustainability, and sustainability-linked (GSSS), blue and diaspora bonds.

GSSS Bonds

These instruments could be contemplated as a viable option for building Caribbean resilience, given the region's development challenges and its vulnerability to the effects of climate change and external shocks. The first green bond from the Latin America and the Caribbean (LAC) region was issued in December 2014. Since then, a broader range of socially conscious debt labels in LAC have risen to also include social, sustainability, and sustainability-linked bonds under the umbrella of sustainable bond issuance.

There are two types of structure in the sustainability debt market: use of proceeds and target-linked. Green, social, and sustainability bonds belong to the first type of structure.[4] Sustainability-linked bonds (SLB) are target-linked instruments that allow financing outside of specific projects or use of proceeds categories. The issuer of an SLB chooses key performance indicators and associated targets that it wants to achieve. There is an element of specific accountability: if the target is not achieved, a step-up mechanism will be applied to the bond's interest rates.[5]

Since December 2014 and up to September 2021, total LAC issuance of GSSS bonds in international markets reached US$ 73 billion. The annual average of cross-border GSSS bonds in the total international debt issuance from the region in this period is 7.1 percent (table 4.1). In the first nine months of 2021, international GSSS bond issuances from LAC totaled US$ 39.2 billion and represented 31.5 percent of the total cross-border bond issuance in the period, a new peak (figure 4.2).

The GSSS bond market may present a unique opportunity to help with the economic recovery from the impact of the COVID-19 pandemic. For example, green bonds can help fund sustainable infrastructure, and social bonds could be a way to raise funds to help fortify health systems or help finance eligible

---

[4] Green and social bonds are any type of fixed income instrument whose proceeds are allocated to projects with clear environmental and social benefits, respectively. In the case of sustainability bonds, proceeds will be allocated to the financing or refinancing of a combination of green and social projects.

[5] After the International Capital Market Association (ICMA) released the Sustainability-Linked Bond Principles (SLBP) in June 2020, the first sustainability-linked bonds (SLBs) were issued in the LAC region in the second half of the year.

Table 4.1 LAC GSSS annual bond issuance in international markets

	US$ Million	Percentage of Total International LAC Bond Issuance
2014	204	0.2
2015	1,049	1.3
2016	3,486	2.7
2017	8,329	5.7
2018	535	0.6
2019	6,451	5.4
2020	13,443	9.3
2021 (Jan–Sep)	39,219	31.5
	72,716	**AVG 2014–2021 (Jan–Sep): 7.1%**

Source: ECLAC 2017c, 29. Updated by author based on data from Dealogic, Climate Bonds Initiative, LatinFinance, press announcements and releases. The table includes issuance from mostly corporate issuers in six countries (Argentina, Brazil, Chile, Costa Rica, Mexico and Peru) and two supranational issuers (CAF Development Bank of Latin America and Central American Bank for Economic Integration (CABEI)). In 2019, Chile became the first sovereign in the Americas to issue a green bond.

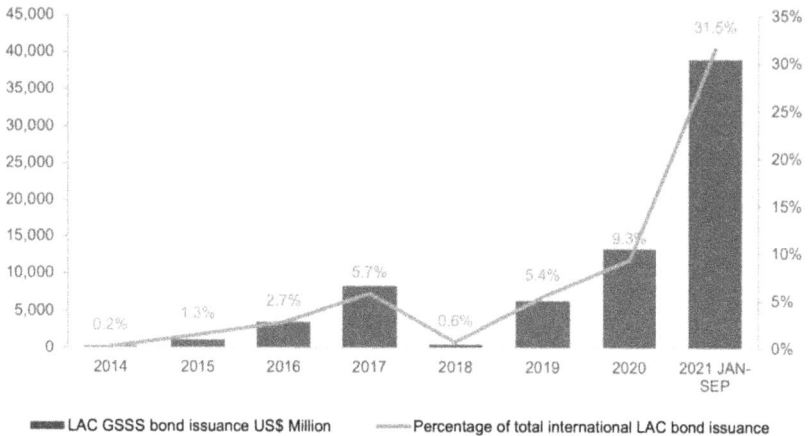

Figure 4.2 LAC GSSS bond issuance in international markets, 2014 to 2021(Jan–Sep)(Left axis, US$ Million; Right axis, percentage).

Source: ECLAC 2021, 8.

social investments related to the pandemic's prevention, containment, and mitigation.

The benefits of promoting the use of these novel instruments include the increased interest in them on the part of countries, companies, and investors worldwide, particularly following the pandemic crisis; a bigger pool of finance, relieving fiscal pressure on governments; and increased participation of the private sector in the mobilization of resources for the development process, by offering a menu of financial instruments that can attract private investors to sustainable projects.

However, there are challenges as well, which include, among others, the lack of taxonomies and definitions of sustainable activities aligned with developing countries' policies, needs, and objectives that could help sovereign and corporate issuers know when to use these instruments as a way of mobilizing resources, not enough transparency or data (it is not easy to track the proceeds of green bonds, for example, until reports for how they have been spent are available), a lack of measurable indicators of the core risk factors and project success, and absence of a standard methodology.

For the most part, Caribbean issuers have been absent from the GSSS bond market.[6] Their absence suggests that size and scale may be an impediment to the use of these new instruments, raising the benefits of cooperation among states, which could pool together regional projects that could simultaneously benefit several countries.

Blue Bonds

Blue bonds are a relatively new form of a sustainability bond (ADB 2021), whereby funds raised are earmarked exclusively for projects dedicated to enhancing ocean and coastal resilience. In 2018, the Republic of Seychelles launched the world's first sovereign blue bond raising a total of US$ 15 million to advance its blue economy. The World Bank helped design the bond.

In early November 2021, IDB Invest, the private-sector affiliate of the Inter-American Development Bank (IDB), announced at COP26 the issuance of the first blue bond in LAC (ten-year notes with a 2.2 percent coupon), raising AUD 50 million (US$ 37.2 million) to fund ocean and freshwater conservation projects (IDB Invest 2021).

Also in November, the Government of Belize financed the buyback of its US dollar bond due 2034 with funding provided by a subsidiary of The Nature Conservancy (TNC) as part of TNC's Blue Bonds for Ocean Conservation

---

[6] In June 2019, Williams Caribbean Capital, incorporated in Barbados, issued a BBD 3 million (US$ 1.5 million) green bond with a four-year tenor in a private placement to finance a solar energy project. The Climate Bonds Standard Board approved the Certification of the Williams Renewable Energy Limited Fixed Rate Notes. This certification scheme is used globally by bond issuers, governments, investors, and the financial markets to prioritize investments which genuinely contribute to addressing climate change. This is a development that warrants monitoring, as it may offer possibilities that could be replicated by other Caribbean corporate issuers.

program. The financial transaction between the Government of Belize and TNC is backed by the proceeds of a blue bond, arranged by Credit Suisse (ECLAC 2021).

Diaspora Bonds

Diaspora bonds are fixed-debt instruments issued by a country to its emigrants outside of the home country at preferential rates. Because of their sheer volume, as well as their consistent and resilient nature, cross-border remittances that flow into Caribbean countries every year have become a vital source of funds. Remittance spending is skewed toward consumption, and the economic impact of remittance flows could be greater if at least some of that money was directed into productive investment. A growing number of countries around the world are seeking to tap into the financial resources of their overseas expatriate populations by channeling part of their savings and remittances into diaspora bonds, which are one way of directing remittances into investment.[7]

Countercyclical Sovereign Instruments[8]

Caribbean countries are considering an array of options to bolster their financial resilience and help transfer risk in cost-effective ways. These options include the ones described in the previous section, which represent ways to channel private-sector resources toward this end. Regarding sovereign instruments, options include building small fiscal buffers by putting aside windfall revenues and obtaining disaster insurance through regional polling mechanisms such as the Caribbean Catastrophic Risk Insurance Facility.[9]

Given the Caribbean's increasing exposure to the risk of exogenous shocks, weather-related or otherwise, the pressing need to explore new and cost-effective instruments to transfer risk is strong. With its second debt restructuring process initiated in 2013, Grenada pioneered a "hurricane clause" in its bonds,

---

[7] The Government of Israel has used these instruments since 1951 and India on a few occasions since 1991 (Ketkar and Ratha 2010). India, Bangladesh, Pakistan, Lebanon, Sri Lanka, and the Philippines have already managed to finance development projects in this way. In Africa, diaspora bonds have so far been issued by six countries – with mixed results (Enders 2020). The suitability of diaspora bonds as a financial instrument in the context of the Caribbean is discussed in Wenner 2015.

[8] The discussion in this section is found in ECLAC (2020, 37).

[9] In 2007, the Caribbean Catastrophe Risk Insurance Facility was formed as the first multi-country risk pool in the world and was the first insurance instrument to successfully develop parametric policies backed by both traditional and capital markets. It was designed as a regional catastrophe fund for Caribbean governments to limit the financial impact of devastating hurricanes and earthquakes by quickly providing financial liquidity when a policy is triggered. See https://www.ccrif.org.

stipulating an immediate, if temporary, debt moratorium if the country were struck by another natural disaster. The move was endorsed by the Paris Club of governmental creditors and held out the promise of vital financial relief at times of distress. In 2019, Barbados also inserted a hurricane clause into its restructured domestic and external debt.

Hurricane-linked clauses have been gaining support from multilateral lenders and the International Capital Markets Association (ICMA), a trade body. To facilitate the use of hurricane-linked clauses by interested sovereigns, ICMA has drafted a standardized clause that would allow stricken countries to defer all principal and interest payment for three years.

The primary benefits of adding a hurricane clause are immediate cash relief and fiscal space in the event of a disaster, avoidance of payment default, and the prevention of further debt restructuring. The amount of cash relief would depend on the amount of debt affected, the number of times a claim is triggered, and the number of deferred payments. In the case of Grenada, its hurricane provisions allowed for a maximum of three claims and up to two deferred payments under each claim (The Commonwealth 2016, 19).

However, there is a risk that hurricane-linked clauses may not provide meaningful relief following hurricanes, at least until a substantial share of the existing debt stock has matured and been replaced by debt containing such clauses. In the case of Barbados, the hurricane clause included in the new bonds offered in the domestic and external debt restructuring will enable the government to capitalize interest and defer principal maturities due on the new bonds for two years following an earthquake, tropical cyclone, or rainfall event covered by its insurance policy. As a result of the restructuring, the totality of Barbados' public debt stock has become climate resilient.

Other options from a sovereign perspective include state-contingent debt instruments, whose premise is to tie a sovereign's payment obligations to its repayment capacity. The debt service burden on these instruments would fall in a downturn, providing countercyclical policy space and helping to reduce the likelihood and severity of a sovereign debt crisis. Sovereign contingent convertible bonds (CoCos) are an example of these instruments. Sovereign CoCos are bonds that would automatically extend repayment maturity when a country receives official sector emergency liquidity assistance.

Necessary Ingredients to Strengthen Resilience: Competitiveness and Convergence

Achieving higher sustainable growth remains elusive, despite years of adjustment. Policy prescriptions including the removal of price controls and subsidies are important but not enough. An adjustment framework for development must stimulate the dynamics for endogenous growth, "so that the industrial structure of production may be transformed, creating new vehicles for the empowerment of peoples which will yield a high-level equilibrium and momentum for sustainable growth" (Dookeran 1996, 10).

There must be internal forces for change that will lead to higher growth. Caribbean economies must strengthen their capacity to adapt to evolving external economic conditions and develop new sources of sustainable growth based on a sound competitiveness agenda that facilitates innovation and entrepreneurship. Failings in the fundamental pillars of competitiveness in the region – institutions, infrastructure, labor market efficiency, and innovation – must be addressed to improve resilience to external shocks. Also, building a competitive agenda requires public–private partnerships that extend the life of single-term government administrations.

Collaboration and coordination are also important ingredients to strengthen resilience in the Caribbean. Anyanwu goes further and points to the need for convergence (Anyanwu 2015). The logic of convergence is to foster cooperation among like-minded states over common interests, by providing information, reducing transaction costs, and facilitating linkages. According to Anyanwu, convergence is about moving beyond boundaries to create economic opportunities, and it calls for bold political and economic decision-making, new and innovative ideas, and integrated interests toward win–win outcomes. It is based on three key points: a new approach to regionalism that focuses on the wider hemisphere, an emphasis on capability building through cooperation and not just a focus on trade and markets, and a strong focus on production integration, competitiveness, and equity of the Caribbean economies in the global order.

In summary, strengthening resilience and engendering regional economic development in a sustainable way would require the Caribbean countries to build their economies on four pillars (Dookeran 2013): *(1) inclusive and equitable development*, with inclusiveness implying the enlargement of the Caribbean, the widening of trade arrangements, and a process to incorporate the private sector and civil society intrinsically into the development process; *(2) transformative and endogenous growth*, which includes the capacity to pool regional resources and restructure domestic and foreign investments/finance, foster new models of public–private partnerships and redefine the role of development finance and equity; *(3) entrepreneurial competitiveness*: in the new frontier of Caribbean convergence, innovation in science, technology, and entrepreneurship must go hand in hand with raising the ambition of the region to engage in global initiatives and in the growing outsourcing opportunities in the world; and *(4) adaptive and realigned institutions*, which require a new adaptive framework and a realignment of regional institutions to achieve the convergence outcome.

Conclusion

In a context where official development assistance (ODA) flows and access to concessional financing have declined, there is a need to access other sources of international financing. For that to happen successfully, new strategies and financial instruments are needed to mobilize resources for the development agenda. Innovative debt-based instruments such as GSSS, blue, and diaspora bonds, among others, could complement international resource flows (ODA, foreign direct investment, and remittances) and mobilize additional resources for development. Mechanisms such as hurricane clauses and state-contingent debt instruments for sovereigns, such as sovereign CoCos, would provide needed countercyclical space.

Strengthening economic relationships and increasing institutional cooperation in the Caribbean will be critical to effectively benefit from these instruments. This will require that the region works together on regional goals and projects that can help overcome their limitations and size constraint. Moreover, these novel instruments and mechanisms will be successful only to the extent that there is a broad collaborative effort – among the public sector, multilateral institutions, the private sector, and international development partners – to design and mobilize resources for regional projects that address the Caribbean's long-term challenges and potential.

References

ADB (Asian Development Bank). 2021. "Sovereign Blue Bonds. Quick Start Guide." https://www.adb.org/sites/default/files/publication/756966/adb-sovereign-blue -bonds-start-guide.pdf.

Anyanwu, David C. 2015. *Caribbean Convergence – An Essay*. Prepared for the Forum on the Future of the Caribbean, Trinidad & Tobago, May. http://www20.iadb.org/ intal/catalogo/PE/2015/15506.pdf.

Briguglio, Lino. 2014. "A Vulnerability and Resilience Framework for Small States." In *Building the Resilience of Small States: A Revised Framework*. London: Commonwealth Secretariat. http://dx.doi.org/10.14217/9781848599185-5-en.

Bustillo, Inés, Helvia Velloso, Winston Dookeran, and Daniel Perrotti. 2018. *Resilience and Capital Flows in the Caribbean*. ECLAC Office in Washington D.C., LC/WAS/ TS.2018/2/-*, October. https://www.cepal.org/en/publications/43420-resilience-and- capital-flows-caribbean.

Dookeran, Winston. 1996. "Crosscurrents in Caribbean Policy Analysis." In *Choices and Change: Reflections on the Caribbean*, Chapter One, edited by Winston C. Dookeran, Inter-American Development Bank.

———. 2013. "A New Frontier for Caribbean Convergence." *Caribbean Journal of International Relations & Diplomacy*, 1 (2): 5–20.

———. 2017. "Vulnerabilities, Fragility and Resilience: Challenges for the Caribbean." Speech prepared for Conference IdA-EU-LAC Foundation 2017: The Caribbean in the Strategic Partnership EU-CELAC, Paris, June.

ECLAC. 2016. "Proposal on Debt for Climate Adaptation Swaps: A Strategy for Growth and Economic Transformation of Caribbean Economies." Economic Commission for Latin America and the Caribbean, Subregional Headquarters for the Caribbean, LC/CAR/L.492, 12 April.

———. 2017a. "ECLAC's Proposal on Debt for Climate Adaptation Swaps: A Strategy for Growth and Economic Transformation of Caribbean Economies." Presentation at CARICOM – United Nations High Level Pledging Conference Building a More Climate– Resilient Community. https://www.cepal.org/sites/default/files/news/files/nydbetreliefcaribbeannovember2017.pdf.

———. 2017b. "Criteria for Access to Concessional Financing Must Change to Support Caribbean Countries with their Reconstruction." Press Release, 24 October. https://www.cepal.org/en/pressreleases/criteria-access-concessional-financing-must-change-support-caribbean-countries-their.

———. 2017c. "The Rise of Green Bonds: Financing for Development in Latin America and the Caribbean." Report prepared by Helvia Velloso, October, LC/WAS/TS.2017/6. https://www.cepal.org/en/publications/42230-rise-green-bonds-financing-development-latin-america-and-caribbean.

———. 2017d. "Financing the 2030 Agenda for Sustainable Development in Latin America and the Caribbean. The Challenges of Resource Mobilization." Forum of the Countries of Latin America and the Caribbean on Sustainable Development, Mexico City, 26–28 April. http://repositorio.cepal.org//handle/11362/41197.

———. 2020. "The Caribbean Outlook: Forging a people-centred approach to sustainable development post-COVID-19." Economic Commission for Latin America and the Caribbean, LC/SES.38/12, 23 October.

———. 2021. "Capital Flows to Latin America and the Caribbean: First nine months of 2021." Report prepared by Helvia Velloso, November, LC/WAS/TS.2021/9. https://www.cepal.org/en/publications/47514-capital-flows-latin-america-and-caribbean-first-nine-months-2021.

Enders, Mira. 2020. "Untapped Potential." D+C Development and Cooperation, 18 March. https://www.dandc.eu/en/article/diaspora-bonds-could-play-bigger-role-development-finance.

ICMA. 2020. "The Sustainability-Linked Bond Principles (SLBP)." https://www.icmagroup.org/assets/documents/Regulatory/Green-Bonds/June-2020/Sustainability-Linked-Bond-Principles-June-2020-171120.pdf.

IDB Invest. 2021. "IDB Invest Issues First Blue Bond in Latin America and the Caribbean." Press Release, 5 November. https://idbinvest.org/en/news-media/idb-invest-issues-first-blue-bond-latin-america-and-caribbean.

Ketkar, Suhas L., and Dilip Ratha. 2010. "Diaspora Bonds: Tapping the Diaspora during Difficult Times." *Journal of International Commerce, Economics and Policy*, 1 (2): 251–63.

McLean, Sheldon, and Don Charles. 2018. "Caribbean Development Report. A Perusal of Public Debt in the Caribbean and Its Impact on Economic Growth." Series Studies and Perspectives, ECLAC Subregional Headquarters for the Caribbean, LC/TS.2017/157, LC/CAR/TS.2017/18, S.17-01291, January.

Mendoza, Patricia, and Sheila Stuart. 2011. "Caribbean Millennium Development Goals Report 2010." Series Studies and Perspectives No.16, LC/L.3537, LC/CAR/L.371, ECLAC Subregional Headquarters for the Caribbean, December. http://repositorio.cepal.org/bitstream/handle/11362/5045/1/S2012371_en.pdf.

Tennant, David. 2007. "Investigating the Performance of Caribbean Commercial Banks in their Mobilization and use of Savings." *Iberoamericana. Nordic Journal of Latin American and Caribbean Studies*, XXXVII (2): 55–88.

The Commonwealth. 2016. *Introducing Hurricane Clauses. Lessons from Grenada's Recent Experience. A Countercyclical Financial Instrument.* Author: Michele Robinson. Edited by Heidi Tavakoli. London: Commonwealth Secretariat.

UNDP. 2015. "Financing for Development Challenges in Caribbean SIDS. A Case for Review of Eligibility Criteria for Access to Concessional Financing." Report prepared for the *United Nations Development Programme* by Professor Compton Bourne, assisted by Megan Alexander, Daren Conrad and Julia Jhinkoo, a publication of the UNDP Trinidad & Tobago Country Office, June 2015.

Wenner, Mark D. 2015. "Can Diaspora Bonds be used in the Caribbean." Inter-American Development Bank, October. https://publications.iadb.org/handle/11319/7257.

Part 3

Development Frontiers

Fixing the Gap Between Theory and Practice

5

The Calculus of Development Insights on the Frontier of Analysis

WINSTON DOOKERAN

Introduction

Renowned scholar Robert Cox, in his seminal article "Social Forces, States and World Orders" (1981), inspired his students to think beyond the boundaries of conventional theorizing by arguing that we live in a time of gradual disintegration of a historical structure (Cox 1981, 127). In his penetrating insights on international political economy, he asserted that politics can never be separated from economics and that theory is always linked to practice (Cox 1981, 128). His treatise was aptly titled "Theory Talks," and while he applied it elegantly in the field of international relations, his urging is equally applicable in the discourse surrounding economic development.

In my book *The Caribbean on the Edge*, I began by noting that "in a period of tense stability in the Caribbean space" (Dookeran 2018, 7), the old premises that inspired development thinking become brittle. I posed the question, in its movement away from survival and toward sustainability, could the Caribbean stand up to recurring risks ahead and forge a confident pathway for sustainable development (Dookeran 2018, 20). In the tradition of Allister McIntyre, I examined the work of one of the Caribbean's most prolific and influential scholars, Arthur Lewis, in an attempt to locate his pioneering contribution to the contemporary context of Caribbean development. Lewis' model of economic growth is rooted in classical analysis and is thus regarded as a profound analysis of the theory of capital and growth in development economics.

This chapter describes the logic and argument of said model, situating it among the literature at the time. It focuses on the underlying assumption of linearity in models of development and applies the much-discussed idea of convergence in the development strategy emerging from the Lewis model. It asks the questions: Does it all fit today? What are the demands on scholarship for growth models in the making?

The Analytics of Vulnerability, Fragility, and Resilience

Much has been said about the vulnerability, fragility, and the quest for resilience of the Caribbean economy; however, these notions should be located analytically. Vulnerability is an inherent condition, dictated by geography, ecology, and location. In this sense, it is a structural variable, an initial condition that circumscribes the growth process. William Demas (1965) spoke of the limitations of small size and the degree of openness of these economies, of the space for diversification, and of the capacity to buffer external shocks. At the same time, fragility is a process variable, largely influenced by institutions and their behavior and the governance process. In periods of transition waves, institutional inertia makes systems more brittle and fragile, thus adding stress to effective performance. Frank Rampersad (1964), in his contribution to the structure and policy analysis of the Trinidad and Tobago economy, alluded to the matrix of resilience. In this analytical frame, resilience is largely but a strategy and policy variable, to insulate the economy from external shocks, to create space for expansion, and to sustain measures for stability, development, and economic growth.

Manfred Jantzen muses in his 2018 article, who are the cutting-edge thinkers today? His answer is that they are "the thinkers in complexity" (Jantzen 2018). He introduced the concept of frontier space as the space created by information. In applying the core growth model into a policy framework, Manfred crafted a frontier development framework that skillfully aligns the economic notions of shocks, vulnerability, and resilience in a governance map that includes the role of the state in development, and he identified strategic variables in policy analysis, as depicted in Figures 5.1 and 5.2.

Figure 5.1 depicts the frontier development framework, while Figure 5.2 superimposes this framework into a One-World–Information-Space. The key strategies focus on the catalytic role of the state, transforming the growth culture, integrating the informal economy, and aligning institutions with performance. Out of this framework analysis, Manfred concluded that the development challenge ahead will call for a reconceptualization of the orthodox growth theory and the resetting of the policy imperatives for equitable and sustainable development.

Applying the complex adaptive system dynamics of small developing states, he illustrated this complexity in the following extract, in his chapter on "Distorted Development in a One-World-Information-Space." The diagram is crystallized by observing the exposure to external shocks resulting in internal changing vulnerability that draws on its resilience and requires a convergence that integrates the wider regional space.

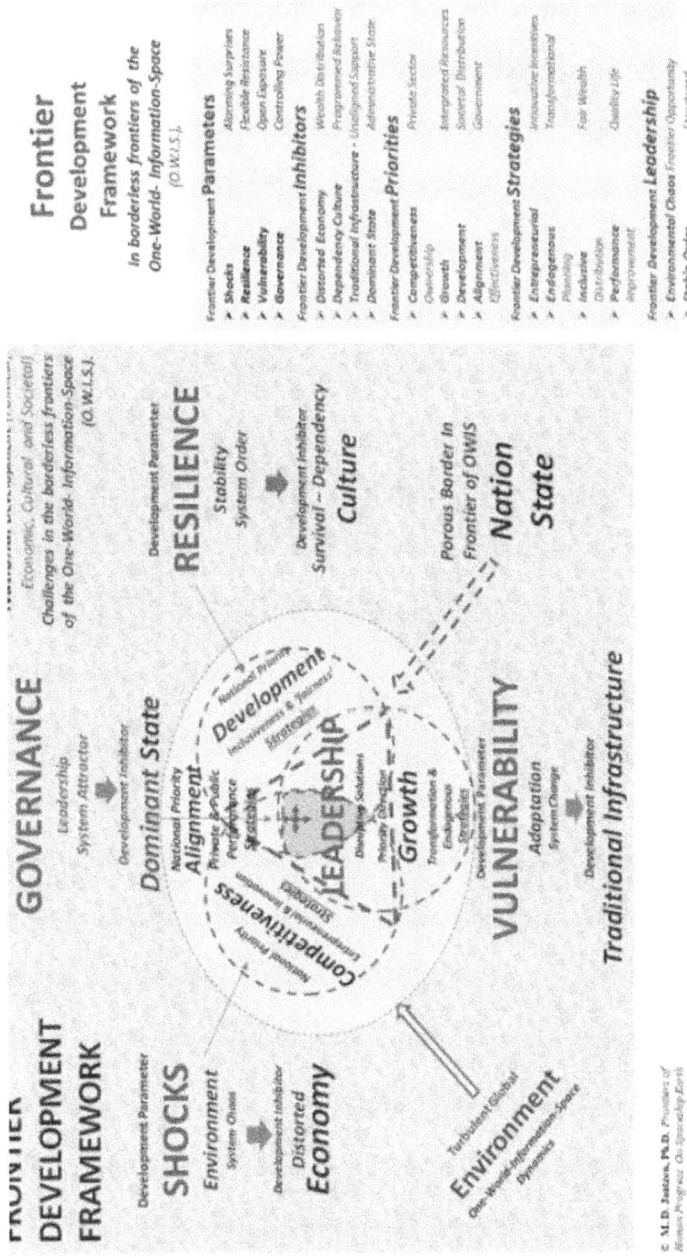

Figure 5.1 Frontier development framework.
Source: Jantzen 2018.

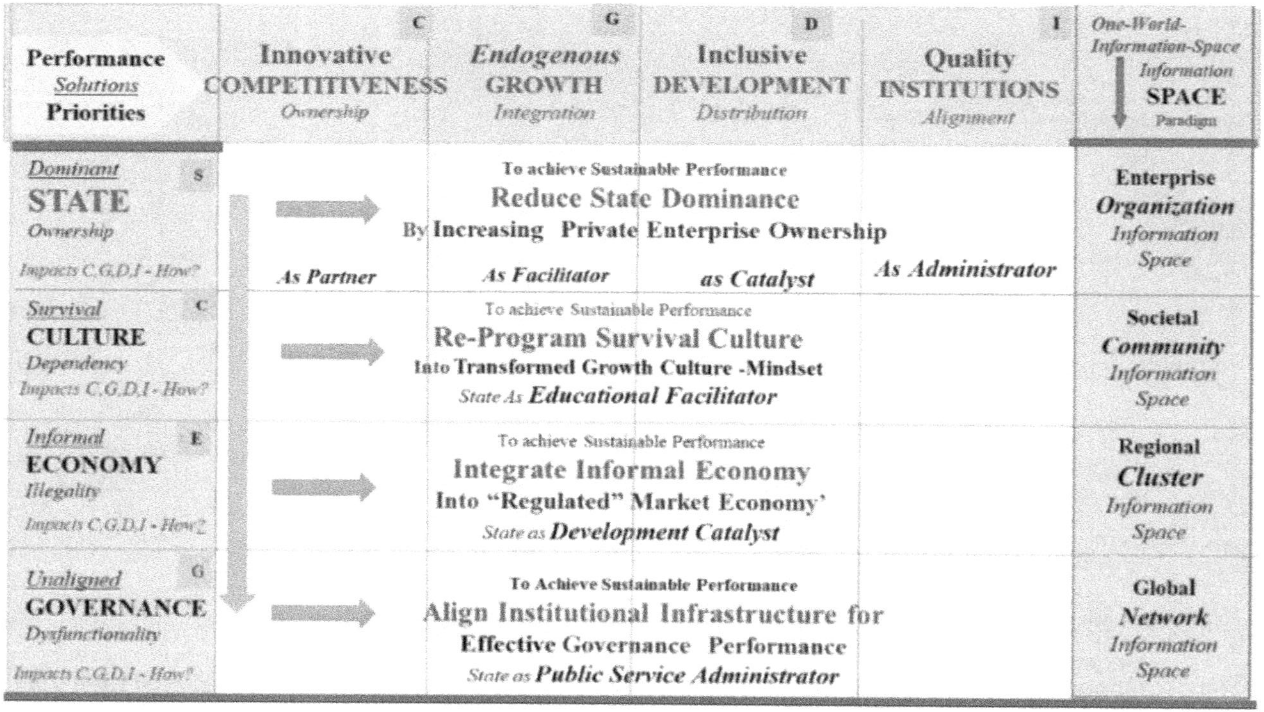

Performance Solutions / Priorities	Innovative COMPETITIVENESS (C) Ownership	Endogenous GROWTH (G) Integration	Inclusive DEVELOPMENT (D) Distribution	Quality INSTITUTIONS (I) Alignment	One-World-Information-Space SPACE Paradigm
Dominant **STATE** (S) Ownership — Impacts C,G,D,I – How?	To achieve Sustainable Performance **Reduce State Dominance** By Increasing Private Enterprise Ownership — *As Partner*	*As Facilitator*	*as Catalyst*	*As Administrator*	**Enterprise Organization** Information Space
Survival **CULTURE** (C) Dependency — Impacts C,G,D,I – How?	To achieve Sustainable Performance **Re-Program Survival Culture** Into Transformed Growth Culture -Mindset State *As Educational Facilitator*				**Societal Community** Information Space
Informal **ECONOMY** (E) Illegality — Impacts C,G,D,I – How?	To achieve Sustainable Performance **Integrate Informal Economy** Into "Regulated" Market Economy' State *as Development Catalyst*				**Regional Cluster** Information Space
Unaligned **GOVERNANCE** (G) Dysfunctionality — Impacts C,G,D,I – How?	To Achieve Sustainable Performance **Align Institutional Infrastructure for** Effective Governance Performance State *as Public Service Administrator*				**Global Network** Information Space

Figure 5.2 Solution priorities in a One-World-Information-Space.

Source: Jantzen 2018.

In the context of a One-World-Information-Space, the COVID-19 pandemic has become a flashpoint, bringing to light long simmering, perturbing issues not addressed by societies and their sovereign nation-states in their development journey. The pandemic may well be the tipping point that heralds in a new global frontier calling for a resetting, reconceptualizing, and redirecting of societal and global priorities with paradigm shifting impact. This may require research-based recontextualization of future societal and global development. (Jantzen 2021)

On the other side of the spectrum, Glenn Sankatsing (2016), in his acclaimed book *Quest to Rescue Our Future*, critiqued traditional development theory by asserting that "development is always from within . . . you can trigger, stimulate, encourage, strengthen, nourish, and support development, but you can never design, blueprint, bring, buy, install, insert, or impose development from outside" (Sankatsing 2016, 34). This raises the dichotomy between endogenous and exogenous factors in the matrix of development and the synergy needed to produce results. Perhaps it was the missing synergy that led Joseph Cox of the Caribbean Community (CARICOM) Secretariat to call for a new model of growth for Caribbean development, a call that has been echoed by several prominent leaders with ever-increasing frequency.

Reframing the Context of Caribbean Development

So where do we go from here? In this period of policy uncertainty, several issues are up for reframing. In the context of Caribbean development, I will focus on four questions:

- Has globalization taken a wrong turn, or is it the next chapter?
- How is the value chain in the global production function changing?
- Is there a new nexus between inequality and economic growth?
- Will currency devaluation fix the global balance of payments issue?

Dani Rodrik (2019), in his lecture titled "Globalization's Wrong Turn – What's Wrong with Globalization, and Can It Be Fixed?" traced the roots to the wrong turn of the 1990s, when globalization seemed to be based on sound economics – that is, the idea that openness to trade would lead economies to allocate their resources to where they would be most productive; capital would flow from countries where it is plentiful to countries where it is needed; and more trade and freer finance would unleash private investment and fuel economic growth. He called this the "hyperglobalist path . . . marked by a fundamental shift in governments' attitudes away from managing capital flows and towards liberalization" (Rodrik 2019, 26).

These sound economic concepts, together with other issues of discontent, give rise to a populist backlash which the hyperglobalist did not foresee, but which "economic theory could have predicted" (Rodrik 2019, 26) but did not. Rodrik appealed for what he called "a saner globalization" (Rodrik 2019, 30), not to resuscitate the Bretton Woods System, but to craft a narrower, healthier globalization; not to return to fixed exchange rates, capital controls, and high levels of trade protection, but rather to "expand the space for governments to pursue domestic objectives" (Rodrik 2019, 31).

Is Rodrik's argument right, or is it that we are now entering a new phase of globalization? The McKinsey Global Institute (2020) agrees with the latter assertion that globalization is not in retreat but has instead morphed into a very different phenomenon, increasingly powered by trade in services and by interregional trade. In other words, this is globalization's next chapter. At the heart of it are the changing dynamics of global value chains in the world's production function. According to the McKinsey Global Institute, the trade intensity of manufactured goods is going down – in other words, more goods are now sold in the country in which they are produced – and over the last five years there has been an increase in the regionalization of the value chain.

The McKinsey Report identified five structural shifts taking place in global value chains, namely:

- Goods producing value chains have grown less trade-intensive.
- Services play a growing and undervalued role in global value chains.
- Trade based on labor-cost arbitrage is declining in some value chains.
- Global value chains are growing more knowledge intensive.
- Value chains are becoming more regional and less global.

Along with these structural shifts in the production function are changes in the geography of global demand, as emerging markets will consume almost two-thirds of the world's manufactured goods by 2025. By 2030, developing countries are projected to account for more than half of all global consumption. The fall in global trade intensity has been partly due to the rise of domestic supply chains in China (McKinsey Institute 2020, 67), and the reality that other developing countries are at an earlier stage of this shift as seen in China. Production networks are consolidating within individual countries such as Vietnam, Bangladesh, Malaysia, India, and Indonesia, and production capabilities and consumption are gradually converging in emerging economies (McKinsey Institute 2020, 70).

According to the McKinsey Global Institute, "digital technologies and data flows are becoming the connective tissue of the global economy" (McKinsey Institute 2020, 59). New technologies are changing costs across global chains.

Digital platforms, logistics technologies, and data processing advances will also continue to reduce cross-border transaction costs and enable all types of flows. Automation and additive manufacturing are gaining traction, for prototypes, replacement parts, toys, shoes, and medical devices. It merits mentioning that these technologies could lead to reshoring, and regionalization, and trade instead of reshoring advanced economies. Given these shifts in value claims, it concludes that companies must reevaluate their strategies for operating globally. This is inclusive of: reassessments of where to compete in the value chain and how to capture value from services, reconsideration of operating footprints to reflect new risks, prioritization of speed to market, and proximity to customers' and suppliers' relationships.

The early literature on the trade-off between economic growth and equality, as articulated in the Kuznets curve and the measurement of the Gini coefficient, was key theoretical insights into the phenomenon of inequality and the persistence of poverty. In recent times, it has reemerged as a political flashpoint, an indicator of public discontent. Pro-poor growth policies became fashionable as inclusive growth became the mantra of the new growth matrix. The center-periphery thesis articulated by Raul Prebisch and others of the Latin American school gained legitimacy, and early empirical works I carried out alongside Ralph Henry on Trinidad and Tobago set the stage for a comprehensive review of restructuring for economic independence in Caribbean societies.

Equality is at the center of economic growth. The Kuznets' (1955) early thesis came under scrutiny, as advocated by the Economic Commission for Latin America and the Caribbean (ECLAC)'s influential school of economic thought. Daniel Perrotti (2018), in an eloquent discourse on the evolution of ECLAC's School of Thought and its influence on the Caribbean, traced ECLAC's Structuralism thesis and the industrialization period in Latin America. He argued that income distribution policies, including agrarian reform, were key policy variables to modify the structure of the economy to reduce the index of dependence. In focusing on the Caribbean, Perrotti challenged the synthesis for absorbing shocks in macro stability, productive transformation with equity, and the right approach to confronting the issue of poverty.

The nexus between inequality and growth was explored further in a recent UNU-WIDER Workshop (2019) by Martin Ravallion in his presentation on "Economic Inequality: Challenges for Policy," where he argued for policymaking that goes beyond slogans. In the very same workshop, speaker Rachel Gisselquist looked at the politics of group-based inequalities in the Global South, contending that politics is central to horizontal inequality as expressed in sustainable development goal (SDG)10 and has potentially big implications for peace development and governance. These conversations underline the multiple factors at play in this nexus. Simultaneously, they demonstrate the missing theoretical link between growth theory and endogenous distribution vectors, driven by state and market interventions. The link between economic growth and redistribution vectors in that growth must be decoupled in the next design of growth models.

The global trading system is under great stress, and underlying it is the issue of the global balance of payments. Concerns over "beggar-thy-neighbor" policy and fears of a currency war have become a focal point for global trade tensions. Competitive devaluation – through exchange rates or tariff changes – is aimed to generate expenditure switching with a balance of payments effects.

In a recent blog of August 2019, International Monetary Fund (IMF) senior economists deemed this argument as a counterproductive policy, claiming that "bilateral tariffs are unlikely to reduce aggregate trade imbalances, instead will simply divert trade elsewhere and harm both domestic and global growth by draining business confidence and investment, disrupting supply chains and increasing costs for producers and consumers" (Gopinath, Cubeddu, and Adler 2019). In turn, the IMF economists resorted to traditional policy advice, such as reducing budget deficits without sacrificing growth, strengthening the competitiveness of export industries, improving investment in the workforce, and encouraging lifelong saving.

The IMF economists concluded that "There are serious problems to contend with, such as rising inequality and sluggish growth. Currencies are neither the hammer nor the nail" (Gopinath, Cubeddu, and Adler 2019).

Arthur Lewis' Model of Economic Growth

Indeed, there are serious problems to contend with, much of which are in the realm of theoretical design. Will the existing reality and the current economic premises fit? Is this a time for theory to talk again, to look at the limitations of linearity in traditional growth models, and to explore the phenomenon of convergence in the policy matrix of the future? In attempting this, I will look at Arthur Lewis' model for economic growth.

Lewis was perhaps the Caribbean's most distinguished and globally acclaimed economist of the early post-independence era. He claimed that his interest lay in "the fundamental forces determining the rate of economic growth" (Lewis 1980, 5) – the subject of his classic 1955 book – and the origin of the model which he attributed to his Nobel Prize. The lineage of Joseph Schumpeter, Frank Knight, Roy Harrod, John Hicks, Theodore Schultz, Arthur Lewis, Robert Solow, and Joseph Stiglitz represented the intellectual heritage of *capital theory and growth in economics.*

Lewis' seminal article of 1954 "Economic Development with Unlimited Supplies of Labor" generated extensive literature at the center of development theory, in his search for applying existing theory to the problems of the developing world. He stated, "This article is written in the classical tradition, making classical assumptions, and asking the classical question" (Lewis 1954, 1). Furthermore, his book *The Theory of Economic Growth* (1955) was praised by Gustav Ranis in his article with John Fei, who affirmed that Lewis' work "revolutionized contemporary thinking on development . . . as he saw the development problem as focusing on a change in basic rules of operation of an economic system" (Ranis and Fei 1961, 4). His analytical frame depicts a two-sector world, focused on organizational dualism and the reallocation process of surplus labor in phases toward modern economic growth. This logic became the basic model of development among the extensive and scrutinizing literature that made economic development respectable in the world of scholarship.

Much of the commentary on his early work was not so much on the policy issues of his argument, but rather the classical assumptions that underlie his analysis and the analytical rigor of his argument, for example, the classical assumption that all profits are saved and all wages are consumed. Ranis summarizes as follows: "the crux of the contemporary critique of the Lewis model is the rejection of an exogenous bargaining wage or consumption share, exceeding the marginal product of labor at any point of time" (Ranis 2004, 11).

Lewis' model was in line with Kuznets' structural analysis of income distribution (Lewis 1955) and no wonder it had a "substantial influence on subsequent work on the relationship between growth and equity" (Ranis 2004, 8). Much effort was placed on the engine of economic growth. In the "State of Development Theory" article, he expressed his views on the drivers of the engine of economic growth as follows: "Every school has offered its candidate for driver of economic growth. The Physiocrats, agriculture; the Mercantilist, an export surplus; the Classicists, the free market; the Marxists, capital; the Neo-Classicists, entrepreneurship; the Fabians, Government; the Stalinists, industrialization; and the Chicago School, schooling" (Lewis 1984, 7).

Lewis as a Development Economist

Lewis, in the "State of Development Theory" (1984), asserted that growth occurs whenever there is a gap between capability and opportunity. Capability covers both domestic and foreign skills, government, savings, and technology. Opportunity can be of any kind, including markets, rainfall, access to licenses, and infrastructure. The engine may be at home or abroad, an innovation, a good site for a transportation center, or much else (Lewis 1984, 8). He concluded that a model for the economy is rather complex – there is one growth theory, but a set of complementary theories – including a theory of government, where the government would appear to be as much the problem as the solution. The analytical challenge is predictability, bringing together the forces of history, the workings of institutions, and the determinants of structure to yield self-sustaining growth, using Rostow's phrase for development.

Essentially, Lewis' notions of dualism and unlimited supplies of labor were the frame for his growth theory of structural change. The offshoots of his model provided insights into development economics, in the mushrooming literature in the field of development economics. Economic development ideas implicitly assumed a linear trajectory – stages of growth (Rostow 1959) – the trade-off in growth and equality (Kuznets 1955), equilibrium and steady states (Harrod 1939 and Domar 1946), and linkage and input–output flows (Leontief 1986). The strategies for economic development were premised on linear processes underlying the basic rules of operation in the economic system. At times, feedback loops were inserted into the analysis, which introduced a dynamic element to the static logic that defined development pathways.

Linearity in Growth Models

In today's discourse on development strategy, the assumption of linearity in the economic development path is being tested by the notion of the Circular Economy. In the linearity notion, the operating system of the economy is based on the "end-of-life" concept, while in the circularity notion, reusing, recycling, and recovering materials in the production/distribution and consumption processes are at the core of the drivers of change in resource efficiency. A recent paper by the Ellen MacArthur Foundation devoted to the study of the Circular Economy highlighted a number of factors that indicated that the linear model is increasingly being challenged by the very context within which it operates and that a deeper change in the operating system of our economy is necessary.

The chapter introduces the dimensions of structural waste. The current economy is surprisingly wasteful in its model of value creation, as significant structural waste was measured in Europe. Material recycling and waste-based energy recovery capture only five percent of the original raw material value, and a business model that commercializes this waste "offers a promising vision for a regenerative and restorative economy of the future" (MacArthur, Klaus, and Stuchtey 2015, 5). The Foundation's latest report "Growth Within" spells out this vision and provides a circular perspective on rethinking value creation in economic systems.

In this vein, a workshop was recently held at the University of Alberta, Edmonton, Canada, titled "The Guyana Project: A New Approach to Sustainable Development in Guyana: Towards a Circular Economy and Resilience in Businesses." Among the project ideas that came out of the workshop was a follow-up on the CARICOM Circular Economy Package for Sustainable Development. In 2017, Platform for Accelerating the Circular Economy (PACE) – a public–private sector collaboration was set up, hosted, and facilitated by the World Economic Forum. This platform encourages developing countries to adopt strategies, both finance and growth, that will accelerate action in Circular Economy initiatives.

Recently, the Economic and Social Council of the United Nations held a plenary session on the application of the principles of the Circular Economy. China, in 2008, based on the 3R Framework – reduce, reuse, and recycle – outlined the Circular Economy Promotion Law of the People's Republic of China and subsequently signed a technical cooperation agreement with the European Union. The overall aim of these developments is to accomplish sustainable development by simultaneously creating environmental quality, economic prosperity, and social equity.

Complexity Analysis – A Nonlinear Design for Development

Linear thinking is the logic frame in the design of growth models, from Rostow's stages of economic growth to Smith's and Ricardo's laws of economics and Marx's deterministic laws of capitalist development. Accordingly, it can be argued that the World Bank/IMF programs of structural adjustment and stabilization are predicated on linear analysis. Linear mathematical models allowed for predictability, but history has shown that the "world does not work that way" (Bryne 1998, 19). In a penetrating article titled "Complexity: An Appropriate Framework for Development" and published in Progress in Development Studies, Rihani and Geyer (2001, 237–45) drew attention to the nonlinear system – that is, complex adaptive system – as a more appropriate framework for the study of development.

Rihani and Geyer (2001) argued that social behavior is based on "order, chaos, and self-organized complexity" and that development studies are about understanding the connectivity of the network system – noting that "a complex system has to adapt in response to changing conditions and survive long enough for the next cycle of adaptation to begin" (Rihani and Geyer 2001, 240). This is the genesis of the nonlinear paradigm in the framework for development. Later, this would lead to designing tools to measure complexity, as an indicator of productive potential and knowledge intensity in the economy. Ricardo

Hausmann (2013) and a group of six authors drew the Atlas of Complexity for countries around the world as a tool to study the productive structure and its potential for change – the diversification process – that may lead to sustainable development.

Such studies aim to measure the future growth potential of an economy by focusing on the production structure and its evolution. In recent times, measures of economic complexity have been used to quantify a country's productive structure and have revived interest in the macroeconomic role of structural transformation (Hausmann et al. 2013). These measures are seen as useful, as they are highly predictive of future economic growth and relevant to social welfare. Economic growth and income levels are linked to poverty levels and social well-being.

More recently, Vito D.P. Servedio and others, in a path-breaking article "A New and Stable Estimation Method of Country Economic Fitness and Product Complexity" on a new approach to macroeconomics, constructed metrics that quantify the "fitness of countries, the quality of their industrial system, and the complexity of commodities by indirectly inferring the technological requirements needed to produce them" (Servedio et al. 2018, 782).

In the analysis of Servedio et al. (2018, 782), the "key idea is to consider the international trade of countries as a proxy of their internal production system." Hence, their work focuses on the network of countries and their exported goods, examining data sets for 161 countries and 4,000 products over the period 1995–2015. In defining the precise strategies to improve countries' economies, they introduce the notion of convergence and make a distinction between *rank and absolute convergence* to ascertain a country's fitness and product complexity. In the analytics, the leading part of fitness is given by diversification, and it was concluded that there is a power-law dependence between inefficiency and the diversification of the country (Servedio 2018).

As such, new metrics– fitness index, index of complexity, diversification, and inefficiency link – all add new ways to measure the production structures of economies. How will macro management influence the production structures of an economy? This topic was taken up in an IMF working paper, using the classical Mundell-Fleming model for open economies. The paper showed that investment to real exchange rate movements varies depending on the production structure of the economy (Boughton 2002). Where there is a high degree of structural economic complexity, the logic of the Mundell-Fleming model holds – that is, investment is positively associated with a real exchange rate depreciation. However, where the degree of complexity is low, the positive impact of a real exchange rate depreciation on price competitiveness tends to outweigh the negative impact associated with the increased cost of imported capital goods.

The distinguishing feature of how investment responds to exchange rate moves lies not so much in whether it is an advanced or emerging economy, but more so on the degree of complexity in the economy. The data set used in this analysis is firm-level investment rather than aggregate investment levels, thus mitigating against potential endogeneity issues, but this may be insignificant as firm-level investment is highly correlated with aggregate investment (Boughton 2002, 7–8).

The missing link between macro management and structural transformation is a key factor in the integration process in the region. Diversification is a huge challenge for the region, not only in response to the issues of expanding economic space or addressing inefficiencies.

These analytics are basic to the design strategies that will populate the cells in Leontief's input–output models, showing how changes in one economic sector affect other sectors. As a strong advocate of relying too much on "theoretical assumptions and non-observed facts," Leontief (1986) felt that too many economists were reluctant "to get their hands dirty" in the actual metrics in the calculus of development.

In specifying the calculus of development, the political setting sets the ceiling, particularly for risk analysis and resource mobilization. In chapter 16, we examine the forces that are shaping the geopolitical framework with an in-depth discourse on the subject, to determine the strategic shifts in the global order and the agenda facing small economies in their quest for growth and development.

Convergence in Growth Models

Out of *The Theory of Economic Growth* came the policy imperative of integration. This led to the flow concept of convergence, which is now one of the more discussed fields in economics. Several approaches to the convergence of economies – real convergence, nominal convergence, and structural convergance – have been studied as an addition to the integration literature. Robert Solow, in his article "A Contribution to the Theory of Economic Growth" (1956) connected growth theories to the definition of convergence. He argued that conditional convergence could be observed due to diminishing returns to capital – a logic of the Lewis model as well.

Economic growth and convergence in the neo-classical growth models look at factors affecting long-run growth, which determines the welfare of countries. Attila Gasper distinguishes between real convergence (Gross Domestic Product per capita), nominal convergence (interest rates), and structural convergence (labor and competitiveness). Steady-state models – a la Harrod and Domar

– and endogenous growth models – Paul Romer with technical change along with Lewis' unlimited supplies of labor model – are logically linked, giving new analytical powers to what Lewis earlier had called "one growth theory." The implication of development policy is that growth and convergence imply a catching-up process, and sustainability feeds on a wider economic space. It also has extended to a discussion of New Frontiers in Caribbean Integration.

The emerging dynamics of convergence are a response to the limitations of the orthodox integration model, the quest for resilience, and self-sustaining growth. The economic logic of convergence is not just about the enlargement of markets and trade, it is about creating a new economic space that is inwardly resilient, globally competitive, and able to capture opportunities in the future. New vulnerabilities emerging out of the structure and size of economies have affected the wiggle room for growth and gave rise to institutional factors in the study of the subject. As such, this brings to the fore theories of institutional change that could shape the outcome of development in society.

Mario Coccia, in an article in the *Journal of Economic Library* on theories of institutional change, define institutions as "rules and expectations that govern human interaction and paths of development in society" (Coccia 2018, 337). He argues that understanding "deinstitutionalization" – the process by which institutions weaken and disappear – is critical to institutional change that brings new ideas, beliefs, and practices. Institutions are resistant to change "which can threaten existing patterns of status, wealth and power" (Coccia 2018, 340). In some cases, institutional change will only take place if the operating space expands to accommodate the changing dynamics of the growth model and new rules are adopted.

Hence, the theory of growth in closed economies takes on a new dynamic in its application to small open economies – the limitations of linearity and the link between growth and convergence – open a new intellectual curiosity on Lewis' forces determining the rate of economic growth and the model's applicability to economic development.

So how shall "theory talk" help in understanding the new geometry of growth models for Caribbean development? The key argument of this discourse is that the growth model should adopt a nonlinear logic to understand the relationships of growth processes. Nonlinearity will embrace the notions of a Circular Economy, convergence spaces, and the changing dynamics of the production function, as it integrates economic theory with the practice of development. This scholarship is in the rich heritage of the ideas and the work of Caribbean economists of the past era, and there cannot be a more fitting tribute to the contribution of Allister McIntyre to Caribbean development.

Conclusion

Indubitably, this COVID-19 pandemic has morphed from a health crisis into a full-blown economic crisis, which has triggered unprecedented repercussions in the global, regional, and domestic economies. In a web article in the *Financial Times*, leading financial writer Martin Wolf describes the pandemic as "a microbe . . . [which has] overthrown our arrogance and sent global output into a tailspin" (Wolf 2020). Similarly, in a previous article[1] I set out the structural impact of COVID-19 on the Caribbean, by highlighting that the coronavirus crisis has prompted a supply shock – reduction of wages and production – which has consequently induced a demand shock, that is, a fall in purchasing power. I postulated that this becomes a "loop-type" cycle of shocks, and the Caribbean economy lacks the necessary buffers and shock absorbers which prevent the adverse impacts of growth.

So, what is the mode of action? A young student remarked that the world must not be intimidated by the academic elite in the classroom or by the polemics of the podium. In looking ahead, the state will be pivotal in directing the progress of development toward equity and egalitarian public values. However, the state-centric growth process is hindered by outdated controls and systems. Market forces alone will not protect the public good. Hence, the state must be neither controlling nor facilitating, but catalytic, if the engineering of a new synthesis between the private and public sectors is to occur. Michael Sabia, in an article in "The Globe and Mail," posed the question, "Is there a public roadmap to build confidence in the public that . . . government action is locked and ready to go?" (Sabia 2020). The primary concerns are certainly the safety and fairness demonstrated to citizens by the state, as journalist Prem Shankar Jha[2] urges that stimulus packages must not be "confidence tricks" played on the people.

Growth models must therefore question its typically linear assumptions and accept that the growth process is a nonlinear one. This pandemic "loop-type" cycle of shocks further compounds the nonlinearity of the growth process. As Mark Cliffe cleverly defined it, "pandenomics" emphasizes the strategies required to restart the economy and contain the "infection curve" despite the biggest economic downturn of the post-war period. Cliffe goes on to assert, "our previous preoccupation with growth, mobility and optimization will

---

[1] Winston Dookeran, "Reflections on the COVID-19 Pandemics and the Caribbean," published in EUCLID Global Health website, 1 April 2020, EUCLID's intergovernmental School of Global Health and Bioethics.

[2] Jha (2020).

likely give way to a new emphasis on equality, sustainability and agility" (Cliffe 2020). Now is the time for the analytics to incorporate the nonlinearity factor into models of growth and the practice of development. Growth theory and practice must not fall into a state of inertia – it must rise above the orthodoxy of thinking in the calculus of development.

References

Boughton, James M. 2002. *On the Origins of the Fleming-Mundell Model.* Washington, DC: International Monetary Fund.

Bryne, D. 1998. *Complexity Theory and the Social Sciences.* London: Routledge.

Cliffe, Mark. 2020. "Pandenomics – Policymaking in a Post-Pandemic World." VOX, CEPR Policy Portal, 13 April. https://voxeu.org/article/pandenomics-policymaking -post-pandemic-world.

Coccia, Mario. 2018. "An Introduction to the Theories of Institutional Change." *Journal of Economics Library*, 5 (4): 337–44.

Cox, Robert W. 1981. "Social Forces, States and World Orders: Beyond International Relations Theory." *Millennium*, 10 (2): 126–55. https://doi.org/10.1177/03058298810 100020501.

Demas, William G. 1965. *The Economics of Development in Small Countries: With Special Reference to the Caribbean.* Kingston, Jamaica: University of the West Indies Press.

Domar, Evsey. 1946. "Capital Expansion, Rate of Growth and Employment." *Econometrica, Journal of the Econometric Society*, 14 (2): 137–47.

Dookeran, Winston. 2018. *The Caribbean on the Edge: An Anthology of Ideas and Writings.* Santiago, Chile: Economic Commission for Latin America and the Caribbean.

Gisselquist, Rachel M. 2019. "The Politics of Group-Based Inequalities in the Global South." presented at the UNU-WIDER Workshop, May.

Gopinath, Gina, Luis Cubeddu, and Gustavo Adler. 2019. "Taming the Currency Hype," 21 August. https://blogs.imf.org/2019/08/21/taming-the-currency-hype/.

Harrod, Roy. 1939. "An Essay in Dynamic Theory." *The Economic Journal*, 49 (193): 14–33.

Hausmann, Ricardo, Caesar Hidalgo, Sebastian Bustos, Michele Coscia, Alexander Simoes, and Muhammed A. Yildirim. 2013. *The Atlas of Economic Complexity: Mapping Paths to Prosperity.* Cambridge, MA: MIT Press.

Jantzen, Manfred. 2018. "Distorted Development in a One-World-Information-Space." Foundation for Politics and Leadership, Arthur Lok Jack Global School of Business, University of the West Indies.

Jantzen, Manfred. 2021 (revised). "Distorted Development in a One-World-Information-Space." Foundation for Politics and Leadership, Arthur Lok Jack Global School of Business, University of the West Indies.

Jha, Prem Shankar. 2020. "Modi's 'Stimulus Package' Is a Gigantic Confidence Trick Played on the People of India." *The Wire*, 18 May. https://thewire.in/political -economy/modis-stimulus-package-is-a-gigantic-confidence-trick-played-on-the -people-of-india.

Kuznets, Simon. 1955. "Economic Growth and Income Inequality." *The American Economic Review*, 45 (1): 1–28.

Leontief, Wassily. 1986. *Input-Output Economics.* Oxford: Oxford University Press.

Lewis, William Arthur. 1954. "Economic Development with Unlimited Supplies of Labour." *The Manchester School,* 22 (2): 139–91. https://doi.org/10.1111/j.1467-9957.1954.tb00021.x.

———. 1955. *Theory of Economic Growth.* Homewood: R.D. Irwin.

_____. 1980. "Autobiographical Note." *Social and Economic Studies,* 29 (4): 1–4.

———. 1984. "The State of Development Theory." *The American Economic Review,* 74 (1): 1–10.

MacArthur, Ellen, Zumwinkel Klaus, and Martin R. Stuchtey. 2015. Growth Within: A Circular Economy Vision for a Competitive Europe, Ellen MacArthur Foundation, McKinsey Center for Business and Environment, Chicago, Illinois, United States

McKinsey Global Institute. 2019. "Globalisation in Transition: The Future of Trade and Value Chains." https://www.Mckinsey.com/Mgi.

Perrotti, Daniel E. 2018. "The Evolution of ECLAC's School of Thought and Its Influence on the Caribbean." In *The Caribbean on the Edge: An Anthology of Ideas and Writings,* 15–18. Santiago, Chile: Economic Commission of Latin America and the Caribbean.

Rampersad, Frank. 1964. *Growth and Structural Change in the Economy of Trinidad and Tobago 1951-1961.* Jamaica: University of The West Indies Press.

Ranis, Gustav, and John Fei. 1961. "A Theory of Economic Development." *The American Economic Review,* 51 (4): 533–65.

Ranis, Gustav. 2004. "Arthur Lewis' Contribution to Development Thinking and Policy." Center Discussion Papers. https://ideas.repec.org/p/ags/yaleeg/28410.html.

Ravallion, Martin. 2019. "Economic Inequality: Challenges for Policy." Presented at the UNU-WIDER Workshop, May.

Rihani, Samir, and Robert Geyer. 2001. "Complexity: An Appropriate Framework for Development." *Progress in Development Studies,* 1 (3): 237–45.

Rodrik, Dani. 2019. "Globalization's Wrong Turn - What's Wrong with Globalisation and Can It Be Fixed?" April. https://drodrik.scholar.harvard.edu/links/globalizations-wrong-turn.

Rostow, Walt W. 1959. "The Stages of Economic Growth." *The Economic History Review,* 12 (1): 1–16.

Sabia, Michael. 2020. "Opinion: In This Pandemic, Governments Will Face Three Tests -Including How Best to Restart the Economy," 23 March. https://www.theglobeandmail.com/business/commentary/article-in-this-pandemic-governments-will-face-three-tests-including-how/.

Sankatsing, Glenn. 2016. *Quest to Rescue Our Future.* Amsterdam: Rescue Our Future Foundation.

Servedio, Vito, Paolo Buttà, Dario Mazzilli, Andrea Tacchella, and Luciano Pietronero. 2018. "A New and Stable Estimation Method of Country Economic Fitness and Product Complexity." *Entropy* 20 (10): 783. https://doi.org/10.3390/e20100783.

Solow, Robert M. 1956. "A Contribution to the Theory of Economic Growth." *The Quarterly Journal of Economics,* 70 (1): 65–94.

Wolf, Martin. 2019. "How Covid-19 Will Change the World." *Financial Times,* 16 June 2020. https://www.ft.com/content/9b8223bb-c5e4-4c11-944d-94ff5d33a909.

6

Small State Diplomacy and Global Competitiveness[1]

WINSTON DOOKERAN AND PREEYA MOHAN

Introduction

In the new geopolitics of today, there has been an "outpouring of anxiety over the future of the liberal order" (Acharya 2017). The spillover of this anxiety has opened a dialogue on the "new globalization" in a period of protectionism, weakening multilateralism, and a political assault on global competitiveness. Acharya (2017, 271) sums up the political architecture of the emerging multiplex world order as follows: "[I]nternational relations scholars should be wary of conventional wisdom and be open to new concepts and theories, and hence to new possibilities of world order that have no precedent in history . . . where scholars and practitioners alike will have to embrace the complexities of this new system."

The latest Global Competitiveness Report states that "governments, businesses, and individuals are experiencing high levels of uncertainty as technology and geopolitical forces reshape the economic and political order that has underpinned international relations and economic policy for the past 25 years" (The Global Competitiveness Report 2018, v). These insights provide the setting for discovering new possibilities for small state diplomacy in improving small state competitiveness and economic advancement in an uncertain economic order.

Competitiveness is not only an economic matter; it is also a foreign policy issue. The Global Competitiveness Report (2018, v) affirmed that "improving competitiveness requires the coordinated action of the state, the business

---

[1] This chapter was previously published in *Small States and Territories* (as Dookeran, W., & Mohan, P. S. (2019). Small state diplomacy and global competitiveness. *Small States & Territories*, Vol. 2, No. 1, 69–82). Kind reprint permission has been granted by the journal for publication of an updated version in this book that includes the COVID-19 pandemic experience.

community and civil society." Further, the report explains that uncertainty among government, businesses, and individuals is being driven by geopolitical forces, which have reshaped the economic and political order with implications for international relations and economic policy. Competitiveness determines a country's global influence and its ability to shape the international dialogue and is the set of institutions, policies, and factors that determine the level of productivity of a country (Global Competitiveness Report 2018).

A competitive economy is productive, and productivity leads to growth and higher incomes, and improved standards of living for all. Global economic institutions must now confront a new quest to design strategies and roadmaps for reform that will build on the achievements of the past, cope with an increasingly new set of ripples that pose risks to the orthodox practice of development, and ignite a search for a new kind of diplomacy. A global dialogue is in the making, and small economies have a vested interest in being part of that dialogue.

In 2015, the UN General Assembly adopted the 2030 Sustainable Development Agenda, along with the 17 Sustainable Development Goals (SDGs) and 169 targets that cover the economic, social, and environmental aspects of sustainable development (United Nations 2015). While all countries and stakeholders are expected to act collaboratively to implement this roadmap, with a central theme of "no one left behind," small states face their own unique challenges that threaten the achievement of the SDGs (United Nations 2015). Alicia Bárcena called for "revitalizing multilateralism" to promote the 2030 Agenda, and it is at the cornerstone of small states' voice and influence in accepting collective responsibility for global challenges (Bárcena 2017). The World Bank in their recent presentation "Small States: A Roadmap for World Bank Group Engagement" explained that these challenges include building resilience to climate change, diversifying their economic base, and developing new systems to generate and attract public and private finance (World Bank 2017).

Small economies lack adequate financial resources for achieving the SDGs, while at the same time there have been new challenges for them in accessing development finance from the international community (World Bank 2017). Additionally, the World Bank's "ease of doing business" index is a key indicator in attracting international investment, and countries, including small states, are ranked against each other. The appropriateness of the index in measuring competitiveness in small states and the amount of information provided by the index on small states have been questioned (Commonwealth Secretariat 2007); more recently, the integrity of the index has come under scrutiny (The Economist 2018). Moreover, small nations are generally more sensitive to and more impacted by international developments, but at the same time have benefited more from globalization (Spolaore 2018).

Recently, there have been indicators that the international economic and political environment has become less supportive of globalization, which may negatively impact small states (Spolaore 2018; Dookeran 2018). It is therefore not only a technical dialogue to come up with solutions to these challenges but also a diplomatic dialogue, since diplomatic interventions are necessary, within global institutions and in the global policy frameworks that are being developed. Diplomatic intervention is an important tool available to small states that can improve their global competitiveness standing (Dookeran 2018).

While small states have fewer resources to devote to the tasks of diplomacy and effective interaction with other states, this shortcoming can be reduced given their large number and common interests through the formation of alliances and networks (Estevadeordal and Goodman 2017). Further, European small states are strategically positioned in regional and international diplomacy to promote a global competitiveness and growth agenda where small states are not left behind (Dookeran 2018) with special conditions for their participation in international affairs, and years of experience in participating in international institutions (Pedersen 1987).

This chapter explores small state diplomacy in affecting international competitiveness with reference to European small states. The concept of small state diplomacy is defined, and three current issues affecting competitiveness and diplomacy are explored: small states' access to development finance, competitiveness measures, and threats to globalization, and small state alliances and networks. The chapter comprises four sections, including this introduction. Section two defines and outlines small state diplomacy. Section three looks at the three current issues in international diplomacy and small states. Section four concludes the chapter.

Small State Diplomacy

Small states operate in the same political and economic environment as large states; in their foreign policy, they pursue the same objectives of security, prosperity, and well-being for their citizens and conduct their diplomacy using the same diplomatic toolbox as large states. The international system contains many small states, which form an integral part of the international order (Keohane 2009).

The number of small states increased significantly in the twentieth century, with the end of both World Wars, the decolonization process in the 1960s, and the collapse of the Soviet Union in 1991 (Veenendaal and Corbett 2014;

Kassimeris 2009). About two-thirds of the member states of the United Nations are small states. In the European Union, there are (at the time of writing) 28 members, and seven are small states (Thorhallsson and Wivel 2006). In other words, small states make up 25 percent of EU membership.

Small states are here defined as states with a resident population of three million or less. In the European Union, they include Cyprus, Estonia, Latvia, Lithuania, Luxembourg, Malta, and Slovenia (Thorhallsson and Wivel 2006). Small states are, therefore, well represented within the European Union and the international community and can influence regional and world politics (Henrikson 2001). Diplomatic means can transform the smallness of small states into an asset when promoting national and international interests (Dookeran 2018).

Small states have fewer resources to devote to the tasks of diplomacy and effective interaction with other states (Henrikson 2001). This includes the resources required for gathering and analyzing relevant information, for elaborating and projecting positions and points of view, and for organizing and deploying alignments and circumstances in support of their positions.

Although their limited resources can put small states in a weaker bargaining position in their interactions with large states, this disadvantage can be reduced, given the large number of small states with common interests (Estevadeordal and Goodman 2017). This may require reliance on collective solidarity and the rule of law, a strict focus on limited objectives, and the adoption of creative solutions (Dookeran 2018).

The role of small states in various multilateral negotiations confirms that small and cohesive groups can have an important effect. For example, the Neutral and Non-Aligned (N+N) countries in the Conference on Security and Cooperation in Europe, the Alliance of Small Island States in climate negotiations, and the Small and Vulnerable Economies group in the World Trade Organisation DOHA round (Panke 2012).

The characteristics of small states influence how they operate in the international system. The characteristics of small states, including their small size, openness, and proneness to natural disasters, and vulnerability to climate change, influence the issues they deem important (World Bank 2017). The effects of small state actions on the international order tend to be more focused (Kassimeris 2009). Small states are attracted to the notions of legitimacy and the rule of law (Pollard 2009). They recognize the valuable role that multilateral diplomacy plays in enhancing their engagement and amplifying their voices on regional or global issues, thus leveling the playing field (Henrikson 2001). Nevertheless, the many complex structures and processes of multilateral diplomacy strain their resources.

Diplomatic Issues in Global Competitiveness

Accessing Development Finance

Financial vulnerabilities are a threat to competitiveness and threaten a nation's ability to finance innovation, spread the benefits of technology, adoption, and provide worker protection in a flexible labor market (World Bank 2017). The World Bank Roadmap for small states specifically linked financing to competitiveness by carefully identifying seven priority action areas, in which there is a need for the development of a global practice: inclusion of vulnerability as a criterion for concessional financing, predictability of affordable financing, debt sustainability, access to new and existing climate financing, capacity building and technical assistance, diversification of small state economies, and access to financial markets (World Bank 2017). Diplomatic interventions for the benefit of small states can play an important role here within the global dialogue, global institutions, and the global policy frameworks that are being framed on development finance (Dookeran 2018).

In July 2015, at the Third International Conference on Financing for Development, development finance entered a new era when the international community agreed to the Addis Ababa Action Agenda (AAAA): a framework and set of commitments for financing the SDGs, which require far more funding than aid can provide. Meeting the SDGs will require an additional USD $2.5 trillion in private and public financing per year and an additional USD $13.5 trillion to implement the 2015 United Nations Climate Change Conference (COP21) Paris climate accord (UNCTAD 2014). The World Bank, together with other multilateral development banks and the International Monetary Fund (IMF), committed to use billions in investment funding, aid, and grants, in innovative ways to increase development finance (World Bank 2017). It is imperative that small nations, including EU states, are able to access these funds successfully, and diplomatic channels can play a key role here (Dookeran 2018).

In seeking development finance, small states – including European small states – may consider taking into account their vulnerability and seek preferential access to concessional finance (Dookeran 2018). Given their small populations, limited geographies, and the difficulties to diversify, small states are particularly vulnerable to external shocks. This vulnerability hinders small states' capacity to progress toward the SDGs. Small states must also seek the small state diplomacy and global competitiveness predictability of affordable financing.

Despite their acute vulnerabilities to shocks, small states are ineligible for concessional financing because of their high per capita incomes. Debt sustainability is another urgent matter facing small states (Bustillo et al. 2018).

Vulnerability to natural disasters, with high costs of recovery, contributes to small states' indebtedness. In addition, limited fiscal space, narrow potential for domestic revenue generation, and the high costs of public services typically exacerbate debt burdens (Bustillo et al. 2018). Because of these debts, small states may not be able to access concessional or market financing (Dookeran 2018).

Small states would do well to invest in building resilience and diversifying their economies to lessen their vulnerability, manage their debt burdens, and attract private-sector financing (Bustillo et al. 2018). Accessing new and existing climate financing is also recommended. Although the international community is giving high priority to climate adaptation and mitigation, small states have difficulty accessing the vast pool of climate funds (World Bank 2017).

Additionally, capacity building and technical assistance in small states must be developed. Many small states face limited human, institutional, and implementation capacity to carry out the tasks needed to absorb development finance and implement the investments necessary to address their vulnerability and lack of resilience. Donor fragmentation in small states hinders the effective use of financing for achieving development outcomes (World Bank 2017).

The World Bank Roadmap identified financial deepening of the private sector – the cascade approach and blended finance approaches – as relevant to enhancing competitiveness strategies in small states in Europe, designed to support progress toward the SDGs at the Third International Conference on Financing for Development in 2015 (World Bank 2017). Blended finance is described as the strategic use of development finance and philanthropic funds to mobilize private capital flows to emerging and frontier market resulting in positive results for both "investors and communities" (World Bank 2017, 16). It offers the possibility to scale up commercial financing for developing countries and to channel such financing toward investments with a development impact. The increasing emphasis on blended finance approaches evokes the need to increase the understanding and transparency of these flows.

The World Bank adopted the cascade approach as a concept to guide its effort to leverage the private sector for growth and sustainable development. The guidelines on how to implement the cascade are very clear. When a project is presented, ask the following question: is there a sustainable private-sector solution that limits public debt and contingent liabilities? If the answer is yes, promote such private solutions. If the answer is no, then ask whether it is because of policy gaps, regulatory gaps, or their weakness. If so, provide World Bank support for policy and regulatory reforms, then assess the risks and see whether World Bank instruments can address them. If it is concluded that the project still requires public funding, only then should that option be pursued (World Bank 2017).

The mandate of the International Finance Corporation, an affiliate of the World Bank Group, is to enhance financial flows for small economies. Capital flows, and their direction and sustainability, are key to building resilience for the economies of small states around the world. Some of the criteria to be considered here include: the predictability of affordable financing, debt sustainability, access to financial markets, and economic diversification. With respect to deepening private-sector involvement, the report says, "the International Finance Corporation is committed to helping expand the limited set of economic opportunities leveraging the full weight of resources of the World Bank group as well as ensuring obstacles for the poor and the bottom 40 percent of the population to access these economic opportunities are reduced" (World Bank 2017, 14).

Small state economies tend to suffer from limited export diversification and productive capacities (World Bank 2017). A lack of economic diversity leaves small states dependent on the economic and political situations of neighboring transit countries, and vulnerable to economic and climate shocks. Small states must enhance their capacity to attract, manage, and invest in both concessional and private-sector resources.

Access to financial markets poses a risk to small states (World Bank 2017). Large financial entities are effectively cutting ties between banks in small states and global finance. A decline in correspondent banking relationships is having damaging results at the individual and community levels, particularly by affecting remittances and complicating the provision of domestic and cross-border payments (Alleyne et al. 2017; Alwazir et al. 2017).

At the 17th annual Small States Forum held in October 2017 in Washington DC, 50 small states banded together and were able to successfully increase their development finance allocation from the World Bank by fourfold after active diplomacy. Members of the Forum welcomed the World Bank's May 2017 Roadmap for Engagement with Small States (Small States Forum 2017). The challenge is to find transformative projects that can absorb and make the most of these extra resources. The Forum also highlighted the importance of mobilizing public and private-sector financing for renewable energy, the green and blue economy, and technology development in building resilience and reducing vulnerability in small countries.

Some small states that are vulnerable to natural disasters, such as Nauru and Palau, do not qualify for the small states' exception from the International Development Association because they are classified as high-income countries, or meet the International Bank for Reconstruction and Development's credit standards and are therefore unable to access resources for clean-up and relief. The 2017 Small States Forum successfully lobbied for the World Bank to explore financing solutions for countries in this category (Small States Forum 2017).

Financial institutions are seeking to "de-risk" and are leading to the withdrawal of correspondent banking relationships in small states, resulting in financial exclusion from the international community. The 2017 Small States Forum proposed establishing a working group to address the development challenges of de-risking in small states and to provide a systematic and comprehensive response, and to explore possible solutions, including blockchain technology (Small States Forum 2017).

Malta, now dubbed "Blockchain Island" (Holotescu 2018), has an opportunity to play a leadership role here for other small states. At the same time, it has been recently accused by the European Union of failing to correctly supervise financial institutions and ensure their compliance with anti-money laundering rules. In November 2018, the European Commission required the Maltese Financial Intelligence Analysis Unit to: improve its methodology to assess money laundering and terrorist financing risks, enhance its monitoring and supervisory strategy, ensure that the authority is able to react at an appropriate time when a weakness is identified, ensure that its decision-making is properly reasoned and documented, and adopt systematic and detailed record-keeping processes (European Commission 2018).

Competitiveness Measures and Integrity

One of the flagship economic reports that measures business competitiveness rankings is the World Bank's "ease of doing business" index. A higher ranking (lower numerical value) indicates that the regulatory environment is more conducive to starting and operating a local business. These indicators carry considerable attention in investment attractiveness and include regulatory hurdles, tax and exchange rate issues, and other measures that make a "better" business environment and improve competitiveness (Dookeran 2018).

The index attracts extensive international media coverage, and its findings are used by countries against each other to improve their competitiveness standing (Dookeran 2018). It may, however, be argued that the "ease of doing business" index is inappropriate for measuring competitiveness in small states, provides limited information on competitiveness in small states (Commonwealth Secretariat 2007), and most recently has been accused of political interference and thus bringing the integrity of the index into question (Dookeran 2018; Morck and Shou 2018).

The "ease of doing business" index has been criticized on technical grounds, with flaws in its definition of competitiveness, model specification, variable choice, causal relationships, and use of data. Focusing on particular sectors, rather than the economy as a whole, and using a smaller number of critical variables may be more appropriate in small states (Commonwealth Secretariat 2007). The rankings are determined through a methodology that sorts the aggregate distance to frontier scores on ten topics – namely, starting a business, dealing with construction permits, getting electricity, registering property, getting credit, protecting minority investors, paying taxes, trading across borders, enforcing contracts, and resolving insolvency (The Global Competitiveness Report 2018). Each topic consists of several indicators, giving equal weight to each topic. The method entails answering measurable questions, and the answers determine a country's score, and its score, relative to those of other countries, determines its global rank and bragging rights.

Critics argue that the index is limited in scope since it focuses on ten topics, with the specific aim of measuring the regulation and red tape relevant to domestic small- to medium-size firms (Morck and Shou 2018). Accordingly, the index does not measure all aspects of the business environment that matter to firms and investors and all the factors that affect competitiveness. The index does not, for instance, measure security, macroeconomic stability, corruption, quality of institutions and infrastructure, and foreign investment regulations.

As an alternative, the Commonwealth Secretariat developed the Small State Manufactured Export Competitiveness Index (SSMECI) (Commonwealth Secretariat 2007). The SSMECI focuses on basic economic fundamentals, including macroeconomic stability, outward-oriented trade policy, high levels of human capital, and efficient infrastructure, and is deemed more appropriate than the 200 sub-indices in the "ease of doing business" index. It emphasizes the ability to produce competitively in small economies. The SSMECI, however, does not have the same international recognition as the "ease of doing business" index.

The "ease of doing business" index covers around 190 jurisdictions but includes less than 20 small states; while the SSMECI covers 47 small states, including the seven EU small states. A large number of small states are excluded from this index, largely because the data requirements for calculating the index are huge, and the data simply do not exist in these countries. Small states have small populations, and often have underdeveloped national statistical systems and institutions; they, therefore, can lack the capacity and demand to collect the extensive data required. Having an appropriate index to measure competitiveness in small states allows for proper benchmarking of small states against each other (i.e., countries with similar characteristics) and provides a yardstick to measure performance.

Small states at the lower end of the ranking could then emulate and learn from the experience and policy strategies implemented by small states at the higher end of the ranking. The SSMECI is constructed by taking into account the data availability in small states and realistic data requirements. Malta and Estonia top the rankings because of their greater access to markets and the positive effect of sustained competitive pressure from their large European members, and as such provide appropriate benchmarks for small countries seeking to improve their competitiveness.

An article in *The Economist* (2018) calls into question the integrity of the "ease of doing business" index and its accompanying reports. The article explains that the compilation of the "ease of doing business" index may have been tainted by the political motivations of World Bank staff (*The Economist* 2018). The story was based on an interview with Paul Romer, the World Bank's chief economist, who pointed out that Chile's ranking in the yearly report had dropped sharply during the presidency of President Michelle Bachelet, a left-leaning politician who took office for the second time in 2014 (Reuters 2018; *The Economist* 2018; Zumbrun and Talley 2018). In small states, with weaker institutions and institutional frameworks and a lack of data, the possibility of political interference may be even larger.

To move the pendulum forward, technical analysis will be needed to build a momentum for effective results. The Global Competitiveness Report recently developed a proposal on "the future of competitiveness benchmarking" which offers an opening for technical negotiations and conceptual innovations in design challenges (Dookeran 2018). This index is a valuable measure of how a country is progressing to build structures and processes to support policy initiatives on a global competitiveness framework. As such, the search for diplomatic interventions becomes necessary, within global institutions and in the global policy frameworks that are being framed, and small states have a role to play.

A global dialogue is in the making with regard to the "ease of doing business" index and measuring competitiveness, and small economies have a vested interest to be part of that dialogue. Small states could coordinate to improve the appropriateness, integrity, and objectivity of international competitiveness indices. It is, therefore, not only a technical dialogue but also a matter of diplomacy.

In an often-cited publication, Long (2017, 9) argued that "small states can influence institutional rules and procedures . . . just as for rules shaped by greater powers." Many scholars argue that small states can "punch above their weight," and "Luxembourg has been a founding model member of European institutions, and it has used this to pressure for favorable EU policies, while seeking to strengthen institutions as a bulwark against historic German French rivalry" (Long 2017, 9). Allegrezza (2018, 135) draws attention to the "competitiveness observatory" set up by the social partners in Luxembourg and the measurement of the competitiveness scoreboard, which was discussed in "a special parliamentary session" on competitiveness and growth.

Threats to Globalization and Alliances and Networks

Small nations are generally more sensitive to and possibly more affected by developments in the international system, which can impact their competitiveness (Spolaore 2018). Small nations are more vulnerable, and the economics of their situation are precarious. The workings of the global system, particularly the globalization of business, may harm their competitiveness even while promoting their freedom. After several decades of an international economic and political environment that has been highly supportive of globalization, there are indications of meaningful change (Spolaore 2018; Rodrik 2018; Llunji 2015).

There are threats to globalization, a rise of populist policies, and increased geopolitical pressure (Dookeran 2018). This new international environment is likely to pose a challenge to small economies and their international competitiveness. The international community, a large part of which is now made up of small states, should be prepared to act, for the global public good, as well as out of sheer political and environmental self-interest, to help safeguard the livelihood of the world's many and varied small states. Small state diplomacy can play an important role here.

In Europe, there is a political backlash against international integration both globally and within the European Union, as demonstrated by BREXIT and the rise of anti-European political movements (Rodrik 2018; Inglehart and Norris 2016). On the one hand, critics have argued that institutional integration in Europe has gone too far, the Euro has failed, and BREXIT is seen as the first step toward European disintegration (Spolaore 2018). Furthermore, the immigration crisis may lead to the return of permanent barriers within Europe (Goodwin and Milazzo 2017).

On the other hand, supporters of European integration attribute the current economic, financial, and political crises to incomplete integration, and seek further integration through a banking union, fiscal union, and full political union (Spolaore 2018). The European integration dilemma involves high economies of scale from commercial integration, common immigration policies, common legal system, and common defense and security, but also high heterogeneity from different preferences, beliefs, and values in large and diverse populations (Spolaore 2018).

Small nations have benefited from increasing international openness. They thrive in an economically integrated world while, at the same time, they are disproportionately hurt by international barriers. Alesina and Spolaore (2003) empirically demonstrate that the conditional correlation between international openness and economic growth for larger countries is 0.150 as against 0.641 for smaller countries. This suggests that while international openness is beneficial on average for countries of all sizes, it is especially beneficial for small countries.

The Commonwealth Secretariat, with small states as the majority of its members, including Cyprus and Malta, carries out policy analysis, consultations, and global advocacy to promote the international trade interests of these countries. As a result, trade between Commonwealth countries has seen phenomenal growth termed the "Commonwealth effect," rising from USD $200 billion in 2000 to more than USD $600 billion in 2015 and projected to surpass USD $1 trillion by 2020 (Commonwealth Secretariat 2015).

Regional public goods have once again been cited as important in the context of twenty-first-century international relations. Heterogeneous preferences negatively affect the provision of public goods which are non-rival in consumption and must be shared by all within a jurisdiction. In contrast, diversity of preferences and traits comes with benefits when considering interactions about rival goods. Egan and Pech (2017) traced the pivotal role of European public goods in the foundations of European integration.

The range of these public goods includes competition policy and market access, common external tariff and trade matters, transportation and cross-border services, environment and negative externalities, economic convergence and income and wealth disparities, macroeconomic stabilization and the -Euro, and internal security and border control (Estevadeordal and Goodman 2017). Egan and Pech (2017, 256) concluded that "despite the growing chorus of disenchantment in Europe with the concerns for inequality, productivity, and migration, there remains a role for regional organizations to act as catalysts for collective action by providing regional public goods." But Egan and Pech (2017, 258) hastens to add that it "can also weaken democratic institutions and can collapse trust in European institutions."

Long (2017, 9) states that "small states have a greater capacity to influence the agenda in world politics and play a critical role in the evolution of European integration than is commonly understood." Inside European institutions, small states can construct a "position of authority" through diplomacy by influencing the "rules and voting procedure" (Long 2017, 9). In this sense, small state diplomacy is an essential component for advancing its interest in global competitiveness. Estevadeordal and Goodman (2017) argue that regional leadership alliances and networks fit together to link public goods with sustainability and, with Acharya (2017), called for a new conceptualization of regionalism that will embrace more complex situations in a changing "balance of power."

Small states can coordinate actions to counterbalance current threats to international integration and globalization, as they have done in the past on monumental international issues, since they are less constrained by political alliances and direct national interests, championing ideas that have led to major international agreements (Súilleabháin 2014). Further, decolonization, the end of bipolarity, democratization, trade liberalization, and the digital revolution are five factors that have given small states more freedom (Henrikson 2001). In addition, small countries may find it easier to respond to citizen preferences in a democratic way (Alesina and Spolaore 2003).

Could small states shift global economic structures to favor their interests? Would small states benefit from open trade systems? How could small states overcome their "smallness" and develop diplomatic leverage? These and other relevant questions, as addressed in the work of Henrikson (2001) and Alesina and Spolaore (2003), provide a critical body of thought that informs the agenda of small state diplomacy and competitiveness in today's world.

Conclusion

This chapter has argued that competitiveness is not only an economic matter but also a foreign policy issue. Competitiveness determines a country's global influence and its ability to shape international dialogue. It requires the coordinated action of the state, the business community, and civil society. Three global issues with implications for competitiveness, and where it is crucial for small states to have a voice, are: accessing development finance; measuring competitiveness, and a changing international political and economic environment that is not as supportive of globalization as in the past.

Small nations are generally more sensitive to and more impacted by such international developments; they also, at the same time, benefit from an economically integrated world and are disproportionately negatively affected by international barriers. It is not only a technical dialogue to come up with solutions to these challenges, but a diplomatic dialogue is also necessary within the global institutions and global policy frameworks that are being developed.

A global dialogue is in the making, and small states are not to be left behind. Diplomatic intervention is an important tool available to small states, and it can improve their global competitiveness. While small states have fewer resources to devote to the tasks of diplomacy and effective interaction with other states, this shortcoming can be compensated by their large number and their common interests through the formation of alliances and networks.

Although it may appear that small states have failed to form alliances and networks, progress has in fact been made. This is shown with the Small States

Forum in improving access to development finance and de-risking in small states, and with the Commonwealth Secretariat in increasing international trade and developing a new competitiveness measure for small states. This progress has been made with different degrees of success or not at the level of success anticipated, which makes the point that more could be done.

The fact remains that there is limited space in the global negotiating agenda for the issues that small states represent. Small states in Europe are strategically placed to bring these issues forward at the regional EU level and through the EU at the international level, to recalibrate their approach to regional and international diplomacy in its quest to promote competitiveness, and to sustain growth and equity in their development goals. As such, they can bring important lessons to the attention of other small nations in the world and add considerably to the expectations of this exercise in global analytical leadership.

COVID-19 has posed a diplomatic challenge for small states with implications for their global competitiveness. Pedi and Wivel (2020) examined the implications of COVID-19 on small state diplomacy. According to these authors, the pandemic has short- and medium- to long-term consequences for diplomacy in small states. In the short term, the acquisition of protective equipment proved to be a challenge at the onset of the pandemic, and small states suffered from high prices and shortages with big countries being better able to secure access. Small states resorted to accepting gifts and entered into purchase agreements with countries such as China and India. Small states were also affected by a fall in remittances and tourism revenues for which many are dependent, and this undermined their ability to meet the challenges of the immediate health crisis and the subsequent economic crisis (Pedi and Wivel 2020; Sindico et al. 2020). In the medium-to-long term, Pedi and Wivel (2020, 613) stated that "COVID-19 is likely to accelerate and deepen the crisis in the liberal international order," as countries closed their borders, focused on domestic crisis management, and competed over production and acquisition of protective equipment, treatments, and vaccines (Nye 2020).

Pedi and Wivel (2020) have also posited that the pandemic has temporarily leveled the playing field between small states and middle powers. Both benefit from "political, economic, military, and societal" shelter from great powers and international organizations, which helps to reduce their risk and better absorb shocks, and speed up recovery, and which have been largely inefficient or absent during COVID-19 (Pedi and Wivel 2020, 614). Pedi and Wivel (2020) further argued that this created incentives and opportunities for small states to take action and seek influence and status during the pandemic through offensive small state strategies that are "smart" and "entrepreneurial." Small states are agile and can foster networks that are informal without creating fears of dominance.

Pedi and Wivel (2020) characterized three patterns of small state diplomacy during the pandemic – regional clusters and networks of cooperation, like-minded states' activism, and status seeking amid the crisis. This allowed small states to act on new opportunities by introducing novel ideas and policies made to fit the COVID-19 context, thereby increasing their international status and influence. These innovative diplomatic initiatives have the effect of mitigating falling economic and health security and represent a first step forward toward building a program to boost competitiveness as outlined earlier in terms of accessing development finance, competitiveness measures and integrity, and threats to globalization, alliances, and networks.

References

Acharya, A. 2017. "After Liberal Hegemony: The Advent of a Multiplex World Order." *Ethics and International Affairs*, September. https://www.ethicsandinternationala ffairs.org/2017/multiplex-world-order/.

Alesina, A., and E. Spolaore. 2003. *The Size of Nations.* Cambridge, MA: MIT Press.

Allegrezza, S. 2018. "The Economy of Luxembourg." In *Small States and the European Union: Economic Perspectives*, edited by L. Briguglio, 135–56. London: Routledge.

Alleyne, T., J. Bouhga-Hagbe, T. Dowling, D. Kovtun, A. Myrvoda, J. Okwuokei, and J. Turunen. 2017. "Loss of Correspondent Banking Relationships in the Caribbean: Trends, Impact and Policy Options." IMF Working Paper WP/17/209. https://www .imf.org/~/media/Files/Publications/WP/2017/wp17209.ashx.

Alwazir, J., M.F. Jamaludin, D. Lee, N. Sheridan, and M.P. Tumbarello. 2017. *Challenges in Correspondent Banking in the Small States of the Pacific.* Washington D.C.: International Monetary Fund. https://www.imf.org/en/Publications/WP/Issues/2017 /04/07/Challenges-in-CorrespondentBanking-in-the-Small-States-of-the-Pacific -44809.

Bárcena, A. 2017. "Multilateralism Is a Key Element in Promoting the 2030 Agenda for Sustainable Development." https://www.cepal.org/en/articulos/2017 -multilateralismo-es-clave-potenciar-la-agenda-2030-desarrollo-sostenible.

Bustillo, I., H. Velloso, W. Dookeran, and D. Perrotti. 2018. *Resilience and Capital Flows in the Caribbean.* Washington D.C.: United Nations Economic Commission for Latin American and the Caribbean.

Commonwealth Secretariat. 2007. *Commonwealth Small States: Issues and Prospects.* London: Commonwealth Secretariat.

———. 2015. *The Commonwealth in the Unfolding Global Trade Landscape.* London: Commonwealth Trade Review.

Dookeran, W. 2018. *The Caribbean on the Edge: An Anthology of Ideas and Writings.* Washington D.C.: United Nations Economic Commission for Latin American and the Caribbean.

Egan, Annabel, and L. Pech. 2017. *Respect for Human Rights as a General Objective of the EU's External Action Research Handbook on EU Law and Human Rights*, edited by Sionaidh Douglas-Scott, Research Handbooks in European Law, 243–66. Edward Elgar, University of Nottingham, UK.

Estevadeordal, A., and L.W. Goodman. 2017. *21st Century Cooperation: Regional Public Goods, Global Governance and Sustainable Development*. London: Routledge.

European Commission. 2018. "Commission Requests Maltese Anti-Money Laundering Watchdog to Step Up Supervision of Banks." https://ec.europa.eu/commission/presscorner/detail/ga/ip_18_6303.

Goodwin, M., and C. Milazzo. 2017. "Taking Back Control? Investigating the Role of Immigration in the 2016 Vote for Brexit." *British Journal of Politics and International Relations*, 19 (3): 450–64.

Henrikson, A.K. 2001. "A Coming 'Magnesian' Age? Small States, the Global System and the International Community." *Geopolitics*, 6 (3): 49–86.

Holotescu, C. 2018. "Understanding Blockchain Opportunities and Challenges." (4) *The 14th International Scientific Conference ELearning and Software for Education Bucharest*, 277–8. https://www.researchgate.net/publication/324209739_Understanding_Blockchain_Opportunities_and_Challenge.

Inglehart, R.F., and P. Norris. 2016. "Trump, Brexit and the Rise of Populism: Economic Havenots and Cultural Backlash." HKS Working Paper No. RWP16-026. https://ssrn.com/abstract=2818659.

Kassimeris, C. 2009. "The Foreign Policy of Small Powers." *International Politics*, 46 (1): 84–101.

Keohane, R. 2009. "Lilliputians' Dilemmas: Small States in International Politics." *International Organization*, 23 (2): 291–310.

Llunji, V. 2015. "Issues of Small States in the Age of Globalization." *European Journal of Social Sciences Education and Research*, 2 (2): 102–7.

Long, T. 2017. "Small States, Great Power? Gaining Influence through Intrinsic, Derivative, and Collective Power." *International Studies Review*, 19 (2): 185–205.

Morck, R., and J. Chenxing Shou. 2018. "On the Integrity of the 'Ease of Doing Business' Indicators," https://www.df.cl/noticias/site/artic/20180712/asocfile/20180712140607/auditoria_banco_mu ndial.pdf.

Nye, J.S. 2020. "No, the Coronavirus Will Not Change the Global Order, Foreign Policy." *Foreign Policy*. https://foreignpolicy.com/2020/04/16/coronavirus-pandemic-china-united-states-power-competition/.

Panke, D. 2012. "Small States in Multilateral Negotiations: What Have We Learned?" *Cambridge Review of International Affairs*, 25 (3): 387–98.

Pedersen, O.K. 1987. "Small States and International Institutions." In *Les Internationales et le problème de la guerre au XXe siècle*, 337–48. Rome, Italy: French School at Rome.

Pedi, R., and A. Wivel. 2020. "Small State Diplomacy after the Corona Crisis." *The Hague Journal of Diplomacy*, 15: 611–23.

Pollard, D. E. E. 2009. "Unincorporated Treaties and Small States." *Commonwealth Law Bulletin*, 33 (3): 389–421.

Reuters. 2018. "Chile Slams World Bank for Bias in Competitiveness Rankings." https://www.reuters.com/article/us-chile-worldbank/chile-slams-world-bank-for-bias-in-competitiveness-rankings-idUSKBN1F20SN?il=0.

Rodrik, D. 2018. "Populism and the Economics of Globalization." *Journal of International Business Policy*, 1 (1): 12–33.

Sindico, F., G. Sajeva, N. Sharman, P. Berlouis, and J. Ellsmoor. 2020. *Islands and COVID-19: A Global Survey*. Strathclyde Centre for Environmental Law and Governance and Island Innovation.

Small States Forum. 2017, October 14. "Chairman's Summing Up. Small States Forum 2017: From Roadmap to Action," https://www.worldbank.org/en/events/2017/10/04/small-states-forum-2017.

Spolaore, E. 2018. Notes Provided by the Author for the Conference: Competitiveness Strategies for the Small EU States: Economic and Social Perspectives, 19–20 April 2018, Luxembourg.

Súilleabháin, A.Ó. 2014. *Small States at the United Nations: Diverse Perspectives, Shared Opportunities*. New York: International Peace Institute.

The Economist. 2018, January 20. "The World Bank 'ease of doing business' Report Faces Tricky Questions" https://www.economist.com/finance-andeconomics/2018/01/20/the-world-banks-ease-of-doing-business-report-faces-tricky-questions.

The Global Competitive Report 2018. Washington DC: World Economic Forum. http://www3.weforum.org/docs/GCR2017-2018/05FullReport/TheGlobalCompetitivenesReport2017%E2%80%932018.pdf.

Thorhallsson, B., and A. Wivel. 2006. "Small States in the European Union: What Do We know and What Would We Like to Know?" *Cambridge Review of International Affairs*, 19 (4): 651–68.

United Nations. 2015. "Transforming Our World: The 2030 Agenda for Sustainable Development." Resolution adopted by the General Assembly on 25 September 2015. http://www.un.org/ga/search/view_doc.asp?symbol=A/RES/70/1&Lang=E.

United Nations Conference on Trade and Development. 2014. *World Investment Report*. Washington DC: UNCTAD. https://unctad.org/en/PublicationsLibrary/wir2014_en.pdf.

Veenendaal, W.P., and J. Corbett. 2014. "Why Small States Offer Important Answers to Large Questions." *Comparative Political Studies*, 48 (4): 527–49.

World Bank. 2017. "Small States: A Road Map for World Bank Group Engagement." http://pubdocs.worldbank.org/en/982421496935264348/Small-StatesRoadmap.pdf#zoom=70.

Zumbrun, J., and I. Talley. 2018, January 12. "World Bank Unfairly Influenced Its Own Competitiveness Rankings." *Wall Street Journal*. https://www.wsj.com/articles/world-bank-unfairly-influenced-its-own-competitivenessrankings-1515797620.

7

Setting the Agenda for the "Circular Economy" of the Caribbean

WINSTON DOOKERAN AND PREEYA MOHAN[1]

Introduction

The Coronavirus disease of 2019 (COVID-19 pandemic) and its accompanying lockdown measures are major driving forces toward a Circular Economy. The pandemic has revealed significant shortcomings in the linear economy, including the vulnerability of global value chains, the depletion of natural resources, and the exacerbation of social inequalities. The new normal puts constraints on the current linear economic model, while there is a search for a new model to emerge which is in line with the fundamentals of the Circular Economy. The imposed lockdowns have exposed the fact that, in the current linear system, what is good for the economy is rarely good for the environment and society. The significant increase and rebound in emissions and pollution to pre-pandemic levels in many countries following the end of the lockdown and stay-in-place measures show that the linear economic model is not an option for a sustainable recovery.

We are forced to think of new ways to make things work, and as such, we are likely to find new ways to produce, distribute, purchase, and consume goods and services. The Circular Economy is not an abstract concept, and its principles can be applied to help us cope in the post-pandemic period. It offers an alternative framework for a more resilient and inclusive economic model for Caribbean small states. The aftermath of the COVID-19 crisis provides a unique opportunity for a resilient recovery, and the transition to a Circular Economy offers a suitable framework to ensure an inclusive and economically, socially and environmentally resilient future for the region. The question that

[1] The authors would like to thank the SALISES, St. Augustine, and its director Professor Hamid Ghany for his support of this research. This paper comes out of the Political Economy research cluster of the SALISES.

arises is, how can a Circular Economy create a more competitive, diversified, and inclusive economy in the post-COVID-19 Caribbean when imports remain high, particularly for energy and food, and when the economies are largely service-oriented particularly tourism?

The concept of the Circular Economy is a new line of thinking on development strategy and aims to present solutions by combining economic growth with social and environmental impact. It goes beyond survivability into sustainability and introduces the reduce, reuse, and recycle concept in the model of production. It therefore questions the orthodox theory of economic growth and raises new premises for growth theory and strategies for development. The concept can be applied to operating systems in different sectors and is acknowledged as an area on the frontiers of economic analysis to provide prescriptions to development challenges.

This new business model changes the roles of the entrepreneur, the household, the firm, and the financier. This chapter examines the conceptual framework and changing perspectives of the Circular Economy thinking and identifies the necessary changes in the strategies for development in Caribbean small states. The chapter describes the Circular Economy as new thinking on development strategy; it presents the Circular Economy as a new growth theory; the financial challenges of implementing Circular Economy principles are laid out; and finally Circular Economy policy actions and applications in the Caribbean Small Island Developing States (SIDS) are explored.

The New Discourse

The concept of the Circular Economy enables industry to grow and prosper while keeping the environment and society intact, ensuring growth for current and future generations. The Circular Economy is a development strategy applied to operating systems in different sectors and is acknowledged as an area on the frontiers of economic analysis to provide prescriptions. It aims at decoupling economic growth from the consumption of finite raw materials. This can be achieved over time by gradually designing out waste from production and other economic activities, keeping raw materials and products in economic use, and regenerating natural systems. The value of raw materials and goods and services is maintained and reused for as long as possible. It must not be confused with recycling since waste is minimized and resource-use maximized as raw materials and products are used again and again to create further value. This can bring about major economic, social, and environmental benefits.

In contrast to the concepts of sustainable development and the green and blue economy, which require effective resource-use and environmentally friendly technologies in isolated areas of the entire production system, the Circular Economy advocates for a broader and more comprehensive innovative design of sustainable solutions over the entire life cycle of products, and for integrated production and consumption patterns within the entire economic system. The Circular Economy looks at the environment as a system to imitate when redesigning production. It rests on value creation through restoration, regeneration, and reuse of resources and inputs. This is enabled by new types of business models and production and consumption that discard ownership and rely on active "users" rather than passive "consumers."

The Industrial Revolution led to technological advances within a linear "take, make, and dispose" model of production, where the majority of feedstock ends in waste and creates unsustainable side effects such as a loss of biodiversity, deforestation, air and water pollution, and natural resource depletion. The planet currently faces challenges of increasingly constrained resources, adding to price volatility of raw materials, and increasingly demanding markets. This requires a movement away from survivability to sustainability and a new economic paradigm of reduce, reuse, and recycle as advocated for in the Circular Economy model of production. The concept of the Circular Economy is new thinking on development strategy and aims to present solutions by combining economic growth with social and environmental impact.

The Ellen MacArthur Foundation (2012) introduces the dimension of structural waste, which is an important concept in the Circular Economy. In the linear economy, waste management is a way to get rid of waste in ways that generate huge losses of valuable resources and have large environmental impacts. In the Circular Economy, waste management is viewed as a recovery of resources process which at the same time minimizes environmental impact. As such, waste management is an important sector of the Circular Economy and has led to the emergence of new business models and types of operators, called scavengers and de-composers, which are capable of extracting resources out of waste by applying innovative recovery technologies and thus adding value to create new production inputs (Ghisellini, Cialani, and Ulgiati 2015).

Circular Economy in the Academic Literature

In academic literature, the Circular Economy cannot be attributed to a single author. Theoretically, the concept originates from ecological and environmental economics, industrial ecology, and general systems theory (Winans, Kendall, and Deng 2017; Ghisellini, Cialani, and Ulgiati 2015; and Ellen MacArthur Foundation 2012). Pearce and Turner (1990) have also presented the "resource products pollution model" which is related to the Circular Economy approach.

The Circular Economy is presented as an alternative to the neo-classical growth model since it takes into account the role of the environment and the interplay between the environment and the economy.

Circular Economy in Action

In recent years, the Circular Economy has gained increasing prominence as a tool which presents solutions to some of the world's most pressing crosscutting sustainable development challenges. The Ellen MacArthur Foundation's mission is to accelerate the transition to a Circular Economy and works with business, government, and academia to build a framework for an economy that is restorative and regenerative by design. In September 2018, the UN General Assembly held a stakeholder workshop titled "Closing the Loop: Unlocking an Inclusive Circular Economy Approach."

In 2017, – Platform for Accelerating the Circular Economy (PACE) – a public–private sector collaboration was set up, hosted, and facilitated by the World Economic Forum. This platform encourages developing countries to adopt strategies, finance, and growth that will accelerate action in Circular Economy initiatives.

Finland is the first country to prepare a national roadmap to a Circular Economy in 2016, under the leadership of the Finnish Innovation Fund Sitra. A Circular Economy roadmap outlines actions that can accelerate the transition toward a competitive and fair Circular Economy. It is a way of involving stakeholders, highlighting best practices, and enabling sustainable change nationally (Jarvinen and Sinervo 2020). In the post-COVID-19 recovery, such a roadmap can provide the compass and the engine for a sustainable recovery (Jarvinen and Sinervo 2020). Table 7.1 outlines the Circular Economy roadmap process.

Insights into Growth Theory

The traditional strategy for economic growth and development in the literature is predicated on linear processes underlining the basic rules of operation in the economic system. At times, feedback loops were inserted into the analysis which introduced a dynamic element to a static logic that defines development pathways. In today's discourse on development strategy, the assumption of linearity in the economic development path is being tested by the notion of the Circular Economy.

In the linearity notion, the operating system of the economy is based on the "end-of-life" concept, while in the circularity notion, reusing, recycling, and

Table 7.1 Circular economy road map process

Step	Details
1. Groundwork and Preconditions	Define the preconditions, create a project plan for the process, define team roles, and make sure there are sufficient resources available.
2. Stakeholders and Participation	Identify key stakeholders and make sure they are committed to the process. Form a steering group and identify needs for other working groups.
3. The Situational Picture	Deepen the understanding about the current state of the circular economy in the country. The situational picture will serve as a solid basis for the next steps.
4. Vision and Goals	Create an inspiring vision for the road map as well as set specific and measurable goals.
5. Focus Areas	Define the focus areas based on the vision and strategic goals. Define the indicators that help measure the transition to a circular economy.
6. Planning the Actions	Plan the actions that lead to the road map goals. At best, the circular economy road map is a combination of strategy and tangible action plan.
7. Compile and Publish	Start compiling the road map. Ask for stakeholder comments. Communicate to inspire others to start their own actions to promote the circular economy.
8. Execution and Implementation	Define the management model of the road map and ensure stakeholder commitment to guarantee strong implementation. Remember to communicate.
9. Evaluation and Revision	Evaluate ongoing projects, explore supplementary actions, and decide on updates. Not to forget securing the maximum impact.

Source: Järvinen and Sinervo, 2020.

recovering materials in the production, distribution, and consumption processes are at the core of the drivers of change in resource efficiency. A recent paper by the Ellen MacArthur Foundation devoted to the study of the Circular Economy stated: "A number of factors indicate that the linear model is increasingly being challenged by the very context within which it operates and that a deeper change of the operating system of our economy is necessary" (Ellen MacArthur Foundation 2012, 3). The Foundation's report, titled "Growth Within," spells out this vision and provides the circular perspective for rethinking value creation in economic systems (Ellen MacArthur Foundation 2015).

What is now emerging in academic and policy literature is a movement from a linear to a circular view on economic growth and sustainable development.

The Industrial Revolution resulted in a linear economic approach of the take, make, dispose model where the majority of feedstock used to make products eventually ends up as waste. The costs of non-renewable natural resources are, however, high, with numerous negative externalities associated with their use, such as air, land, and water pollution, climate change, and loss of biodiversity. The destructive nature of the linear economy is clearly identified, and the potential for an alternative circular approach is becoming increasingly appealing.

If linear economic principles remain the norm of business practices and consumption patterns, the outcome is likely to be shortages of resources, growing price volatility, and continued environmental degradation. The necessity to transition to an alternative economic model is evident. Further, recent international trends including the higher cost associated with natural disasters, climate smart technologies, a rapidly growing middle class, an emerging green and blue economy, and new governance processes where governments alone do not play an important role but also the private sector and civil society provide tools to move to a Circular Economy model.

The Circular Economy decouples economic growth from resource constraints. Economic activities make more effective use of materials, thus retaining as much of their value as possible by circulating them at their highest value at all times. The economic benefits of products and materials cycling through the system will not be accompanied by the degradation of natural capital, since stocks of non-renewable resources are controlled, and renewable resources are used whenever possible. The Circular Economy reduces negative externalities as it reveals and designs out waste, pollution, and toxic materials. Moreover, a transition to a Circular Economy may generate positive externalities since innovative technologies and new business models would be developed. The aim of the Circular Economy is to decouple the creation of wealth and jobs from the consumption of non-renewable resources by maximizing resource productivity and minimizing waste generation.

Circular Economy versus Linear Economy

The Circular Economy differs from a linear economy fundamentally from the perspective of what sustainability is, and the quality of reuse practices. On the one hand, a linear economy works according to the "take-make-dispose" production process. Resources are extracted from the earth, and goods and services are produced for consumption and are used until they are discarded and disposed of as waste. Value creation occurs by maximizing the number of goods and services produced and consumed. On the other hand, a Circular

Economy works according to the reduce, reuse, and recycle approach. Reuse is intended to be carried out as much as possible. Natural resource extraction is minimized as much as possible by using less as inputs into the production process. Goods and services are produced from reused parts and materials, and after discarding a product, materials and parts are recycled. Value is created by focusing on value retention. A residual stream should be reused for a function that is equal, referred to as functional reuse or of a higher value, called upcycling than the initial function of the material stream. The Circular Economy is different from the linear economy in the area of sustainable exploitation of natural resources, and also in social responsibility and more uniform development of the economy.

The linear economy is associated with eco-efficiency and the Circular Economy with eco-effectivity, where the difference lies in the quality of reuse of materials such as inputs into the production process (Braungart, McDonough, and Bollinger 2007). The key assumption in the transformation of linear to Circular Economy is a feedback circle that returns the collected and recycled waste into the production cycle as a valuable raw material. This ensures that the value of the material is either retained or enhanced, while within a linear economy, reuse is mainly seen in downcycling practices, and a product or part of a product is used for a low-grade purpose, which reduces the value of the material.

A single type of waste may be recycled several times and reused in subsequent cycles of production processes. The goal of the Circular Economy is to achieve 100 percent reuse of materials and make waste zero percent (Bocken, Bakker, and De Pauw 2016 and Ellen MacArthur Foundation 2012). While in the linear economy model there are elements of reuse and minimizing waste in raw material extraction, and of increasing recycling, in the Circular Economy the goal is to make a full 100 percent transition.

In the Circular Economy system, the added value of a product is kept longer in use before it becomes waste. Nevertheless, a small amount of waste may not be recycled and is finally disposed of in an environmentally harmless way. The fundamental principle is thus efficient use of material resources, waste collection, recycling, and reuse in the production process. It is an approach that rationalizes and enriches the relationship between production and consumption since it returns the effects of consumption into the production process.

The Circular Economy approach requires the transformation of value chains and consumption patterns so that the value of products, components, materials, and resources is maintained throughout the product's useful life. This transformation is challenging, and switching to a waste-free economy means changes along the entire value chain from product design to production to distribution and final use. While the transition to a Circular Economy makes economic sense, production processes will not automatically become circular. These changes will only occur when supported by business models and enabled by consumer behavior, legislation, finance, and education. These enablers can reinforce each other and accelerate the change from a linear to a Circular Economy.

Issues in Financing

The Circular Economy requires a different way of doing business and consequently a different financial system to meet different financial needs. This new business model changes the roles of the entrepreneur, the household, the firm, and the financier. The transition to the Circular Economy is estimated to save USD $1 trillion yearly worldwide by 2025 (World Economic Forum, Ellen MacArthur Foundation, and McKinsey and Company 2014). Finance is, however, a critical barrier and enabler in the transition toward a Circular Economy (Fischer and Achterberg 2016; Sonerud 2014 and Eijk 2015). Public and private finance can enable firms and households to make the transition to a Circular Economy on a financial level.

Circular Economy finance is defined as any type of financial instrument where the investments will be exclusively applied to finance or refinance, in part or in full, new and or existing eligible businesses or projects in the Circular Economy (Achterberg, Hinfelaar, and Bocken 2016). The Circular Economy aims to make efficient use of the resources that we already have. Finance plays an important role in facilitating this transition by financing businesses and projects which adopt a Circular Economy approach. Resources must remain functioning at their highest potential for as long as possible so that they are not consumed, but re-enter into the production process and create value again and again.

Businesses and proposals based on a Circular Economy model that generate long-term positive economic, social, and environmental impact should be considered for Circular Economy finance. The financial sector must understand the rationale and investment opportunities of circular businesses which include higher resource and asset productivity, mitigation of input price volatility, increased quality of earnings, and reduced climate risks, in order for banks to express an interest in supporting and financing the Circular Economy (Rabobank 2015). Understanding how circular business models differ from traditional business models and what their barriers to financing are, is highly relevant for financiers. Circular business could be identified by banks through their business culture and operating characteristics.

While circular business models offer economic, social, and environmental benefits, they can be perceived as highly risky by banks (Linder and Williander 2015; FinanCE Working Group 2016; and ING 2015). Moreover, small- and medium-size enterprises with new innovative business ideas face an even lower chance of obtaining finance, although larger corporations also face challenges in attracting funding to transform their business model toward a circular one since the investment costs can be high (Fischer and Achterberg 2016 and ABN Amro 2018). Circular business models also pose challenges to standard banking solutions, and if a transition is to be made various restructuring and innovations in the financial sector must take place (FinanCE Working Group 2016).

Circular businesses have a different revenue structure compared to traditional businesses. The firm's product is no longer sold, but periodic fees are paid by customers for using the product since the product provider retains ownership of the product. The firm's cash flows are then spread out over time, and the firm still requires an initial upfront investment. This results in a longer payback period, which increases the risk of default from the bank's perspective and increases the demand for working capital, resulting in a decline in short-term margins. The trade-off between short-term margins and long-term stability of cash flows impacts the perceived creditworthiness and stability of the firm or entrepreneur seeking to adopt to a Circular Economy model. The firm's balance sheet keeps growing with each additional customer, and this then creates a capital demand in order to finance the long-term ownership of these assets. Further, since customers and firms are used to owning products and may not, yet value used products, there is a high market risk due to uncertain market demand for the products offered.

The assets in the Circular Economy model are less adequate as collateral since they are generally less capital-intensive than traditional economic models. They are generally of a lower value and are fairly illiquid, as they are not readily available to be sold off by the company. Circularity cannot be achieved without value chain collaboration. Products and materials should be shared throughout the value chain to assure shared responsibility, and transparency and circularity, based on shared risks and returns. From a financial risk perspective, this level of collaboration means an increase in interdependence between companies since the success of the individual company depends on other actors.

Caribbean Small States

The Circular Economy has gained prominence in Caribbean small states in recent years as a viable approach to sustainable development. It offers an alternative framework for a more resilient and economically, environmentally, and socially inclusive growth model in the region. Countries in the region have either implemented or are planning Circular Economy policies and public initiatives. In the context of the post-COVID-19 recovery, the Circular Economy is gaining additional attention as a solution to increase resilience and to mitigate future external shocks in the Caribbean. Given the high levels of inequality and poverty in the Caribbean, the transition to a Circular Economy needs to be compatible with, and even a promoter of, these social objectives. Climate change, a fragile environment, and exposure to hurricanes also pose serious threats to sustainable development of these small islands where the concentration of their population and economic infrastructure is in coastal zones.

The transition to a Circular Economy in the Caribbean has been primarily in waste collection, management, and recycling, which are at the lower end of the Circular Economy hierarchy (Schröder, Lemille, and Desmond 2020). Countries have implemented various waste management and recycling initiatives and a ban on single-use plastic and Styrofoam. Caribbean countries are abundant in biodiversity and wildlife with rich marine life and fertile land. However, growing populations and increased consumption of resources have made small states vulnerable to high concentrations of solid waste and plastic litter, and marine debris beyond the capacity for these islands to cope. According to Mohee et al. (2015), waste management is a matter of great concern for SIDS, and on average, the waste generation rate in these islands is high and amounts to 1.29 kg per capita per day. Further, illegal dumping, landfilling, and backyard burning are prevalent and favored over sustainable waste treatment technologies such as composting, anaerobic digestion, and recycling.

Sustainable waste management practices are only now emerging in Caribbean island states, but with many challenges still hindering the implementation of these practices. There are also outdated waste collection vehicles and narrow roads which are inaccessible. In these small states, tourism (WTTC 2018) is a major economic earner and depends on an attractive environment, cultural uniqueness, social interaction, security, and well-being, while at the same time the development of tourism itself can destroy these special resources which are critical for the success of the industry. SIDS are also heavily dependent on hydrocarbons for energy, which contribute to greenhouse gas emissions and are costly for them to import.

The transition to a Circular Economy in the Caribbean requires significant investments in infrastructure for waste collection, management, and recycling (SchröderLemille, and Desmond 2020). Financing for the Circular Economy in the Caribbean is currently limited mainly to the provision of international development finance for waste management and recycling, rather than businesses offering circular products. While there could be substantial changes across the region in waste management, which will need to be financed, it is important to attract both domestic and foreign investments beyond waste management into circular businesses to make the transition to a Circular Economy possible.

The public and private finance in small states must now be geared to engage in new frontiers for commercial funding in a future Circular Economy. This would therefore require a new understanding of the opportunities that may arise from the implementation of an impending Circular Economy. While circular business models offer economic, social, and environmental benefits, they can be perceived as highly risky by banks, and this problem is even more pronounced in Caribbean SIDS given the risk-averse attitude by banks to the private sector (Worrell, Cherebin, and Polius-Mounsey 2001).

The Caribbean banking sector already provides a low source of funding to households and the private sector for activities outside of the Circular Economy. Given the nature of the Circular Economy including uncertain market demand for its products, the lack of assets to be used as collateral that are illiquid, and the sharing of products and materials throughout the value chain, make it even harder to attract financing from the banking sector. Caribbean banks can enable the Circular Economy by developing valuation and risk models that suit the characteristics of circular businesses.

Caribbean Policy Action

The following lists action points taking place in Caribbean SIDS geared toward transitioning to a Circular Economy. The overall aim of these actions is to accomplish sustainable development by simultaneously creating environmental quality, economic prosperity, and social equity.

(a) Caribbean SIDS Public Initiatives

Caribbean SIDS have implemented various public initiatives that made some degree of progress in moving toward a Circular Economy. The Barbados Returnable Containers Act was passed since June 1, 1986, and has increased recycling on the island. In September 2016 Aruba, Bonaire, and Curacao identified common opportunities and challenges in waste management and established the Caribbean Waste Collective, which aims to create a new sector by turning waste into value. On July 1, 2016, Antigua and Barbuda imposed a ban on single-use plastic bags, and this was followed by a ban on the import of all plastic bags. On July 1, 2017, a Styrofoam ban took effect. Aruba and

Dominica have successfully secured public support for a plastic bag ban, and Trinidad and Tobago has proposed a Styrofoam ban. Jamaica launched the Jamaica Plastics Project supported by the United Nations on July 5, 2017, for properly managing plastics through regulations.

(b) Latin American and Caribbean Circular Economy Coalition

The Caribbean together with Latin America has established a regional coalition on the Circular Economy.[2] It aims to develop a common regional vision and strategy on the Circular Economy in order to have a bigger impact, to build cooperation, and have a regional platform to exchange best practices and provide technical support. The coalition is governed by a Steering Committee, supported by Strategic Partners and a Secretariat and provides an open platform where all governments, private sector, institutions, nongovernmental organizations, intergovernmental and international/regional organizations working on the Circular Economy can participate and contribute to.

(c) UN Sustainable Development Goals

The United Nations sees much promise to accelerate the implementation of the 2030 Sustainable Development Agenda through a Circular Economy approach in various areas such as climate change, ocean action, and food waste and loss, which requires a joint effort by stakeholders from all sectors. The Economic and Social Council of the United Nations held a plenary session on the Application of the Principles of the Circular Economy to further this agenda. Additionally, an October 2018 United Nations Environment Programme report, titled "Waste Management Outlook for Latin America and the Caribbean," concluded that the region inadequately disposes of 145,000 tons of waste every day and urgently needs a new economic growth model that would not lead to environmental degradation (UN Environment 2018).

(d) University of Alberta, Guyana, and Energy

A workshop was held at the University of Alberta in Edmonton, Canada, in August 2018 titled "The Guyana Project: A New Approach to Sustainable Development in Guyana: Towards a Circular Economy and Resilience in Businesses." The workshop presented an overview of Guyana and the Caribbean region, with reference to the Circular Economy, and the United Nations 2030 Agenda and the Sustainable Development Goals and identified and

---

2 https://pacecircular.org/latin-american-caribbean-circular-economy-coalition

discussed Circular Economy project ideas. Among the project ideas that came out of the workshop was a follow-up on the CARICOM Circular Economy Package for Sustainable Development and a sustainable energy sector. In St. Lucia, private recyclers have been recovering significant amounts of used oil on the island and from cruise ships and are selling it to the local industry for boiler fuel. This initiative can be expanded to other islands under the Guyana Project.

(e) Sustainable Islands Platform (SIsP)

The SIsP developed by the Inter-American Development Bank is looking at the best ways to support the Caribbean in its pursuit of sustainability and prosperity under three founding pillars including the Circular Economy together with Climate Resilience and Blue Economy.[3] It encourages island leaders to reimagine integrated sustainability solutions that examine the linkages and interactions between their economies, societies, and the environment within the context of an oceanic development space.

(f) The Circular Economy Platform of the Americas (CEP-Americas)

The CEP-Americas is committed to engage with like-minded individuals and organizations to explore, identify, and realize innovative solutions inspired by the Circular Economy principles to address economic and social challenges in the region.[4] The initiative is focused on promoting, introducing, and applying the concept of the Circular Economy across multiple sectors of the economy. This will serve as a major step to achieving sustainable development and to help mitigate climate change through sustainable and eco-effective production.

Conclusion

The Circular Economy is more than just a buzz phrase. It represents a serious paradigm shift. It tackles the issue of limited resources in a serious way and must be accepted as a reality for the transformation of the economy in the post-COVID-19 era. It requires the redesign of the structure for economic growth and development, and a new research agenda and policy action has emerged out of this. If Caribbean small states are not to be left behind, the concept of the Circular Economy must be expanded and deepened and enter into their research agenda, policy agenda, operational agenda, and finance agenda. To do

---

[3] https://www.sustainableislandsplatform.org/
[4] https://www.sustainableamericas.com/circular-economies-program.

so, adequate resources must be applied to research, action, and policy. Setting up a task force for small states is the first step in the right direction.

References

ABN AMRO. 2018. "Circular Economy Finance Guidelines." https://www.ing.com/Newsroom/News/ABN-AMRO-ING-and-Rabobank-launch-finance-guidelines-for-circular-economy.htm.

Achterberg, Elisa, Jeroen Hinfelaar, and Nancy Bocken. 2016. "Master Circular Business with the Value Hill." http://www.circle-economy.com/financing-circular-business.

Bocken, Nanacy M.P., Ingrid de Pauw, Conny Bakker, and Bram van der Grinten. 2016. "Product Design and Business Model Strategies for a Circular Economy." *Journal of Industrial and Production Engineering*, 33 (5): 308–20. doi: 10.1080/21681015.2016.1172124.

Braungart, Michael, William McDonough, and Andrew Bollinger. 2007. "Cradle-to-Cradle Design: Creating Healthy Emissions – A Strategy for Eco-effective Product and System Design." *Journal of Cleaner Production*, 15 (13–14): 1337–48.

Eijk, Freek van. 2015. "Barriers & Drivers towards a Circular Economy." Netherlands: Acceleratio. https://www.circulaironndernemen.nl/uploads/e00e8643951aef8adde612123e824493.pdf.

Ellen MacArthur Foundation. 2012. "Towards the Circular Economy Vol. 1: An Economic and Business Rationale for an Accelerated Transition." https://ellenmacarthurfoundation.org/towards-the-circular-economy-vol-1-an-economic-and-business-rationale-for-an.

———. 2015. "Growth Within: A Circular Economy Vision for a Competitive Europe." McKinsey Center for Business and Environment and Ellen MacArthur Foundation. https://www.mckinsey.com/business-functions/sustainability/our nsights/growth-within-a-circular-economy-vision-for-a-competitive-europe.

FinanCE Working Group. 2016. "Money Makes the World Go Round - and Will It Help Make the Economy Circular as Well?" http://sustainablefinancelab.nl/files/2016/04/FinanCE-Digital.pdf.

Fischer, Aglaia, and Elisa Achterberg. 2016. "Create a Financeable Product-as-a-Service Business in 10 Steps." http://circleeconomy.com/financing-circular-business.

Ghisellini, Patrizia, Catia Cialani, and Sergio Ulgiati. 2015. "A Review on Circular Economy: The Expected Transition to a Balanced Interplay of Environmental and Economic Systems." *Journal of Cleaner Production*, 114 (15): 11–32.

ING. 2015. "Rethinking Finance in a Circular Economy; Financial Implications of Circular Business Models." https://www.ing.com/MediaEditPage/Financing-the-Circular Economy.htm.

Jarvinen, Laura, and Riku Sinervo. 2020. *How to Create a National Circular Economy Road Map A Guide to Making the Change Happen*. Helsinki: The Finnish Innovation Fund Sitra. https://www.sitra.fi/en/publications/how-to-create-a-national-circular-economy-road-map/#why.

Linder, Marcus, and Mats Williander. 2015. "Circular Business Model Innovation: Inherent Uncertainties." *Business Strategy and the Environment*, 26 (2): 182–96.

Mohee, Romeela, Sumayya Mauthoor, Zumar M.A. Bundhoo, Geeta Somaroo, Nuhaa Soobhany, and Sanjana Gunasee. 2015. "Current Status of Solid Waste Management in Small Island Developing States: A Review." *Waste Management*, 43: 539–49.

Pearce, David W., and R. Kerry Turner. 1990. *Economics of Natural Resources and the Environment*. Baltimore: The John Hopkins University Press.

Rabobank. 2015. "De Potentie van de Circulaire Economie." https://economie.rabobank .com/publicaties/2015/juli/de-potentie-van-de-circulaire economie/.

Schröder, Patrick, Alexandre Lemille, and Peter Desmond. 2020. "Making the Circular Economy Work for Human Development." *Resources, Conservation and Recycling*, 156: 104686.

Sonerud, Beate. 2014. "Meeting the Financing Needs of Circular Business." https://ec .europa.eu/environment/ecoap/about-eco-innovation/policies-matters/eu/study examines-financing-barriers-facing-circular-economy-business-models_en.

Winans, Kiara, Alissa Kendall, and H. Deng. 2017. "The History and Current Applications of the Circular Economy Concept." *Renewable and Sustainable Energy Reviews*, 68: 825–33.

World Economic Forum, Ellen MacArthur Foundation, & McKinsey & Company. 2014. *Towards the Circular Economy: Accelerating the Scale -Up Across Global Supply Chains*. Geneva: World Economic Forum. https://doi.org/10.1162 /108819806775545321.

World Travel and Tourism Council. 2018 (WTTC 2018). *Travel and Tourism Economic Impact 2018 Caribbean*. United Kingdom: World Travel and Tourism Council.

Worrell, DeLisle, Desiree Cherebin, and Tracy Polius-Mounsey. 2001. "Financial System Soundness in the Caribbean: An Initial Assessment." IMF Working Paper WP/01/123. Washington, International Monetary Fund.

UN Environment. 2018. "Waste Management Outlook for Latin America and the Caribbean." United Nations Environment Programme, Latin America and the Caribbean Office. Panama City, Panama. https://www.unep.org/ietc/resources/ publication/waste-management-outlook latin-america-and-caribbean.

8

What Drives Economic Complexity?

Panel Data Evidence from Latin America and the Caribbean

VAALMIKKI ARJOON

Introduction

The production structure of economies plays a pivotal role in driving their growth, export competitiveness, and income generation. Economic complexity has emerged as an important measure of the degree of sophistication of these production structures (see Hidalgo et al. 2007; Hausmann, Hwang, and Rodrik, 2007; Hausmann et al. 2014; Hidalgo and Hausmann 2009). Specifically, countries with higher levels of economic complexity have several diverse industries that place greater emphasis on using technical knowledge, innovation, and superior technologies to produce a mix of commodities for both local consumption and export. What is also distinctive about these knowledge-based commodities is that they have low ubiquity, as they can only be produced by a few countries. By the same token, countries with low economic complexity have less diversified production structures. The items which they produce are usually also available from many other countries in the international market, as they do not require significant technical expertise and advanced scientific knowledge for production. In this line of thinking, a more complex production structure is associated with a higher knowledge base, skilled labor force, and diversification. Therefore, transforming the production system to one that is more complex can derive several benefits for the whole economy. For instance, a diversified economy with several industries that use high-tech equipment and innovative production strategies can improve productivity, lower the cost of production, and therefore stimulate increased output levels, bringing higher GDP growth. The existence of several diverse industries also creates more productive employment opportunities and lowers income inequality (see Hartmann et al. 2017). Economic complexity also increases export competitiveness, since having a diverse product line that is only manufactured by a few other countries protects the economy from international commodity price fluctuations, contributes to the stability of export earnings, and improves the balance of payments (see Sepehrdoust, Setarehie, and Davarikish 2020). Motivated by these clear benefits of economic complexity, this chapter investigates what drives economic complexity in a panel of economies in Latin America and Caribbean (LAC).

This study is related to a new and emerging literature on economic complexity and its importance for economic prosperity. Studies including Hidalgo et al. (2007), Hausmann, Hwang, and Rodrik (2007), Hidalgo and Hausmann (2009), and Hausmann et al. (2014) introduced the economic complexity metric to quantify the capabilities of the factors of production, and the sophistication and diversity of a country's production structure. The authors stress that the production of any commodity requires knowledge. Economic complexity, therefore, reflects the degree of knowledge that economies possess, as diverse and unique product lines require relatively more skills and technical know-how to produce. They also show that complexity drives income levels and future growth – a result that is also corroborated by Felipe et al. (2012), Caldarelli et al. (2012), Cristelli, Tacchella, and Pietronero (2015), and Zhu and Li (2017). This positive effect of complexity on growth is further enhanced by improvements in human capital, both in the short and long term (see Zhu and Li 2017). Complexity is also shown to lower income inequality, as a complex production structure has several diverse economic sectors, allowing for increased employment opportunities (see Hartman et al. 2017). It further encourages greater foreign direct investment (FDI), as foreign firms may be attracted to the increased levels of productive knowledge, human capital performance, and economic growth, commonly featured in economies with a complex production structure (see Sadeghi et al. 2020).

Indeed, such findings highlight that development efforts should focus on generating conditions that allow the emergence of greater complexity. Gala et al. (2018) document that complexity improves with an increase in manufacturing and sophisticated jobs in the services sector. Recently, Nguyen, Schinckus, and Su (2020) find that it also improves with patents and financial development. Patents signify the creation of new knowledge and innovation, while financial development enables greater funding opportunities for the creation of these patents. Complexity also progresses due to trade liberalization, as is shown by Sepehrdoust, Setarehie, and Davarikish (2020), since it allows for more imports of medium and final capital goods for the production process and increased FDI. However, research into what drives complexity is still limited, and the existing studies only focus on the effect of a narrow range of socioeconomic factors on complexity. As such, the current understanding of what influences complexity is under-investigated. This article therefore contributes to the literature by investigating the influence of a series of financial development, institutional quality, and macroeconomic indicators on economic complexity.

The rationale for assessing the effects of these variables is as follows. A large literature has shown that a developed financial system is growth enhancing, as it allows for more funds to be channeled into the most profitable uses (see Levine 2005, for a review of these studies). It is therefore reasonable to expect that financial development may affect the complexity of an economy's production structure, as greater access to capital might promote the financing of research and innovation-led sectors, together with the ability to import more sophisticated technologies, which have direct implications for export diversity. Weak institutions such as significant procedural hurdles that entrepreneurs and firms endure when doing business, poor contract enforcement, and corruption cause meager economic performance (see Kolstad and Søreide 2009). This may also influence complexity by affecting the willingness of entrepreneurs to invest and state officials misusing funds which otherwise could have been used to increase technical skillsets and create more diverse industrial activities. Several macroeconomic variables may also impact complexity, such as FDI, increased wealth creation, and government investment expenditure, if directed to building diverse and sophisticated economic sectors.

The analysis is conducted using data from eighteen LAC economies – which is another major contribution of this chapter, as there is no other empirical investigation on economic complexity for this region. Indeed, LAC economies demonstrated strong growth performance from 2000 to 2019, averaging 2.53 percent. However, despite implementing several financial reforms and increasing the scope of financial services since the 1970s, access to finance and financial inclusion remains an obstacle for many firms in the region. Furthermore, institutional quality in the region continues to languish due to corruption by state officials, political instability, inept implementation of the rule of law, and little improvements in procedural bureaucracy in state agencies – all of which erode the region's economic well-being. Further, countries in this region have varying levels of complexity. For instance, out of 133 countries globally, Mexico is ranked in the nineteenth position with a score of 1.29. Costa Rica is ranked forty-seventh with a score of 0.33. These scores suggest a more sophisticated and diverse production structure, that is, higher complexity, relative to economies such as Panama and Jamaica, both ranked seventy-fourth and ninety-second with scores of −0.24 and −0.58, respectively, suggesting lower complexity. Taken together, these features make the LAC region an ideal setting to develop a better understanding of what drives economic complexity.

The empirical strategy relies on panel co-integration methods. The results show that improvements in institutional quality, specifically greater control of corruption and economic freedom, lead to an increase in economic complexity. In contrast, the financial development variables, including private-sector credit and international reserves, have a negative effect. This effect, however, is reduced with improvements in institutional quality. The macroeconomic fundamentals, including debt and gross fixed capital formation, are also found to stymie economic complexity, while FDI and GDP per capita have positive effects. The results further show that institutional quality mitigates the negative effect of gross fixed capital formation and debt.

The rest of this chapter is organized as follows. The second section discusses the empirical strategy, and the third section describes the data used in this study. The fourth section reports the empirical findings. Conclusions and policy recommendations are set out in the final section of this chapter.

Empirical Strategy

In this section, I present the main empirical models and the econometric methods used to estimate these models.

Baseline Model

The first step in our empirical strategy is to analyze the effect of institutional quality and financial development on economic complexity. For this purpose, the following baseline regression is estimated:

$$EC_{i,t} = \alpha + \eta \varphi_{i,t} + \lambda \gamma_{i,t} + \varepsilon_{i,t} \tag{1}$$

with $i = 1, \ldots, 19$ countries over $t = 1, \ldots, 19$ years. The dependent variable $EC_{i,t}$ denotes economic complexity. $\varphi_{i,t}$ is a vector of institutional quality variables including control of corruption (CONTROL_CORRUPT) and economic freedom (ECON_FREEDOM). $\gamma_{i,t}$ is a vector of financial development indicators, namely private-sector credit (PS_CREDIT), international reserves (INTL_RESERVES), and broad money (BM).

The dependent variable $EC_{i,t}$ is measured using the economic complexity index, from MIT's Observatory of Economic Complexity (Simoes and Hidalgo 2011). This index measures how sophisticated a country's production structure is, by capturing information on (1) its economic diversification and (2) the ubiquity of its products (Hidalgo and Hausman 2009). Economic diversification denotes the extent to which a country produces and exports a diverse range of products. The ubiquity of these products reflects the number of countries that make these products. Therefore, countries with a higher EC have more sophisticated production structures, as they manufacture a diverse mix of products for exports, which are only produced and exported by few other countries, making them less ubiquitous. On the contrary, countries with a lower *EC* have less sophisticated production structures, as they tend to produce and export a few diverse and highly ubiquitous commodities, as these commodities are also produced in many other countries.

To compute the index, Hausman et al. (2014) first uses export data to determine the revealed comparative advantage (RCA) of a country *i*, defined as *i*'s total share of global exports of product *p* divided by *i*'s share of the total global exports:

$$RCA_{i,p} = \frac{X_{i,p}\big/\sum_{p'} X_{ip'}}{\sum_{i'} X_{i'p}\big/\sum_{i'p'} X_{i'p'}}$$

(2)

where $X_{i,p}$ is the total export of country *i* in product *p*. A value greater than 1 implies that country *i* has a comparative advantage in product *p*. The RCA is then used to define a matrix $M_{i,p}$ which takes a value of 1 if country *i* has an RCA for product *p* and 0 otherwise:

$$M_{i,p} = 1 \text{ if } RCA_{i,p} \geq 1$$

$$M_{i,p} = 0 \text{ if } RCA_{i,p} < 1$$

(3)

From this matrix $M_{i,p}$ we can define economic diversification as the number of products exported by a country with comparative advantage and ubiquity as the number of countries that export a product with a comparative advantage.

$$Diversity = k_{i,0} = \sum_{p} M_{i,p}$$

$$Ubiquity = k_{p,0} = \sum_{i} M_{i,p}$$

(4)

The following matrix is then constructed, which connects countries exporting similar products weighted by the inverse of the ubiquity of a product, and normalized by the diversity of a country:

$$\tilde{M}_{ii'} = \frac{1}{k_{i,0}} \sum_{p} \frac{M_{i,p} M_{i',p}}{k_{p,0}}$$

(5)

The $EC_{i,t}$ index is then computed as:

$$EC_i = \frac{K_c - \langle K \rangle}{std(K)} \qquad (6)$$

where K_i is the eigenvector $\tilde{M}_{ii'}$ associated with the second largest eigenvalue, given that the vector associated with the largest eigenvalue is a vector of ones which are not informative.

Turning to the independent variables, I measure CONTROL_CORRUPT using the World Bank's control of corruption index. This index specifically gauges the degree and frequency of corruption in government administrations, public institutions, and private companies, where a higher value indicates less corruption. It assumes that corruption increases transaction costs and uncertainty in economic transactions. ECON_FREEDOM is measured using the index of economic freedom provided by the *Wall Street Journal* and the Heritage Foundation. It captures a multitude of the political and economic institutional features of a country, which include the following. First, it incorporates information on the rule of law, measuring (for instance, how well a country protects private and intellectual property rights) the risk of expropriation of assets, degree of investor protection, and government integrity. Second, it also considers the size of the government, including fiscal health, tax burdens, and government spending. The third institutional feature is regulatory efficiency, such as the time taken and cost involved in starting a business, obtaining licenses and permits, and getting electricity. Fourth, the index also captures the openness of the market, such as trade, investment, and freedom (such as the extent of government regulations and intervention into the activities of financial firms). A higher index suggests better institutional quality in the country. For the financial development variables, PS_CREDIT denotes domestic credit (loans) to the private sector expressed as a percentage of GDP. INTL_RESERVES is measured using the total US dollar value of the international reserves owned by a country expressed as a percentage of GDP, while BM is measured as the total money supply (M2) as a percentage of GDP.

Model Extension

The second step in the empirical strategy considers an extension to the baseline model in eq. (1), which examines the impact of key macroeconomic fundamentals on economic complexity. The extended model also allows us to assess the robustness of the baseline model result. The model is specified as:

$$EC_{i,t} = \alpha + \eta \varphi_{i,t} + \lambda \gamma_{i,t} + \mu \xi_{i,t} + \varepsilon_{i,t} \qquad (7)$$

where $\xi_{i,t}$ is a vector of macroeconomic variables including gross fixed capital formation (*GFCF*), government debt (*DEBT*), FDI, and GDP per capita (*GDP_PC*).

GFCF is measured as government investment expenditure expressed as a percentage of GDP. This is government expenditure on areas intended to increase value added and future production levels in the economy, such as investing in infrastructure (factory upgrades, roads, highways, ports, and other transportation networks), research and innovation, and developing productive capacity. *DEBT* is measured as the total government debt to GDP ratio. This debt consists of liabilities that require payments of interest or principal by the government in the future. *FDI* denotes the net inflows of foreign direct investment expressed as a percentage of GDP, indicating the level of investment made by international entities in the domestic economy. Finally, *GDP_PC* is used as a proxy of a country's economic wealth.

Econometric Methods

The first step in the econometric analysis involves testing whether each of the variables in eqs (1) and (7) are stationary. For this purpose, the panel unit root tests of Levin, Lin, and Chu (2002) (LLC) and the Fisher-Phillips Perron (PPF) tests proposed by Maddala and Wu's (1999) are applied. These tests assume that the null hypothesis is an individual unit root process. The PPF test further accounts for unobserved country heterogeneity, which is a key advantage over the LLC test.

Once the panel unit root tests indicate the presence of a unit root in each variable, I then apply the panel co-integration test of Pedroni (1999, 2004) to determine whether there is a co-integrating (long-run) relationship among these variables. This test controls for unobserved country heterogeneity by allowing for differences in the co-integration vectors among the countries in our panel. It involves estimating eleven statistics to test for co-integration – eight based on the "within" dimension and three based on the "between" dimension. Each of these tests focus on the null hypothesis of no co-integrating relationship.

While Pedroni's (1999, 2004) procedure tests for co-integration, it does not estimate the long-run relationship between economic complexity and the independent variables in eqs (1) and (7). Therefore, once the presence of co-integration is established, I then apply two methods proposed by Kao and Chiang (2000) to estimate the long-run relationship – Fully Modified OLS (FMOLS) and Dynamic OLS (DOLS). Both of these methods are superior to other panel estimators such as pooled OLS, since they correct for serial correlation in the errors and potential endogeneity bias among the regressors, which are normally found in long-run relationships.

The FMOLS estimator is derived by correcting for endogeneity and serial correlation to the OLS coefficient estimates in eqs (1) and (7) and is defined as:

$$\beta_{j,FMOLS} = \frac{\left[\sum_{i=1}^{N} \left(\sum_{t=1}^{T} \left(X_{i,t} - \bar{X}_i \right) EC_{i,t}^+ + T\hat{\Delta}_{\varepsilon\mu}^+ \right) \right]}{\left[\sum_{i=1}^{N} \sum_{t=1}^{T} \left(X_{i,t} - \bar{X}_i \right)' \right]} \tag{8}$$

where $\beta_{j,FMOLS}$ is the FMOLS coefficient estimates for each independent variable j in eqs (1) and (7), N = eighteen countries (cross-sections) that comprise our sample and T = nineteen years. $T\hat{\Delta}_{\varepsilon\mu}^+$ corrects for serial correlation and $EC_{i,t}^+$ is the transformed dependent variable which corrects for any endogeneity bias among the regressors.

The DOLS estimator overcomes serial correlation and endogeneity issues by augmenting eqs (1) and (7) to include lags and leads of the first difference of the $I(1)$ regressors. The DOLS model is specified as:

$$EC_{i,t} = \alpha_i + X_{i,t}' \beta_{j,DOLS} + \sum_{l=-Q}^{Q} \eta_{i,l} \Delta X_{i,t+l} + v_{i,t} \tag{9}$$

where X' denotes the regressors from eq. (1), $\Delta X_{i,t+1}$ accounts for any endogeneity among the regressors. $\beta_{j,DOLS}$ is the DOLS coefficient estimates and is given by:

$$\beta_{j,DOLS} = \frac{\sum_{t=1}^{T} z_{i,t} EC_{i,t}^+}{\sum_{i=1}^{N} \left(\sum_{t=1}^{T} p_{i,t} p_{i,t}' \right)}; \tag{10}$$

where $p_{i,t} = \left[X_{i,t} - \bar{X}_i, \Delta X_{i,t-Q}, \ldots, \Delta X_{i,t+Q} \right]$ is a $2(Q+1) \times 1$ vector of regressors.

Data

All variables in eqs (1) and (7) are measured annually over the period 2000 to 2018. The data are collected for a sample of eighteen countries from the LAC region, including Argentina, Bolivia, Brazil, Chile, Columbia, Costa Rica, Dominican Republic, Ecuador, El Salvador, Guatemala, Jamaica, Honduras, Mexico, Nicaragua, Panama, Paraguay, Trinidad and Tobago, and Venezuela. Table 8.1 presents the definitions of each variable and the data source.

Time plots of the dependent variable EC for each country in our sample are presented in figure 8.1. Among the countries, seven of them show negative indices for the full sample period, namely Chile, Ecuador, Guatemala, Honduras, Nicaragua, Paraguay, and Venezuela. Consistent negative indices suggest that

Table 8.1 Variable definitions

Variable	Definition	Data Source
EC	Economic complexity index	Atlas of Economic Complexity, Centre for International Development, Harvard University
CONTROL_ CORRUPT	Control of corruption index	World Bank Worldwide Governance Indicators
ECON_FREEDOM	Index of economic freedom	The Heritage Foundation and *Wall Street* Journal
PS_CREDIT	Credit to the private sector (% of GDP)	World Bank World Development Indicators
BM	Broad money (M2) (% of GDP)	Inter-American Development Bank
INTL_RESERVES	International reserves (% of GDP)	Inter-American Development Bank
GFCF	Gross fixed capital formation (% of GDP)	Inter-American Development Bank
DEBT	Government debt (% of GDP)	Inter-American Development Bank
FDI	Net foreign direct investment inflows (% of GDP)	Inter-American Development Bank
GDP_PC	GDP per capita	Inter-American Development Bank

Notes: All variables are measured annually for the period 2000 to 2018.

these countries may have the least sophisticated production structure in our sample, as they have limited diversification and produce mainly commodities that are highly ubiquitous. This may be due to most of these countries being dominated by natural resource and extraction industries. For instance, the largest industry and exporter in Chile is the copper industry, which accounts for 37.47 percent of their exports. Paraguay's largest industry is based on soybeans, making up 35.75 percent or the largest share of its exports. Both Venezuela and Ecuador focus heavily on petroleum and its related products, which form 75.84 percent and 33.46 percent of their exports, respectively. Other economies such as Honduras, and to a lesser extent Nicaragua, have a fairly large ICT export sector (17.25 percent and 9.35 percent), which suggests investment in technological innovation, but their products may also be produced and exported by many countries globally. This, together with a less diversified production structure, is likely accounting for their persistent negative index.

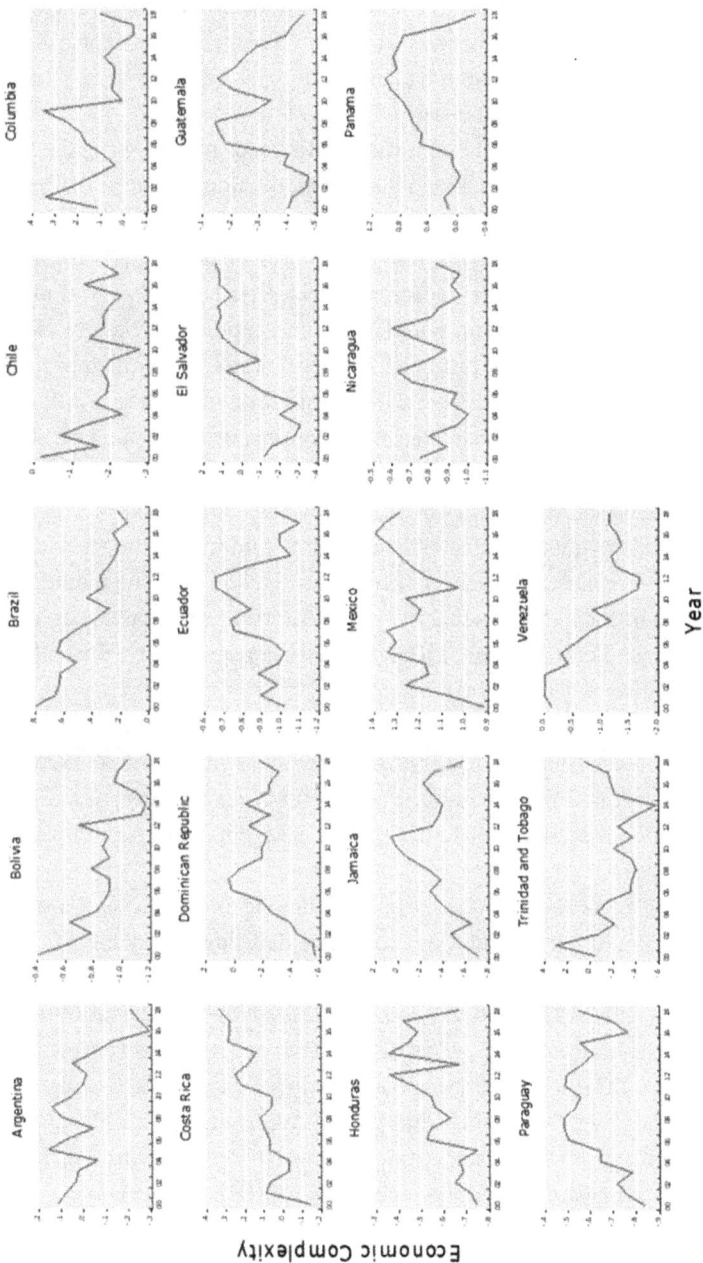

Figure 8.1 Economic complexity index.

Countries such as Trinidad and Tobago and Jamaica experience a very short window of positive complexity, but the index is mainly negative for the majority of the sample period. Again, this is because both Trinidad and Tobago focus heavily on its extractive industries with over 75 percent of its exports based on hydrocarbon commodities and its derivatives. For Jamaica, over 88 percent of its exports come from the tourism sector.

The figure also shows that Brazil and Mexico enjoy positive *EC* indices for the overall sample period, reflecting a diverse production structure that produces less ubiquitous commodities. For instance, in Mexico, over 25 percent of their exports comprise of a diverse range of motor vehicle-based commodities, including cars, tractors, parts for motor vehicles, trailers and semi-trailers, and parts for aircrafts. They also manufacture and export a variety of electronic items such as telephones, insulated electrical wires, transmission apparatus for radio and televisions, monitors and projectors, to name a few. Electronic items account for over 15 percent of its exports. Such a production structure may suggest a more sophisticated production structure that uses technological equipment and innovation. Costa Rica and El Salvador both appear to improve in their *EC*, moving from negative to positive values over the sample period. This is because Costa Rica diversified its production into the manufacturing of equipment such as medicinal instruments, orthopedic appliances, sporting equipment, and optical fibers. El Salvador also appears to have diversified into ICT and a diverse range of textile items.

Descriptive statistics for the variables in our analyses are presented in table 8.2. The distributions of all variables are highly non-normal, skewed, and more concentrated than the normal distribution with longer tails. The panel co-integration methods applied in this study are robust to these features of the data.

Table 8.3 presents pairwise correlation among the variables, as observed over the sample period 2000 to 2018. The dependent variable *EC* appears to be highly positively correlated with both institutional quality variables: *CONTROL_CORRUPT* and *ECON_FREEDOM*. Two of the three financial development indicators (*PS_CREDIT* and *BM*) are negatively correlated with *EC*. Further, *EC* is also negatively correlated with two of the macroeconomic fundamentals *DEBT* and *GFCF*, but positively correlated with *FDI* and *GDP_PC*. The table also reveals some other noteworthy correlations. For instance, *DEBT* has a negative correlation with *PS_CREDIT*. This may suggest that government debt in the form of loans from banks crowds out private-sector borrowing. *FDI* is positively correlated with both institutional quality variables, which could potentially imply that foreign firms are more inclined to invest in the local economy when there is less corruption and bureaucracy involved to

Table 8.2 Descriptive statistics

	EC	CONTROL_CORRUPT	ECON_FREEDOM	FS_CREDIT	BM	INTL_RESERVES	DEBT	GFCF	FDI	GDP_PC
Mean	-0.141	-0.341	61.472	31.849	30.442	13.279	49.868	20.663	2.829	6127.016
Median	-0.180	-0.413	62.000	27.130	28.020	12.390	40.810	20.430	2.475	5091.000
Maximum	1.393	1.592	79.000	92.410	83.520	51.340	251.450	41.260	14.580	21179.160
Minimum	-1.684	-1.400	36.100	7.520	5.210	0.990	16.181	11.080	-3.360	885.230
Std. Dev	0.593	0.629	8.404	19.045	15.292	8.046	32.937	4.501	2.751	3890.737
Skewness	0.484	1.382	-0.433	1.114	1.160	2.469	2.635	1.117	0.482	0.888
Kurtosis	3.391	5.010	3.452	3.820	4.977	11.474	12.474	6.349	3.846	3.162
Jarque-Bera	12.495	133.781	10.936	64.614	106.498	1102.246	1346.666	185.656	18.783	36.424

Table 8.3 Pairwise correlation coefficients

	EC	CONTROL_CORRUPT	ECON_FREEDOM	PS_CREDIT	BM	INTL_RESERVES	GFCF	DEBT	FDI	GDP_PC
ECI	1									
CONTROL_CORRUPT	0.308**	1								
ECON_FREEDOM	0.404**	0.658**	1							
PS_CREDIT	-0.311**	0.468**	0.357**	1						
BM	0.311**	0.377**	0.320**	0.761**	1					
INTL_RESERVES	-0.251**	0.063	-0.034	0.115*	-0.048	1				
GFCF	-0.125**	0.060	0.084	0.274**	0.363**	-0.162**	1			
DEBT	-0.158**	-0.125**	0.055	-0.115*	-0.279**	-0.019	-0.107*	1		
FDI	0.322***	0.278**	0.285**	0.343**	0.186**	0.020	0.423**	-0.027	1	
GDP_PC	0.354**	0.413**	0.077	0.215**	0.351**	-0.075	0.130**	-0.229**	-0.006	1

Notes: ***, **, and * denote statistical significance at the 1 percent, 5 percent, and 10 percent levels, respectively.

acquire permits. *DEBT* and *GFCF* are negatively correlated, which could point to governments not spending debt financing on building productive capacity, but instead using it for recurrent expenditure.

The results of the unit root tests are presented in table 8.4. Each variable when first differenced is stationary at the 1 percent significance level and therefore meets the criteria for the panel co-integration test.

Table 8.5 shows the outcome of the Pedroni (1999; 2004) co-integration analysis. With the exception of the weighted *v*–Stat, the results of the within and between-group tests offer strong support for the existence of a long-run relationship among the variables in eq. (1).

Table 8.4 Panel unit root test results

	LLC	PPF
EC	−1.095	40.739
Δ*EC*	−17.429***	271.011***
CONTROL_CORRUPT	−0.483	39.686
Δ*CONTROL_CORRUPT*	−15.217***	265.816***
ECON_FREEDOM	−0.368	34.121
Δ*ECON_FREEDOM*	−8.796***	213.104***
PS_CREDIT	0.589	16.097
Δ*PS_CREDIT*	−10.533	77.972***
BM	−0.4061	18.897
Δ*BM*	−10.439***	114.530***
INTL_RESERVES	1.644	13.318
Δ*INTL_RESERVES*	−11.073***	163.274***
DEBT	−0.234	40.879
Δ*DEBT*	−10.803***	167.584***
GFCF	0.679	15.884
Δ*GFCF*	−13.405***	232.603***
FDI	1.3924	18.094
Δ*FDI*	−12.449***	177.123***
GDP_PC	1.1855	29.257
Δ*GDP_PC*	−15.158***	85.493***

Notes: LLC and PPF represent the panel unit root tests of Levin, Lin, and Chu (2002) and the Fisher-Phillips Perron panel unit root tests of Maddala and Wu (1999), respectively. The lag length is selected using the Schwarz information criterion (SIC). The bandwidth is selected using the Newey–West method, while Bartlett is used as the spectral estimation. Test statistics are reported. ***, **, and * denote statistical significance at the 1 percent, 5 percent, and 10 percent levels, respectively.

Table 8.5 Pedroni panel co-integration test results

	Within Dimension (Panel Statistics)		Between dimension
	Weighted Statistics		
v – Stat	1.731**	−4.222	
	(0.028)	(0.974)	
Rho	2.701***	5.851*	6.378**
	(0.003)	(0.061)	(0.040)
PP	−9.535***	−6.313***	−8.490***
	(0.000)	(0.000)	(0.000)
ADF	−7.357***	−5.667***	−5.467***
	(0.000)	(0.000)	(0.000)

Notes: Test statistics are reported with p-values in parenthesis. ***, **, and * denote statistical significance at the 1 percent, 5 percent, and 10 percent levels, respectively.

Table 8.6 Baseline specification results

	FMOLS	DOLS
CORRUPT	0.1628***	0.3287***
	(0.0000)	(0.0000)
ECON_FREEDOM	0.0211***	0.0121***
	(0.0000)	(0.0000)
PS_CREDIT	−0.5611***	−0.3316***
	(0.0000)	(0.0000)
INTL_RESERVES	−0.0094***	−0.0136***
	(0.0000)	(0.0000)
BM	0.0195***	0.0153***
	(0.0000)	(0.0000)

Note: ***, **, and * denote statistical significance at 1 percent, 5 percent, and 10 percent, respectively.

Table 8.6 presents the results of the baseline regression eq. (1). We find that CONTROL_CORRUPT is positively associated with the EC. Indeed, lower corruption improves the efficiency of state expenditure, as government officials are more likely to direct expenditure in developing new and productive sectors in the economy to build export complexity, rather than allocating it to specific sectors where they can extort bribes. When state funds are lost to corruption, there is less left for the state to invest in technological advancement and scientific knowledge required for creating new and diverse industries, thereby limiting complexity. Moreover, corruption can also impede diversification and complexity, as it may be associated with artificial bottlenecks in the supply chain.

For instance, in many LAC economies, customs can delay access to important raw materials and machinery, unless bribes or special favors are paid. This impedes the production process, which naturally has negative implications for complexity. It may also lower the confidence of local and foreign private-sector entities, deterring them from expanding and diversifying their operations. Lower corruption levels, however, may encourage the private sector to expand and diversify their operations, invest in technology or even establish new business ventures altogether, which can have positive implications for export diversity and complexity.

We also find that *ECON_FREEDOM* has a positive effect on *EC*. This suggests that in general, improvements in the health of institutions encourage the production of a more sophisticated mix of export commodities. For instance, those economies that promote intellectual property rights have a low risk of asset expropriation and protects minority investors. This might generate added private-sector confidence and encourage them to expand or diversify the scale of their operations. It may also motivate them to invest in more advanced technologies and make efficient use of factor endowments for a faster and less costly manufacturing process. This also improves product sophistication and diversity for export. Further, complexity increases when the private sector experiences less bureaucracy when trying to accomplish essential procedures with public service entities. These may include registering a new business, obtaining permits and licenses, submitting documents and payment for international trade, getting electricity, to name a few. In the LAC region, these procedures can be generally lengthy with high costs, creating obstacles in the overall supply chain. When these procedures are made simpler and less costly, it enables for faster and more diverse commercial and industrial activities, which improve complexity. For instance, in the LAC region, it takes an average of 191 days to obtain a building permit (World Bank 2019). Reducing this time can help a small manufacturing firm to establish a new factory in a timely manner, thereby facilitating an increase in its production line for export.

Turning to *PS_CREDIT*, we find that it is negatively associated with *EC*. It is possible that this result is driven by inequities in the provision of credit financing to the private sector. For instance, due to intense competition for loans, small and medium-sized enterprise (SME) firms in the LAC region find it more difficult to acquire credit from financial institutions, as they are regarded as riskier with a higher chance of default (Presbitero and Rabellotti 2016; Wang 2016; Broome, Moore, and Alleyne 2018; Williams 2018). This limits their ability to invest in technological advancement and technical knowledge in order to expand and diversify their product mix. Large companies, which are far fewer in number, tend to receive the greater part of credit financing. Much of these funds are likely spent on importing final goods for resale in the country in which they are operating and not necessarily to further develop export capacity or a more sophisticated and diverse mix of export products. It is also possible that the majority of credit financing allotted to generate export production focuses on a limited range of commodities. This might be due to these commodities earning high export revenues historically and being considered as less risky, compared to investing in a new range of products. These reasons might account for the negative association between private-sector credit and complexity.

Similar to *PS_CREDIT*, we also find that *INTL_RES* has a negative association with the *ECI*. A large portion of the firms in the LAC region tend to focus heavily on importing final goods for resale in the local market. Therefore, an increase in foreign currency reserves is likely to cause these firms to increase imports of final goods. Those firms involved in manufacturing activities may use this currency to import more of the same raw materials and machinery to increase production of the items that they historically produce, especially if they perceive these items to earn sustainable export revenues. They may not be willing to take on additional risk and venture into a different and innovative production line by using the foreign currency to import new and more advanced inputs for production, which could then foster increased complexity.

However, the third indicator of financial development *BM* appears to be positively related to *ECI*. Indeed, increased financial development reflects higher liquidity available to firms in the private sector and state enterprises. This gives them the ability to invest in greater technological innovation and skills training for the production of more sophisticated and diverse export commodities. In addition, financial development is associated with increased financial services and a better functioning financial market. These can mobilize finances to more productive physical capital, which can boost the production of diversified and unique product lines for export.

I also examine whether institutional quality causes a differential response of *EC* to financial development. For this purpose, eq. (1) is re-estimated to include an interaction term between institutional quality and financial development as follows:

$$EC_{i,t} = \alpha + \eta \varphi_{i,t} + \lambda \gamma_{i,t} + \delta \left(\varphi_{i,t} \times \gamma_{i,t} \right) + \varepsilon_{i,t} \qquad (11)$$

A significant coefficient on the interaction term δ would suggest that institutional quality does indeed affect the relationship between financial development and *EC*.

Table 8.7 shows the FMOLS and DOLS regression estimates when *CORRUPT_CONTROL* is interacted with the financial development variables.

Table 8.7 Interaction effects of corruption and financial depth on economic complexity

	FMOLS			DOLS		
	(1)	(2)	(3)	(4)	(5)	(6)
CORRUPT_CONTROL	2.2395***	2.1794***	3.2723***	1.8016***	1.6136***	2.4868***
	(0.0000)	(0.0000)	(0.0000)	(0.0000)	(0.0000)	(0.0000)
ECON_FREEDOM	0.0221***	0.0259***	0.0293***	0.0192***	0.0192***	0.0215***
	(0.0000)	(0.0000)	(0.0000)	(0.0000)	(0.0000)	(0.0000)
PS_CREDIT	−0.7141***	−0.3850***	−0.4474***	−0.6037***	−0.2904***	−0.2856***
	(0.0000)	(0.0000)	(0.0000)	(0.0000)	(0.0000)	(0.0000)
BM	0.4439***	0.0192*	0.4802***	0.3426***	0.0308***	0.3274***
	(0.0000)	(0.0573)	(0.0000)	(0.0000)	(0.0000)	(0.0000)
INTL_RESERVES	−0.1197***	−0.1368***	−0.7696***	−0.1135*	−0.1481***	−0.5938***
	(0.0000)	(0.0000)	(0.0000)	(0.0600)	(0.0000)	(0.0000)
CORRUPT_CONTROL×PS_CREDIT	0.5503***			−0.4373***		
	(0.0000)			(0.0000)		
CORRUPT_CONTROL×BM		−0.5660***			−0.4166***	
		(0.0000)			(0.0000)	
CORRUPT_CONTROL×INTL_RESERVES			−1.2185***			−0.8481***
			(0.0000)			(0.0000)

Note: ***, **, and * denote statistical significance at 1 percent, 5 percent, and 10 percent, respectively.

Moving across each column, we find the results generally corroborate our findings for the baseline model eq. (1) in table 8.5. In addition, the interaction terms are all positive and statistically significant, suggesting that increased control of corruption mitigates the negative effects of *PS_CREDIT* and *INTL_RES* on *EC* and enhances the positive association between *BM* and *EC*.

The result for *CORRUPT_CONTROL×PS_CREDIT* in column (1) may be explained by the following reason. Indeed, lower corruption may arise because of increased regulations and standards for processing loans to avoid asymmetric information and adverse selection issues.

There may be less incidence of bankers accepting bribes and favors for granting loan financing to specific members of the private sector. This suggests a more efficient allocation of loans across the private sector, allowing for credit to be redirected to the most productive firms. These firms can use this credit financing to invest in technological innovation, to produce diverse and sophisticated items for export.

A potential explanation for the positive coefficient on *CONTROL_CORRUPT×INTL_RES* in column (3) is as follows: Increased control of corruption suggests less opportunity for government officials to misuse foreign currency or corruptly increase their own holdings of foreign currency, which in fact belong to the state.

These foreign reserves may instead be allocated to industries, allowing them to import more cutting-edge technologies and other factor inputs to diversify into a more sophisticated production base for export.

In column (2), a possible reason for the result for *CONTROL_CORRUPT×BM* may be that with greater control over corruption, firms pay less bribes and therefore have more of their own internal financial resources available to them to invest in producing complex commodities. Moreover, less corruption can increase the private sector's confidence and therefore more firms would be inclined to spend their financial resources on new technical innovation to manufacture sophisticated export commodities.

Similar results are shown in table 8.8 when we interact *ECON_FREEDOM* with financial development. The point estimates on the interaction terms are all positive and statistically significant, suggesting that *ECON_FREEDOM* can also be regarded as an important channel to improve the effect of financial development on complexity.

These findings can be attributed to various reasons. Improvement in economic freedom involves better contract enforcement and property rights. It also means there are fewer procedural bottlenecks in the supply chain, thereby making it easier for firms to access licenses and permits from state entities.

Table 8.8 Interaction effects of economic freedom and financial depth on economic complexity

	FMOLS				DOLS	
	(1)	(2)	(3)	(4)	(5)	(6)
CORRUPT_CONTROL	0.1101***	0.2212***	0.2023***	0.3272***	0.3063***	0.3402***
	(0.0000)	(0.0005)	(0.0000)	(0.0000)	(0.0000)	(0.0000)
ECON_FREEDOM	0.0036***	0.0119**	0.0232***	0.0070**	0.0054*	0.0080***
	(0.0000)	(0.0456)	(0.0000)	(0.0139)	(0.0619)	(0.0064)
PS_CREDIT	−0.8386***	−0.1397***	−0.1525***	−0.4190***	−0.2793***	−0.2844***
	(0.0000)	(0.0000)	(0.0000)	(0.0000)	(0.0000)	(0.0000)
BM	0.4265***	0.5876***	0.1594***	0.2708***	0.0607	0.2738***
	(0.0000)	(0.0000)	(0.0000)	(0.0000)	(0.3980)	(0.0000)
INTL_RESERVES	−0.1038***	−0.1280***	−0.1838***	−0.1952***	−0.1668***	−0.3293***
	(0.0000)	(0.0000)	(0.0000)	(0.0000)	(0.0001)	(0.0000)
ECON_FREEDOM×PS_CREDIT	0.0063***			0.0023*		
	(0.0000)			(0.0524)		
ECON_FREEDOM×BM		0.0070***			0.0035***	
		(0.0001)			(0.0000)	
ECON_FREEDOM×INTL_RESERVES			0.0045**			0.0120***
			(0.0173)			(0.0000)

Note: ***, **, and * denote statistical significance at 1 percent, 5 percent, and 10 percent, respectively.

It may also make it less burdensome, in terms of documentary compliance and customs delays, to access imports of essential inputs to production. This would encourage and speed up additional private-sector activities, including where more firms make use of credit financing, their own internal financing and foreign exchange to invest in technical inputs to production and scientific knowledge. These can lead to a greater mix of diverse and sophisticated products for export, in turn improving EC.

The estimation results of the extended model eq. (7) are presented in table 8.9. Again, these results largely confirm the findings for the baseline model eq. (1) in table 8.6. FDI is shown to improve EC. Indeed, increased FDI involves foreign investors and multinationals establishing operations in the host economy, leading to the development of new industries.

When setting up their operations, they bring advanced equipment and technologies, together with broadened managerial perspectives and technical

Table 8.9 Model extension regression results

	FMOL S	DOLS
	(1)	(4)
CORRUPT_CONTROL	0.0596***	0.2475***
	(0.0000)	(0.0000)
ECON_FREEDOM	0.0288***	0.0184***
	(0.0000)	(0.0000)
PS_CREDIT	−0.4403***	−0.3142***
	(0.0000)	(0.0000)
BM	0.2879***	0.1748***
	(0.0000)	(0.0000)
INTL_RESERVES	−0.1093***	−0.1672***
	(0.0000)	(0.0000)
DEBT	−0.1649***	−0.0974***
	(0.0000)	(0.0099)
FDI	0.0205***	0.0038
	(0.0000)	(0.6612)
GDP_PC	0.1840***	0.1331***
	(0.0000)	(0.0000)
GFCF	−0.6949***	−0.3738***
	(0.0000)	(0.0001)

Note: ***, **, and * denote statistical significance at the 1 percent, 5 percent, and 10 percent, respectively.

skills. These promote a lower cost of production and better productivity. All of these may promote increased export potential of diverse and sophisticated products.

Further, local companies over time may adopt some of the new technologies and innovative means of production introduced by the foreign company, allowing these local companies to diversify into new and complex products for export.

There may also be backward and forward linkages, also enabling increased activity and growth of domestic companies in other sectors through business dealings and partnerships. For instance, local companies in downstream industries may use the products created by the foreign entity as intermediate inputs for the production of new and sophisticated items for export purposes.

In Trinidad and Tobago and Brazil, for example, foreign companies in the upstream hydrocarbon sector supply oil and natural gas to local companies, which are used as inputs to produce other hydrocarbon-based commodities such as ammonia and methanol. Similar practices occur in Chile for copper.

A higher *GDP_PC* signals increased wealth in the economy, which is found to improve *EC*. As wealth increases, more local investors may be inclined to set up new ventures, while existing firms will have more funds available to diversify their operations.

Increased wealth in the economy may also encourage spending on research and innovation into the production of new and sophisticated goods for export purposes. It can similarly be used to deepen investments in underdeveloped sectors that have potential to manufacture complex products.

GFCF appears to have a negative relation with *EC*. This may suggest that in general, the government investment expenditure in LAC economies focus largely on limited industries which they conventionally regard as less risky and higher revenue generators. They may be less willing to invest into developing new industries, especially those that require technological innovation and knowledge base, as they may regard these industries to have a high level of uncertainty.

In contrast, when traditional industries stop providing a healthy source of national income, causing governments to have less revenues, then they may be more inclined to invest and diversify into innovative and newer industries, thereby increasing *EC*. The result may also be attributed to possible lower productivity and "value for money" in investment expenditure. For instance, the state may employ contractors who may overcharge when implementing capital projects. Some projects may also have long gestation periods due to low labor productivity and bureaucratic obstacles including delays in awarding construction permits, getting electricity, and imported equipment. These obstacles mitigate the extent to which any investment in new and diverse industries can be successful. There may also be instances where the state may prefer to focus most of their investment in specific industries, rather than build new ones, as they may find it easier to extort bribes and engage in other corrupt practices within these industries.

The results also show that *DEBT* has a negative effect on *EC*. A possible reason for this result is that government borrowings might not be well-spent on building productive capacity and developing new sectors. Indeed, many LAC economies use some debt financing to spend on recurrent budgetary expenditure, which carries lower rates of return (see Pessino, Izquierdo, and Vuletin 2018).

In addition, if the debt becomes too high, then it becomes difficult to repay. As such, the state may have to use part of their national savings to service the debt, which crowds out potential investment in new industries for the development of sophisticated commodities. Increasing debt levels can also negatively impact the economy's credit ratings. This can impair investor confidence, which can adversely affect complexity in a variety of ways.

For instance, it may lower investors' willingness to diversify their operations or set up new ones, particularly for developing complex products. It may also cause international suppliers of imported inputs used in the production process, such as raw materials machinery and technologies, to limit favorable credit terms, as they may become wary that the country may not be able to honor their payments in a timely manner. This can reduce the imports of such inputs necessary to facilitate the production of diverse and innovative items.

I also empirically show that bureaucratic obstacles and corrupt practices by state officials can influence the effect of *GFCF* and *DEBT* on *EC*. This is achieved by re-estimating eq. (7) to include an interaction term between the institutional quality variables and (1) *GFCF* and (2) *DEBT*.

The results are given in tables 8.10 and 8.11, respectively. In each case, the interaction terms are positive and statistically significant, suggesting that increased control of corruption and lower bureaucratic bottlenecks can indeed reduce the negative effect of *GFCF* and *DEBT* on *EC*.

A potential reason for this result is that better institutional quality enables for state funds and government expenditure to be directed to the most productive sectors, which use technical knowledge to foster diverse production.

Policy Implications for the COVID-19 Pandemic

The COVID-19 pandemic has highlighted the importance of having a complex economic structure. Indeed, the pandemic resulted in the closures of numerous businesses globally, including major suppliers of raw materials, machinery, and

Table 8.10 Interaction effects of institutional quality and gross fixed capital formation on economic complexity

	FMOLS		DOLS	
	(1)	(2)	(3)	(4)
CORRUPT_CONTROL	6.4657***	0.2447***	3.1082***	0.8011***
	(0.0000)	(0.0000)	(0.0002)	(0.0012)
ECON_FREEDOM	0.0401***	0.0418***		0.0202***
	(0.0000)	(0.0000)		(0.0000)
PS_CREDIT	−0.3862***	−0.3206***		−0.2617***
	(0.0000)	(0.0000)		(0.0001)
BM	0.3350***	0.2077***		0.2032***
	(0.0000)	(0.0000)		(0.0008)
INTL_RESERVES	−0.0506***	−0.0323***		−0.1731***
	(0.0000)	(0.0000)		(0.0032)
DEBT	−0.0420***	−0.0672***		0.0039
	(0.0000)	(0.0000)		(0.9458)
FDI	0.0101***	0.0027**		0.0055
	(0.0000)	(0.0390)		(0.6743)
GDP_PC	0.2787***	0.4211***		0.1785***
	(0.0000)	(0.0000)		(0.0000)
GFCF	−1.5012***	−1.9531***		−0.7602***
	(0.0000)	(0.0000)		(0.0001)
CORRUPT_CONTROL×GFCF	2.1618***			0.9789***
	(0.0000)			(0.0006)
ECON_FREEDOM×GFCF		0.0289***		
		(0.0000)		

Note: ***, **, and * denote statistical significance at the 1 percent, 5percent, and 10 percent, respectively.

technology for manufacturing firms operating in LAC. Many global shipping companies were also forced to halt their activities, so even if suppliers were still functioning, manufacturers faced significant delays in accessing their inputs for the production process. These supply chain disruptions could be avoided if LAC economies were more complex, thereby allowing them to source the inputs needed for the production process locally. The pandemic also significantly increased the worldwide demand for pharmaceutical drugs, which threatened to limit its accessibility for many LAC economies. Several countries faced delays in receiving medication from their usual suppliers due to the pressure of higher global demand and supply chain issues. This not only led

Table 8.11 Interaction effects of institutional quality and debt on economic complexity

	FMOLS		DOLS	
	(1)	(2)	(3)	(4)
CORRUPT_CONTROL	1.3667***	−0.1522***		0.7013***
	(0.0000)	(0.0000)		(0.0060)
ECON_FREEDOM	0.0286***	−0.0176***		0.0189***
	(0.0000)	(0.0000)		(0.0000)
PS_CREDIT	−0.4398***	−0.3526***		−0.3002***
	(0.0000)	(0.0000)		(0.0000)
BM	0.3294***	0.2175***		0.1812***
	(0.0000)	(0.0000)		(0.0000)
INTL_RESERVES	−0.0787***	−0.0659***		−0.1498***
	(0.0000)	(0.0000)		(0.0000)
DEBT	−0.3471***	−1.0397***		−0.1524***
	(0.0000)	(0.0000)		(0.0037)
FDI	0.0191***	0.0105***		0.0079
	(0.0000)	(0.0000)		(0.4681)
GDP_PC	0.2147***	0.3639***		0.1488***
	(0.0000)	(0.0000)		(0.0000)
GFCF	−0.6206***	−0.4396***		−0.3942***
	(0.0000)	(0.0000)		(0.0000)
CORRUPT_CONTROL×DEBT	0.3499***			0.1250*
	(0.0000)			(0.0688)
ECON_FREEDOM×DEBT		0.0156***		
		(0.0000)		

Note: ***, **, and * denote statistical significance at 1 percent, 5 percent, and 10 percent, respectively.

to a shortage of medication in certain countries, but also increased its prices. These consequences emphasize the importance of countries in the LAC region to bolster investments in research and production of pharmaceuticals, which is just one example where countries may improve their complexity.

The empirical results in this chapter can be applied to help LAC economies shape their policies to better overcome the economic challenges brought by the pandemic, through building greater complexity. This primarily involves making more efficient use of scare financial resources, eliminating unethical financial practices, and fixing institutional quality. To cope with the economic fallout due to the lockdowns imposed by the governments, countries would have received additional financing from multilateral agencies including the

IMF, World Bank, IADB, and CAF.[1] For instance, the IMF made US$ 250 billion available in financing for its member countries through a Rapid Credit Finance Facility, to mitigate the fallout of the pandemic. Some countries that benefitted from this financing include Bolivia (US$ 327 million), Dominican Republic (US$ 250 million), Ecuador (US$ 643 million), and Jamaica (US$ 520 million), to name a few. Central banks also created additional liquidity and lowered their repo rates, to make more finances available for the state and the private sector. Governments of the LAC region must be careful to not misappropriate these funds and ensure that none are lost due to corrupt activities by state officials. Instead, governments ought to carefully allocate a portion to technological advancement and scientific knowledge required for creating new and diverse industries. There should also be more equitable allocation of finances by banks to the private sector, especially to small firms, as they were more disadvantaged by the pandemic relative to large companies. Greater access to financing would allow them to not stay afloat but also to diversify their operations. The state also ought to urgently improve institutional quality, as this will simplify procedures in state agencies and render them less costly. This is necessary to create, accelerate, and diversify commercial and industrial activities in the private sector. Foreign exchange should also be spent on increasing research, technology, and innovative production, and to establish new sectors and develop existing ones. Using these approaches to build additional complexity will enable LAC economies to accelerate their recovery from the economic fallout due to the COVID pandemic. With higher complexity, these countries will also ultimately reduce their dependency on other economies for essential products, including inputs in the manufacturing process, food items, and pharmaceuticals to name a few, thus rendering the LAC more self-sufficient, export competitive, and better able to withstand future global economic shocks.

Conclusion and Policy Suggestions

Economic complexity involves creating a sophisticated production structure using technical knowledge to manufacture diverse commodities for the domestic market and for export – commodities that are only produced by a few other countries at most. Indeed, countries that have achieved high levels

---

[1] The IMF and the G-20 also implemented the Debt Service Suspension Initiative (DSSI) where creditors suspend debt repayments for some of the world's poorest countries.

of complexity enjoy increased employment, export competitiveness, growth, and lower income inequality. These clear benefits underscore the need to understand what drives economic complexity.

Using panel co-integration techniques and data from eighteen LAC countries, this chapter examines how institutional quality, financial development, and macroeconomic fundamentals influence economic complexity.

The empirical results show that institutional quality in the form of greater control of corruption and economic freedom leads to improvements in complexity.

In contrast, financial development appears to worsen complexity, but this effect is mitigated when institutional quality improves. Such a result might suggest that despite increased financial services and a greater flow of financial resources, capital may not be allocated to the most productive sectors and to invest in technical knowledge enabling varied sophisticated products to be manufactured. However, institutional quality improves the allocative efficiency of these finances, channeling them to develop more diverse sectors to produce less ubiquitous items for export.

The analysis further finds that government debt and government investment expenditure also have negative effects on complexity, but the negative effect of government investment expenditure is also mitigated with advancements in institutional quality. Again, this might suggest allocative inefficiency in state expenditure, but this inefficiency is lessened with improvements in institutional quality. Other macroeconomic indicators including FDI and GDP per capita are also found to improve complexity.

The findings of this study have important policy implications. First, it highlights a need for a more equitable distribution of capital by financial institutions, so that an increased number of SMEs can invest in building technical skills and acquiring technologies. This can enable them to produce diverse and innovative items for export.

Second, increasing the allocative efficiency in how funds are channeled by financial institutions and state expenditure can also ensure that monies are spent on creating a more diverse and sophisticated production structure.

Third, complexity in LAC economies can also benefit from improved institutional quality including lower corruption and less procedural bureaucracy that firms endure from state agencies. Lower corruption allows the state to invest in research, innovation, and building new industrial sectors, instead of projects where there is a greater risk of monies being lost due to bribery or extortion. Less bureaucratic bottlenecks in state agencies also allow firms to receive licenses and permits, submit trade documents, and make payments faster, which reduces delays in their operations. It also builds the private sector's confidence to invest in new production lines.

Establishing these conditions can effectively enhance complexity in LAC economies, which is not only essential to overcome the economic setbacks due to the pandemic but also to build economic resilience to future global economic shocks.

References

Broome, Tracey, Winston Moore, and Philmore Alleyne. 2018. "Financing Constraints and the R&D Decision in the Caribbean." *Entrepreneurship & Regional Development*, 30 (9–10): 964–86.

Caldarelli, G., M. Cristelli, A. Gabrielli, L. Pietronero, A. Scala, and A. Tacchella. 2012. "A Network Analysis of Countries' Export Flows: Firm Grounds for the Building Blocks of the Economy." *Plos one*, 7 (10): e47278.

Cristelli, Matthieu, Andrea Tacchella, and Luciano Pietronero. 2015. "The Heterogeneous Dynamics of Economic Complexity." *PloS one*, 10 (2): e0117174.

Felipe, Jesus, Utsav Kumar, Arnelyn Abdon, and Marife Bacate. 2012. "Product Complexity and Economic Development." *Structural Change and Economic Dynamics*, 23 (1): 36–68.

Gala, Paulo, Jhean Camargo, Guilherme Magacho, and Igor Rocha. 2018. "Sophisticated Jobs Matter for Economic Complexity: An Empirical Analysis Based on Input-Output Matrices and Employment Data." *Structural Change and Economic Dynamics*, 45: 1–8.

Hartmann, Dominik, Miguel R. Guevara, Cristian Jara-Figueroa, Manuel Aristarán, and César A. Hidalgo. 2017. "Linking Economic Complexity, Institutions, and Income Inequality." *World Development*, 93: 75–93.

Hausmann, Ricardo, César A. Hidalgo, Sebastián Bustos, Michele Coscia, and Alexander Simoes. 2014. *The Atlas of Economic Complexity: Mapping Paths to Prosperity*. MIT Press.

Hausmann, Ricardo, Jason Hwang, and Dani Rodrik. 2007. "What You Export Matters." *Journal of Economic Growth*, 12 (1): 1–25.

Hidalgo, César A., and Ricardo Hausmann. 2009. "The Building Blocks of Economic Complexity." *Proceedings of the National Academy of Sciences*, 106 (26): 10570–75.

Hidalgo, César A., Bailey Klinger, A.-L. Barabási, and Ricardo Hausmann. 2007. "The Product Space Conditions the Development of Nations." *Science*, 317 (5837): 482–87.

Kao, Chihwa, and Min Hsien Chiang. 2000. "On the Estimation and Inference of a Cointegrated Regression in Panel Data." In *Nonstationary Panels, Panel Cointegration, and Dynamic Panels*, Vol. 15, 179–222. Emerald Group Publishing Limited, Bingley.

Kolstad, Ivar, and Tina Søreide. 2009. "Corruption in Natural Resource Management: Implications for Policy Makers." *Resources Policy*, 34 (4): 214–26.

Levin, Andrew, Chien-Fu Lin, and Chia-Shang James Chu. 2002. "Unit Root Tests in Panel Data: Asymptotic and Finite-Sample Properties." *Journal of Econometrics*, 108 (1): 1–24.

Levine, Ross. 2005. "Finance and Growth: Theory and Evidence." *Handbook of Economic Growth*, 1: 865–934.

Maddala, Gangadharrao S., and Shaowen Wu. 1999. "A Comparative Study of Unit Root Tests with Panel Data and a New Simple Test." *Oxford Bulletin of Economics and Statistics*, 61 (S1): 631–52.

Nguyen, Canh Phuc, Christophe Schinckus, and Thanh Dinh Su. 2020. "The Drivers of Economic Complexity: International Evidence from Financial Development and Patents." *International Economics*, 164: 140–50.

Pedroni, Peter. 1999. "Critical Values for Cointegration Tests in Heterogeneous Panels with Multiple Regressors." *Oxford Bulletin of Economics and Statistics*, 61 (S1): 653–70.

———. 2004. "Panel Cointegration: Asymptotic and Finite Sample Properties of Pooled Time Series Tests with an Application to the Ppp Hypothesis." *Econometric Theory*, 20 (3): 597–625.

Pessino, Carola, Alejandro Izquierdo, and Guillermo Vuletin. 2018. *Better Spending for Better Lives: How Latin America and the Caribbean Can Do More with Less*. Vol. 10. Inter-American Development Bank.

Presbitero, Andrea F., and Roberta Rabellotti. 2016. "Credit Access in Latin American Enterprises." In *Firm Innovation and Productivity in Latin America and the Caribbean*, Inter-American Development Bank, edited by Matteo Grazzi and Carlo Pietrobelli, 245–83. New York: Palgrave Macmillan.

Sadeghi, Pegah, Hamid Shahrestani, Kambiz Hojabr Kiani, and Taghi Torabi. 2020. "Economic Complexity, Human Capital, and FDI Attraction: A Cross Country Analysis." *International Economics*, 164: 168–82.

Sepehrdoust, Hamid, Maryam Setarehie, and Razieh Davarikish. 2020. "The Impact of Government Trade Liberalization Policy on the Economic Complexity of Developing Countries." *Quarterly Journal of Applied Theories of Economics*, 7 (1): 211–38.

Simoes, Alexander James Gaspar, and César A. Hidalgo. 2011. "The Economic Complexity Observatory: An Analytical Tool for Understanding the Dynamics of Economic Development." *Workshops at the Twenty-Fifth AAAI Conference on Artificial Intelligence*.

Wang, Yao. 2016. "What Are the Biggest Obstacles to Growth of Smes in Developing Countries?–An Empirical Evidence from an Enterprise Survey." *Borsa Istanbul Review*, 16 (3): 167–76.

Williams, Kevin. 2018. "Has the Finance–Growth Link Been Broken? Panel Data Evidence from Latin America and the Caribbean." *Economia*, 19 (3): 404–23.

World Bank. 2019. *Global Financial Development Report 2019/2020: Bank Regulation and Supervision a Decade after the Global Financial Crisis*. The World Bank.

Zhu, Shujin, and Renyu Li. 2017. "Economic Complexity, Human Capital and Economic Growth: Empirical Research Based on Cross-Country Panel Data." *Applied Economics*, 49 (38): 3815–28.

Part 4

Recovery Process

Flows and Frameworks

9

Good Governance and Economic Reconfiguration

Policy Responses in Trinidad and Tobago to the COVID-19 Pandemic

SHANE JUSTIN PANTIN

Introduction

The June 2020 issue of *Global Economic Prospects* report published by the World Bank stated that "COVID-19 has inflicted a high human toll worldwide and triggered a severe regional and global economic downturn. It has affected the regional economy through both domestic and external channels" (The World Bank 2020, 69). This cogent observation also extends to Caribbean states, as they will grapple with the fallout from the economic backlash of the predicted downturn. To mitigate the decline, now more than ever, regional governments would have to apply political mechanisms that would create a level of trust between the government and the citizen to work together for an efficient and effective recovery. This chapter explores how good governance can assist in mobilizing this response. First, it outlines the ambit of good governance; second, it briefly explores the global and regional economic issues at play; third, it explores Trinidad and Tobago's response to address the economic crisis by drawing on a report prepared for the Road Map to Recovery Committee (Dookeran 2020); and fourth, it discusses and analyzes how good governance can assist in responding to the issues.

Definition, Background, and Theoretical Underpinning of Good Governance

The distinction between governance and good governance has practical and theoretical significance.[1] The World Bank sees governance as "the manner

---

[1] While there are subtleties to how governance is defined, the study largely limits the understanding of governance to the role the state plays in guiding society. However, it will draw upon empirical as well as theoretical aspects of governance in some areas.

in which public officials and institutions acquire and exercise the authority to shape public policy and provide public goods and services" (World Bank 1994, xiv). Asaduzzaman and Virtanen describe it as ". . . the political field and political activity . . ." that is the ". . . vital task of every national government," given the elements of leadership, management, and security governments provide a population (Asaduzzaman and Virtanen 2016, 124). Other perspectives of governance have varying subtleties deriving from the historical and social contexts as well as drawing from governance theory and practice.[2] However, this discussion adopts a limited and grounded understanding of governance by focusing on the political process.

Commentators have stated that "Good governance became important as an issue for developing countries from the late 1980s onwards when two international funding organisations began to emphasise it. The World Bank and the IMF (International Monetary Fund) started paying attention to policy processes in states for which funding was being considered" (Munshi, Abraham, and Chaudhuri 2009, 3). Neoliberal movements in the Western world exemplified by policies from Margaret Thatcher's Conservative government in the United Kingdom and Ronald Reagan's Republican government in the United States assisted in shifting the focus to governance issues in less developed states and changing the approach to aid funding. Conditionality is a fundamental part of the World Bank's and IMF's lending policies aligned to neoliberal thought.[3]

By the late 1980s, noninterference was not creating the type of results desired, and the two lending institutions included principles of good governance as part of their loan agreements. Neoliberal thinkers also promoted the idea that a state-led approach to development had created problems for many nations. Less government was viewed as the superior method and, therefore, countries that sought aid funding had to reduce government intervention. Good governance was linked to the trajectory of development becoming both theory and a praxis.

---

[2] Governance theory, for which a large volume of literature has emerged within the past thirty years, has allowed theoreticians to contextualize governance. For example, some theories link governance to the power wealthy organizations use to influence political policy. Other theoretical positions understand governance through the hierarchy of governance structures from public authorities to ministries to local government councils in visualizing how the political mechanics operate. Then there are those perspectives that see governance as networks of policymaking which regulate and direct behavior.

[3] Conditionality refers to the requirements for borrowing from the World Bank and the IMF.

Several important publications emerged that set the discussion for good governance. But two important reports are the *Sub-Saharan Africa: From Crisis to Sustainable Growth* (The World Bank 1989) and the *Governance and Development* (The World Bank 1992). The former discussed the stagnation and decline of many sub-Saharan nations' post-colonialism (The World Bank 1989, 1). In 1992, the World Bank's *Governance and Development* showed that "it (the World Bank) focused its attention on the topic of governance as a necessary precondition for development. In that report the World Bank explored the meaning of governance and its importance for long-term sustainable development" (The World Bank 1992, 1). The *Governance and Development* report recognized that part of the "failings" of these nations to "progress" from stagnation or decline was attributed to not only the system of governance[4] but also to the characteristics of that governance (The World Bank 1992, 3).

Good governance literature and analysis have since grown and have become part of overall development theory. As a theory, Woleola J. Ekundayo explains that fundamental aspects of good governance theory include accountability, control, responsiveness, transparency, public participation, economy, efficiency, and so on (Ekundayo 2017, 154). Furthermore, it involves, "an efficient public service, an independent judicial system and legal framework to enforce contracts and responsible administration of public funds" (Ekundayo 2017, 154). Additionally, good governance should address market failures and ensure institutional reforms capable of making markets work better (Jomo and Chowdhury 2012, 1). Therefore, good governance emerged as a response to the lack of sufficient progress in postcolonial countries and to create a better framework for how international organizations collaborated with nations (Munshi, Abraham, and Chaudhuri 2009, 3).[5]

---

4 In Governance and Development, governance is defined as "the manner in which power is exercised in the management of a country's economic and social resources for development."

5 The authors state that "Good governance has been in discussion primarily because of the importance given to it by many international organisations, including the World Bank, International Monetary Fund (IMF), Organization for Economic Cooperation and Development (OECD), Asian Development Bank (ADB), Department for International Development (DFID) and Canadian International Development Agency (CIDA)."

Good Governance Indicators

While each international institution has its own measures, the United Nations has recognized eight major characteristics to measure good governance. Good governance *is participatory, consensus oriented, accountable, transparent, responsive, effective and efficient, equitable, and inclusive,* and follows the *rule of law* (Munshi, Abraham, and Chaudhuri 2009). On the one hand, it assures that corruption is minimized, that the views of minorities are taken into account, and that the voices of the most vulnerable in society are heard in decision-making. It is also responsive to the present and future needs of society (Economic and Social Commission for Asia and the Pacific 2009). On the other hand, "poor governance is readily recognisable. Some of its major symptoms include the diversion of public resources for private gains, absence of law or arbitrariness in its application, excessive rules which impede the functioning of markets, allocation of resources in a manner that is inconsistent with the priorities of development, and a decision-making process that is not transparent" (Munshi, Abraham, and Chaudhuri 2009, 5).

Each of these characteristics has indicators that rank the success or failure of achieving a certain outcome. For example, corruption is linked to accountability and transparency, and it is one of the problem issues that confront many postcolonial states. Low to zero levels of corruption in a state testifies to that state's capability in having an effective governance structure. It is suggested that corruption is not common in developed states and where it does occur, officials are brought to justice. However, in states that are less developed, corruption is one of the ways of getting things done rather than through legitimate avenues; for example, "procuring a license for an activity, without offering bribes, in cash or in kind, to layers of public officials" (Ghosh and Siddique 2015, 11) will not be successful.

Another measure is to assess the level of participation of citizens in important policy formulations. For example, one way of participation is through a process called deliberative democracy. Ghosh and Siddique explain that "deliberative democracy . . . entrusts the power of decision-making to randomly selected representatives of the public following intensive processes of deliberation. The role of experts in the process is to inform the deliberations, and the role of the traditional structures of power within society is to implement the outcomes from the deliberations" (Ghosh and Siddique 2015, 47). This type of approach, for good governance theorists, is considered a progressive approach and assists in providing a positive indicator.

Poverty reduction is another measure that is linked to how well a governing structure is effective, efficient, equitable, and inclusive. Grindle has stated that it is all too clear that when "governments perform poorly, the consequences are wasted resources, undelivered services, and denial of social, legal, and economic protection for citizens—especially the poor" (Grindle 2004, 525). Reducing levels of poverty is one of the important areas for many postcolonial societies including Trinidad and Tobago. Over the past thirty years, there has been a remarkable improvement in these indicators, but there is still much work to be done. As Grindle notes: "For many reform-minded citizens in developing countries, as well as for academics and practitioners in the international development community, good governance has become as imperative to poverty reduction as it has become to development more generally" (Grindle 2004, 525).

The sample of indicators is also used as measures to assess Trinidad and Tobago's developmental status and trajectory. Analysts have used corruption indicators and poverty levels to make recommendations about Trinidad and Tobago's development. Other measures such as crime and economic indicators also serve to highlight the effectiveness of governance.

Criticisms

The premise and measures of good governance have not gone without criticisms. One of the first criticisms stemmed from the World Bank's and the IMF's failure to effect economic and social changes in African states where social and economic models could not be easily adapted in sub-Saharan Africa. Therefore, the blame for the lack of success fell on the governance system of those countries. For there to be stable macroeconomic development, it had to be coupled with "public sector management, financial management, the modernization of public administration, and the privatization of state-owned enterprises" (Santiso 2001, 5). A second criticism is that models used to assess good governance derive from the functionalist school of thought that provided societies with ideal-type models (Jomo and Chowdhury 2012, 6). According to conflict theorists, functionalists ignored the exploitative historical relationship between developing and the developed states. A third criticism deals with the indicators adopted for good governance practice. Such systems are "riddled with systematic biases due to selection problems, perception biases, as well as survey design and aggregation problems" (Jomo and Chowdhury 2012). Therefore, what may be corrupt in one society might not seem corrupt in another; data might be subjectively interpreted and exaggerated. A fourth but not final criticism deals with flawed assumptions of good governance. As with the indicators, theorists believe that assessing whether governance is good or not good is culturally insensitive because it did not examine sociocultural contexts and as such creates many problems when adapting it in different societies.

Good governance theorists have addressed these criticisms. One approach is to argue that good governance is more objective and practically achievable than other theories assessing systems of accountability and transparency. A second approach has been explained by Merilee S. Grindle, who suggests that instead of looking at good governance, theorists should look at good *enough* governance where the standard is an achievable one based on the social and economic context of a society (Grindle 2004).

Global and Regional Economic Issues

Criticisms aside, as national economies experience rising unemployment, poverty, and corruption, governments will experience difficulties if they are not deploying policies that are fair, efficient, and effective. The pandemic has magnified these problems, and the effects on the Caribbean economy will present a political challenge. Reports from the Economic Commission of Latin America and the Caribbean have painted a challenging landscape across all sectors. For example, some studies predict losses in the tourism industry and contractions in the energy sector (*The Caribbean Outlook*, 2020, 7). Another example is that of debt servicing, a major issue for Caribbean states. Some commentators analyzing the global system view it asymmetrically where the developed world has a privileged position and is able to adapt to crises whereas in the Caribbean region failure to adapt places it in a disadvantaged position. The challenge before the pandemic was to align the Caribbean economy to embrace technological and institutional upgrades that allow it to be part of the developed world's economic architecture, especially in generating valuable foreign exchange earnings to service debts. The pandemic has certainly slowed that the report *Building a New Future: Transformative Recovery with Equality and Sustainability* states, for example, that should economically vulnerable countries continue to borrow in foreign currencies, could lead to further deficits and slower growth (Economic Commission for Latin America and the Caribbean, *Building a New Future* 2020, 19).

This situation is in juxtaposition with other aforementioned regional problems. For Caribbean states, climate change is part of the agenda in light of the effects human activity has on the environment and consequently on their economies. According to the report, it is not surprising that the pandemic is being assessed as an environmental phenomenon as human encroachment upon fragile ecosystems unleashes new types of diseases (Economic Commission for Latin America and the Caribbean, *Building a New Future* 2020, 36).

These challenges are occurring even though Caribbean economies are still reeling from the effects of the financial crisis of 2008-2009, and analysts are already assessing the cost of recovery. The estimated cost of a short- to mid-term recovery is substantive as large-scale borrowing is expected at a time when the debt burden is high (Economic Commission for Latin America and the Caribbean, *The Caribbean Outlook* 2020, 11).

The backdrop is certainly not an optimistic one. But as the saying goes, "never let a good crisis go to waste." Opportunities have arisen and new ways of doing things, the "new normal," has emerged. This is an opportunity for political and economic leaders of the Caribbean to embrace these new changes in charting a new future. The pandemic has forced many to accept the new realities, and it has also meant that the Caribbean must not attempt to return to the "old normal" lest it be unprepared for the next crisis. Some Caribbean sectors have already begun adapting. For example, at the University of the West Indies, all three campuses are conducting virtual classes; the Judiciary of Trinidad and Tobago has begun to roll out electronic platforms for customer services and litigation; schools are conducting virtual classes; and media companies are using new technologies for covering the news and broadcasting. All this has meant a new unmeasured sector of the economy has emerged and requires analysis of its economic impact.

Roadmap to Recovery

While these new avenues are emerging, addressing the current crisis is important. In July 2020, the prime minister of Trinidad and Tobago established a Road Map for Recovery committee. The committee had an assemblage of persons from the public sector, private sector, labor, civil society, and academia to advise on the way forward in addressing the economic and social issues of the pandemic. A report followed which outlined various recommendations for the recovery of Trinidad and Tobago's economy. The report stated that the current crisis represents a "loop-type" cycle of shocks between demand and supply, but expressed the view that old policies that dealt with previous recessions will not be able to successfully navigate out of the current predicament (Dookeran 2020, 2).

Six recommendations made in the report are:

1. Increase the Capacity for Net Inflow of Foreign Exchange and Capital;
2. Catalyze Growth;
3. Restore Purchasing Power;
4. Source Funding to Meet Demands on Private and Public Expenditure;

5. Introduce a "Liveable Basic Income" for the Poor; and
6. Rebuild "Buffers" to Strengthen the Immunity of the Economy.

As the report explains, the pandemic has resulted in:

> … a supply shock – reducing wages and production, which in turn fuels a demand shock – a fall in purchasing power: resulting in a "loop" cycle of shock. This is coupled with an after-shock in the energy market, a key pillar of the economy, with future ripples to come from dramatically falling growth rates in the world economy. The size, speed and depth of these hits have contracted our economic base by an estimated 20-25 per cent.(Dookeran 2020, 2)

The recommendations are aimed at getting "the economy 'back on its feet' – to snap back into activity – and walk a new road where there will be absorbers and buffers for immunity in the economy" (Dookeran 2020, 3). Briefly, some of the elements of these recommendations are notable; for example, to restore purchasing power parity the report recommended that the Central Bank engage in buying and selling long-term government bonds (Dookeran 2020, 7); to reduce the finance gap in private and public expenditure will require some sort of "stimulus package" (Dookeran 2020, 8); growth can be achieved by extensively supporting small ventures and by expanding commercial activities (Dookeran 2020, 12); requests for financial assistance from the IMF and World Bank using careful negotiation strategies can help increase foreign exchange (Dookeran 2020, 13); replenishing the nation's sovereign wealth fund (Heritage and Stabilization Fund) can create the necessary immunity to shocks (Dookeran 2020, 15); and extending the National Insurance Boards' insurance coverage to the self-employed will help reduce financial difficulties of persons in this category (Dookeran 2020, 15).

The main driver of this plan will be the state, but the report was wary of unchecked state intervention (Dookeran 2020, 11). Thus, the report put forward the idea of government partnering with the private sector, stating that "The new incarnation of this dichotomy is the 'private public partnership'" (Dookeran 2020, 11). Government policy has reflected some of this approach from the report as seen in the budget statements made in Trinidad's Parliament for the year 2020/2021, where plans were outlined for economic diversification and a public–private partnership. Time will tell whether the recommendations and the planned course of action will assist in the recovery efforts. However, whatever the planned set of prescriptions, the main thrust should be to engender a sense of trust and confidence between citizens and public institutions to help rectify issues arising out of the pandemic.

Partnering for Good Governance

The report recognized that a successful macroeconomic strategy needs citizen and government partnership. So far, there have been positive responses from citizens of those nations that have used a partnership approach to institute economic recovery programs. Part of this success, some commentators say, are the good governance mechanisms that have aided this recovery. Therefore, Trinidad and Tobago's political apparatus can gain from this experience. For example, Germany seemed to be on course to experience some form of economic recovery and has handled the effects of the pandemic using methods that can continue this recovery even if there are further waves of the virus (Sullivan 2020). The advanced economies of the Asia-Pacific region such as South Korea, Australia, Singapore, and New Zealand, who are deemed good governance exemplars, are also showing strong growth rates largely because of their handling of the health protocols in their countries and because of trust in place between citizens and government (Ostry 2020).

Trinidad and Tobago share similar values to these countries regarding respect for democracy, transparency, accountability, and human rights. The nation's governance model is an inheritance from the United Kingdom's Westminster model (Ghany 2012, 124). For the average citizen of Trinidad and Tobago, the notion of governance is the application of a set of principles and the delivery of social conditions that create a stable, healthy, peaceful, successful, and equitable social and physical environment. A study undertaken by Raymond Mark Kirton, Marlon Anatol, and Niki Braithwaite concluded that citizens "support the electoral and democratic processes of the country. Additionally, there is a tradition of free and fair elections, belief in the rule of law, and the perception that the citizen's rights and freedoms are recognized and protected under the Constitution" (Kirton, Anatol, and Braithwaite 2010, 105). But this perception does not end there. Effective governance links with the day-to-day experience of citizens. Presently, the situation of crime, ethnic, and racial discrimination, poverty, unemployment, health care, and infrastructural development remain critical issues that shape opinion regarding effective governance (Deosaran 2019; Pantin 2009). Some of these opinions were translated by political figures who understand the mood of the people. For example, noted Trinidadian social activist and political leader, David Abdullah, was reported to have stated that "good government . . . takes into consideration and seeks the well-being of every citizen" (Trinidad and Tobago Guardian 2012). Similar sentiments were reported to have been stated by Winston Dookeran, a noted Trinidadian political leader and advocate for good governance where he stated, "a caring government must use our precious national resources to address the critical issues of today" (Newsday 2005).

Therefore, the prevailing desire for change in various sectors of life places emphasis not only on the way the system organizes and distributes the resources but additionally on how that interaction is conducted. As the pandemic continues, now more than ever good governance is needed for an effective recovery.

However, the national perception has not been positive regarding confidence in public institutions. Reported opinion polls released in 2019 by Nigel Henry highlighted the feelings among the population. There were low levels of confidence in the delivery of services by many institutions. Some 56 percent of the population believed that there was a crisis in the level of crime, 40 percent believed that the economy was at a critical point, 38 percent believed that corruption was rife, and 34 percent believed that national infrastructure was long overdue for improvement (Sunday Express 2019). These numbers are problematic if the government wishes to have the citizenry on board for a recovery effort.

The recommendations of the report coupled with a strong desire to instantiate good governance therefore will augur well for the nation. Much of the recommendations will require trade-offs in one way or the other for citizens. For example, as part of the proposal to increase the capacity for net inflow of foreign exchange and capital, the report highlighted that the International Monetary Fund (IMF) is providing financial assistance for which Trinidad and Tobago is eligible. It further stated that some Latin American and Caribbean countries have already accessed this funding under the IMF's Rapid Financing Instrument (Dookeran 2020, 13). So there is a possibility of Trinidad and Tobago accessing those funds. However, some economists and commentators have always been wary of accessing loans from the IMF and the heavy conditionalities that are mounted on nations. Additionally, a further debt burden means a further hit to the debt-GDP ratio. Therefore, the downside of such a proposal is justifying to national populations the need to go through the IMF, even in the difficult times the nation is experiencing.

This is where the role of good governance comes into play. Citizens having trust in their institutions and their leaders serve as the foundation for governments to communicate policy conditions acceptable to the populace. It will help in stemming criticism that funds will be used for ulterior purposes or are mismanaged, or that one group will experience more than another, or that the economic strain will be placed unfairly on some (Prasad 2020).[6]

---

6 The case of Fiji is one where there has been loss of trust and confidence in public institutions severely affecting national development.

Trinidad and Tobago, therefore, has to approach the next few months and perhaps years with the urgency required to ensure the population is well aware of the challenges ahead once the government develops transparency and accountability for its actions.

Even with the distribution of the various vaccines to mitigate the effects of the virus, there will be much work to do for an economic recovery where health protocol restrictions are eased and a return to pre-pandemic routine may be expected. There will be both optimism and uncertainty among people, especially regarding their economic livelihoods. While the recommendations of the report have outlined the process of economic recovery, it can also be seen as reconfiguring the economy. Should the government embrace the recommendations of the report, the reconfigured economy in the post-pandemic period will not be one bound by the linear models but will be immune to loop-cycle shocks (Dookeran 2020, 3). An admirable aspect of the report is that rather than suggesting a return to "normal," sustainability of the recommendations is a sounder approach to the post-pandemic strategy.

Therefore, it is not only the recovery that requires principled governance, longer-term success requires it as well. Given the nation's heavy reliance on foreign exchange, the large gap between the well-to-do and the less well-to-do in society and the need to have income levels reflecting the daily lives of people, it would be prudent to include the first, third, and fifth recommendations in the agenda for recovery. Recommendations two, four, and six address the issue of sustainability given that growth, sourcing funds, and crafting economic policies may take some time. Further to this, is addressing the mood of a population which has lost confidence in the public institutions to serve their interest. The vision of a nation operating under good governance principles which was a whisper before the pandemic is now a shout for the recovery and sustainability of a post-pandemic nation.

Conclusion

Good governance is therefore an important part of any macroeconomic recovery program. The pandemic exemplifies a critical situation where accountability and transparency are needed to build trust and confidence for any rebuilding process. The upside is that Trinidad and Tobago has an environment ripe for the application for principles of accountability to be applied and flourished, and perhaps the pandemic provides just such an opportunity. The political leaders will have to make the necessary effort not just focusing on a macroeconomic recovery plan, but also in weaving together good governance principles in its recovery program. An approach that simply applies economic measures sans good governance may not have effective and lasting results.

References

"Abdulah: Citizens Yearn for Good Governance." *Trinidad and Tobago Guardian*, 17 June 2012.

Asaduzzaman, Mohammed, and Petri Virtanen. 2016. "Governance Theories and Models." In *Global Encyclopedia of Public Administration, Public Policy, and Governance*, edited by Ali Farazmand, 1–13. Cham: Springer International Publishing.

Deosaran, Ramesh. 2019. "Crime, Gangs and Politics." *Trinidad Express*, Updated 13 March, accessed 21 September 2019. https://trinidadexpress.com/opinion/columnists/crime-gangs-and-politics/article_b07f6522-45ef-11e9-84f7-3f0f1706234a.html.

"Dookeran Calls for 'Principled Leaders' Who Must Listen to the People." *Newsday*, 15 September 2005, 5.

Dookeran, Winston C. 2020. *Resetting Macroeconomic Setting*. Trinidad and Tobago: Government of Trinidad and Tobago.

Economic Commission for Latin America and the Caribbean. 2020. *Building a New Future: Transformative Recovery with Equality and Sustainability*. Santiago: Naciones Unidas Comisión Económica para América Latina y el Caribe (CEPAL).

Economic Commission for Latin America and the Caribbean. 2020. *The Caribbean Outlook: Forging a People-Centred Approach to Sustainable Development Post-Covid-19*. Santiago: Naciones Unidas Comisión Económica para América Latina y el Caribe (CEPAL).

Economic and Social Commission for Asia and the Pacific. 2009. "*What Is Good Governance?*" Accessed 21 September 2019. https://www.unescap.org/sites/default/files/good-governance.pdf.

Ekundayo, Woleola J. 2017 May. "Good Governance Theory and the Quest for Good Governance in Nigeria." *International Journal of Humanities and Social Science*, 7 (5): 154–61.

Ghany, Hamid. 2012. "The Relevance of the Senate in a Modern Democracy." In *Evolution of a Nation Trinidad and Tobago at Fifty*, 79–100. Hertfordshire: Hansib Pub..

Ghosh, R.N., and M.A.B. Siddique (eds.). 2015. *Corruption, Good Governance and Economic Development:Contemporary Analysis and Case Studies*. Toh Tuck Link, Singapore: World Scientific Publishing Co. Pte. Ltd.

Grindle, Merilee S. 2004. "Good Enough Governance: Poverty Reduction and Reform in Developing Countries." *Governance: An International Journal of Policy, Administration, and Institutions*, 17 (4): 525–48. https://doi.org/10.1111/j.0952-1895.2004.00256.x.

Jomo, Kwame Sundaram, and Anis Chowdhury. 2012. *Is Good Governance Good for Development?* London: Bloomsbury Academic.

Kirton, Raymond Mark, Marlon Anatol, and Niki Braithwaite. 2010. *The Political Culture of Democracy in Trinidad and Tobago*. St Augustine: The University of the West Indies.

Munshi, Surendra, Biju Paul Abraham, and Soma Chaudhuri. 2009. *The Intelligent Person's Guide to Good Governance*. Edited by Biju Paul Abraham and Soma Chaudhuri. Los Angeles and London: SAGE.

Ostry, Jonathan D. 2020. "Imf: Everything You Need to Know About Asia's 'Multispeed' Recovery." *World Economic Forum*, 23 October. https://www.weforum.org/agenda/2020/10/asia-multispeed-recovery-coronavirus-covid-economies-economics/.

Pantin, Dennis. 2009. "Requirements of Good Governance." *Trinidad and Tobago Guardian*, 18 July.

"Pass Mark for the Pm." *Sunday Express*, 8 September 2019, 4–5.

Prasad, Biman Chand. 2020. "Responding to Covid-19: Time to Refocus on Pacific Governance." *Devpolicy Blog from the Development Policy Centre*, 13 October. https://devpolicy.org/responding-to-covid-19-time-for-pacific-governments-and-donors-to-refocus-on-governance-20201013-2/.

Santiso, Carlos. 2001. "Good Governance and Aid Effectiveness: The World Bank and Conditionality." [In English]. *The Georgetown Public Policy Review*, 7 (1): 1–22.

Sullivan, Arthur, 2020. "Will the German Engine Power Europe?" DW.COM, 29 September. Accessed 9 November 2020. https://www.dw.com/en/germanys-pandemic-recovery-raises-age-old-questions-about-european-economy/a-55090733.

The World Bank. 1989. *From Crisis to Sustainable Growth - Sub Saharan Africa: A Long-Term Perspective Study*. Washington, DC: The World Bank.

The World Bank. 2020. *Global Economic Prospects, June 2020*. Washington, DC: World Bsnk.

The World Bank. 1994. *Governance: The World Bank's Experience*. Washington, DC: The World Bank.

The World Bank. 1992. *Governance and Development*. Washington, DC: The World Bank.

10

Resetting Regionalism for Convergence and Post-Pandemic Recovery for Caribbean Economies

DAVID ANYANWU

Introduction

The global economy is undergoing major transformations, accelerated by the COVID-19 pandemic that calls for new development strategies. In the Caribbean Community (CARICOM), parallel threats linked to public health, economic and social crises, and the environment have brought regional economies to a standstill. This is not unexpected considering that the 1985 seminal study of the Commonwealth Secretariat on small states highlighted the economic weakness of Caribbean economies. These weaknesses are marked by the economies' vulnerability to ecological forces and their dependence on undiversified economic structures, a narrow resource base, relative openness, high infrastructural costs, remoteness, and high dependence on external trade (Commonwealth Secretariat 1985, 21–2). The evolving context has also called into question conventional wisdom on growth and economic development in the Caribbean and beyond. These, alongside deep-rooted structural challenges, suggest the need for new models which force Caribbean economies to rethink both domestic policies and approaches to partnerships and international cooperation required to address the region's enduring challenges and accelerate post-pandemic recovery.

Trade plays an important role in the development agenda of Caribbean economies, supporting economic growth through job creation and poverty reduction. Table 10.1 groups Caribbean countries according to their major source of export earnings. It shows that most Caribbean economies are service economies, reliant primarily on tourism.

Notwithstanding their relative openness and embrace of trade liberalization, Caribbean economies' trade performance both within the region and extra-regionally have been poor. Their heavy dependence on commodity exports, imported intermediate goods, and hydrocarbons for production is also

Table 10.1 Economic profile of Caribbean economies

Services Dependent	Light Manufacturing Dependent	Agriculture and Food Dependent	Natural Resources Dependent
Antigua and Barbuda	Haiti	Guyana*	Suriname
The Bahamas		Belize	Trinidad and Tobago
Barbados			Guyana
Dominica			
Grenada			
Jamaica			
St. Kitts and Nevis			
St. Lucia			
St. Vincent and the Grenadines			

Source: Author's compilation (2020).

Table 10.2 Caribbean economies export of goods and services

Exports of goods and services (% of GDP)				
	2016	2017	2018	2019
Barbados	43.1	42.1	41.2	42.0
Belize	52.6	54.9	57.7	57.7
Grenada	49.3	51.3	55.0	54.5
Guyana	41.1	40.4	35.4	33.0
Jamaica	31.8	34.6	37.9	38.0

Source: World Bank (2020).

problematic and foundational to regional economies' high extra-regional dependence. Table 10.2 shows the export numbers for some economies. With the phase-out of preferential trade arrangements, the expected benefits of Free Trade Agreements (FTAs) and Partial Scope Agreements, including to overcome the challenges related to smallness, have not materialized as inherent structural rigidities remain problematic (Mclean and Khadan 2015, 5–29).

Similarly, the region's significant reliance on tourism weakens their posture as recently demonstrated by the impacts of a highly contracted global tourism industry crippled by pandemic-related travel restrictions.

With minimal economic and financial buffers, high extra-regional dependence leaves Caribbean economies vulnerable to external shocks, falling commodity prices, and volatility. Since the outbreak of COVID-19 in late 2019, economic conditions have worsened dramatically. The volatility of commodity prices over the past decade and the onset of the COVID-19 pandemic have led to a further shrinking of their global exports. The pandemic imposed substantial job losses in key sectors such as tourism, which is a major employer in all tourism-dependent Caribbean economies. Unemployment rates remain very high, and gains made in poverty reduction over the last decade are increasingly threatened. Over the past five years, unemployment rates have averaged near or above double-digit levels in most countries in the region. Progress toward further reduction of poverty has been relatively slow and remains uneven in the region.

The sudden but deep impact of COVID-19 was expected to trigger severe economic depression and have long-lasting effects. As these effects ripple through the region, disruption to global supply chains will drive commodity and transport costs and increase trade tensions among countries. Reignited nationalist sentiments in many parts of the world and increasingly restrictive trade rules that further fuel protectionism are indicative of emergent effects of the pandemic.

Strategic rivalry between the United States and China, Russia-Ukraine war, aftereffects of BREXIT, oil price wars, and the unending crisis in Venezuela are also just some examples of the geopolitical tensions that have become more dangerous and consequential for small Caribbean economies than imagined. At a regional level, CARICOM has been unable to adopt a coordinated political and economic approach to the Venezuelan crisis, leaving member states such as Trinidad and Tobago to singlehandedly deal with a migrant crisis.

Regional Effects of COVID-19 and Related Shocks

Challenges posed by COVID-19 are also manifesting at a time during which processes of globalization (such as financial liberalization and deregulation which have made the world increasingly interconnected and interdependent for the last three decades) have become more problematic for most, particularly small developing countries. The interconnectedness of the global economy has made these economies more vulnerable to shocks, including natural and man-made disasters.

It is already established that Caribbean economies, like other vulnerable economies, often face disproportionate effects of macroeconomic shocks for reasons including their geography, macroeconomic fundamentals, and government action (WTO 2021). Current account deficits of economies were identified as a key macroeconomic indicator that contributed to the vulnerability of wealthier emerging economies and poorer high-income countries to higher growth collapses during the 2008 global financial crisis (Didier, Hevia, and Schmukler 2012).

The COVID-19 pandemic caused contractions across most Caribbean economies and significantly impacted labor productivity and output. The Economic Commission for Latin America and the Caribbean (ECLAC) has noted that the Latin America and the Caribbean region are likely to experience a setback of ten years in income levels per inhabitant and a greater increase in unemployment (13.5 percent by the end of 2020), both of which, in turn, will produce a significant deterioration in poverty and inequality levels (Mclean and Khadan 2015, 5–29).

With financial instability more frequent and systemic, and inequality increasingly problematic, there is greater impetus for Caribbean economies, given their limited buffers, to consider alternative approaches toward better economic outcomes for their citizens.

As expected and shown in table 10.3, FY20 growth in several countries, including tourism-dependent Caribbean economies was negatively impacted by the pandemic. The sharp fall in global commodity prices was a headwind for much of the region, and particularly for Trinidad and Tobago which has been deeply impacted by the decline in global energy prices. Growth in the Caribbean experienced a 1.8 percent contraction in 2020, or a 3.1 percent contraction if Guyana is excluded due to the country's rapidly developing oil sector (World Bank 2020).

Table 10.3 Selected Caribbean country forecasts

Caribbean Country Forecasts (Annual percent change)					
	2017	2018	2019	2020	2021f
GDP at market prices (2010 US$)					
Belize	1.9	2.1	0.3	−13.5	6.7
Dominica	9.5	0.5	9.6	−4.0	4.0
Grenada	4.4	4.2	3.1	−9.6	6.5
Guyana	2.1	4.1	4.7	51.1	8.1
Haiti	1.2	1.5	−0.9	−3.5	1.0
Jamaica	1.0	1.9	0.7	−6.2	2.7
St. Lucia	2.2	1.4	1.4	−8.8	8.3
St. Vincent and the Grenadines	1.0	2.0	0.4	−5.5	4.0
Suriname	1.8	2.6	2.3	−5.0	3.0

Source: World Bank (2020).

Falling tourism activity and remittance inflows were also expected to be a severe drag on growth in a large swath of economies in the subregion (World Bank 2020) as COVID-19 cases remained high in North America and Europe. The adoption of vaccine mandates, quarantine requirements, mandatory testing, travel insurance coverage as means to curb the spread of COVID-19 impacted tourism negatively, resulting in negative balance sheets for tourism operators and tourism-dependent economies. Similarly, travel advisories issued by public health authorities in source countries have also contributed to the slump.

At the height of the pandemic, most Caribbean islands were classified by the US Centers for Disease Control and Prevention as "Level 4" based on what it assessed to be very high rates of COVID-19, which meant travel to those countries was not recommended. Other countries including Canada published similar travel advisories. The complexity and inconsistency in application of the pandemic-related travel rules across jurisdictions had a debilitating impact on tourism economies and would have contributed to the performance of the sector.

Despite the decline in 2020 and 2021, an economic recovery is underway in the region, but the pandemic still casts shadows on much of the region. Delays in the sourcing and financing of COVID-19 vaccines in the global south frustrated FY2021 forecasts and could suggest that 2022 estimates may not be attainable after all.

As figure 10.1 shows, going forward, most Caribbean economies led by Guyana were expected to experience economic growth in 2022. However, GDP for Jamaica and Belize in 2022 respectively was forecast to be lower in 2021, and Suriname and Haiti are expected to experience minimal growth compared to others. The outcome remains uncertain as new strains of COVID-19 evolve. Despite the optimism, it is difficult to imagine a post-pandemic recovery scenario for Caribbean economies that does not require new forms of strategic partnerships that could create economic and financial spaces that can allow them to begin to reignite their economies.

Indeed, these strategic partnerships appeared lacking as governments struggled to access COVID-19 vaccinations for their residents as richer countries amassed more than they needed. As figure 10.2 shows, by the end of 2020, COVID-19 vaccines were not administered in any developing and/or low-income country, and by end of 2021, vaccination rates in the Caribbean remained relatively below the world average.

While the World Health Organization (WHO) initiative COVAX offered the best chance for the poorest countries to obtain significant quantities of the vaccine in 2021, the initiative, which is dependent on funding from wealthier countries, was challenged due to funding and supply concerns. Despite calls by

GDP real growth rate in the Caribbean in 2021 and 2022

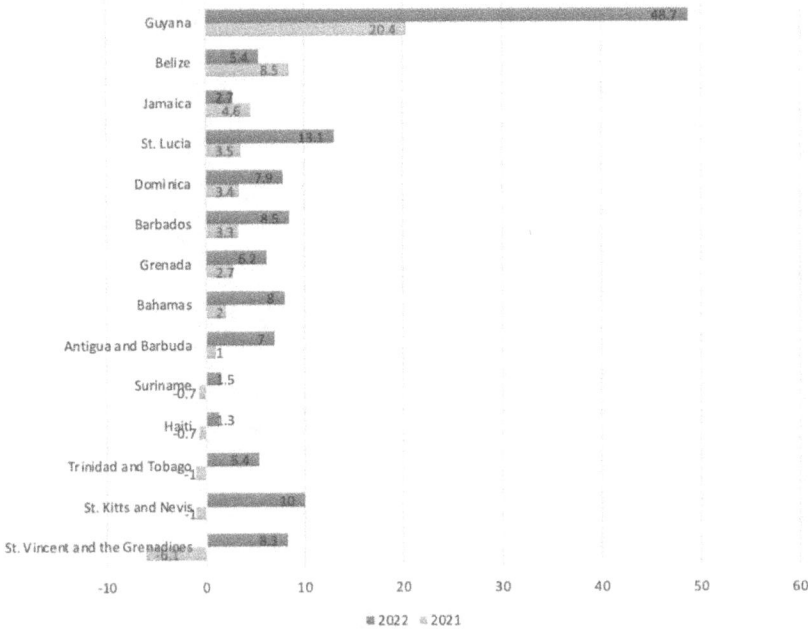

Figure 10.1 GDP real growth rate in the Caribbean in 2021 and 2022.

Source: Teresa Romero, Statista, October 2021.

the WHO and global civil society for governments to make vaccine protecting against COVID-19 a public good, the hoarding of the vaccines by rich countries that secured more doses than their populations needed revealed the broader challenge some governments faced in their bid to protect their populations from the virus and reopen their economies. More importantly, it reinforced the need for an alternative form of deepened cooperation based on convenience, which can offer the additional policy and diplomatic space for invested Caribbean governments to negotiate and pursue these kinds of strategic interests.

Small economies are also increasingly caught stranded as bigger economies pursue mutually benefiting trade pacts beyond traditional spaces. As multilateral institutions are increasingly weakened by global forces at work, extra-regional cooperation is needed to buttress long-term prospects. Such coalitions are critical to reform capitalism and strengthen multilateral institutions. As ECLAC noted in its 2020 International Trade Outlook for Latin America and the Caribbean, countries, particularly the major trading economies, in seeking to overcome differences in the multilateral spaces such as the WTO, are leaning toward regional agreements to achieve a minimum level of trade cooperation.

% of Population Fully Vaccinated in the Caribbean

Country	%
Antigua and Barbuda	60.81
Belize	51.67
Barbados	50.12
Trinidad and Tobago	48.33
Dominica	39.73
Suriname	39.49
Bahamas	38.36
Guyana	33.73
Grenada	31.66
St. Lucia	27.21
St. Vincent and the Grenadines	23.73
Jamaica	19.67
Haiti	

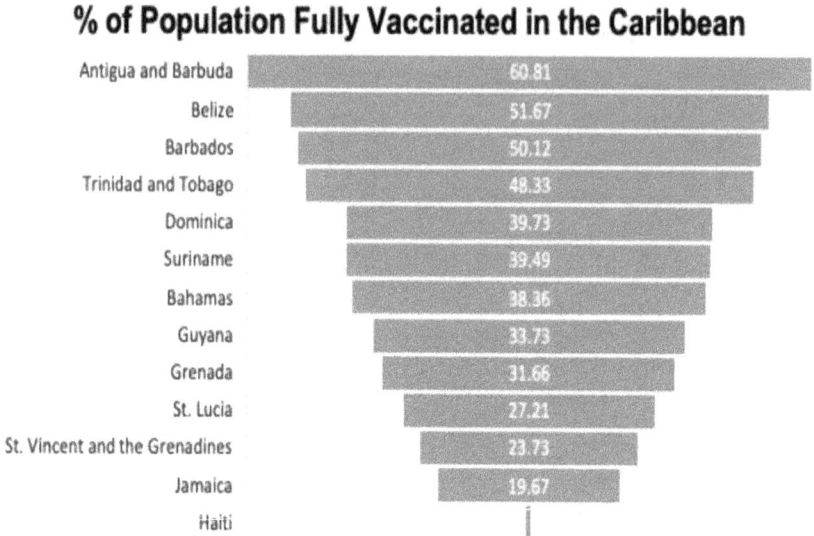

Figure 10.2 Percentage of population fully vaccinated in the Caribbean.
Source: John Hopkins Coronavirus Resource Centre. 2022.

The Canada-United States-Mexico Agreement which entered into force in July 2020, the Regional Comprehensive Economic Partnership agreement signed in November 2020 between fifteen Factory Asia countries to form the so-called African Continental Free Trade Area and the Comprehensive and Progressive Agreement for Trans-Pacific Partnership (CPTPP) are examples of such recent configurations (ECLAC 2021). It is worth noting that the origins of CPTPP date back to the 2006 Transpacific Strategic Economic Partnership Agreement (TPSEP) signed by Brunei, Singapore, New Zealand, and Chile in 2006. These countries saw value in converging beyond geographical borders in a trade agreement.

Inter-regionalism and Intra-regionalism

Regionalism (and increasingly open regionalism) is defined in terms of "networks" as opposed to "blocs," as countries actively pursue arrangements that can provide the policy space necessary to reframe the terms of their engagement with the rest of the world.[1]

In analyzing the different perspectives on "region" as a subsystem in the global system, and the levels and directions of cooperation among states within

---

[1] New technologies have played a role in this regard by allowing for interconnection in trade among people and markets.

and across "regions," the concepts of inter-regionalism, trans-regionalism, and other forms of cooperation such as extra-, cross-, pan-regionalism come to mind. In the last two decades, inter-regionalism and trans-regionalism have been used to reflect the marked growth in regional projects between and among countries and regions. Inter-regionalism is defined as the political and/or economic relationship between two regional arrangements. In suggesting that economic distance is no longer a defining facet of trade competitiveness (Jules 2015, 37–57), it challenges the long-held importance attached to geographic proximity. On the other hand, trans-regionalism denotes less institutionalized arrangements between regions (Tsardanidis 2010, 2) and the creation of common spaces (such as economic, political, financial, social-cultural, and so on) between and across regions in which principal actors such as states and their organizations can collaborate and have integrative links (Dent 2003, 223–35) (Ruland 2002, 1–9).

Both frameworks are helpful, but the latter offers more for the convergence thesis given its premise on cooperation and multilateral market-driven consensus, which is distinct from south–south regionalism defined by trade-based rules, bipolarity, regional trade agreements, tariff reductions, and technical assistance (Jules 2015, 37–57). This is an important distinction that supports the premise that trans-regional arrangements do not necessarily require institutionalized relations but are grounded in common ideological, pragmatic preferences and principles (Luzina et al. 2019, 166–76).

Both inter-regionalism and trans-regionalism represent an effort to resolve one of the central problems of contemporary trade policy: how to achieve compatibility between the explosion of regional trading arrangements around the world and the global trading system (Bergsten 1997, 545–65). The idea is that despite geographical spread, market-driven integration provides a strong foundation for economic cohesion between countries.

This is the antithesis of a protectionist and inward-looking approach that has dogged traditional regional groupings/blocs and which is increasingly more prevalent today. In addition to prioritizing the commonality of economic interests, the success of interactions within the trans-regionalism framework is dependent on agreed economic interests and interstate agreements (Heifetz 2016, 19–42), thereby reiterating the notion of a coalition of the willing.

Overview of Caribbean Integration

A theory-based explanation of the Caribbean integration as consisting of a set of concentric circles representing the different levels of integration in the region offers a fair insight into the long-varied history of the region's integration movement. The varied definitions of the Caribbean are reflected in regional configurations such as the Association of Caribbean States (ACS), CARICOM, and the Organization of the Eastern Caribbean States (OECS).

The ACS reflects the Greater Caribbean interpretation, consisting of the Anglophone, Dutch, Spanish, and French Caribbean, and Latin American countries that are "washed by the Caribbean Sea" (Ramphal and West Indian Commission 1994).

CARICOM comprises the English-speaking Caribbean, in addition to Suriname and Haiti. CARICOM is located at the outer layer of these concentric circles compared to the OECS, a more integrated subregional grouping of the English-speaking islands in the Eastern Caribbean (Girvan 2013, 1–32) which will be in the core.[2]

Despite the similar identity and the seeming interdependence of the economies, CARICOM, unlike the OECS, has not been able to implement a single economy. As such, the Caribbean Single Market and Economy (CSME) which was born by the Revised Treaty of Chaguaramas in 2001 is yet to be implemented in its entirety.

Internally, attempts to deepen CARICOM economic integration have been hampered partly by inconsistencies within the grouping including the diversity in language, population size, and pace of economic development of some members. The diagnosis of the stalemate in CARICOM is often attributed, even by political leaders, as an "implementation deficit"; but it appears the stalemate is derived from a "design deficit" which has limited deepened integration. Since the revised treaty, some 57 percent of the actions required to establish the CSME have been completed, primarily in the areas of intra-CARICOM goods trade and common market in services and skilled labor. Progress has been limited in areas such as customs union and in the harmonization of regulations and policies to support a single economic space, capital mobility, and processes related to intraregional labor movement (Al Hassan et al. 2020).

Importantly, CARICOM's external relations are characterized by a shift away from relations with predominantly traditional North American and European transatlantic partners to a more diverse set of relationships with new partners. These developments have both positive and negative implications in terms of their ability to raise CARICOM's profile on the global stage and provide

---

[2] Member States of the OECS are Anguilla, Antigua and Barbuda, British Virgin Islands, Dominica, Grenada, Montserrat (Montserrat is an overseas territory *of the United Kingdom*), St. Kitts and Nevis, St. Lucia, St. Vincent and the Grenadines.

alternatives to "North-South" development cooperation, as well as undermine regional progress and development if not managed properly (Montoute 2015).

Indeed, these concentric circles of Caribbean integration have been born out of the need for significant changes in order for the region to maintain some sort of strategic relevance in what was an increasingly unfavorable global economic environment. Over the years, integration has increasingly moved, not necessarily by choice, from *de jure* state-driven regionalism to *de facto* market regionalism (Breslin and Higgott 2003, 167–82), given that an unfavorable global economic environment has required and continues to demand at every point that states maintain an agile stance in seeking out safe havens for their interests.

It also has required that Caribbean governments think beyond the geography and economic, demographic, political, and institutional linkages and interactions which have formed the basis of Caribbean integration for the last half century. Collectively, CARICOM's external endeavors have represented the most challenging issues on CARICOM States' foreign policy agenda.

Toward a Convergence Approach

The "political imperative for convergence" and the need for "appropriate correcting mechanisms" were identified as important during the discussions on "Regional Economic Integration: Caribbean Convergence and Competitiveness" in the 2012 Caribbean Growth Forum as well as the Forum of the Caribbean held in Trinidad and Tobago in May 2015.

The call for convergence beyond CARICOM is rooted in the argument that the current integration framework is neither equipped to address the full scope of the development challenges the region faces nor does it support the quest for policy space in multilateral forms required to ensure that the range of issues of critical importance to the Caribbean can be prioritized.

For long, the Caribbean integration problematic has been attributed to weak implementation and/or the unwillingness of states to take intentional steps to bring into local law the provisions of the revised treaty. Similarly, the inadequacies of the current structures to respond to the development needs of member states have made implementation unattractive for member states. It could be argued that no matter how well the CSME is implemented, it may not be sufficient to overcome the inherent limitations related to smallness and volatility and, as such, unable to keep pace in the current global economic and political context and challenges.

Convergence beyond geographical proximity and borders is also discussed as a point of departure for the future given the possibility it offers. The Greater

Caribbean region, for example, denotes geographically those nations that are washed by the Caribbean Sea. It includes most of the islands of the Lesser and Greater Antilles as well as territories in Central America (Costa Rica, Belize, Panama, Honduras) and Northern South America such as Colombia and Venezuela.

Convergence is presented as a potential development approach that may offer Caribbean economies the kinds of instruments and policy and diplomatic spaces necessary to respond to ongoing major transformations in the global economy that are not readily available in existing structures such as FTAs, traditional multilateral organizations, development banks, and economic cooperation bodies. Even where existing structures are found lacking, it is important to note from the onset that the convergence approach is not argued to supplant any institutions but instead to bolster them by offering more opportunities for cooperation and investment in ways that are required for today's challenges.

While the interoperability of the convergence process with subregional and regional integration processes as well as concerns about institutional redundancy are viable ones, they do not represent an inevitable obstacle. Instead, convergence will add future value to the workings of the integration process and support existing structures.

Even a more integrated Greater Caribbean market of 300 million inhabitants would constitute an important insurance policy against supply or demand shocks produced outside the region. See tables 10.4 and 10.5. It will facilitate market integration, reduce transaction costs, production, trade, and distribution barriers, facilitate integration of national firms and businesses into regional value chains, and foster regional joint action and the free movement of capital and skilled labor.

Integration by convenience is significant given that they represent 48.9 percent of the GDP of Latin America and the Caribbean and 44 percent of its population.[3] A strategically reinvigorated international cooperation that offers an open economic space for the flow of goods, services, capital, technology, and so on can present a more promising path to resilience and offer innovative forms of public–private partnership focused on production integration, distribution, and competitiveness supporting trade and markets. It could present significant benefits to tackle challenges related to climate which is driving the increases in extreme weather events such as hurricanes, tropical storms, and floods. It

---

[3] Based on the author's tabulation.

Table 10.4 Population of countries of the Greater Caribbean

Subregion	Year	Subtotal
CARICOM	2019	18,664,458
Central America, Venezuela, and Colombia	2019	270,600,938
ALL		289,265,396

Source: World Bank (2020).

Table 10.5 GDP (current US$ billions): Countries of the Greater Caribbean

Subregion	Subtotal
CARICOM	84,789.34
Central America, Venezuela, and Colombia	2,410,793.32
ALL	2,495,582.66

Source: World Bank (2020).
2014 data.

could also expand the scope for greater trade and security cooperation, and help build viable and dependable regional supply chains for greater economic security in the future.

Convergence entails exploring opportunities for deeper cooperation beyond geographical limits. In the Greater Caribbean context, the removal and/or reduction of barriers to investments and trade would be an enormous step toward a more converged and integrated economic space.

The Guiana Shield is one such example. Convergence within the Guiana Shield presents additional opportunities for Guyana and Suriname, which alongside French Guiana, Venezuela, and small parts of Colombia and northern Brazil cover an area of 3,700,000 square kilometers rich in diverse resources from oil and natural gas, to diamonds, bauxite, and gold. The subregion also has one of the largest rainforests in the world which is rich in biodiversity. While traditionally the integration among the shield countries has been characterized by weak action between the states (Gustavo and Superti, 2016, 43–67) and territorial disputes, there is an opportunity for these territories, through a convergence of their economies, to propel economic growth, improve the social and economic outlooks of their citizens, and enhance their post-pandemic recovery posture.

Such deepened cooperation is driven solely at the national level and through existing regional structures such as CARICOM, the ACS, and the Union of South American Nations (UNASUR).

The proposed bridge over the Corentyne River connecting Suriname and Guyana and the "Open Skies Agreement" are examples of recent bilateral cooperation and/or joint-action initiatives that both governments undertook to reduce barriers, improve market access, enhance national competitiveness, and create investment and developmental opportunities for both countries.

Similarly, the strategic dialogue and cooperation agreement signed by both governments on November 25, 2020 – the forty-fifth anniversary of diplomatic relations between Guyana and Suriname – is designed to provide a formal mechanism for future collaborative efforts. However, more can be achieved within a convergence, as countries of the Guiana are well positioned to drive deepened cooperation toward expanded hydro-energy production, agricultural development, and the promotion of sustainable ecotourism (Lewis 2017); all are critical for post-pandemic economic growth, if they are able to overcome common differences and historical mistrust.

On the Caribbean side, the complementarity of economies of the Greater Caribbean is an important consideration in discussing the potential of their convergence. Complementarity measures the degree to which the export pattern of one country matches the import pattern of another, and this can be assessed in terms of their trade and production structures to prospect the outcomes of bilateral trade and economic arrangements. A high degree of complementarity is assumed to indicate more favorable prospects for a successful trade arrangement.

Convergence is likely to be most effective and lead to trade growth and development if Caribbean economies share a strong level of trade complementarity with countries of the Greater Caribbean. An analysis (Mclean and Khadan 2015) of the comparative advantage of the CARICOM economies (exporting country) to the comparative disadvantage of the importing partner, weighted against world trade, is shown in table 10.6.

As an alternative development approach, convergence can offer a more robust post-pandemic recovery for Caribbean economies. Coordination around areas where it is generally accepted that limited capacity exists such as in regional

Table 10.6 Trade complementarity between CARICOM and Latin America

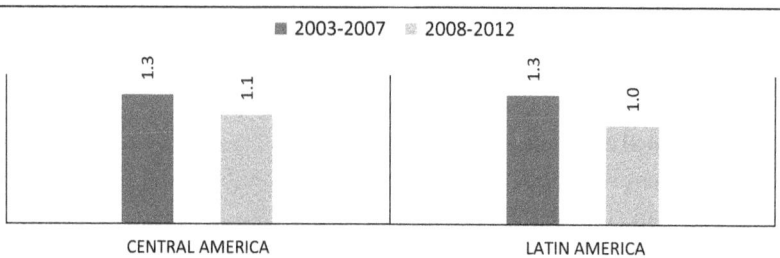

Source: Jeetendra Khadan and Roger Hosein (2013).

pandemic surveillance and vaccine development and research will be critical for future outbreaks. COVID-19 has not only exacerbated the public health challenges in countries and exposed severe shortcomings in national medical infrastructure, but it also revealed the stark inequalities between countries, both in their responses to the pandemic and in their access to vaccines to contain the outbreak.

While supplies improved, the politicization of vaccines by global powers and the proliferation of misinformation, conspiracy theories, and disinformation by radical but powerful anti-vaccine personalities and groups further exacerbated vaccine hesitancy, and proved problematic for Caribbean governments that struggled to increase vaccination rates amid high hospitalization and death rates. Given the slower pace of vaccination in low- and middle-income countries, the majority of African and Caribbean countries climbed their way out of the pandemic much more slowly than the rest of the world.

The WHO emphasized the need for international cooperation in vaccination campaigns, noting that a global pandemic requires global efforts to end it. In that context, the role that convergence can play in facilitating collective and joint action in the Greater Caribbean around vaccine sourcing and distribution can be significant, even if it is explored for future outbreaks. Convergence will provide opportunities to maximize the success of health diplomacy and the transfer of technologies and collaboration on science and innovation. It can facilitate an economic platform for deepened cooperation among countries of the Greater Caribbean to negotiate development finance with international financial institutions from both a short- and long-term perspective (Dookeran 2020, 1). It will also provide an additional platform to promote their interests both within the broader Latin America region, across the hemisphere, and globally. It is through strategic realignments such as this that the Caribbean economies can create the policy space necessary to navigate the global economic environment, bolster post-pandemic recovery, build buffers against economic and financial shocks, expand market access for goods and services, and create opportunities for development finance.

It is true that the case for wider and deeper regional economic integration and cooperation has been made before in the context of the ACS and the Free Trade of the Americas, respectively. The latter never materialized. But the ACS, which was established to provide the space for regional cooperation beyond immediate economic concerns, did not meet the expectation given its focus on areas such as tourism, sustainable tourism, and natural disasters (Dookeran 2020, 2). It is also important to note the similarity of Caribbean Basin economies as often having presented the most significant obstacles to meaningful regional cooperation and a successful integration project. The banana wars of the 1990s, the negative impact of the North American Free Trade Agreement on Caribbean apparel exports, and the asymmetry of the economies are just examples of factors that have fueled mistrust in the past and can potentially slow convergence. For example, the concern that the Dominican Republic would side with Central American countries and not CARICOM on regional and global trade issues has contributed to the mistrust that exists today and, by extension, has impacted regional economic activities in the Greater Caribbean. Despite these historical facts, deepened regional cooperation among the Greater Caribbean economies will be crucial to revamp the current development model, control the pandemic, and ensure a sustainable and speedier economic recovery.

Role of the State

This new paradigm of economic cooperation in the Greater Caribbean calls for good leadership capacity defined as bold political and economic decision-making. The role of the state in catalyzing growth and development is essential. As a potentially significant (but not new) diplomatic challenge, significant investments in economic diplomacy will be necessary to the extent that it may require a shift in thinking toward a new approach in both domestic and international spaces.

This catalytic role of the state is required at pivotal and precarious points when conventional models to economic development have been ineffective. A shift toward new approaches based on convenience and strategic interest in exploiting opportunities that surface during and beyond the pandemic is therefore required in order to improve national competitiveness through collective and joint action among like-minded economies. This is also necessary to create knowledge platforms necessary to build among many things, surveillance and response capacity for future crises, including on climate action.

It also entails the intentional application of strategic foresight in policymaking to ensure a better understanding of the key uncertainties and possible future developments that could have short-, medium-, and long-term implications for public health, security, and national economy in general. Strategic foresight can allow for better articulation and championing of more innovative and forward-looking policy actions and strategies for economic development, including measures that drive joint action in a convergence of like-minded economies.

The catalytic impulse relates to the boldness and commitment to test new waters toward widening, deepening, and strengthening the region's cooperation with like-minded countries in the Greater Caribbean to fuel growth and respond to challenges in today's global economic environment.

In terms of leadership capacity, the role of initiators relates to the foresight and the ability necessary to anticipate the need and importance of convergence as a way of creating and/or broadening the policy and economic space to drive Caribbean development and developing necessary supporting arrangements to get the rest of the leaders and governments on board. Initiators can be described as those that have special vision (the "visionaries"), courage, and ability to look beyond the initial limitations as well as to articulate that vision for those who are resistant and protective of their own domains. It is through good leadership and effective diplomacy that Caribbean economies, and indeed other small developing states, can carve out the appropriate policy spaces conducive for articulating and promoting their interests in multilateral arenas that currently afford them very little wiggle room to respond to the changing global economic and political landscape.

The development of regionalism in Southeast Asia relied on cooperative and transformative leadership. Such leadership relates to the recognition of "the need to synergize the national and regional nexus – to attain an 'equilibrium' between the demands of national priorities and dynamics in the region" (Natelegawa 2018, 3). Thus, ensuring that national interest and the region's collective interests are not inherently in conflict. Similarly, the ASEAN achievement would not have been possible without the requisite leadership if one considers the history of Southeast Asia, such as the divide between the so-called ASEAN and non-ASEAN Southeast Asian countries. Leadership is important for igniting a beyond-the-region or beyond-CARICOM outlook. It is important to spur convergence of the Greater Caribbean economies toward a positive post-pandemic economic recovery, growth, and development.

Conclusion

Caribbean governments, like the rest of the world, will face formidable policy challenges as they seek to overcome the wide-ranging and long-lasting health, financial, macroeconomic, and social impacts of COVID-19. With multilateral cooperation under strain, an adjusted approach is necessary for sufficient post-pandemic recovery, and to treat other enduring economic and financial challenges. As an ongoing process that must be accelerated, convergence could position the future direction of the Caribbean region in a world in which increasingly stringent trade and financial rules continuously pit wealthy countries against the poorest amid debilitating international structures that limit their policy options, making it extremely difficult to create viable policy and diplomatic spaces to successfully influence the international economic or financial architecture. This chapter acknowledges that problem-solving approaches are not limited to regional arrangements, but Caribbean economies might find more benefits through coalitions of the willing. Finally, good leadership has been discussed in the context of the catalytic role of the state in driving economic development, and as necessary to ignite and accelerate convergence and create an effective policy space for collective and joint action among like-minded economies, including for post-pandemic recovery.

References

Al Hassan, Abdullah, Mary Burfisher, Julian Chow, Ding, Fabio Di Vittorio, Dmitriy Kovtun, Arnold McIntyre, et al. 2020. *Is the Whole Greater than the Sum of Its Parts? Strengthening Caribbean Regional Integration.* IMF Working Paper. Vol. WP/20/8. Washington DC: International Monetary Fund.

Bergsten, C. Fred. 1997. "Open Regionalism." *The World Economy*, 20 (5): 545–65. https://doi.org/10.1111/1467-9701.00088.

Breslin, Shaun, and Richard Higgot. 2003. "New Regionalism(s) in the Global Political Economy: Conceptual Understanding in Historical Perspective." *Asia Europe Journal*, 1: 167–82.

Commonwealth Secretariat, ed. 1985. *Vulnerability: Small States in the Global Society.* Report of a Commonwealth Consultative Group. Geneva: Commonwealth Secretariat.

Dent, Christopher. 2003. "From Inter-Regionalism to Trans-Regionalism? Future Challenges for ASEM." *Asia Europe Journal*, 1 (2): 223–35.

Didier, Tatiana, Hevia Constantino, and Sergio Schmukler. 2012. "How Resilient and Countercyclical Were Emerging Economies during the Global Financial Crisis?" *Journal of International Money and Finance*, 31 (8): 2052–77.

Dookeran, Winston. 2020. *Geo Political Shifts in the Pandemic World Order.* Virtual Symposium, Faculty of Medical Sciences, St. Augustine.

ECLAC (Economic Commission for Latin America and the Caribbean). 2021. *International Trade Outlook for Latin America and the Caribbean, 2021.* Santiago: Economic Commission for Latin America and the Caribbean (ECLAC). Summary (LC/PUB.2021/14-P/Rev.1).

Girvan, Norman. 2013. "Re-Inventing the CSME." Edited text of address to The Caribbean Association of Judicial Officers, 3rd Biennial Conference, Accra Beach Hotel, Bridgetown, Barbados, 27 September.

Gustavo, Paulo, and Eliane Superti. 2016. "Integration and International Security in the Guyana Shield: Challenges and Opportunities." *Revista de Geopolítica*, 7 (1): 43–67. http://www.revistageopolitica.com.br/index.php/revistageopolitica/article/view/148.

Heifetz, B.A. 2016. "Trans-Regionalization of the Global Economic Space." *Society and Economy*, 6: 19–42.

Jules, Travis. 2015. "A Stich in Time Saves Caribbeanization: Meta-Steering and Strategic Coordination in an Era of Caribbean Trans-Regionalism." *Caribbean Journal of International Relations & Diplomacy*, 3 (2): 37–57.

Lewis, David. 2017. "The Guiana Shield: A Zone of Southern Caribbean Integration and Sustainable Development." *Commentary, Center for Strategic and International Studies* (blog), 28 November. https://www.csis.org/analysis/guiana-shield.

Luzina, T.V., E.A. Dudareva, E.M. Akhmetshin, V.V. Yankovskaya, Y.S. Berdova, and G.E. Emaletdinova. 2019. "The International and Legal Framework for Transregionalization of Trade and Economic Cooperation of the BRICS Countries." *European Research Studies Journal*, XXI (Special 3): 166–76. https://www.ersj.eu/journal/1370.

Mclean, Sheldon, and Jeetendra Khadan, 2015. *An Assessment of the Performance of CARICOM Extraregional Trade Agreements, an Initial Scoping Exercise.* Santiago: ECLAC.

Montoute, Anita. 2015. "CARICOM's External Engagements: Prospects and Challenges for Caribbean Regional Integration and Development." *Policy Brief*, May. OCP Policy Center.

Natelegawa, Marty. 2018. *Leadership and Regionalism in Southeast Asia.* Brisbane: Griffith Asia Institute.

Ramphal, Shridat S., and West Indian Commission. 1994. *Time for Action: Report of the West Indian Commission.* Largo: International Development Options; Kingston, Jamaica.

Ruland, Jurgen. 2002. "The European Union as an Inter- and Transregional Actor: Lessons for Global Governance from Europe's Relations with Asia." In *National Europe Centre Paper*. Vol. 13, Australian National University.

Tsardanidis, Charalambos. 2010. "Interregionalism: A Comparative Analysis of ASEM and FEALAC." In *Asia and Latin America: Political Economic and Multilateral Relations*, edited by Dosch Jörn and Jacob Olaf, 218–20. London: Routledge.

World Bank. 2020. *Global Economic Prospects, June 2020.* Washington D.C.: World Bank.

World Trade Organization. 2021. *World Trade Report, Economic Resilience and Trade.* Geneva: WTO.

11

The Trend in External Financing to the Caribbean

Is It in the Right Direction?

HELVIA VELLOSO[1]

Introduction

The increase in financial depth since 2003 has translated into greater availability of funding for the Latin America and Caribbean region and into better access to external financing. In the period of strongest regional growth before the global financial crisis of 2008–2009, the regional cost of accessing external financing was the lowest since the 1970s (Ocampo 2016). However, not all countries had the same opportunities to access external financing, as these depend on, among other factors, the size and openness of their economies, the depth of their financial systems, and their production structures.

Physically located in one of the most disaster-prone regions in the world, the Caribbean countries must rely on international financing to expand their limited fiscal capacity to respond to external shocks, which tend to be persistent and long-lasting. Nonetheless, some official sources of financing have been on a downward trend in recent years. The counterpart of this decline has been an increase in private sources of financing, including foreign direct investment,

[1] Economic Affairs Officer of the United Nations Economic Commission for Latin America and the Caribbean (ECLAC), Office in Washington, DC. The views and opinions expressed are my own and do not necessarily reflect the opinions of ECLAC or the countries it represents.

Acknowledgments: I would like to thank Winston Dookeran, for generously sharing his deep knowledge of the Caribbean region with me during his yearlong stay in Washington, DC. It was through the work we did together then that the main concepts and ideas for this chapter were developed. I am also thankful to Inés Bustillo, for her comments on the topics discussed in this chapter.

remittances, and private portfolio flows, which so far have not been enough to offset the loss of official assistance.

This chapter looks at the trends in international capital flows to the Caribbean – including foreign direct investment, portfolio flows, remittances, and official development assistance – since the 1980s. It also takes a closer look at the Caribbean countries' access to international debt markets from 2000 to 2020, examining key characteristics of debt securities, such as issuance volume, spreads, and credit ratings.

Trends in External Financing Flows to the Caribbean

A key development regarding external financing flows to the Caribbean is the downward trend of official development assistance (ODA) relative to average gross national income (GNI) from 1990 to 2016. In 2016, flows of ODA reached a historic low and represented 1 percent of Caribbean GNI. The 1.9 percent average for the 2010s marks a significant drop from the 5.6 percent average for the 1980s and 1990s (figure 11.1).

In contrast, private capital flows have been on the rise. Net foreign direct investment (FDI) and net personal remittance flows have become the top two sources of external financing since the 1990s. Net portfolio investment flows have been less significant and more unpredictable (figure 11.2).

FDI flows were on an upward trend until 2008, and following the global financial crisis, on a downward trend until 2012. Although there has been a partial recovery since then, flows have become more volatile. FDI flows go mainly to natural resource and service sectors, thus tying in directly with the region's trade specialization patterns and increasing exposure to sector-dependent shocks (box 11.1). Caribbean economies receive substantial FDI flows relative to their size with an average ratio of inward FDI to gross domestic product (GDP) in the 2010–2020 period of 3 percent. In almost half of the economies, inward FDI as a share of GDP exceeded 6 percent, making them sensitive to variations in these inflows (figure 11.3). In terms of amount, the top three recipients of FDI flows in the 2010–2020 period were Guyana, Jamaica, and the Bahamas (figure 11.4).

While countries in the Caribbean share many similarities, the subregion is also marked by heterogeneity. Population size and per capita income levels, for example, differ quite widely within the region. Some are commodity exporters, while most are service-oriented economies. Growth has also been uneven in the subregion. Similarities include proximity to major markets in North and South America, and for most countries, a transition from agriculture or mining to a service-driven economy, anchored on tourism and financial services. Another

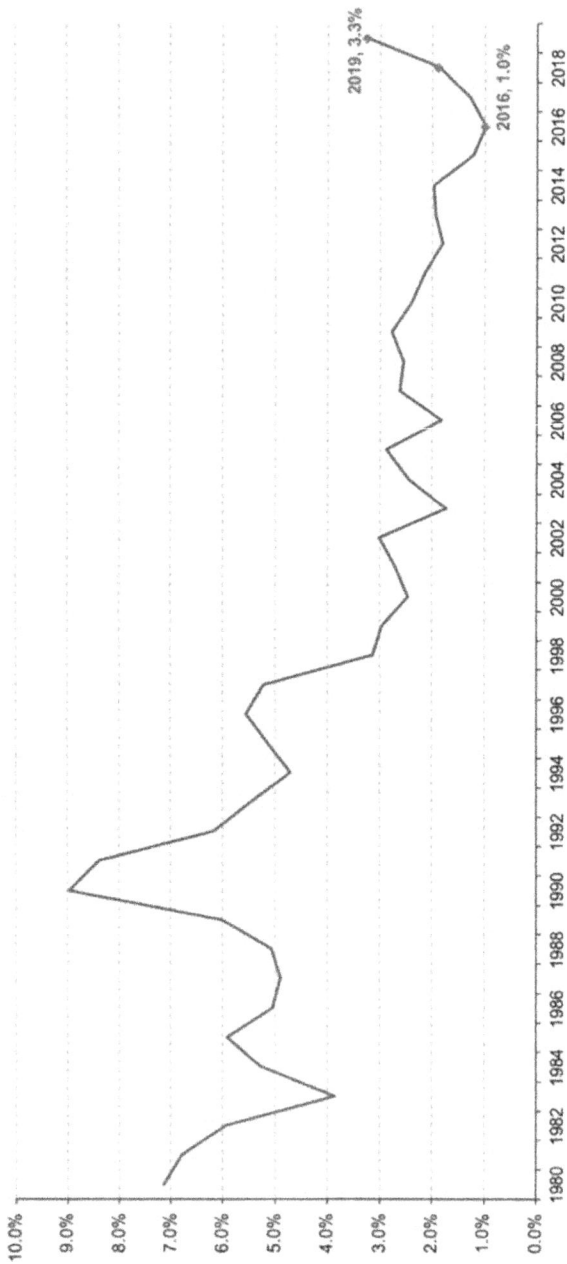

Figure 11.1 The Caribbean (thirteen countries): ODA net flows, 1980–2019 (*Simple average, as a percentage of GNI*).

Source: OECD and World Development Indicators for Antigua and Barbuda, the Bahamas, Barbados, Belize, Dominica, Grenada, Guyana, Jamaica, Saint Kitts and Nevis, Saint Lucia, Saint Vincent and the Grenadines, Suriname, and Trinidad and Tobago. Data was extracted on January 20, 2022.

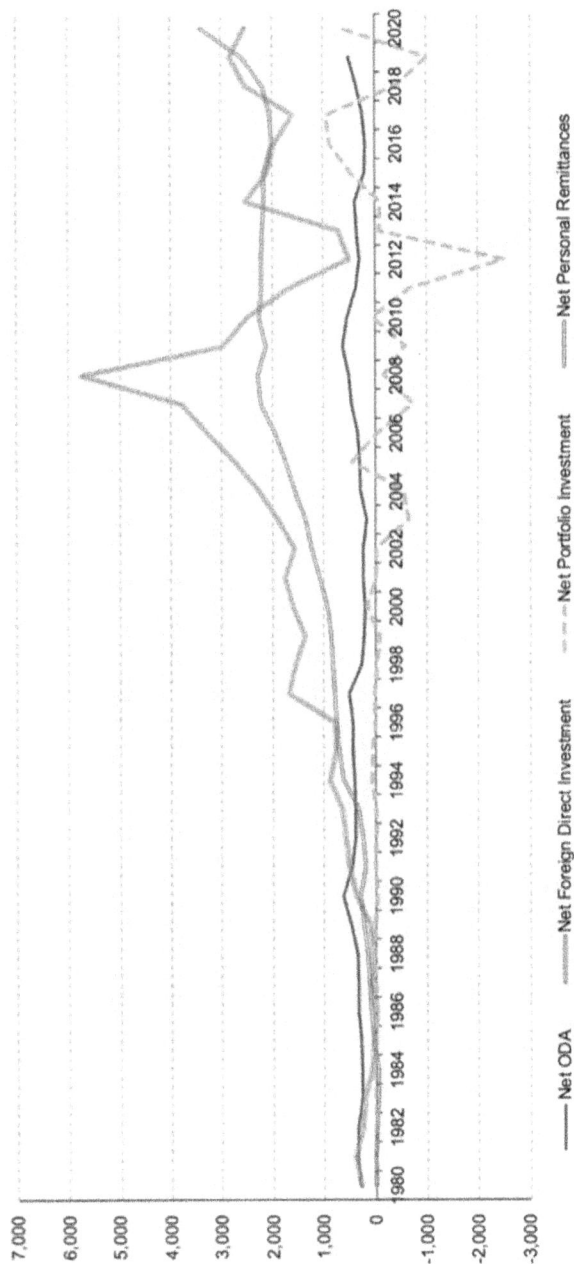

Figure 11.2 The Caribbean (thirteen countries): main external financing flows, 1980–2020 (*In current US$ millions*).

Source: ECLAC, based on data from OECD, CEPALSTAT, and World Development Indicators for Antigua and Barbuda, the Bahamas, Barbados, Belize, Dominica, Grenada, Guyana, Jamaica, Saint Kitts and Nevis, Saint Lucia, Saint Vincent and the Grenadines, Suriname, Trinidad and Tobago. Data was extracted on January 20, 2022.

Notes: (1) Portfolio investment flows are defined as cross-border transactions and positions involving equity or debt securities, other than those included in direct investment or reserve assets. Negative net flows represent outflows and positive net flows represent inflow. (2) For ODA flows, 2019 is the last year of data available.

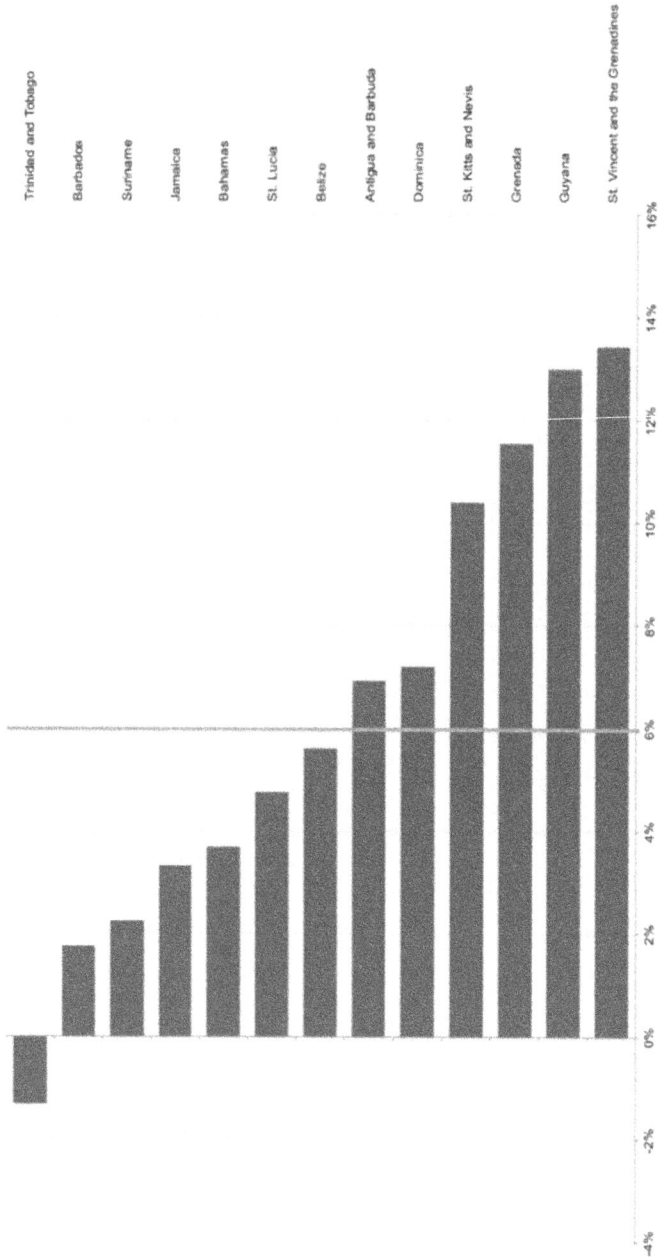

Figure 11.3 The Caribbean (thirteen countries): FDI inflows by country, 2010–2020 (*As a percentage of GDP*).

Source: ECLAC, CEPALSTAT.

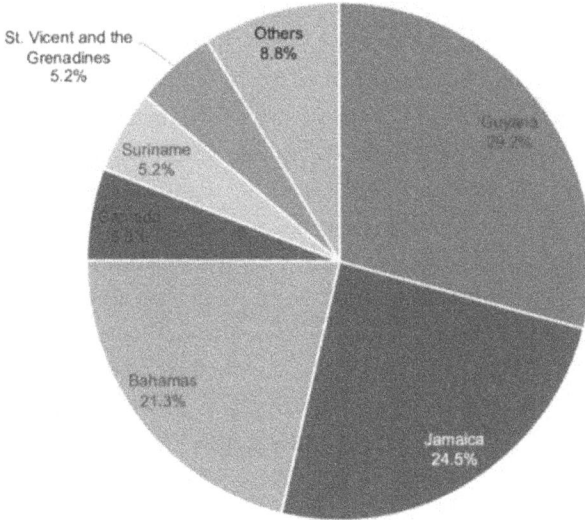

Figure 11.4 Top Caribbean recipients of FDI, 2010–2020 (*As a percentage of total FDI*).
Source: ECLAC, CEPALSTAT.

similarity is that domestic private investment is strongly driven by public investment, which highlights the importance of FDI as a source of investment financing.

BOX 11.1: FDI IN THE CARIBBEAN

FDI is narrowly based in terms of origin, with a great portion coming from a limited number of countries, especially Canada and the United States. As a result, shocks that affect these countries of origin are quickly transmitted to the Caribbean. Investment decisions made in Europe, the United States, or Asia can have large effects on the levels of investment, employment, or tax receipts in Caribbean economies because of the relative size of individual companies in those economies. Policies designed to maintain or attract FDI, including those aimed at making it easier to do business, are thus particularly important because policy changes may affect individual companies' decisions, directly impacting local economies.

Sectoral Trends

The Caribbean consists of several groups of economies, each with its own economic story reflecting its strengths and weaknesses. There are some sectoral trends that are common to the whole subregion, however. For many economies, the tourism sector is the largest earner of foreign exchange and the primary destination for investment. The second most important sector is natural resources. The third category is export-oriented FDI – FDI that seeks to exploit local production advantages to supply an external market. This is not a single sector but includes both export-oriented manufacturing and various export-oriented services, such as offshore education and business process outsourcing.[2] The final category is market-seeking FDI – defined as FDI whose purpose is to produce and sell a product in a specific market, rather than export it. This also encompasses various sectors, mostly in services (banking, retail, energy) but also in small-scale manufacturing.[3]

FDI Impact on Balance of Payments and Economic Growth

With respect to the *balance of payments*, the impact of FDI is ambiguous. While it is true that economies with temporary current account deficits may be able to offset them with a capital account surplus, many economies in the Caribbean have permanent current account deficits, and the continuous inflow of FDI that would be required to offset them would lead to a large build-up of foreign capital. Furthermore, such inflows are then associated with outflows of capital in the form of income from FDI. On average, outflows of income from FDI are equivalent to more than three-quarters of FDI inflows in the Caribbean, and they are particularly substantial in Barbados, Suriname, and Trinidad and Tobago.

The degree to which FDI crowds out local investment also affects its impact on the balance of payments. A local investment will not give rise to an influx of capital at the time the initial expenditure is carried out and does not lead to significant outward current transfers compared with a similar amount of FDI. Export receipts can rise whatever the source of the investment. Although local investment may seem more likely to have a beneficial long-term impact on the balance of payments than a similar amount of FDI, it is important to remember that FDI is often sought by

---

[2] BPO is the most important type of export-oriented service in the Caribbean (it includes call center services at the lower end, and technical support, accounting, and even management in the high end).

[3] For a more detailed and deeper analysis of FDI in the Caribbean, see ECLAC 2015, Chapter II.

countries because local firms do not have the resources to make the same types of greenfield investments that large multinational corporations do.

Besides the impact on the balance of payments, there is potential to positively affect *economic growth* in the different economies. Many Caribbean economies have long been suffering from a lack of competitiveness, and FDI could help to transform them. However, evidence for a transformative impact is limited.

Are FDI Promotion Policies Effective?

The impact of the extensive use of FDI promotion policies in the Caribbean is a subject of debate. The effectiveness of different policies of this type has not been sufficiently researched in the Caribbean context, making them difficult to justify when governments are suffering from significant revenue shortfalls. Investment incentives have been too often granted based on individual negotiations between investors and policymakers. Unfortunately, this is not always a relationship between equals in the Caribbean, with investors having substantially more bargaining power.

The result of such unbalanced relationships and of the fact that many Caribbean economies offer very similar products has been a race to the bottom between the different governments, which match one another's incentive offers. Caribbean governments should thus be encouraged to cooperate more energetically on reducing the FDI promotion policies available to investors, particularly those that do not seem to directly affect the variables which governments wish to act upon, such as employment creation. Only if governments cooperate closely through forums like CARICOM and OECS can they stand up to the market power of some of the larger corporate players in the region.[4] In particular, rather than having blanket fiscal subsidies, they could target specific sectors with reforms that can increase the local benefits of FDI.

Source: ECLAC 2015, Chapter II.

---

[4] CARICOM, the Caribbean Community, is a group of twenty countries: fifteen Member States and five Associate Members. Except for Belize, all Members and Associate Members are island states. The Organization of Eastern Caribbean States (OECS) is an international intergovernmental organization dedicated to economic harmonization and integration, protection of human and legal rights, and the encouragement of good governance among independent and nonindependent countries in the Eastern Caribbean.

Migrant remittances to the Caribbean have also increased substantially, becoming the most dynamic component of international capital flows together with FDI and exceeding 8 percent of GDP in some countries. Following the global financial crisis of 2008–2009, while FDI flows to the Caribbean have declined and become more volatile, flows of net personal remittances remain resilient and have overtaken FDI as the largest source of foreign financing to the Caribbean in seven of the past ten years.

In the case of portfolio investment, inflows increased from 2014 to 2017, following some critical debt restructurings.[5] However, they represent a much smaller share of the total and have shown more unpredictability. In 2018 and 2019, for example, there were outflows due to an increase in global volatility and risk aversion, but in 2020 inflows increased again. Because of their volatility and small role in the region, these flows are often overlooked as a source of financing, but through innovative debt instruments and increased cooperation they could play a more active role in the mobilization of resources toward development objectives.

The relative scale of the different sources of external financing is highly heterogeneous across Latin America and the Caribbean. There are countries such as Haiti in which ODA and remittances together account for practically the whole of the external financing flows received. Conversely, these flows play a lesser role in upper middle-income countries, where most financing comes from FDI, and depending on the period, portfolio investment flows. According to ECLAC, a breakdown of external financial flows to Latin America and the Caribbean reveals notable differences between the three principal subregions – the Caribbean, Central America, and South America – and that a country's per capita GDP is a strong predictor of its main sources of financial flows (ECLAC 2017, 21–22). On average, between 2017 and 2019, countries with per capita GDP significantly lower than the regional average tended to receive over 60 percent of their flows from ODA and remittances, while those with per capita GDP around or above the regional average attracted more capital in the form of FDI and portfolio flows, with remittances and ODA representing about 21 percent of their total financial flows on average (figure 11.5).

---

[5] Some of these debt restructurings include Belize (2013, 2017), Jamaica (2010, 2013), Grenada (2013, 15), St. Kitts and Nevis (2011), Antigua and Barbuda (2010).

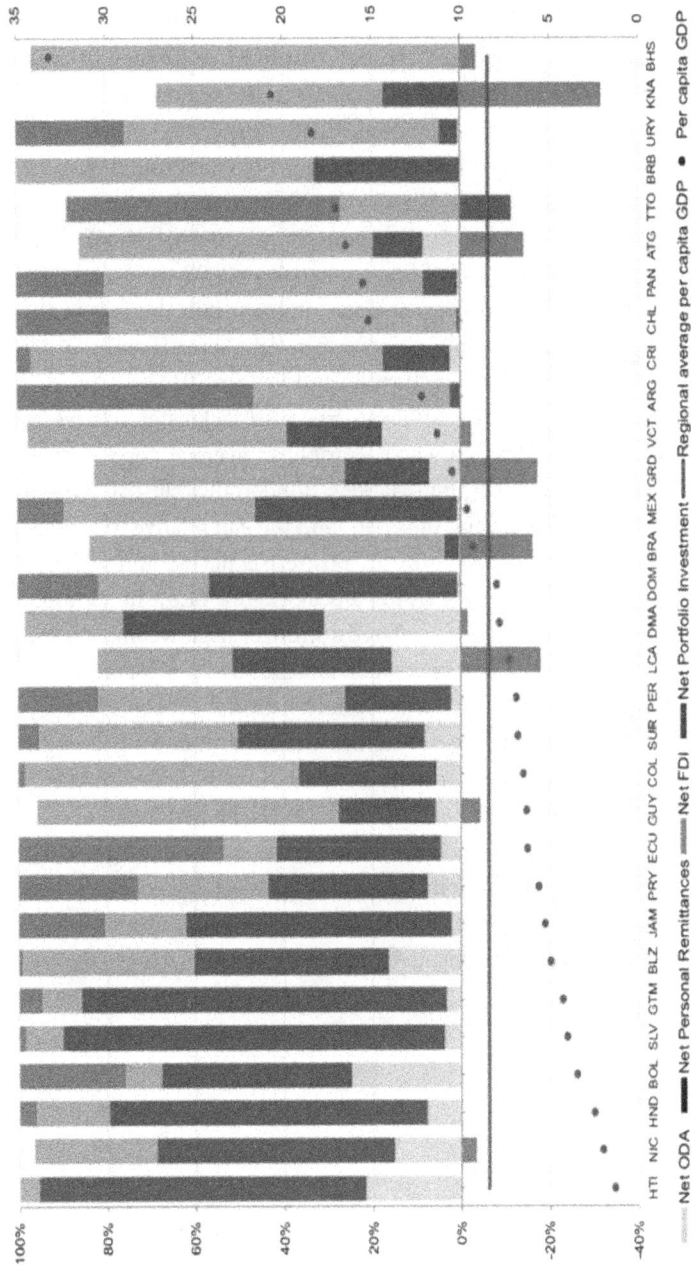

Figure 11.5 Composition of external financial flows: selected LAC countries (*Percentage of all flows (left scale); per capita GDP in US$ thousands (right scale); 2017–2019 three-year average*).

Source: ECLAC 2017, 22, based on data from OECD, CEPALSTAT, and World Development Indicators. Chart has been updated by author to 2019, latest data available for ODA flows (data extracted on January 20, 2022).

Note: Venezuela, for which full information for the reference period was not available, was not included.

Constrained Access to International Debt Markets

Access to international debt markets and flows of private capital toward Latin America and the Caribbean has increased significantly in the past twenty years. However, Caribbean countries have not borrowed as frequently or in as favorable terms as some of the larger economies in the region, as they face peculiar constraints in attracting global capital. Their narrow range of economic activities, limited economies of scale, and vulnerability to economic shocks are among the factors that impair access (Bustillo and Velloso 2013).

Vulnerability tends to increase during periods of external shocks and financial turbulence. During the global financial crisis of 2008–2009 and later bouts of volatility, the Caribbean felt a stronger impact than the rest of the LAC region, with larger increases in their sovereign debt spreads and sharper downgrades in their credit risk ratings (Bustillo and Velloso 2014).[6]

The post-crisis recovery in the Caribbean was also lackluster relative to the recovery of the LAC region as a whole. Caribbean average bond spreads measured by the JPMorgan Emerging Markets Bond Index (EMBI) Global Index increased more sharply during the crisis, and the gap relative to average spreads for the LAC region continued in the post-crisis period and widened from late 2010 to late 2012, when it reached a peak (figure 11.6). In addition, Caribbean sovereign credit risk ratings suffered a stronger negative impact, and new debt issuance as a share of the region's total issuance had not yet recovered by the end of 2012.[7] The Caribbean access to international debt markets has improved since late 2012, but access is still more limited than for the larger countries in the Latin America and Caribbean region.

In 2020, the Caribbean was hit hard by the COVID-19 pandemic and its impact on the tourism sector. As a result, following the pattern during periods of external turbulence, Caribbean bond spreads on average spiked more than spreads for the LAC region as a whole, while new debt issuance and sovereign credit risk ratings suffered a larger negative impact.

---

[6] For debt issuance, spreads. and credit ratings' behavior during more recent bouts of volatility. see recent issues of Capital Flows to Latin America and the Caribbean, Part II, ECLAC Washington Office, periodical publication.

[7] McLean and Charles (2018) show that the global financial crisis also negatively affected economic growth in the Caribbean.

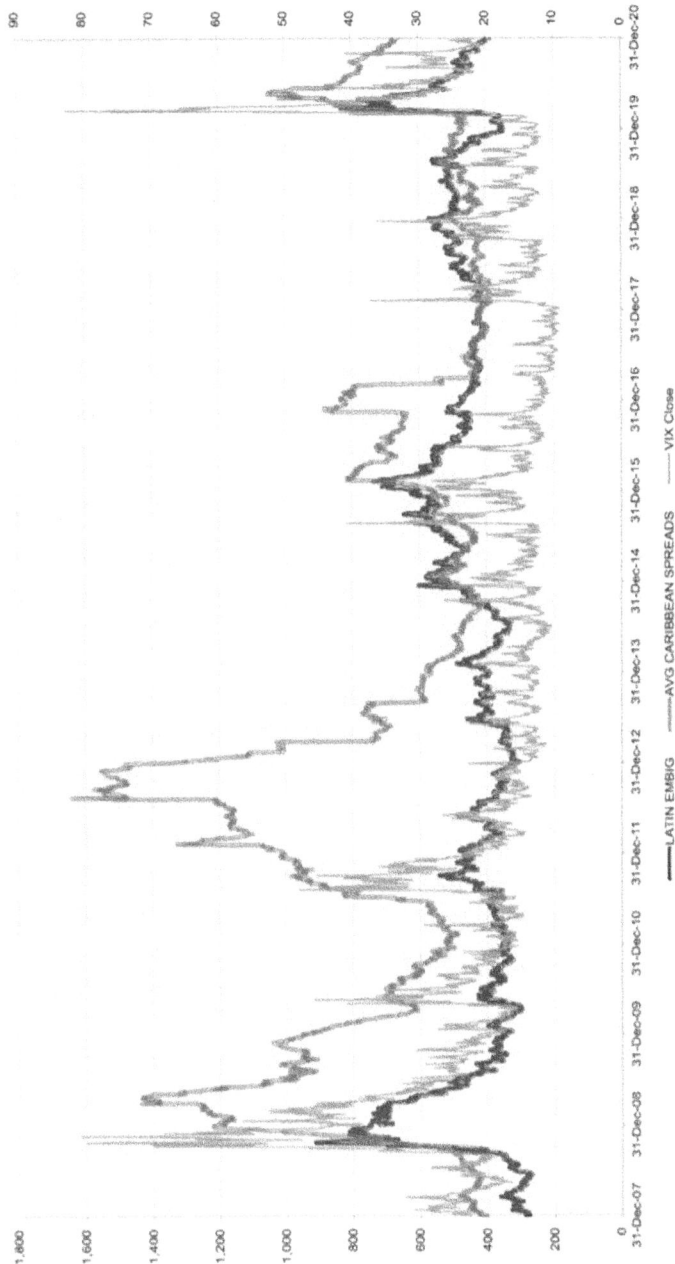

Figure 11.6 JPMorgan EMBIG and CBOE volatility index: Dec 2007–Dec 2020 (*Left scale: basis points; right scale: VIX close*).

Source: ECLAC, based on data from JPMorgan Emerging Markets Bond Index Global (EMBI Global) and the Chicago Board Options Exchange VIX Index.

International Debt Issuance: 2000–2020

The volume of LAC international bond issuance rose considerably in recent years, from US$ 40 billion in 2000 to US$ 145 billion in 2020. The 2020 total was second only to the historic record of US$ 146 billion reached in 2017 (ECLAC 2021a, 7). Caribbean international debt issuance remained a small share of the regional total during this period, however (figure 11.7).

In 2011, this share reached its lowest level since 2003, as Caribbean economies struggled to return to pre-global financial crisis levels on account of their close ties with the US economy and vulnerability to its business cycle. The share increased from 2011 to 2015 but has declined since, as commodity producers have been affected by a decline in commodity prices and service producers by natural disasters. In 2018, the Caribbean issuance share reached its lowest level of the 2000–2020 period as a return of volatility to global financial markets negatively impacted overall bond sales. After a slight uptick in 2019, there was another decline in this share in 2020, as the Caribbean was hard-hit by the COVID-19 pandemic.

Debt issuance in international markets has shown more volatility and cyclicality in the Caribbean than in the LAC region as a whole (figure 11.8). During the global financial crisis, it fell more in the Caribbean than in the rest of the region. Although issuance in the rest of the region started to recover in 2009, in the Caribbean it continued to fall until 2010, only reverting to an upward trend in 2011. Caribbean issuance in international bond markets reached a peak in 2014, following a series of debt restructurings. It was on a downward trend again until 2018, reflecting the adverse impact of lower commodity prices on commodity-producer countries, and of the storms that ravaged the region in that period on tourism and other service sectors. Although it ticked up in 2019, as lowering global interest rates supported bond activity, it declined in 2020 (while debt issuance for the LAC region as a whole actually increased), as tourism and other service sectors were heavily impacted by the pandemic.

Caribbean international debt issuance, sovereign and corporate combined, totaled US$ 36.4 billion in the 2000–2020 period and represented 2.2 percent of the LAC region's total. Seven Caribbean countries tapped international debt markets during this period. The top three issuers in the region were Jamaica, Trinidad and Tobago, and the Bahamas (figure 11.9).

One of the main debt financing trends in LAC in the past decade was a shift in external funding from sovereign to corporate and bank debt. Following this overall trend, Caribbean corporate bond issuance rose from zero in the 2000–2004 period to 54 percent of total issuance in 2005, surpassing sovereign issuance for the first time and for eleven of the fifteen years thereafter. In 2020, as a result of the COVID-19 pandemic, the Caribbean corporate share fell to only 15 percent, the lowest since 2008 (figure 11.10).

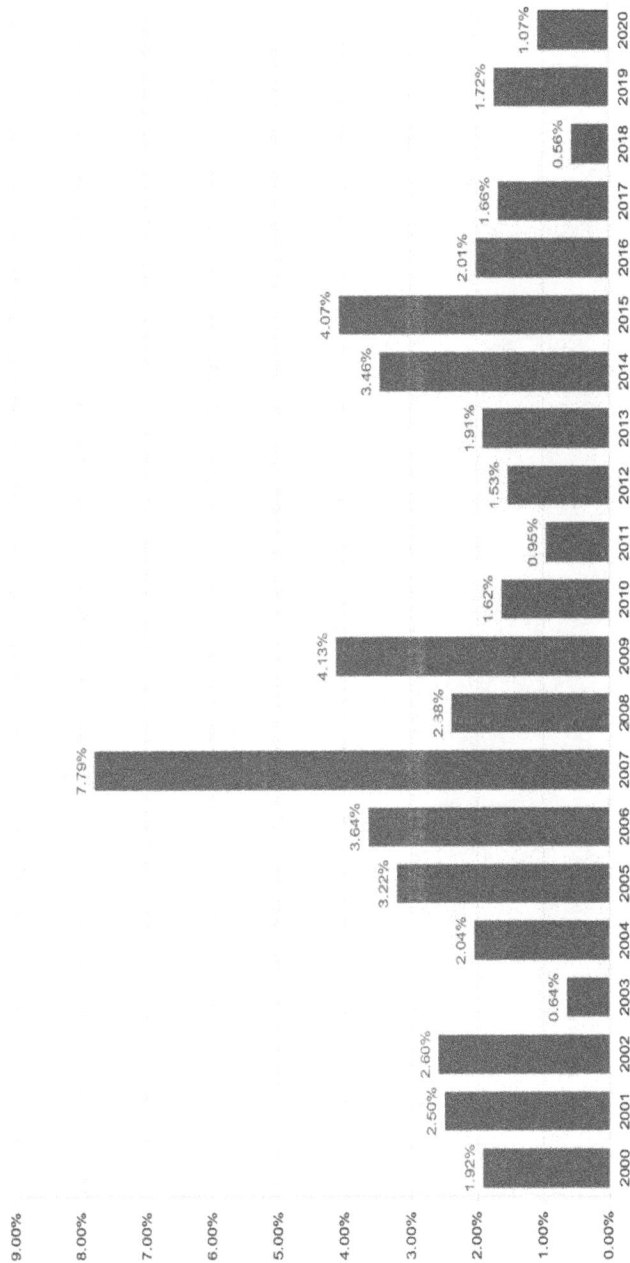

Figure 11.7 The Caribbean (seven countries): annual debt issuance in international markets as a share of the regional total, 2000–2020 (*Percentage*).

Source: Bustillo, Velloso, Dookeran and Perrotti (2018, 23), based on data available for the Bahamas, Barbados, Belize, Grenada, Jamaica, Suriname, and Trinidad and Tobago. Updated by author to 2020.

Note: in 2007, two unusual big issuances from two companies – Petroleum Co. of Trinidad and Tobago (US$ 750 million) and Digicel Group Ltd (US$ 1.4 billion) – increased the participation of the Caribbean in the total regional amount issued.

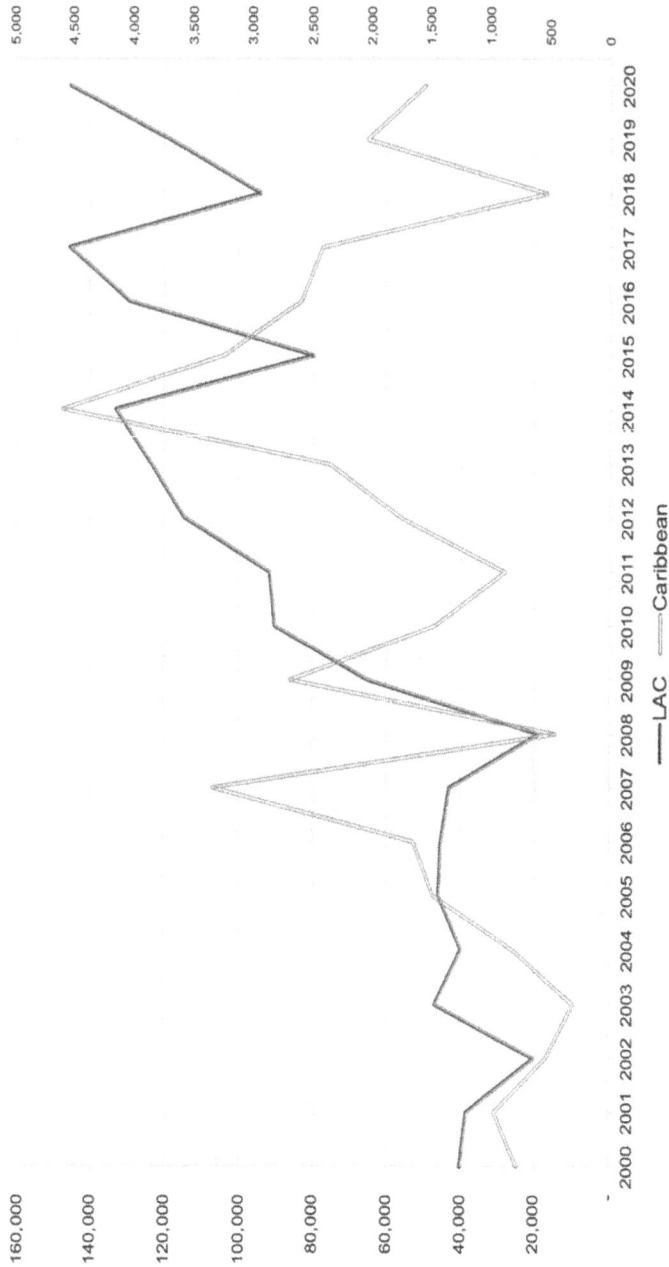

Figure 11.8 Annual debt issuance in international markets: the Caribbean vs LAC, 2000–2020 (*US$ Millions*; *LAC issuance (left scale)*; *Caribbean issuance (right scale)*).

Source: Bustillo, Velloso, Dookeran and Perrotti (2018, 23), based on data available for the Bahamas, Barbados, Belize, Grenada, Jamaica, Suriname, and Trinidad and Tobago. Updated by author to 2020.

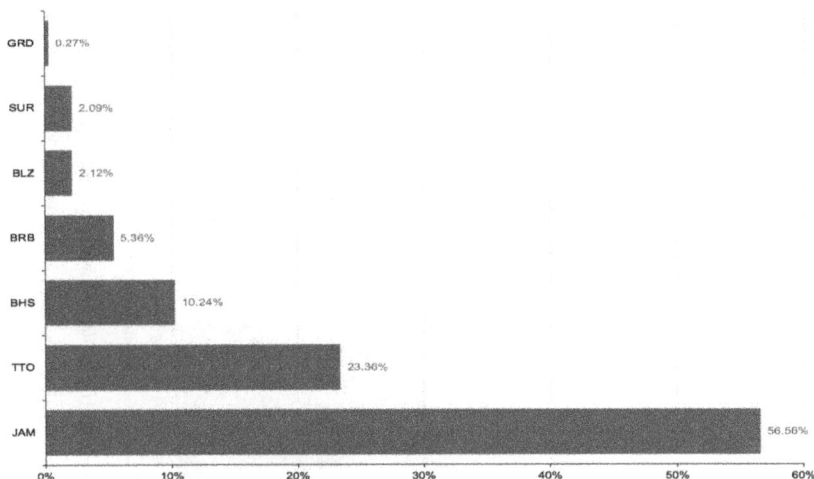

Figure 11.9 The Caribbean (seven countries): country shares of international debt issuance, 2000–2020 (*Percentage*).

Source: Bustillo, Velloso, Dookeran and Perrotti (2018, 24), based on data available for the Bahamas, Barbados, Belize, Grenada, Jamaica, Suriname, and Trinidad and Tobago. Updated by author to 2020.

Only a small number of Caribbean companies have tapped international markets, and most are either transnational corporations or state-owned, with state-owned companies representing about a third of the total Caribbean corporate issuance in international debt markets in the 2005–2020 period. More than half of the Caribbean total international corporate debt issuance in the period was issued by Digicel Group, a telecommunications conglomerate based in Jamaica.

Companies based on only four Caribbean countries – Jamaica, Trinidad and Tobago, Barbados, and the Bahamas – have tapped international bond markets. The top two corporate issuers were Jamaica and Trinidad and Tobago, with a share of 56 percent and 31 percent, respectively. Among all corporate issuers that were state-owned, 81 percent were from Trinidad and Tobago, including Consolidated Energy, Trinidad Generation Unlimited, Petroleum Company of Trinidad and Tobago, National Gas Company, First Citizens Bank, and Telecommunications Services of Trinidad and Tobago. Ninety percent of the Caribbean issuances took place in two sectors, telecommunications and energy, including power and oil and gas (figure 11.11).

Sovereign Debt Spreads

The severe fiscal and economic challenges faced by the Caribbean due to recurrent natural disasters and vulnerability to external shocks have contributed

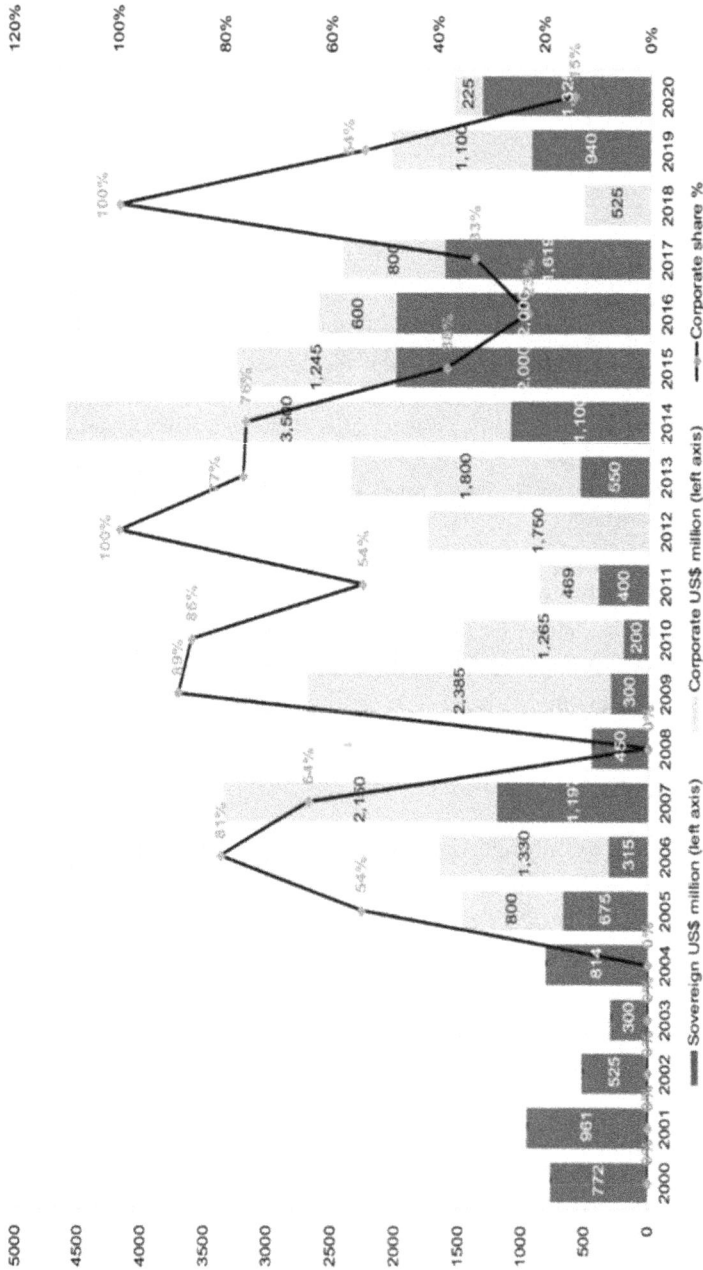

Figure 11.10 The Caribbean (seven countries): sovereign and corporate debt issuance in international markets, 2000–2020 (*Left scale: US$ Millions; right scale: Percentage*).

Source: Bustillo, Velloso, Dookeran and Perrotti (2018, 25), based on data available for the Bahamas, Barbados, Belize, Grenada, Jamaica, Suriname, and Trinidad and Tobago. Updated by author to 2020.

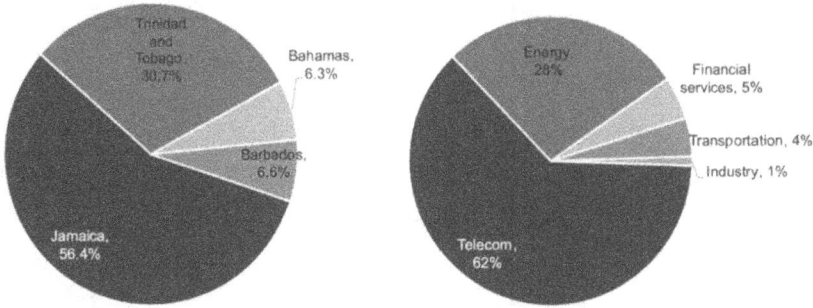

Figure 11.11 The Caribbean (four countries): country shares and sectoral composition of international corporate debt issuance, 2005–2020 (*Percentage*).

Source: Bustillo, Velloso, Dookeran and Perrotti (2018, 26), based on data available for the Bahamas, Barbados, Jamaica, and Trinidad and Tobago. Updated by author to 2020.

to an increase in the cost of borrowing abroad as measured by the JPMorgan Emerging Market Bond Index Global (EMBIG) spreads.

For some of the economies of the region, it is difficult to get a foothold in the capital markets borrowing, because bonds' benchmark sizes – US$ 500 million is JPMorgan Emerging Market Bond Index minimum – are in general too high for the size of their economies. The region's high level of indebtedness has compounded the problem.

From late 2010 to late 2012, the spread gap between the Caribbean countries and the EMBIG Latin component widened by almost 1,000 basis points due to the high number of defaults in the Caribbean. The spread gap closed in 2014, as successful bond restructurings lowered spreads. In 2015, the gap was reversed, with Caribbean spreads lower than the EMBIG Latin component by fifty basis points at the end of the year. The gap reopened in 2016, however, primarily because of a widening of more than 1,000 basis points in Belize's spreads, as the country attempted to negotiate a restructuring of its 2038 US$ 547 million bond, known locally as the "super bond" (Box 11.2), before a US$ 13 million coupon payment in February 2017. After a deal between the government and 87 percent of bondholders was reached in March 2017, the spread gap receded, but reopened in the second half of 2019 and remained open in 2020, as Caribbean countries were hit hard by the COVID-19 pandemic and collapse of the tourism sector, and by the decline in commodity prices early in the year. At the end of December 2020, the Caribbean debt spread average was 288 basis points higher than the EMBIG Latin component (figure 11.12). In the case of Jamaica and Trinidad and Tobago, their spreads were lower than the EMBIG Latin component in the past six years (figure 11.13).

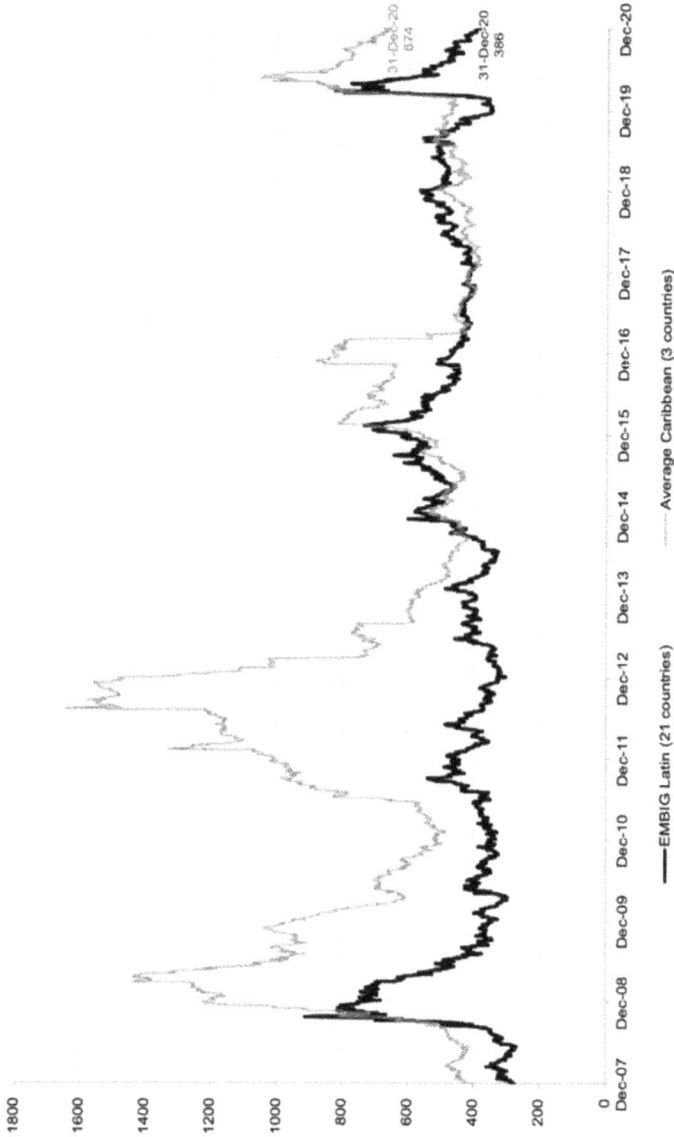

Figure 11.12 EMBIG average spreads: the Caribbean (three countries) versus LAC (twenty-one countries), Dec 2007–Dec 2020 (*Basis points*).

Source: Bustillo and Velloso (2013, 117), based on available data from JPMorgan Emerging Markets Bond Index Global (EMBI Global). Data updated to 2020 by author.
Notes: (1) The EMBIG Latin includes Argentina, Belize, Bolivia, Brazil, Chile, Colombia, Costa Rica, Dominican Republic, Ecuador, Guatemala, Honduras, Jamaica, Mexico, Panama, Paraguay, Peru, El Salvador, Suriname, Trinidad and Tobago, Uruguay, and Venezuela. (2) The Caribbean average is based on daily data available for Belize, Jamaica, and Trinidad and Tobago (no daily data is available for Suriname, which was added to the EMBIG index following its cross-border debut in October 2016 with the issuance of a US$ 550 million 2026 sovereign bond with a 6.25 percent coupon; its spread was 1,860 basis points at the end of December 2020).

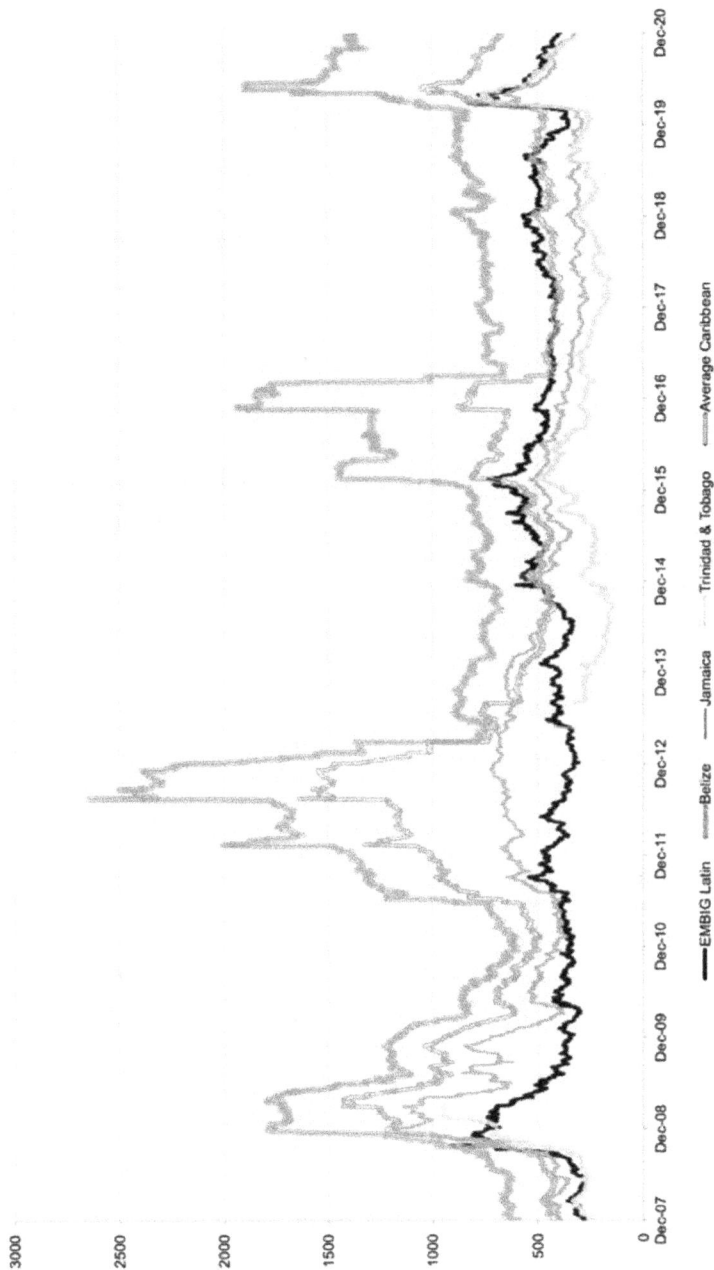

Figure 11.13 Caribbean EMBIG spreads by country, Dec 2007–Dec 2020 (*Basis points*).

Source: ECLAC (2020b, 33), based on available data from JPMorgan. Triridad and Tobago was out of the JPMorgan EMBIG index from March 2009 to August 2013.

BOX 11.2: BELIZE'S "SUPER BOND"

The behavior of Belize's spread in the past fifteen years reflects the restructuring of its US$ 547 million 2029 "super bond." The Government of Belize undertook four sovereign debt restructurings within a relatively short time span. Following default in August 2006, the bond – which originally carried an interest rate averaging more than 11 percent – was restructured in early 2007 as a "super bond." It was restructured again in February 2013 as "Super bond 2.0," following another default in August 2012, in 2017, and in 2020.

The 2006–2007 Restructuring

In 2006–2007, facing an acute external liquidity shortage due to high debt service burden, Belize exchanged its various external debt instruments, including both loans and bonds, into one single US dollar-denominated bond ("super bond") with face value of US$ 547 million. The exchange lengthened maturity and lowered coupon rates. The debt restructuring provided a significant liquidity relief, but solvency concerns remained unresolved.

The 2012–2013 Restructuring

Six years later, the Belizean authorities, this time driven mainly by a substantial increase in the coupon rates and future fiscal solvency concern, launched a second external debt restructuring, with a modest face-value haircut as well as cash-flow relief through changes in both coupon and maturity structures.

In March 2012, the Government of Belize announced the commencement of a comprehensive review of external public-sector debt and contingent liabilities. On August 21, 2012, the Government of Belize missed a US$ 23 million coupon payment on the "super bond" resulting in Standard and Poor's downgrading the country to a default rating. On September 20, 2012, after the expiration of the thirty-day grace period, the government announced that it would make a partial payment of US$ 11.6 million, roughly half of the interest owed to bondholders. The Coordinating Committee of Belize Bondholders described the government's announcement as a step in the right direction and agreed not to seek legal remedies for sixty days to provide enough time for the two sides to finalize negotiations on the debt restructuring process. Negotiations began on October 2, and an exchange offer was made on February 15, 2013. On March 8, 2013, the government announced that the holders of 86 percent of the country's US dollar bonds due in 2029 had decided to participate in the restructuring and exchange their bonds for new US dollar bonds *due in 2038.*

The 2016–2017 Restructuring

Starting in 2016, the Belizean authorities had attempted to negotiate a restructuring of the 2038 US$ 547 million bond, before a US$13 million coupon payment on February 20, 2017. The government claimed that it could not meet scheduled repayments falling due in 2017 or in the medium term. Belize's attempts to negotiate a deal with creditors were met with strong resistance from bondholders, but as both parties conceded that the debt terms were unsustainable, a deal between the government and 87 percent of bondholders was reached in March 2017.

In the revised terms of the 2017-2018 restructuring exercise, there was no principal haircut; instead, approximately US$526.5 million of new 2034 bonds were issued without face-value reduction. They reduced the coupon rate by 1.83 percent and introduced a fixed coupon rate of 4.9375 percent. There was an extension of the grace period by 11 years, with amortization starting from 2030 and the maturity was shortened by 4 years, among other terms. (BBN 2021)

Belize also committed to taking IMF assistance in case it missed primary surplus targets in the coming years.

The 2020–2021 Restructuring

Following the strong hit to Belize's tourism sector and overall economy from the COVID-19 pandemic, risks of entering a distressed debt exchange increased. On August 10, 2020, the Government of Belize announced it had reached an agreement with the bondholders of its US dollar bonds due in 2034 on amendments to the terms of such bonds, which led to a downgrade in its credit rating to selective default by Standard and Poor's. On November 5, 2021, it announced the settlement of the offer to purchase its US dollar bond due in 2034, redeeming all notes that had not yet been tendered. As a result, the government said "Belize has reduced the principal amount of its external indebtedness by approximately US$ 250 million (representing approximately 12% of Belize's gross domestic product), significantly improving the sustainability of its financial position" (PR Newswire 2021). This operation was financed with funding provided by a subsidiary of The Nature Conservancy (TNC) as part of TNC's Blue Bonds for Ocean Conservation program, which uses private capital to refinance the public debt of participating countries to support durable marine conservation efforts and sustainable marine-based economic activity.

The financial transaction between the Government of Belize and TNC is insured by the US International Development Finance Corporation and is backed by the proceeds of a blue bond, a type of Environmental, Social and Governance (ESG) instrument, arranged by Credit Suisse, a bank. The payback is due over nineteen years with a coupon that begins below that of the 2034 bond being restructured but rising above it over time. The transaction will enable the country to not only reduce its debt burden but also generate an estimated US$ 180 million for marine conservation, in support of its commitment to protect 30 percent of its ocean by 2026, strengthen governance frameworks for domestic and high sea fisheries, and establish a regulatory framework for coastal blue carbon projects.

Source: Prepared by the author, based on Bustillo, Velloso, Dookeran, and Perrotti 2018, 28, ECLAC 2021a, 32, ECLAC 2021b, 30–31, Asonuma et al. 2014, BBN 2021, and PR Newswire 2021.

Evolution of Credit Ratings

The evolution of credit ratings in Latin America and the Caribbean closely followed the region's business cycle. During the financial shocks of the second half of the 1990s, many countries in the region were downgraded, but there was a trend toward improved credit quality from 2004 to 2008, which was interrupted by the global financial crisis (figure 11.14).

In parallel with the increase in EMBIG spreads, Caribbean countries experienced downgrades in their credit risk rating during the global financial crisis, and many of them have yet to regain their previous rating. In 2020, with the COVID-19 pandemic crisis, Caribbean countries again experienced sharp credit rating downgrades. Because of the small size and underdeveloped

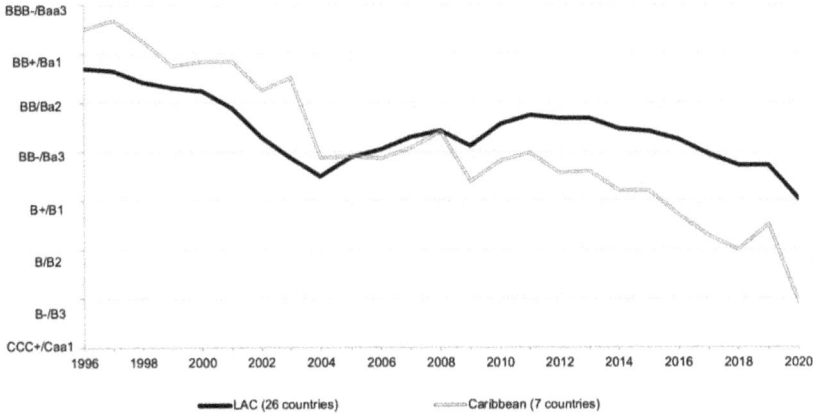

Figure 11.14 The evolution of credit ratings in Latin America and the Caribbean (twenty-six countries), 1996–2020 (Average credit rating: Fitch, Moody's, and Standard & Poor's).

Source: Bustillo, Velloso, Dookeran and Perrotti (2018, 29), on the basis of data available from Fitch, Moody's, and Standard & Poor's, for Argentina, Bahamas, Barbados, Belize, Bolivia, Brazil, Chile, Colombia, Costa Rica, Cuba, Dominican Republic, Ecuador, El Salvador, Guatemala, Honduras, Jamaica, Mexico, Nicaragua, Panama, Paraguay, Peru, St. Vincent and the Grenadines, Suriname, Trinidad and Tobago, Uruguay, and Venezuela. The Caribbean average rating includes seven countries: Barbados, the Bahamas, Belize, Jamaica, Suriname, St. Vincent and the Grenadines, and Trinidad and Tobago. Investment grade: BBB-/Baa3 and above. Data updated to 2020 by author.

capital markets in many of their economies, credit ratings can potentially play an important role in investors' decisions toward the region. Together, the three main credit rating agencies – Fitch, Moody's, and Standard & Poor's – provide ratings for about seven Caribbean countries, including Barbados, the Bahamas, Belize, Jamaica, Suriname, Trinidad and Tobago, as well as Saint Vincent and the Grenadines, which received a rating for the first time in 2016 from Moody's.

Overall, Caribbean credit quality started from a better position in the mid-1990s than the rest of the LAC region, but since then it has been on a decline, as the subregion has struggled with stagnant economic growth, recurrent natural disasters, and fiscal deterioration (Bustillo, Perrotti, and Velloso 2018 and 2019). High levels of debt as a share of GDP and limited fiscal space slow down policy response during economic downturns. Most of the credit rating downgrades that took place in the aftermath of the global financial crisis and during the COVID-19 pandemic were motivated by worsening fiscal conditions, as financial and economic instability brought about by the crises weighed heavily on the countries' fiscal accounts.

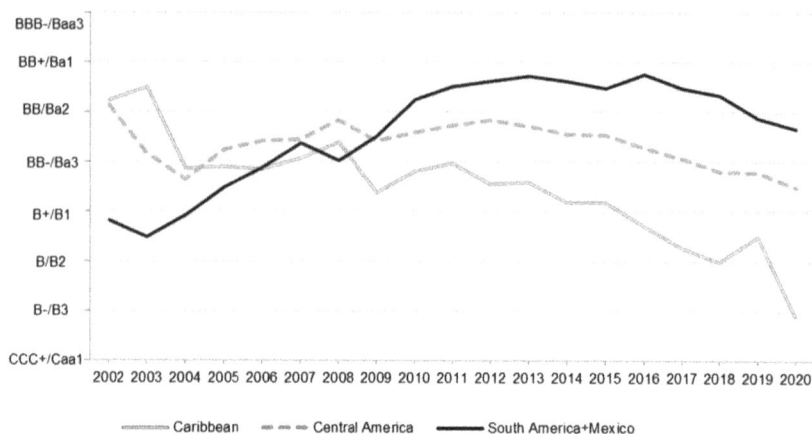

Figure 11.15 Average credit ratings by region, 2002–2020 (Average credit rating: Fitch, Moody's, and Standard & Poor's).

Source: Bustillo, Velloso, Dookeran and Perrotti (2018, 31), based on data from Fitch, Moody's, and Standard & Poor's. Data updated to 2020 by author.

For South America and Mexico, credit quality recorded an upward trend from 2003 to 2016. Since then, the number of downgrades has increased, but on average creditworthiness remains a lot higher than in 2003. That's not the case for Caribbean countries (figure 11.15).

The Caribbean countries suffered downgrades following the onset of the 2008 financial crisis, and although there was an incipient recovery in creditworthiness from 2009 to 2011, the downward trend resumed after that until 2018. By the end of 2017, ten years after the global financial crisis, most of the rated Caribbean countries had not yet recovered the credit rating standing they held at the onset of the global financial crisis. There was a slight improvement in the Caribbean countries' credit ratings in 2019 followed by a sharp decline in 2020. Four Caribbean countries – the Bahamas, Belize, Suriname, and Trinidad and Tobago – were downgraded in 2020. Belize and Suriname, due to their debt restructuring processes, were downgraded multiple times, by multiple agencies, as they sought to restructure their external debt amid an economic downturn exacerbated by the COVID-19 pandemic. As of December 2020, credit ratings for all Caribbean countries remained lower than in 2007 (table 11.1).

For the purposes of this section, sovereign ratings were converted to numerical values and averaged across the three main credit rating agencies: Fitch, Moody's, and Standard & Poor's (table 11.2).

Table 11.1 Credit ratings before and after the global financial crisis (2007 and 2017) and at end of 2020

	S&P			Moody's			Fitch		
	2007	2017	2020	2007	2017	2020	2007	2017	2020
BHS	A-	BB+	BB-	A3	Baa3	Ba2	n/a	n/a	n/a
BRB	BBB+	CCC+	B-	Baa2	Caa3	Caa3	n/a	n/a	n/a
BLZ	B	B-	CCC+	Caa1	B3	Caa3	n/a	n/a	n/a
JAM	B	B	B+	B1	B3	B2	B+	B	B+
SUR	B+	B	CCC	B1	B1	Caa3	B	B-	C
VCT	n/a	n/a	n/a	n/a	B3	B3	n/a	n/a	n/a
TTO	A-	BBB+	BBB-	Baa1	Ba1	Ba1	n/a	n/a	n/a

Source: Bustillo, Velloso, Dookeran, and Perrotti (2018, 31), on the basis of data from Fitch, Moody's, and Standard & Poor's. Data updated to 2020 by author.

Looking Ahead

The Caribbean economies are characterized by small populations and land masses, limited human capital, and recurrent external shocks. They also rely on international finance to supplement domestic savings and mitigate risks, including from natural disasters. In a context of lower ODA flows and concessional financing than in the recent past, the socioeconomic challenges facing the Caribbean economies, which have been aggravated by the impact of the COVID-19 pandemic, will demand new sources of international financing and the participation of the private sector, as the amount of resources necessary to meet these challenges far exceed the scope of traditional financing for development.

The trends regarding access to international financing in the past twenty years indicate that Caribbean debt issuers are not sufficiently large or creditworthy to raise funds in international debt markets in as favorable terms as issuers from some larger Latin American countries. Greater and improved cooperation among Caribbean economies, and with the international community, may offer them a way to overcome the constraints of limited economies of scale and less favorable access to international capital. In this context, new debt instruments – such as ESG fixed-income securities and state-contingent debt, among others – and mechanisms (such as the inclusion of natural disaster clauses in the contractual terms of a debt instrument) could become an option to bolster resilience and help transfer risk in cost-effective ways, offering a viable alternative for the mobilization of external resources toward a sustainable recovery and development.

Table 11.2 Credit rating scale

	S&P	Score	MOODY'S	Score	FITCH	Score
Upper investment grade	AAA	22	Aaa	22	AAA	22
	AA+	21	Aa1	21	AA+	21
	AA	20	Aa2	20	AA	20
	AA-	19	Aa3	19	AA-	19
	A+	18	A1	18	A+	18
	A	17	A2	17	A	17
	A-	16	A3	16	A-	16
Lower investment grade	BBB+	15	Baa1	15	BBB+	15
	BBB	14	Baa2	14	BBB	14
	BBB-	13	Baa3	13	BBB-	13
Noninvestment grade	BB+	12	Ba1	12	BB+	12
	BB	11	Ba2	11	BB	11
	BB-	10	Ba3	10	BB-	10
Lower noninvestment grade	B+	9	B1	9	B+	9
	B	8	B2	8	B	8
	B-	7	B3	7	B-	7
	CCC+	6	Caa1	6	CCC+	6
	CCC	5	Caa2	5	CCC	5
	CCC-	4	Caa3	4	CCC-	4
	CC	3	Ca	3	CC	3
	c	2	C	2	C	2
Default	SD	1		1	RD	1
	D	0		0	D	0

Source: Bustillo and Velloso (2013, 104), on the basis of data from Fitch, Moody's, and Standard & Poor's.

References

Asonuma, Tamon, Gerardo Peraza, Kristine Vitola, and Takahiro Tsuda. 2014. "Sovereign Debt Restructurings in Belize: Achievements and Challenges Ahead." IMF Working Paper. WP/14/132, July.

BBN 2021. "Where did the Superbond Come From?" 19 March. https://www .breakingbelizenews.com/2021/03/19/where-did-the-superbond-come-from/.

Bustillo, Inés, and Helvia Velloso. 2013. "Debt Financing Rollercoaster. Latin America and Caribbean Access to International Bond Markets since the Debt Crisis, 1982-2012." Serie Libros de la CEPAL No. 119 (LC/G.2570-P, Sales No. E.13.II.G.12. Copyright © United Nations), September. https://repositorio.cepal.org/handle/11362 /2635.

———. 2014. "Access to International Capital Markets: Recent Developments in Central America and the Caribbean." ECLAC Office in Washington D.C., 23 April, LC/WAS/L.129. https://repositorio.cepal.org/handle/11362/37855.

Bustillo, Inés, Daniel Perrotti, and Helvia Velloso. 2018. "Sovereign Credit Ratings in Latin America and the Caribbean: Trends and Impact on Debt Spreads." *Series Studies and Perspectives* No. 18. ECLAC Office in Washington D.C., December, LC/TS.2018/107. https://www.cepal.org/en/publications/44336-sovereign-credit-ratings-latin-america-and-caribbean-trends-and-impact-debt.

———. 2019. "Sovereign Credit Ratings in Latin America and the Caribbean: History and Impact on Bond Spreads." *Economía*, 20, no. 1 (Fall): 155–96. Published by Brookings Institution Press. doi: https://doi.org/10.1353/eco.2019.0011.

Bustillo, Inés, Helvia Velloso, Winston Dookeran, and Daniel Perrotti. 2018. "Resilience and Capital Flows in the Caribbean." ECLAC Office in Washington D.C., LC/WAS/TS.2018/2/-*, October. https://www.cepal.org/en/publications/43420-resilience-and-capital-flows-caribbean.

ECLAC. 2015. "Foreign Direct Investment in Latin America and the Caribbean, Chapter II: Foreign Direct Investment in the Caribbean." Copyright © United Nations, June 2015, Santiago, Chile. S.15-00534. http://repositorio.cepal.org/bitstream/handle/11362/38215/S1500534_en.pdf.

———. 2017. "Financing the 2030 Agenda for Sustainable Development in Latin America and the Caribbean. The Challenges of Resource Mobilization." Forum of the Countries of Latin America and the Caribbean on Sustainable Development, Mexico City, 26–28 April. http://repositorio.cepal.org//handle/11362/41197.

———. 2021a. "Capital Flows to Latin America and the Caribbean: 2020 Year-in-Review in Times of COVID-19." Report Prepared by Helvia Velloso, March, LC/WAS/TS.2021/1. https://www.cepal.org/en/publications/46697-capital-flows-latin-america-and-caribbean-2020-year-review-times-covid-19.

———. 2021b. "Capital Flows to Latin America and the Caribbean: First Nine Months of 2021." Report Prepared by Helvia Velloso, November, LC/WAS/TS.2021/9. https://www.cepal.org/en/publications/47514-capital-flows-latin-america-and-caribbean-first-nine-months-2021.

McLean, Sheldon, and Don Charles. 2018. "Caribbean Development Report. A Perusal of Public Debt in the Caribbean and Its Impact on Economic Growth." *Series Studies and Perspectives,* ECLAC Subregional Headquarters for the Caribbean, LC/TS.2017/157, LC/CAR/TS.2017/18, S.17-01291, January.

Ocampo, J.A. 2016. "Latin America and World Economic Turmoil." Chapter II in *Neostructuralism and Heterodox Thinking in Latin America and the Caribbean in the Early Twenty-First Century, ECLAC Books,* No.132 (LC/G.2633-P/Rev.1), Economic Commission for Latin America and the Caribbean (ECLAC). https://repositorio.cepal.org/bitstream/handle/11362/40121/S1600999_en.pdf?sequence=1&isAllowed=y.

PR Newswire. 2021. News provided by The Government of Belize. "Belize Announces Successful Settlement of Cash Tender Offer and Redemption of All of Its U.S. Dollar Bonds due 2034," 5 November. https://www.prnewswire.com/news-releases/belize-announces-successful-settlement-of-cash-tender-offer-and-redemption-of-all-of-its-us-dollar-bonds-due-2034-301417916.html.

12

Financing for Quality Investment

The Search for Fresher Sources

MIRIAM L. CAMPANELLA AND WINSTON DOOKERAN

Introduction

Growth in both advanced and emerging economies is slowing. For 2019, the world Gross Domestic Product (GDP) was expected to grow by around three percent, the slowest growth rate since 2009. The slowdown in world GDP growth reflected a range of factors, but it coincided with an escalation in trade tensions. For example, since 2018 the United States (US) gradually raised tariff rates on key trading partners, most notably China (see Bank of England's Inflation Report 2019). US tariff rates on Chinese exports were around five times higher than they were in 2017, with Chinese tariff rates on US exports around two and a half times higher. The direct impact of these measures on the world economy is likely to be relatively small. As laid out in the Inflation Report, tariffs introduced to date will reduce world GDP by around a quarter percent over the forecast, via their direct effects on the real economy, for example, through reduced trade flows and higher import costs. However, indirect effects, such as the impact of trade tensions on sentiment, are important as well. Firms are less likely to increase investment if they are uncertain about future trading relationships. Since the Ukraine–Russia war conflict, and the sanctions being imposed on Russia by the US, Europe, and Western allies, a new era of global isolationism, supply interruptions, and rising commodity prices has increased considerably the level of uncertainty, especially in trade matters.

Concerns around rising trade tensions and measures of uncertainty about economic policy have risen sharply. The Bloomberg measure of global economic policy uncertainty increased over 2018 and reached record highs in June (Figure 12.1).

Measuring policy uncertainty has led to the construction of the index of Global Economic Policy Uncertainty (GEPU). In discussing this index, Davis remarked, "The elevated levels of global policy uncertainty in the past five years compared even to the crisis years of 2008-09 is remarkable. They have contributed to the

Standard deviations from average

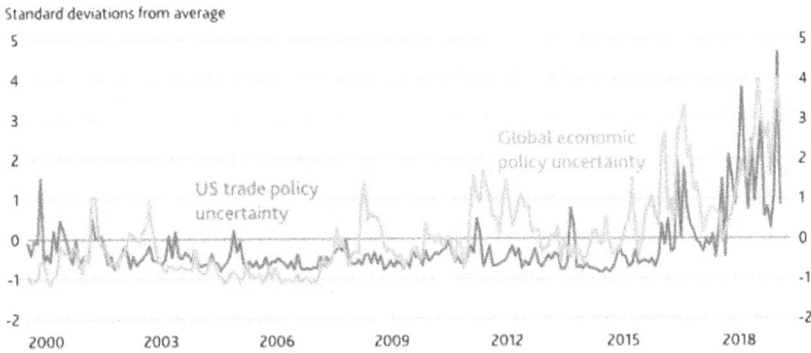

Figure 12.1 Measures of policy uncertainty.

Source: Global Economic Policy Uncertainty index January 1997–May 1997. https://www.policyuncertainty.com

disappointing performance of the global economy in recent years. By how much is an open question and an active area of research? (Davis 2016, 8)."

This measure of policy uncertainty will increase significantly due to the continuing military clashes and devastation in the Ukraine-Russian war, and its global impact on energy supplies and commodity trade disruptions. Against this uncertain scenario, large and small countries, no matter in which continent they are located, all share the "growth challenge" (Dookeran 2019), matching limited resources and updating infrastructure in the midst of environmental challenges. Updated infrastructure and its value chain are the bedrock of economic opportunity. They facilitate trade, increase productivity, promote knowledge sharing, and create an environment for economic and even social innovation. For this reason, quality infrastructure development is both a top responsibility and a high priority of the state.

Eager to unlock the potential of their respective economies, Asia, Latin America, and Caribbean (LAC) states – to varying degrees – are pursuing their own infrastructure "build-out programs." Increasing urbanization, population growth, and rising energy demand are fueling increases for energy, transport, and digital connectivity expansion. However, budgetary, technical, and bureaucratic constraints across the region mean that states on their own have been unable to meet the domestic demand for infrastructure needs. Therefore, attempting to bridge the infrastructure gap is a critical catalyst in development for all – small, medium, or large economies.

The financing of quality investment and the provision of liquidity are the lifeblood of any economic system. The task is to shore up sufficient finance to ensure there is enough liquidity to support a growing and resilient economy.

Reliance on international finance, locked into the dollar and US jurisdictional powers, has often turned out to be risky and costly. US financial sanctions, abrupt changes in the Federal Reserve monetary policies, or – as recently – the eruption of the financial crisis, caused via dollar shortage, has painful consequences for emerging economies. Disconnections from the dollar capital markets affect a government's infrastructure build-out programs and can hamper that economy from catching up.

Therefore, it may be asked where must one turn to, in order to tap into the liquidity that is necessary to meet the challenges of these current high level of uncertainties? Increasingly, global markets will face unbearable forex (FX) risks. How will governments avoid disconnection from the capital market, FX risk, and/or abrupt interruption of liquidity to long-term investments?

This chapter suggests that boosting the use of local-currency beyond trade financing makes sense in the current dilemma. Established and renewed finance outlets and central banks' Bilateral Swap Agreements (BSAs) are first on the list of international alternative finance sources. The currency exchange fund (TCX) which promotes local-currency financing to reduce the currency risk when international investors provide debt to borrowers in developing countries can expand. So far, TCX has operated in poor countries. It should now expand its reach and raise the stakes in providing financing for infrastructure programs. Signing BSAs with central banks in developed and emerging economies could help diversify from the vagaries of the dollar, and open new doors for financial sustainability. It may also encourage more monetary discipline.

Since 2010, China has pursued the internationalization of the Renminbi (RMB), which has rendered BSAs to be more than simply short-term trade arrangements. These instruments now apply to long-term infrastructure investments, like the Belt and Road Initiative (BRI). Recently, the European Commission and the European Central Bank (ECB) are considering BSAs to relaunch the internationalization of the Euro.

The chapter develops as follows. Section one measures the mismatch between the Sustainable Development Goals (SDG) and the finance gap. Section two explains international capital markets and the hard-currency risk. Section three identifies tools to hedge local-currency financing.

Metrics in Mismatch: SDGs and Finance Gap

According to the Organisation for Economic Co-operation and Development (OECD), "delivering the Sustainable Development Goals (SDGs) and the Paris Agreement will require more resources than are currently being spent on development outcomes, not least in developing countries" (OECD 2018).

Blended finance, an approach that mixes different forms of capital to support development, is emerging as a solution to help achieve the "billions to trillions" agenda. Scaling up blended finance without a sound understanding of its potential and its risks, however, may have unintended consequences for development cooperation providers (OECD 2018).

At the Rio+20 conference, which took place in Rio de Janeiro in June 2012, member states called for a prioritization of the sustainable development agenda. The conference eventually led to the 2015 UN Sustainable Development Summit and to the launch on January 1, 2016, of the 2030 Agenda for Sustainable Development and its 17 SDGs. Meeting the SDGs will require an additional USD $2.5 trillion in private and public financing per year. Based on estimates for 2017, an additional USD $13.5 trillion to implement the Paris Climate Accord will be required. The concept of blended finance can contribute to raising the private financing needed. This was raised as a solution to the funding gap in the outcome document of the Third International Conference on Financing for Development in July 2015.

A recent survey conducted on behalf of the World Economic Forum identified 74 pooled funds and facilities representing USD $25.4 billion in blended finance assets, with the funds affecting over 177 million lives. This is evidence of the tremendous potential of blended finance to close the funding gap required to finance the ambitious SDGs agenda and deliver development outcomes. The concept has been gaining popularity lately within the world of international development finance. The development finance institutions offer co-investment opportunities to align capital toward meeting the SDGs. Actually, over 90 percent of cross-border debt financing to low and lower middle-income countries is denominated in foreign currency, principally the US dollar. Almost 100 percent of equity flows are subject to FX risk, while FX debt burdens rise, therefore the achievement of the minimum SDGs is jeopardized.

The SDGs and the Addis Ababa Action Agenda (2019) point toward deploying blended finance to reduce FX risk in developing countries to achieve long-term sustainability, including:

- reducing the percentage of cross-border flows where the borrower bears FX risk on an unhedged basis and;
- increasing the amount of domestic financial intermediation (in the financial and capital markets) in local-currency.

In addition, the finance lines of central banks have now begun to introduce Currency Swap Arrangements (CSAs). Since 2008, CSAs – largely adopted by the People Bank of China (Public) – helped to keep trade going during the financial crisis. This played a major role in launching the internationalization of the use of the Chinese RMB (Campanella 2014). That strategy, neglected for too long by the ECB, is now likely to further the use of the Euro in the payment system and in BSAs with partner economies (Campanella 2019). The Eastern Caribbean Central Bank headquartered in St. Kitts and Nevis could play a critical role in activating swap lines with foreign central banks, especially with the ECB, given that the EU is their second trade partner after the US .

Achieving the SDGs requires improved policies and governance and higher levels of public and private investment. According to a recent study, annual financing needs for meeting the SDGs in LAC are estimated to range between USD $1.5 trillion and USD $2.5 trillion (Castellani et al. 2019). Castellani, Larrinaga, Panizza, and Zhou's study finds that the gap between fiscal balance and investment will rise from USD $170 billion (3.1 percent) in 2015 and will surpass USD $1.4 trillion (12.4 percent of the region's GDP) by 2030, if the SDGs were to be reached. The total public investment gap of LAC countries was close to USD $170 billion (3.1 percent of the region's GDP) and that the gap will reach USD $501 billion (4.4 percent of the region's GDP) by 2030 (Figure 12.2).

As Castellani et al remark, at first glance, the gap's increase is somehow surprising as the region's GDP per capita is expected to increase during this period, which may encourage private–public sector joint financing and a fall in direct public investment needed. However, "the increase in GDP per capita will be accompanied by a structural transformation of the region's economies away from agriculture and manufacturing and towards the service sector" (Castellani

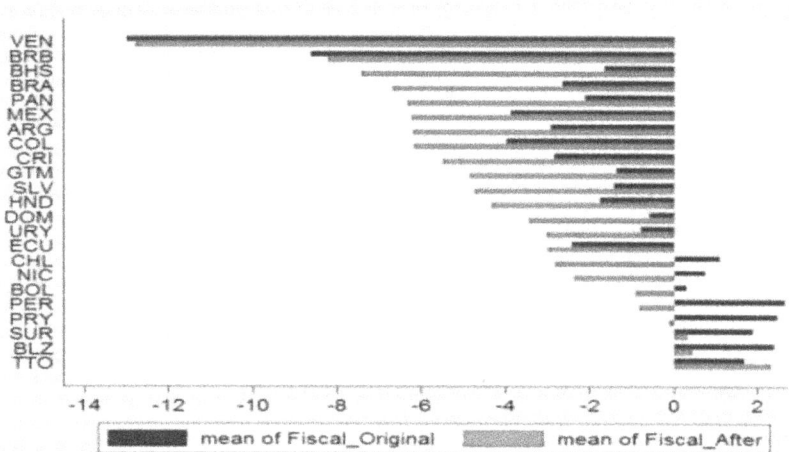

Figure 12.2 Investment gaps and fiscal balance (percentage of GDP).
Source: Castellani, Olarreaga, Panizza and Zhou, 2019.

et al. 2019, 38). This, in turn, will lead to a larger public investment gap by 2030. In 2030, the gap to reach the SDGs would reach USD $1,406 billion (12.4 percent of the region's GDP) (Castellani et al. 2019, 38).

These estimates, although not factoring in the positive effect of public investment on growth and the fiscal balance, still leave a gap that must be filled by deficit financing. Castellani et al warn "those larger Latin American economies would need substantial fiscal deficits (ranging from 7.5 percent in Brazil to three percent in Chile) sustained for a period of 15 years to close the investment gap" (Castellani et al. 2019, 32).

How could the multilateral development banks (MDBs) help countries in the region to close these gaps? In addition, do they have the financial capacity to do so? On the policy advice side, MDBs can help countries to design fiscal reforms aimed at limiting the budgetary implications of scaling up public investment and creating an enabling environment for promoting greater private-sector participation in infrastructure projects. MDBs can also help countries to develop policies that can promote domestic savings and therefore limit the current account implications of scaling up public investment (Cavallo and Serebrisky 2016, 9). On the financing side, MDBs' impact on large countries on their development indicators may be limited, while their impact on small countries may have economy-wide effects. For this reason, Castellani et al suggested that strategically MDBs should concentrate on lending to small countries (Castellani et al. 2019, 35).

International Capital Markets and the Hard-Currency Risk

Developing and emerging economies, however, have precarious access to the international capital markets, and they are prone to lose market access during recessions. Losing access to international financial flows can lead to budgetary cuts, which, besides deepening the recession in the short term, may also have long-term implications as these cuts tend to be concentrated on public investment (Easterly, Irwin, and Servén 2008, 4) and infrastructure investment.

At the core of international funding is the foreign exchange risk. Borrowing in strong currencies causes a significant barrier to sustainable development, particularly in agriculture, food security, SMEs, infrastructure, energy, and environment/climate change projects, sectors that are at the core in achieving the SDGs.

Hard-currency finance still dominates financing flows from development finance institutions (DFIs) and other public lenders into low- and middle-income countries. Unfortunately, given the often very volatile exchange rates in such countries, the volume of local currency required to service hard-currency debt will be very hard to predict and would typically increase significantly over time.

The effects of significant depreciation in an economy carrying a large hard-currency public and/or private debt stock are multiple. These may include financial distress at the borrower's level, increased non-performing loans in the financial sector, and a resulting credit freeze. These fiscal difficulties with numerous trickle-down effects, increased utility tariffs, imported inflation, and a resulting higher cost of living have a downside impact on the confidence of foreign and local investors alike. There is, therefore, arguably a serious flaw in hard-currency-denominated development finance, as the exchange rate risk that comes with it may partially undo the intended positive development outcome.

Hedging Local-Currency Financing

When development finance emerged in the mid-last century, with its initial heavy bias toward infrastructure, there were no realistic alternatives to US funding, nor did foreign investors wish to take any exchange rate risk. As a result, governments and parastatals borrowed in hard currency to fund public-sector infrastructure investments. Meanwhile, international private infrastructure developers insisted on having USD indexed off-take agreements – where buying a utility, typically a power or water utility, bears the long-term exchange rate risk – and accordingly, as the revenue under the off-take agreement is USD linked, would also fund their projects with hard-currency debt. This became the norm for many decades.

The intervening period has seen dramatic improvements in the conditions for local-currency financing. Target markets themselves have grown in depth and structure, as savings cultures have evolved, and capital markets have developed. There is also greater availability of instruments designed to unlock those markets, such as DFI guarantee programs and other capital-market development initiatives. GuarantCo, which provides guarantees to support locally sourced local-currency funding of infrastructure development, is an example. International hedge markets have also developed, now within the reach of commercial banks in emerging markets. Also, emerging are specialized hedging instruments like the Currency Exchange Fund (TCX) that offers currency hedges without tenor limitations in developing countries. In short, the availability of local-currency finance instruments, both from domestic and international sources, has grown significantly.

The increase is a steady rise in local-currency transactions across many sectors, with the microfinance and SME sectors having seen the largest rise.

Local currency has become the default choice in these sectors due to several factors, including regulations that prevent hard-currency lending to local-currency earning customers. Lenders sensitive to social impact investment supported the establishment of TCX which offers hedging products to investors in these markets.

The greater incidence of local-currency transactions beyond microfinance demonstrates that the supply of local-currency funding products is not necessarily a constraint anymore. Some recent examples are a USD $85 million Kenyan Shilling facility from Kenyan and international banks for M-Kopa, an off-grid solar distribution company, a USD $20 million Rwandan Franc loan by a Rwandan bank to Boxx, and Philippine Peso bonds issued by a renewable energy developer and guaranteed by GuarantCo. Some examples in which the TCX hedges are used are as follows:

1. Nine-year USD $35 million Georgian Lari loan to the Georgian water utility.
2. Nine-year USD $50 million Peso loan for an Argentinian public transportation project.
3. Eight-year USD $20 million loan for a Nigerian university project.
4. USD $100 million of long-term local-currency loans to power utilities in Uruguay, Costa Rica, and Jamaica.

The internal financials of the above-noted examples show how hard-currency is largely demand-driven, while the supply of local currency is not constrained. Persistent beliefs around the availability of local-currency, such as its relative cost, volume, and tenor, and the presumed need for hard-currency debt to fund hard-currency equipment purchases are unfounded. First, there is no empirical evidence supporting the notion that local currency is generally more expensive than the hard currency. On the contrary, for the required long-term financing structures needed for most infrastructure projects, local currency is, over time, generally a more cost-effective solution.

Second, dollar-denominated equipment purchases do not necessitate dollar debt; they simply mandate the purchase of dollars at some point to make payments. Regarding tenors and volumes, the previous examples show that the range of tenors and volumes – across multiple currencies – is competitive with the dollar alternative. Consequently, Cubb et al. affirmed that "many reasons that once ruled out local-currency, no longer stand today" (Cubb, Durland, and Horrocks 2017).

One key driver of the persistence of hard-currency infrastructure funding in developing markets is the hard-currency off-take agreement model, where exchange rate risk is borne by the off-taker, for example, the national power utility.

Project developers, investors, lenders, and even host governments have become so accustomed to this model that it is now hard to depart from it. The USD off-take agreement is used to purchase goods in advance and so provide project financing for future expansion. There are many variants of such agreement.

One is to move toward local-currency off-take agreements and hence to local-currency project finance, which will stimulate local debt and capital markets to the extent available and otherwise take the FX risk outside the country and onto the books of foreign lenders and/or their hedge providers. To avoid industry disruption, however, this would have to be phased in gradually, allowing stakeholders to adapt, and for debt and hedge markets to adjust and scale up. An example of this gradual approach is in Nepal, where projects below a certain threshold were chosen for a Rupee off-take contract. Another way is to hedge a utility's currency mismatch resulting from USD off-take agreements. TCX and GuarantCo are working with several African utilities toward that objective. GuarantCo enables sustainable infrastructure projects in Africa and Asia. GuarantCo provides a local-currency credit solution to unlock the potential of local capital markets and help close the infrastructure funding gap in low-income countries.

In sum, developments and the examples given above validate that "long-term local-currency lending to infrastructure sectors in developing countries is possible and is happening" (Cubb, Durland, and Horrocks 2017).

Given the systemic risk that comes with hard-currency finance and given the enormous funding volumes that emerging and developing countries will be taking on to develop their infrastructure sectors, a continued exclusive reliance on hard currency is not sustainable. Over time, the development of international and domestic local-currency markets and the changing attitude of all stakeholders will have to move hand-in-hand and step-by-step to realize a gradual but vital transition to a much greater share of local currency in the financing of infrastructure sectors and of developing economies in general (Cubb, Durland, and Horrocks 2017).

Hedging Local Currency

Recently, a new repo facility, Foreign and International Monetary Authorities (FIMA) was set up by the Federal Reserve Bank of the United States. The Fed is offering dollars to central banks in CSAs, accepting local currency in exchange. FIMA account holders consisting of most central banks with accounts at the Federal Reserve Bank of New York are eligible to apply in order to use this facility. The Federal Reserve must approve such an application. Mexico and Brazil recently signed up for swap deals to increase their supply of US dollars.

The facility is yet to extend to small countries, but there is no rule that debars their participation. The currency exchange fund (TCX) promotes local-currency financing to reduce the currency risk that arises when international investors provide debt to borrowers in developing countries. So far, TCX has operated in low-income countries, and at a very low finance scale. There is scope to identify additional hedging risk instruments that will meet the market demands for higher finance scale projects, particularly for infrastructure programs.

The TCX offers an innovative paradigm in terms of the diversity and nature of investors involved, such as government institutions, DFIs, and specialized microfinance investment vehicles. The fund is unique in terms of the problem that it seeks to address, namely the availability of local-currency lending in developing and emerging countries where there are no liquid, sustainable financial markets, and ensuring additionality. The use of hedging products and the diversity of partners that enables the fund to hold a diversified portfolio of currencies and thus mitigate risks are also innovative.

The central banks' finance lines extend to the CSAs. Since 2008, CSAs – largely adopted by the People's Bank of China – helped to keep trade going during the great financial crisis. This played an important role in encouraging the use of central bank finance lines and the pursuit by China of the internationalization of the RMB.

Unlike the earlier usage of BSAs in trade financing, China's BSAs are not short-term trade arrangements. These instruments are now in use for channeling long-term infrastructure investments (BRI). The Bank of China has also compiled the BRI RMB exchange rate investments index to help customers identify risks aimed at increasing currencies of the emerging markets to enrich the product line of financial hedging tools. Box 12.1 on the concept, structure, and logic of the TCX explains further this finance model.

BOX 12.1 TCX

The TCX is a fund managed by TCX Investment Management Company BV, a private company that was established in 2007 by a group of development finance institutions following an initiative by the Netherlands Development Finance Company (FMO). The Dutch government is among investors and, together with the German government, it provided risk capital to facilitate the participation of other investors. The fund provides over-the-counter derivatives to hedge the currency and interest rate mismatches that are created when international investors lend to financial institutions in developing countries in their local currencies.

The TCX is mandated to develop markets for long-term exchange rate risk and interest rate risk hedging products, primarily cross-currency swaps, in developing countries and emerging economies where such markets do not yet exist. By contributing to the reduction of market risks associated with currency mismatches, the fund gives borrowers in these countries access to long-term financing in their own currencies and risk management products that help manage exchange rate risks. With such access, borrowers are protected from growing debt burdens, financial losses, reduced abilities to repay debt and possibilities of default linked to high currency volatility, all of which can undermine their businesses and the economic development of their countries.

Partners: The TCX has 22 investors including: development finance institutions from the Netherlands, Germany (the Kiwi, German Investment and Development Corporation [DEG] and European Fund for Southeast Europe), France (Proparco and the French Development Agency [AFD]), Belgium, Austria, Japan and Spain; international finance institutions, namely the European Bank for Reconstruction and Development, International Finance Corporation, Inter-American Development Bank, African Development Bank and Development Bank of Southern Africa; and specialized microfinance investment vehicles, including Oikocredit, Oxfam Novib, Triple Jump, ASN Bank, BlueOrchard and Grameen Crédit Agricole Microcredit Foundation.

Investors in the fund must be professional investors from outside the United States, subject to prior approval of the fund manager and existing shareholders in the TCX and subject to a minimum initial investment of USD $5 million.

How does it work? Access to TCX hedging products is granted to TCX investors, their clients, parties introduced by TCX investors, and trading counterparties such as broker-dealers. Counterparties that have not invested in the TCX can hedge their currency risks with equity or debt instruments received from TCX investors directly with the fund after a counterparty onboarding process has been concluded and commercial and International Swaps and Derivatives.

Association agreements have been signed. Results: Since its launch in 2007, TCX has hedged USD $1.5 billion in loans to borrowers in developing and emerging countries, covering around 70 currencies, and particularly benefiting microfinance institutions and SMEs. The fund has absorbed approximately USD $890 million in currency.

This box is reproduced from: https://www.tcxfund.com/concept-structure/

Furthermore, according to the City of London:

> . . . the Bank of China's currency services currently covers 62 currencies among which 51 of them are from emerging markets and 28 are from countries along the BRI. Bank of China's diverse product line also encompasses an array of hedging tools including the spot/forward settlement and sale of foreign exchange, spot/forward foreign exchange trading, and foreign exchange swap, currency swap, non-deliverable forward and option. The Bank of China leverages its international financial market experience and expertise to help clients identify trends and trading opportunities. The bank uses a mixture portfolio of hedging tools to customize risk management solutions for projects to help a great number of companies going global hedge and avert risks. The total amount of transactions over the last five years has reached USD $470 billion, or GBP £ 357 billion (among which transactions in HKD hit USD $359 billion, or GBP £272.69 billion).
>
> (City of London 2018)

Furthermore, the Bank of China has expanded its currency services to the City of London. In a Bloomberg publication of January 23, 2022, Miaojung Lin and Evelyn remarked that in spite of the low ebb in the United Kingdom's relations with China, Chinese banks in London are "essential conduit to potentially staggering flows of Chinese money and investment" to London. "Change is good, change brings opportunities," they said. Such opportunities to make London 'a global hub for innovation in finance are in the City of London," (Corporate Plan 2018-232018, 3).

Business Must Take a Lead

Business enterprises must acquire the hedging tools for innovative finance, more so in this COVID-19 times. Hill, in her commentary on the COVID-19 World Survey, cautions that "every hedging policy needs to be built around the business and its current needs, not around how the market appears to be behaving." As such, they offer a guide to FX policy creation: define what you are trying to achieve in your strategy, identify FX exposures, quantify risk, set up FX hedging program, and specify the workflow with a trusted communication policy (Hill 2022).

Digital Infrastructure Financing

Funding digital infrastructure in the aftermath of the COVID-19 pandemic will be a heavy demand on Caribbean countries, as well as other small economies in the world. Funding for reaping the benefits of infrastructure, technology, and institutions in this age of the digital economy will be a huge task ahead. A mix of funding avenues to meet this challenge for the Caribbean will require access to market and bank funding, but also an internationally coordinated program with the multilateral banks, and members of the G20 countries. Only Guyana, with its new-found oil finds could, today, find resources from within the country. Finance Minister Ashni K Singh in the budget speech of January 26, 2022, while confirming this, also spoke to "transforming infrastructure" as a conceptual change in the focus of development. (See Budget Speech, *Steadfast Against All Challenges: Resolute in Building One Guyana, January 26, 2022.*)

Diversifying Funding Sources

The diversity of funding sources is of utmost importance for Emerging Market Economies (EMEs) portfolio finance. In diversifying funding sources, Caribbean economies can reduce the risk of sudden reversals of credit from foreign developments in a single or multiple creditor country. The rise of diverse local-currency lending and hedging outlets has eaten into the dominance of foreign banks. Yet, the large diversification of the type of funding provided by creditors requires fine-tuned regulatory infrastructures in determining the risk of credit reversals.

In the Caribbean, reliance on bank funding to meet the demands of COVID-19 is evident by a loan of USD $80 million from the Caribbean Development Bank (CDB) and to bond issues of governments taken up by the commercial banks. The recently announced increase, effective August 23, 2021, in the special drawing rights (SDRs) of the IMF, base will address the long-term global need for reserves and help Caribbean countries. The SDR currency basket comprises of the US dollar, Euro, Chinese Yuan, Japanese Yen, and UK Pound Sterling. This window will help countries cope with the pandemic and support the survival and recovery of the regional economy.

Caribbean economies must strike the right balance between overcoming the pandemic, designing a recovery program, and rebuilding their economies. Reliance on banking finance may not be sufficient. In a recent article, *Miles to Go*, Duttagupta and Pazarbasioglu call for the designing of "macro-financing tools to monitor risks to the overall economy from the non-bank financial sector" (Duttagupta 2021, 5). They argue that "liquidations may lead to a wave of bankruptcies and risks of creating zombie firms that can operate on excessive credit support but cannot invest in new activity" (Duttagupta 2021, 3) – the road ahead could be somewhat bumpier, they exclaimed.

Conclusion

EMEs and particularly small economies are always in search of a wider access to international finance. The sources of such finance often face sudden reversals and rising costs. The credit rating status of these countries set standards that affect access, availability, and cost. In diversifying funding sources, Caribbean economies can reduce the risk of sudden reversals of credit in international finance and its exposure to single or multiple creditor countries. As such, the rise of diverse local-currency lending and hedging outlets provides a buffer and a supplementary window for mobilizing financial resources for development. This will also reduce the dependence on international banks and activate idle financial resources in the local economy. However, there is an urgent need to fix and fine-tune the regulatory structures and practices in financial hedging, to mitigate risks and encourage the effective use of local financing for the hard currency needs of development projects.

There are many miles to travel and confidence to instill, if Caribbean countries were to embark on the search for fresher finance sources for a quality investment.

References

"The 12 Global Economic Indicators to Watch." Bloomberg.com. Bloomberg, n.d. https://www.bloomberg.com/graphics/world-economic-indicators-dashboard/.

Campanella, Miriam. 2014. "The Internationalization of the Renminbi and the Rise of a Multipolar Currency System." The European Centre for International Political Economy.

Campanella, Miriam. 2019. "Turning China Money Reserves into Capital." ResearchGate, October 2019. https://www.researchgate.net/publication/336365040_Turning_China's_Money_Reserves_into_Capital.

Castellani, Francesca, Marcelo Olarreaga, Ugo Panizza, and Yue Zhou. 2019. "Investment Gaps in Latin America and the Caribbean." International Development Policy | Revue Internationale de Politique de Développement. Institut de Hautes Etudes Internationales et du Développement, 1 June. https://journals.openedition .org/poldev/2894.

Cavallo, Eduardo A., and Tomas Serebrisky. "Saving for Development: How Latin America and the Caribbean Can Save More and Better." Inter-American Development Bank, 13 June 2016. https://publications.iadb.org/publications/english

/document/Saving-for-Development-How-Latin-America-and-the-Caribbean-Can
-Save-More-and-Better.pdf.

City of London, Corporate Plan 2018–2023, City of London Corporation, London.
https://democracy.cityoflondon.gov.uk/documents/s117505/Appendix%203%20-
%20Corporate%20Plan%202018-2023.pdf.

Cubb, Chris, Justice Durland, and Paul Horrocks. 2017. "Achieving Sustainable
Development through Local Currency Financing." https://www.a-id.org/2017/05/05/
achieving-sustainable-development-through-local-currency-financing/.

Davis, Steven J. "An Index of Global Economic Policy Uncertainty." National Bureau
of Economic Research. Working Paper 22740. https://www.nber.org/system/files/
working_papers/w22740/w22740.pdf.

Dookeran, Winston. 2019. "Theory Talks: Are Current Models of Economic Growth
Adequate for Caribbean Development- A Tribute to Sir Alister McIntyre." Presented
to a Symposium at the Institute of International Relations, UWI, St Augustine,
11 September, Trinidad and Tobago.

Duttagupta, Rupa, and Pazabasioglu. Summer 2021. "Miles to Go." https://www.imf.org
/external/pubs/ft/fandd/2021/06/pdf/the-future-of-emerging-markets-duttagupta
-and-pazarbasioglu.pdf.

Easterly, William, Timothy Irwin, and Luis Servén. 2008. "Walking up the Down
Escalator: Public Investment and Fiscal Stability." OUP Academic, 28 January.
https://academic.oup.com/wbro/article-abstract/23/1/37/1673672.

European Central Bank. 2021. "The International Role of the Euro." https://www.ecb
.europa.eu/pub/pdf/ire/ecb.ire202106~a058f84c61.en.pdf.

"European Commission Directorate-General for Trade." Caribbean - Trade - European
Commission. https://ec.europa.eu/trade/policy/countries-and-regions/regions/
caribbean/.

GEPU (Global Economic Policy Uncertainty Index). https://www.policyuncertainty
.com/media/Global_Annotated_Series.pdf.

Guarantco. https://guarantco.com/about-guarantco/.

Hill, Eleanor. "Stronger FX Hedging Strategies: A Pandemic Game Changer." European
Association of Corporate Treasures. https://www.eact.eu/articles/fx-hedging-game
-changer/.

"Home | Sustainable Development." United Nations. https://sdgs.un.org/.

"Inflation Report - August 2019." 2020. Bank of England, 5 November. https://www
.bankofengland.co.uk/inflation-report/2019/august-2019.

International Monetary Fund. 2021. "Special Drawing Rights Allocation." https://www
.imf.org/en/Topics/special-drawing-right/2021-SDR-Allocation.

Miaojung Lin, and Evelyn Yu. 2022. "City of London's $10 Trillion Chinese Hub Plans
for Growth." *Bloomberg* 'Business Commentary', 24 January 2022.

Ministry of Finance, Guyana Budget Speech, 26 January 2022 – "Steadfast Against All
Challenges: Resolute in Building One Guyana." https://www.parliament.gov.gy/
documents/sittings/23110-budget_speech_2022.pdf.

OCED (Organisation for Economic Co-operation and Development). 2018. "Making
Blended Finance Work for the Sustainable Development Goals." https://www.oecd

.org/dac/making-blended-finance-work-for-the-sustainable-development-goals
-9789264288768-en.htm.

United Nations. 2015. "Addis Ababa Action Agenda: Sustainable Development
Knowledge Platform." United Nations. https://sustainabledevelopment.un.org/index
.php?page=view&type=400&nr=2051&menu=35.

United Nations. 2019. "2019 ECOSOC Forum on Financing for Development
Follow-up |." https://www.un.org/ecosoc/en/events/2019/ffd-forum.

13

Frontiers, Flows, and Frameworks

Resetting Caribbean and Pacific Policies Post-Pandemic

KHUSHBU RAI

Introduction

Time and again much evidence have been harvested observing efforts of integration in the Caribbean and the Oceania Pacific to address the inherent and linked problems derived from the regions' size, isolation, and islandness. Other obstacles would also be their distance from major markets, the smallness in their production scale, limited export base, and low domestic demand. Parallels are drawn mostly regarding their institutional weaknesses, restraining infrastructure, digital divide, and production homogeneity. One simple justification for comparing the Pacific countries with the Caribbean nations is that small islands share enough economic characteristics that similar economic policy prescriptions could be applied (Thorburn 2007, 243). A clear juxtaposition includes the geographical features of the islands. The Oceania Pacific is widely spread, very far as they are from each other, bringing along with them diverse ethnicity and cultures. The Caribbean islands are physically close to one another and although there are linguistic differences, they do share many ethnic and cultural similarities. The asymmetrical relations with their empowering neighbors have signaled the importance of regional integration and openness. Despite the many natural and economic constraints enumerated above, both the regions have recorded progress overall, although the intraregional gains and growth may have been uneven.

Regional integration in its essence still stands as an elusive goal despite numerous deep-rooted attempts throughout history. Fundamentally, regionalism can be looked at through multiple facets, such as harmonizing macroeconomic policies, liberalizing trade, resource management, disaster rehabilitation, provision of education, judicial services, international policing, and much more. Although accomplishing regionalism has been an age-old conundrum for both the regions, it has always been perceived as a means to an end. As the regions' resetting agenda is unfolded in the discussions that follow, the narration will touch on these various aspects, from both a historical viewpoint and a more present-day perspective.

It is useful to first put things into perspective: Regionalism cannot be a blanket policy. Nevertheless, the pandemic has brought the realization of how interconnected the regions are, so much so that the responses and recovery strategies are almost comparable. As regions are highly susceptible to climate change, the Caribbean and the Pacific had already been developing plans for fostering resilience to the climate crisis, which dawned with some predictability. But COVID-19 stunned the nations, fracturing even the most advanced economies and creating room for confusion and uncertainty. In combating either crises, "there is a dearth of moral leadership, a resurgence of nationalism, and competition between nations, all struggling to deal with their own problems" (Wilkinson 2020, 1).

Against this backdrop, this chapter outlines a comparative analysis of the resetting agenda in the Caribbean and the Pacific regions in the context of regional integration. While chronicling the historical encounters of the regions, section two provides a gestalt from periods of colonialism to the struggles of sovereignty; from the formation of regional structures to the arrangements of regional agreements which are today the pinnacle of regionalism for both the Pacific and the Caribbean. The chapter endeavors to compare two regions that are further apart but share a commonality in the concept of regional integration. Section three highlights the development of the regional trade arrangements and some hinging controversies. Thereafter, the chapter describes some of the transformations that COVID-19 has imposed upon the regions along with the actions taken by governments in the Caribbean and the Pacific to spearhead the *great reset*.

Tying the Two Realms Together

Oftentimes the Pacific Island Countries and the Caribbean Island Nations are projected together to gauge the progress of their economic and political integration. This is justifiable due to various similarities between the two; however, there also subsists nuanced differences. Here, an overview of the regions' journey through time is presented, dating back to the colonial periods. While acknowledging the likenesses, the scrutiny sheds light on features that set the regions apart. Alongside historical and geographical differences, there are also hints of subtleties in the influence the metropolitan neighbors have on the distinct regions.

Colonial Legacy

The initial scrutiny brings to attention an account of the regions' colonial history in order to showcase how it had impacted the regions. Not sequenced chronologically, however, it may be delineated that colonial legacy for the Pacific and the Caribbean are two sides of the same coin. Ostensibly, the distinctiveness and the elusive resemblances have shaped the development and execution of intra- and extra-regional arrangements.

Pacific colonization[1] came hand in hand with German imperialism. As history would see it, this was also the motivation for the emergence of Great Britain's influence in the region. At first, Great Britain was skeptical to annex the extensively scattered South Pacific Islands region; nonetheless, when Germany set in to annex New Guinea, Britain quickly occupied Papua. The two (Papua and New Guinea) got transferred to the Commonwealth of Australia following World War I, administered by the League of Nations. Samoa and Micronesia also got occupied by the British, adding the two island nations to the list of its existing annexed nations – Fiji and the Solomon Islands. The Kingdom of Tonga was the only Pacific nation never to be colonized; however, this did not stop the British culture from influencing Tongan lifestyles. Further, in rivalry with Great Britain, the French also began their exploration of the Pacific region. Largely in the name of patriotism and in part, due to scientific research, France established strategic navy bases and commercial interests in Tahiti, New Caledonia, Wallis and Futuna, and so on.

Looking at the Antillean Islands, alternatively known as the Caribbean region, which were first a means of port entry, a trade hub, and later European countries' foremost overseas colonies. In a strife for colonial powers among Europe, Great Britain, and the United States, the Caribbean Basin witnessed one of its worst tragedies, which got chronicled as the "Cuban missile crisis" of 1962. The swelling interests from these powerful giants were primarily because of the missiles threat posed by the Soviet Union. The supranational interests from West Europe (mainly Britain, Spain, and France) and North America (particularly the United States) in Caribbean islands' natural resources began as early as 1492. Purportedly, not much has changed to date since the Caribbean island nations continue to be the source of natural resources for its neighbors'

---

[1] France colonized Tahiti (1842), New Caledonia (1858), Wallis and Futuna (1886); Britain colonized Fiji (1874), Solomon Islands (1890), Samoa (1899); Germany colonized New Guinea (1885); the United States colonized Hawaii (1898)

industrial manufacturers and are heavily dependent on imports with a very limited export base themselves.

Although the regions are at varying levels of integration, the presence of colonialism was a considerable stepping-stone for both. For the Caribbean, the first true form of regionalism was under the West Indies Federation (established in 1958), with the aim of politically uniting as one voice to negotiate independence from the British rule (Will 1991). Shortly after, the Federation came to an end (1962) due to concerns over nationalism. Debates continued over issues of establishing free trade and customs union; however, the conflict of interests among the Caribbean island governments eclipsed the success of the Federation. Nevertheless, the venture sowed the idea of bringing the Caribbean island nations to cooperate subsequently.

As for the Pacific countries, though dependence upon colonial administrators is self-explanatory, the Pacific micro-states attracted interests from outside powers with no former colonial history. Such overtures had been expressed by the Soviet Union, China, and Japan through diplomatic ties, trade links, aids, and assistances. The North Pacific countries have their eyes set on the vast fisheries endowment of the Pacific Island Countries. British, American, and European heritages are echoed through the social, political, and economic development in the regions. None of these groups wished to see their influence on the Pacific region diluting and as such clashes and conflicts were unavoidable.

Role of Regional Hegemons

Contemporary Pacific and Caribbean countries are theoretically governed by a rule of law and a parliamentary system, but if one takes a closer look, they are bound to discover that the regions' colonial histories have nurtured deep-rooted attitudes of autocracy and dependency, be it on the communities, the governments, or through hegemony.

Both the Pacific and the Caribbean realize that one of the few available options toward development is regional integration – politically, economically, and functionally. In the earlier stages, this was brought to the limelight by foreign policy analyst Georges Fauriol (1984), who added to his notes that small states do not have a foreign policy; they merely have a policy of existence. Some twenty years later, an Oceania security expert reiterated the same: "helpless pawns in the game of international relations" (Lawson 2003, 8). The Economist Intelligence Unit assessment reported that while internal characteristics such as level of development, institutions, and leadership do matter, small states' policy and international relations are largely defined by larger, more powerful actors and situations (Hey 2003, 7). Hence, for the Caribbean and the Pacific, the overarching hegemon would be the United States, Australia, and New

Zealand, respectively. Additionally, another new development to note in any current discussion of larger powers and their influence in the small island states of Caribbean and the Pacific is the emerging role of Asian countries in terms of aid provision and infrastructural developments.

Differences are a matter of influence too when it comes to regional cooperation; foremost, the Pacific islands are geographically more isolated than the Caribbean island states, not only within the region but also in terms of distance from the nearest metropolitan markets. The Caribbean falls within the immediate region of the United States due to its proximity; however, the US is not recorded to play a critically constructive role in the region. In contrast, the giants Australia and New Zealand have a direct and active role in the Pacific's regional development. As will be discussed in detail later, these challenging times make evident the transformative roles the regional guardians play.

Concerns over Sovereignty

Whereas regionalism can promise numerous advantages, it can also form pitfalls. The most worrisome of the drawbacks for developing countries like the ones in the Pacific and the Caribbean is the creation of winners and losers, where the relatively larger economies happen to bulldoze the gains of the relatively smaller economies. All in all, concerns over sovereignty have been the underlying issue of not reaching the desirable level of integration regionally. It is perceived that nationalistic political interests of individual countries are the prime obstruction in deepening the regional integration process. If present realities were to be taken seriously, both regions would need to rethink regionalism with a fundamentally different approach.

For regionalism to grow from strength to strength, Dookeran (2018) writes about *plural leadership* – a synergy between hegemonic and integrationist forms. Such inter-regionalism is characterized by the absence of any "one" supreme leader or even a supra-authority and allows for flexibility in negotiations without a conflicting tone. In practical terms, multiplex regionalism has been seen to be possible, best exemplified in the Association of Southeast Asian Nation (ASEAN) region, the Pacific Alliance (Nolte and Wehner 2013), and the Forum of East Asia Latin Asia-African Cooperation, among others.

A half-century ago, the World Trade Organization held steadfast to the view that bilateral and regional trade agreements were distractions on the path of free global trade. Trade experts lamented such agreements averring that they fragment the international trading ecosystem. Over time its position softened, professing that reconciliation between regionalism in trade and global trade liberalism is palatable after all. The complementarity began being emphasized, suggesting that regionalism can attain multilateralism, and in turn global integration. Although a reasonable ˙rhetoric, cautions must be taken regarding small island developing economies, as will be evident in the following deliberations.

The Route to Regional Integration

The Caribbean and the Pacific alike have not always been able to keep abreast with technological advancements and evolving international trading patterns. With the unprecedented scenario that the pandemic presents, working together as a united region is no longer a mere preference, but rather a necessity. Although it appears that economic integration has not been realized to its optimality, yet in both the regions, many regional organizations have been orchestrated to assist the efforts of further economic cooperation. These organizations enhance regionalism in the arenas of education, trade, government administration, resource management, disaster rehabilitation, justice, and law and order. Given the present ordeal, the University of the South Pacific and the Pacific Islands Forum Fisheries Agency are two of the most essential regional structures in the Pacific region. While the former ensures to nurture education and scientific research for a secured future, the latter is critical in facilitating conservative fisheries policies for sustainable economic development. There are many other organizations, such as the likes of the Pacific Islands Forum Secretariat (PIFS), the Secretariat of the Pacific Community, and so on, which continue to be in the headlines for their vigorous diplomacy on harmonizing as One Blue Pacific Continent.[2] Likewise, for the Caribbean island nations, the University of the West Indies was established with the aim to develop one economic and culturally knowledgeable community. There exists a judicially synchronized body for the Caribbean Community under the Caribbean Court of Justice and several regional arrangements that bring the Caribbean Community together.

Against the limitations of distant geography, underdeveloped and/or developing economies, and slim markets, without a strong presence of such regional bodies, the island states would become negligible; they would lose their voice and stand internationally. It is evident that the regional leaders are aware of the gravity of the situation. From this standpoint, the following reflects upon

---

[2] One Blue Pacific Continent – eighteen Pacific Island Nations collectively driven by their Pacific Ocean identity toward achieving regional peace, security, social-economic-political inclusion and growth.

what gathered the "equals" among the "un-equals" between the two regions by first revisiting the development of the numerous regional trade arrangements.

Historical Account of Trade Integration

Small island economies, the likes of the Pacific countries and the Caribbean countries, resolute toward open trade via regional trade agreements. Such negotiations herald an opportunity for developing countries to gain based on their comparative advantage. Along with that comes an implicit anticipation of improved market access, gains from competitiveness, stronger bargaining power, and opportunities for economic growth through augmented exports, declining imports, and increased employment.

As alluded to earlier, the West Indies Federation (1958–1962) was basically a political union that held any economic integration secondary. Due to this and the insular nationalist interests of the dominant parties, the West Indies Federation collapsed. In 1968, the Caribbean Free Trade Association (CARIFTA) was formed to expand regional trade and economic growth of the Caribbean as a regional community, following which came the Caribbean Regional Secretariat and Caribbean Development Bank. To an extent, scholars believed CARIFTA was much more successful than its predecessor (Rolfe 2007 and Bishop and Payne 2010). It had liberalized trade in manufactured commodities, facilitated trade in agricultural goods, and enhanced economic cooperation. The shortfall of CARIFTA was that it created wide wealth disparities. The larger island nations in the Caribbean had an unfair advantage over the smaller economies from the Eastern Caribbean. Hence, CARIFTA agreements became compromised and had to be transformed into the Caribbean Community and Common Market (CARICOM) in 1973. Under CARICOM, the target was to obtain a common market alongside functional collaboration under educational, health, and foreign policy mandates. The Organization of Eastern Caribbean States (OECS) was also established around the same period (1981) to protect the member nations' sovereignty and harmonize foreign policy (OECS 2005). In 1989, the common market was resuscitated by CARICOM Single Market and Economy (CSME) and was officially launched in 2006 (Bishop and Payne 2010, 12). The CSME has been the driving force behind the Caribbean region's formation of a trade bloc, functional cooperation on issues of the currency union, and macroeconomic policing.

In comparison, negotiations on regional trade agreements in the Pacific began under the South Pacific Bureau for Economic Cooperation in 1972, with the key role to promote trade between the Pacific and Europe. It was amid these consultations that Pacific leaders began negotiating preferential trade agreements individually with the giant markets such as the European Union, Australia,

New Zealand, and others. As such the notion of a lack of political commitment to develop one Pacific community by the island nations' governments started brewing. With the drive to mediate trade disputes, the Melanesian Spearhead Group was formed in 1987 where the prime players were mainly islands from the Melanesian subregion. The islands in the Micronesian subregion formed a Compact of Free Association (COFA) with the United States to access financial, health, and education support. In 1981, the South Pacific Regional Trade and Economic Cooperation Agreement (SPARTECA) brought along some positive trade results for the region as the islands received "duty free and unrestricted access on a non-reciprocal basis to the Australian and New Zealand markets" (MFAT 1996, 25). While a few commended SPARTECA, there were others who criticized the same as a strategy for hegemony and fostering dependency. The Pacific Island Countries Trade Agreement (PICTA) and Pacific Agreement on Closer Economic Relations (PACER) agreements came into force in 2001 and 2009, respectively. It was designed to enhance trade between the fourteen member countries by reducing tariff barriers to zero, allowing a period of protection for selected products in order to support infant industries.

Despite significant efforts to integrate the regions, there are existing arguments for growing competition rather than cooperation within the Pacific and the Caribbean regions. Both the regions are re-tuning their strategies given the present pandemic impediment to achieve a paradigm shift in regionalism. The discussion below deliberates on what pressing the reset button means for the two regions.

History in the Making – The Journey from Response to Recovery

In the Pacific, it is currently observed that while making slow recovery, the pandemic had almost annihilated many island economies mostly because of the impact on tourism travel bans, the plummeting of remittance flows, and the hindrance to trade and supply chain activities. Border closures had also aggravated problems for the aviation and shipping industries. Alongside a decline in exports of fisheries and mineral resources, loggings, and agricultural goods, women's economic and social security had been harshly affected (FEMM 2020). In response measures, the Pacific governments quickly redirected expenditure into health, education, and social welfare. As part of their fiscal stimulus, the banking sector reduced their interest rates to make borrowing more affordable, increased economic subsidies, particularly for small local businesses, raised social protection measures, provided tax concessions for employers, and revised their emergency budgets to be growth conducive. The

Asian Development Bank, the World Bank, and the Australian and New Zealand governments promptly pledged additional streams of funding as a reflection of global solidarity. Post-pandemic, much of the debate revolves around budget issues, the looming debt trap and how to stabilize inflation. The government revenues have taken a colossal plunge and expanded government debts, which will highly likely obstruct future growth patterns. In the immediate run, all construction and investment projects (which would have created employment) have halted. Pacific governments' weakness was basically exposed through their social protection regimes, where a better part of the economy hinged on the informal sectors and/or subsistence living while the welfare assistance mainly indemnified those in formal employment. The social insurance is dominated by pension or provident funds; in an event of a shortfall in the provident funds, the governments stepped in to directly subsidize the balance. This economic stimulus, although welcomed at present, brings into question the sustainability of such policies. The silver lining while tackling the pandemic for the Pacific has been the realization that civil societies, NGOs, and faith-based organizations in the region have a significant role in ensuring sustainability. The Pacific governments have unveiled a strategy of investing in local communities over profit-making during these catastrophic times.

Equally, with the unfolding of the pandemic in the Caribbean region, early controls were implemented with punitive actions. Reportedly, the swift response in managing the outbreak came from the region's familiarity of briskly preparing for other natural disasters frequenting the Caribbean island states (Hambleton et al 2020, 2). Despite their prompt response, because of preexisting fragilities, the region is facing intense unemployment and poverty. The governments have responded by supporting displaced workers, businesses, and the most affected individuals with financial and food services, as well as increasing expenditure on the health services and social security. To keep these island economies from crashing completely, the states injected funds by borrowing, and they now find themselves in heavy debt obligations (MacDonald 2020). While the exports of natural reserves such as gold, nickel, bauxite, oil, and natural gas assist the islands to stay afloat, much like the Pacific, the Caribbean nations also profoundly rely on international tourism. Though the borders are slowly reopening, it is projected that the tourism markets will only recover in the longer run. Further, with a large diaspora working mostly in North American countries, the region has been cushioned through disastrous times with the inflow of remittances. However, with the advanced economies collapsing, the reality of the times questions the feasibility of depending on remittances for rescue. Essentially, COVID-19 is just one of the issues thrown in the blend of chaos in the region. It does not help that the region continues to face natural calamities owing to climate change, setting the island economies back to square one in their economic and social recovery.

The Pacific COVID-19 Developments

In the thick of the pandemic, countries globally had been weighing their option to ease border/movement restrictions in order to save jobs but with a risk of COVID-19 cases running amok. It is widely acknowledged that the dilemma is perhaps the starkest for the Pacific island countries. As the tourism industry was the hardest hit sector in the Pacific, Australia and New Zealand had proposed the idea of a travel bubble based on a trans-Pacific agreement. Although there was a mixed reaction from a few Pacific states, the concept largely generated enthusiastic support from Fiji, Cook Islands, Papua New Guinea, among all others.[3] The Pacific countries had been successful in keeping the virus at bay in the earlier stages of the pandemic. The Delta variant unfortunately brought about unimaginable problems with only one single conceivable solution – mass vaccination coverage. Once again, geographical remoteness proved to be the Pacific's downfall. To make matters worse, the ultimate challenge for most of the countries was not vaccine supply, but rather the demand. Coupled with limited health sector capacity and rampant spread of misinformation, Pacific had been faced with further obstacles in ensuring maximum inoculation of its population. Owing to government efforts (and to an extent "no jab, no job" policy), a tally today will note that many Pacific islanders have received their second, or even third shot of vaccine.

Meanwhile, the regional hegemons are addressing another prominent issue given the significance of remittances and the loss of employment in the islands. By renegotiating the PACER Plus agreement to cement the deliverables for economic integration, an opportunity beckons for the island states to continue exporting labor to the Australian and New Zealand markets, but now under legally binding clauses (Prasad 2020). This situation is also in response to the shortage of workers in the horticultural industry in the host countries. At the same time, their temporary migrant labor schemes are considering issuing temporary visas to continue with the Australia's Seasonal Worker Program and New Zealand's Recognized Seasonal Employment program in the near future (Sherrell and Howes 2020). It is promising to note that Australia has a two-year strategic plan in place to break away from the continuation of creating

---

[3] Palau, one of the few countries to still have diplomatic ties with Taipei, is in the process of pursuing a travel corridor with Taiwan.

aid dependency and rather provide a new path to the Pacific aid program in overcoming the imminent debt trap (DFAT 2020, 18). Australia and New Zealand, the region's guardians, have been actively involved in every dialogue of resetting the regionalism agenda, juggling the fine line between codependency and interdependency. It is agreed that these two giants are the Pacific nations' oldest and most trusted allies, but the unprecedented events have allowed the islands to nurture partnership with other foreign players such as Singapore (assisted in developing a contact tracing app), South Korea, Taiwan (travel-bubble arrangement), China (financial aid), Europe, and the United States, among others.

There exist worries that the region could potentially be exploited by multinationals or other powerful players during this period of heightened susceptibility. For instance, the United States has renewed its interest in the islands that fall under the COFA in offering development aid and visa-free access in exchange for strategic advantage over the Micronesian subregion for defense (Firth 2020). Observers hint toward the entwined geopolitics in the resurgence of Unites States' influence, especially given that China's presence in the Pacific region has been growing exponentially. With geopolitical tensions running high, the Pacific leaders are being strategical in an approach they commonly refer to as – 'friends of all, enemies to none'

Further, in envisioning the great reset, the Forum Economic Ministers Meeting 2020 (PIFS 2020, 3) committed to certain undertakings; a few of the critical ones were as follows. Investing to bridge the digital divide through innovative use of online technologies to support education and businesses with the assistance of the Council of Regional Organizations in the Pacific agencies. The governments are channeling public–private partnerships to promote digital trade, a task that had been held off for far too long due to connectivity challenges in the Pacific. Lastly, but certainly not the least, coordinating with traditional development partners – bilateral, multilateral, and regional – to build disaster rehabilitation plans and strengthen economic/environmental resilience in preparing for fast-approaching climate change calamities.

The Caribbean Reset Agenda

CARICOM's mandate of bringing the Caribbean together as one community was exemplified best during the outbreak. The member nations' governments were freely sharing information and experience in order to curb the spread of the virus further. The Caribbean Disaster Emergency Management Agency together with the Caribbean Public Health Agency has been involved in providing the entire region with resources and medical personnel to support the testing and tracing process (Hambleton et al. 2020). Additionally, through the CARICOM collaborative framework, the Caribbean Development Bank and the University of the West Indies also contributed technical and financial assistance to bolster response efforts.

If scrutinized closely, observe that unlike the Pacific that benefitted much from the inclusive support of their regional hegemons, the Caribbean islands did not find a similar leadership from their metropolitan neighbors, the United States, and to an extent the United Kingdom, who were grappling to manage their own state of affairs. To make matters worse, it became much more difficult for the region to procure personal protective equipment (PPE) since the United States had constricted the exports of critical medical gear. By means of CARICOM, PPE was procured from China and Taiwan; the Caribbean Development Bank availed emergency loans to some member states. The Caribbean countries demonstrated unity and promptly coordinated regional measures to integrate in a time of dire need. The region has been considered to have contained the contagion relatively better than Brazil, Mexico, and Peru (MacDonald 2020).

According to a Trinidadian economist, when the global economy has taken a leg down, it is pointless to gauge Caribbean's recovery in GDP values; rather, she argues, the focus should be on development indicators such as health, education, life expectancy, overall well-being, and political solidarity (Marla Dukharan 2020). With building resilience for the future in perspective, the Caribbean countries are emphasizing growth in the renewable energy sector as well as redistributing resources to the agricultural industry. Agricultural development in the region is seen not only from a food security standpoint but also to diversify exports portfolio and the creation of employment for the locals. She further draws attention to how the Caribbean governments are rapidly shifting toward integrating technologically – for instance, making online transfers for social welfare, insurances, and other payments. The pandemic has forced the region to embrace the universal truth of going digital.

Another facet where Caribbean countries have integrated effectively is in unifying logistical standards to safely administer the transportation of commodities and people within the region (UNCTAD 2020). To ensure a strategy that goes beyond recovery of the Caribbean islands, the region is focusing on ocean and trade governance policies for sustainability and resilience. Put simply, the region is seeking to economically diversify by considering how to produce value-added products and services within their ocean-based value chains, including through the development of linkages with the private sector in the form of public–private partnerships as well as to ensure food security in the wake of climate change.

Conclusion

Clearly, there are symptoms of mounting regional consciousness within both the Caribbean and the Pacific regions. On one end of the spectrum, COVID-19 has decimated the economies economically; however, on the other end, it has also been instrumental in accentuating the integrational work within the regions exponentially. In the wake of the pandemic, the island economies have been applauded for their decisiveness in proactively closing off borders and implementing lockdowns. Almost like an epiphany, the virus has reminded the islanders how interdependent the regional ecosystem is, especially at a time when the entire world is preparing for the worst effects of climate change.

The hesitation of trading off sovereignty for better regional engagement has been a sensitive issue for both the Pacific and the Caribbean countries. The Pacific countries have lagged in political integration and have been reluctant to transfer power to a supranational authority to allow a wider scale of integration. The concerns over sovereignty stand out like a sore thumb. Nonetheless, the discussion here has suggested a way around surrendering sovereignty and imbibing plural leadership. Arguably, the Caribbean is more regionally mature than the Pacific, although there is much to be learned from the other regions, such as ASEAN, the European Union, and others.

All in all, hitherto, the Caribbean and the Pacific economies have targeted similar areas in aligning their reset agendas and rethinking regionalism. Sustaining the blue economy and its reserves, fisheries in particular, has clearly received much emphasis. In realizing that dependency on tourism may not be sustainable after all, both regions are channeling resources in the agriculture and technological development, with urgency. Domestically, the governments are seen to explore more public–private partnerships and acknowledge the contributions of civil societies as well as local communities in readapting development goals. The paradigm shift in contemporary regionalism got more intense with the changing roles of the regional hegemons; the "new normal" is demanding a shift from competition to cooperation.

References

Bishop, L. Matthew, and Antony Payne. 2010. "Caribbean Regional Governance and the Sovereignty/ Statehood Problem." The Centre for International Governance Innovation. *The Caribbean Papers: A Project on Caribbean Economic Governance*, no. 8. https://www.cigionline.org/sites/default/files/caribbean_paper_8_0.pdf.

DFAT. 2020. "Partnerships for Recovery: Australia's COVID-19 Development Response." *Australian Government Department of Foreign Affairs and Trade*. https://

www.dfat.gov.au/sites/default/files/partnerships-for-recovery-australias-covid-19
-development-response.pdf.

Dookeran, Winston. 2018. "The Caribbean on the Edge. An Anthology of Ideas and Writings." *Economic Commission for Latin America and the Caribbean Washington Office.* https://www.cepal.org/es/publicaciones/43984-caribbean-edge-anthology -ideas-and-writings.

Dukharan, Marla. 2020. "Caribbean Crisis Recovery: Interview." *Cayman Compass - Podcast: Caribbean Economies Face the Great Reset.* https://www.caymancompass .com/2020/09/13/podcast-caribbean-economies-face-the-great-reset/.

Fauriol, A. Georges. 1984. "Foreign Policy Behaviour of Caribbean States: Guyana, Haiti and Jamaica." *University Press of America,* 16 (2): 445. https://doi.org/10.7202 /701863ar.

FEMM. 2020. "Forum Economic Ministers Meeting." *Statement on the Economic and Social Impacts of COVID-19 on the Pacific.* Accessed 21 September 2020. https:// www.forumsec.org/wp-content/uploads/2020/08/2020-Forum-Economic-Ministers -Meeting-Statement-on-COVID-19.pdf.

Firth, Stewart. 2020. "American Strategic Considerations Drive Compact Negotiations in Micronesia: Part 1." *DevPolicy Blog.* https://devpolicy.org/american-strategic -considerations-drive-compact-negotiations-in-micronesia-part-1-20200806/.

Hambleton, R. Ian, M. Selvi Jeyaseelan, and M. Madhuvanti Murphy. 2020. "COVID-19 in the Caribbean Small Island Developing States: Lessons Learnt from Extreme Weather Events." *The LANCET Global Health,* 8 (9): 1114–15. https://www.thelancet .com/journals/langlo/article/PIIS2214-109X(20)30291-6/fulltext.

Hey, A. K. Jeanne (ed.). 2003. *Small States in World Politics: Explaining Foreign Policy Behaviour.* Lynne Rienner Publishers, Inc. http://ams.hi.is/wp-content/uploads/2014 /03/Small-States-in-World-Politics_Explaining-Foreign-Policy-Behavior.pdf.

Lawson, Stephanie. 2003. "Security in Oceania: Perspectives on the Contemporary Agenda." In *Security in Oceania: In the 21st Century,* edited by Eric Shibuya and Jim Rolfe, 7–23. Honolulu, Hawaii: Asia-Pacific Centre for Security Studies.

MacDonald, B. Scott. 2020. "COVID-19, the Caribbean and What Comes Next." *Global Americans: Smart News & Research for Latin America's Changemakers.* https:// theglobalamericans.org/2020/07/covid-19-the-caribbean-and-what-comes-next/.

MFAT. 1996. "Ministry of Foreign Affairs and Trade (New Zealand)." In *The South Pacific Forum: Regional Cooperation at Work,* Information Bulletin No. 56. Wellington: Ministry of Foreign Affairs and Trade.

Nolte, Detlef, and Leslie Wehner. 2013. "The Pacific Alliance Casts Its Cloud over Latin America." *German Institute of Global and Area Studies Focus,* no. 8: 1–10. https:// www.academia.edu/5664802/The_Pacific_Alliance_Casts_Its_Cloud_over_Latin _America.

OECS. 2005. "Organization of Eastern Caribbean States: Mission and Objectives." https://www.oecs.org/about_mission.htm.

PIFS. 2020. "Pacific Islands Forum Secretariat: 2020 Forum Economic Ministers Meeting." https://www.forumsec.org/wp-content/uploads/2020/08/2020-Forum -Economic-Ministers-Meeting-Outcomes.pdf.

Prasad, C. Biman. 2020. "Time for a Pacific Community." *DevPolicy Blog*. https://devpolicy.org/time-for-a-pacific-community-20200421/.

Rolfe, Jim. 2007. "Many Small States, Two Regions, Different Constructions." *Social and Economic Studies*, 56 (1/2): 96–134. https://www.jstor.org/stable/27866498.

Sherrell, Henry and Stephen Howes. 2020. "COVID-19 and the Horticultural Sector: Addressing the Pending Labor Supply Shortfall." *DevPolicy Blog*. https://devpolicy.org/covid-19-and-the-horticultural-sector-addressing-the-pending-labour-supply-shortfall-20200321/.

Thorburn, Diana. 2007. "The 'Patch' and the 'Backyard': Caribbean and Pacific Small Islands and Their Regional Hegemons." *JSTOR*, 56 (6): 240–60.

UNCTAD. 2020. "COVID-19 in the Caribbean and the Central America Region: Identifying Blue Pathways to Move Forward in a COVID-19 Context and Beyond." *The United Nations Conference on Trade and Development*. https://unctad.org/en/Pages/DITC/Trade-and-Environment/Oceans-Economy-COVID19.aspx.

Wilkinson, Emily. 2020. "Covid-19: A Lesson in Leadership from the Caribbean." Accessed 20 September 2020. https://www.odi.org/blogs/16959-covid-19-lesson-leadership-caribbean.

Will, W. Marvin. 1991. "A Nation Divided: The Quest for Caribbean Integration." *Latin American Research Review*, 26 (2): 3–37. http://www.jstor.org/stable/2503626.

Part 5

Resetting Diplomacy

Regionalism and Geostrategic Shifts

14

CARICOM's External Engagements

What Are the Prospects for Caribbean Regional
Integration and Development in a Post-COVID
Environment?[1]

ANNITA MONTOUTE

Introduction

Caribbean international relations are in a state of flux, reflecting changes in
the global political economy, shifting priorities and development agenda of
traditional and emerging partners, and the region's own evolving needs and
challenges. As European and US policymakers are redefining their strategies
toward the Caribbean region, a growing number of new partnerships are
offering greater flexibility for these mostly island countries. The nationalist
agenda of the recent US Republican administration under Donald Trump
brought into sharp focus the need to look beyond traditional relationships. The
current Democrat administration under President Joe Biden offers potential
opportunities but also uncertainties, particularly considering the impact of the
COVID-19 pandemic on the United States. As the region continues to endure
the adverse impacts of the COVID-19 pandemic, the importance and necessity
of diverse partnerships and regional cooperation are further illuminated. The
pandemic has also confirmed the benefits but also exposed the limits of regional
integration. The chapter discusses these developments and the implications for
the future of regional integration and development.

The Caribbean Community's (CARICOM) external relations are geared
toward meeting its development objectives, as CARICOM's former secretary-

---

[1] An earlier version of this work was published by the German Marshall Fund and
can be accessed at https://www.policycenter.ma/publications/caricom%E2%80%99s-
external-engagements-prospects-and-challenges-caribbean-regional-integration   .
Kind permission has been granted by the German Marshall Fund for publication of
an updated version in this book.

Table 14.1 CARICOM's international development partners

Traditional Country Donars	Emerging Country Donors	Multilateral Agencies
Canada	South Korea	IDB
United Kingdom	India	CDB
United States	Singapore	World Bank
Spain	Mexico	Commonwealth Secretariat
Italy	Brazil	UNDP
Germany	Chile	United Nations Environmental Programme (UNEP)
Japan	Argentina	Global Environment Fund (GEF)
Australia	Cuba	United Nations Development Fund for Women (UNIFEM)
European Union	Turkey	United Nations Population Fund
Austria	Russia	The United Nations Economic Commission for Latin America and the Caribbean (UNECLAC)
	Kazakhstan	United Nations Children Fund (UNICEF)
		Centres for Disease Control (CDC)

Source: CARICOM Secretariat (n.d.).

general Irwin LaRocque outlined in May 2014 (LaRocque 2014a) (see table 14.1 for a list of CARICOM's international development partners). CARICOM's development agenda as laid out in the CARICOM Secretariat Strategic Framework 2022 – 2030 is as follows: enhanced living standards, work, production and productivity, full employment of labor and other factors of production, accelerated economic development and convergence, expanded external trade and economic relations, international competitiveness, greater economic leverage in external relations and enhanced functional cooperation.

CARICOM's external relations are characterized by a shift away from relations with predominantly traditional North American and European transatlantic partners to a more diverse set of relationships with new ones. These developments have both positive and negative implications. On the one hand, they expand avenues supporting CARICOM's development initiatives, raise CARICOM's profile on the global stage, and complement and provide alternatives to "north–south" development cooperation. On the other hand, if not adequately managed, they pose challenges of overlapping agendas and can hinder regional integration and undermine development.

Caribbean Regional Integration

There are varied definitions of the "Caribbean," as reflected in regional configurations. The Association of Caribbean States (ACS) reflects the Greater Caribbean interpretation, consisting of the Anglophone, Dutch, Spanish, and French Caribbean (the latter are associate members), and Latin American countries whose shores are washed by the Caribbean Sea. CARICOM comprises the Anglophone Caribbean plus Suriname and Haiti. Within CARICOM, there is a subregional grouping of the English-speaking islands in the Eastern Caribbean: The Organization of the Eastern Caribbean States (OECS). The OECS is more integrated than CARICOM; it is a full-fledged economic union (Girvan 2013).

Aside from the ACS, the nonindependent territories[2] share membership with some Caribbean states (mostly the insular Caribbean)[3] through the Caribbean Development and Cooperation Committee of the Economic Commission for Latin America and the Caribbean (ECLAC). The Caribbean Forum of the African, Caribbean, and Pacific (OACP) Group of States (CARIFORUM) – consisting of CARICOM, Cuba, and the Dominican Republic – is based on the region's external trade and economic relations with Europe within the wider ACP framework (Girvan 2001). For the purpose of this chapter, the Caribbean refers to CARICOM, comprising fifteen members[4] and five associate members.[5] CARICOM excludes Spanish-speaking Latin American countries, which are beyond the scope of this chapter.

The Caribbean integration project emerged after the collapse of the British West Indies Federation in 1962. In 1965, the Caribbean Free Trade Association (CARIFTA) was established and transitioned to a common market through the Treaty of Chaguaramas in 1973, at which point it adopted the name Caribbean Community. In 1989, in response to globalizing forces, CARICOM decided to widen and deepen its integration process. The ACS reflects the widening process, whereas deepening took the form of the CARICOM Single Market and Economy (CSME). However, the completion of the CSME has been stalled due to capacity, implementation, institutional, political, and economic challenges (for details of the challenges plaguing the completion of the CSME, see, for example, Bishop

---

[2] Territories that have not received political independence from the United States, the United Kingdom, France, and the Netherlands.
[3] The insular Caribbean refers to the island territories of the Caribbean.
[4] Antigua and Barbuda, Bahamas, Barbados, Belize, Dominica, Grenada, Guyana, Haiti, Jamaica, Montserrat, St. Kitts and Nevis, St. Lucia, St. Vincent, Suriname, and Trinidad and Tobago
[5] Anguilla, Bermuda, British Virgin Islands, Cayman Islands, and Turks and Caicos Islands.

et al. 2011, 13); the deadline was moved from 2008 to 2015 (Girvan 2013) and subsequently to 2019 to coincide with the end of the CARICOM strategic plan.

Coordinating Policy

According to Norman Girvan, only some elements of CARICOM's regional integration – functional and security cooperation – are "doing reasonably well" (Girvan 2013, 2). Although some progress has been made in developing a framework for enhanced foreign policy coordination, challenges remain. CARICOM's foreign policy objectives are to enhance foreign and economic policy coordination, expand trade and economic relations, and exercise greater leverage and effectiveness in its external relations. These objectives are to be achieved through the Council for Foreign and Community Relations (COFCOR), the Council for Trade and Economic Development, and joint negotiations, respectively (Inter-American Development Bank 2005).

With a changing global environment, CARICOM took steps to enhance the coordination of its foreign policy and external relations, and COFCOR was charged with this responsibility. In 2002, COFCOR adopted a revised foreign policy framework to strengthen and expand external cooperation (Granderson 2012). In 2004, the bureau of COFCOR was granted an enhanced role in "promoting more regular consultation and coordination among member states" (Inter-American Development Bank 2005, 48). Despite these efforts, the operationalization of foreign policy coordination is largely left to regional leaders and institutions to handle, which makes the process ad hoc for the most part (Inter-American Development Bank 2005).

COFCOR faces many challenges: the divergent interests of member states, failure of member states to provide new or revised foreign policy positions, tardiness of member states in providing information necessary for communication, analysis, and coordinating positions, communication and coordination with national agencies limited to foreign ministries, limited resources for engaging in complex technical negotiations, and an expanded international agenda (Granderson 2012). Economic foreign policy coordination is more advanced than in the noneconomic realm.

Like COFCOR, the Caribbean Regional Negotiating Machinery (now the Office of Trade Negotiations) – the regional body set up in 1997 to conduct external trade negotiations – faced challenges in coordinating trade positions of the member states, including the reluctance of member states to surrender sovereignty to a regional body, overlapping mandates with the CARICOM Secretariat, divergent trade interests of member states, inadequate resources and capacity of some member states to make informed decisions, and inadequate funding to conduct research and employ staff (Inter-American Development Bank 2005). Bringing the Caribbean Regional Negotiating Machinery (CRNM) formally under the umbrella of the CARICOM Secretariat as the Office of Trade Negotiations in 2009 was an attempt to address member states' concerns about sovereignty and the CRNM's role vis-à-vis the CARICOM Secretariat (Bishop et al. 2011, 22).

The limits of CARICOM's foreign policy coordination can be seen in concrete cases of disunity among member states on issues of importance. In the 1990s, CARICOM countries were split in their position on the US Ship Rider[6] issue. In 2015, regional leaders could not agree on one candidate for the Commonwealth secretary-general post. In 2017, the Caribbean was divided on the United Nations vote on the United States' motion on recognizing Jerusalem rather than Tel Aviv as the capital of Israel. Currently, there is still no unified position on the One China Policy, neither is there agreement between member states on their response to the political crisis in Venezuela.

The division between CARICOM member states over Venezuela illuminates how national interests pose challenges to having a regional foreign policy position. On January 10, 2019, the Organization of American States (OAS) Permanent Council approved a resolution to not recognize the second term of Venezuelan president Nicolas Maduro Moros. The Bahamas, Guyana, Haiti, Jamaica, and Saint Lucia voted for the resolution. Dominica, St. Vincent and the Grenadines, and Suriname voted against it. St. Kitts and Nevis, Trinidad and Tobago, Antigua and Barbuda, Barbados, and Belize abstained, while Grenada was absent.

Guyana has a long-standing border dispute with Venezuela, and Jamaica recently re-acquired Venezuela-owned shares in Petrojam, which may explain their opposition to the Maduro regime. Others who opposed the resolution are members of the Bolivarian Alternative for the Americas (ALBA) and recipients of assistance from Venezuela through the Petrocaribe initiative. The majority of CARICOM member states seem to have supported non-intervention. The Bahamas and Haiti took a similar position as major Western powers in recognizing Opposition Leader Juan Guaido as Interim president of Venezuela. Additionally, not all CARICOM governments took part in a meeting at the United Nations that CARICOM had initiated to discuss the crisis (Nichols 2019).

---

6 Shiprider refers to bilateral agreements between various Caribbean countries and the United States in 1996 and 1997 to curb drug trafficking from South American countries to North America and Europe in light of the region's role as a transshipment point for the illicit trade between these two zones (Ferguson 2012).

Mapping CARICOM's Partnerships

CARICOM's external engagements take into account developments in the global political economy in which traditional partners – the United States and the European Union, in particular – are major global actors when they formulate their strategic options. Other players became increasingly important from the 2000s, including the BRICS group (Brazil, Russia, India, China, and South Africa – China being the dominant partner), members of the Organization of the African, Caribbean and Pacific (OACP) States, Japan, South Korea, Turkey, Singapore, the Gulf States, and the countries of Latin America. In response, CARICOM revised its external relations priorities to maintain and strengthen relations with the European Union, the United Kingdom, the United States, and Canada, while deepening relations with Latin America and building relationships with nontraditional partners like the United Arab Emirates, Austria, Italy, Spain, Australia, Russia, Turkey, and India.

CARICOM seeks to consolidate relations with China and strengthen relations with international, regional, and subregional organizations. However, these relationships are not equal. Traditional relationships are substantial and are characterized by greater stability than new relationships. Although significant, more recent partnerships are more volatile in nature (Colin Granderson, email interview, December 1, 2014).

Traditional Partners

Despite waning interest on the part of traditional partners, they remain high priorities for CARICOM. For example, the United States continues to be a significant partner because of its powerful position in the hemisphere and the world as well as its contribution to the security, economic, and financial realms in the region (Colin Granderson, email interview, December 1, 2014).

In 2016, the Caribbean's relationship with the United States took a further deep nosedive as has typically been the case under Republican administrations. The United States' interest in the Caribbean plummeted even more with Donald Trump's presidency and his "America First" and "Making America Great Again" policy positions. Not only was the Caribbean neglected under the Trump presidency save for matters relating to US security interest such as Venezuela's political crisis and China's presence in the region, Trump's actions also encouraged and reinforced fragmentation among CARICOM member states. A case in point was Trump's invitation and promise of investment opportunities to the five countries[7] which supported the United States' rejection of Maduro as the legitimate president of Venezuela.

The recent Democratic win promises both challenges and opportunities for the Caribbean. It was predicted that a Biden presidency could potentially have several benefits: increased US interest in multilateralism – which typically benefits smaller and economically weaker states – global affairs and the Caribbean, more US travel to the Caribbean owing to a successful Biden post-pandemic economic recovery plan, reduced polarization in the OAS (Jessop 2020), and a rolling back of US divide and rule tactics in the region. However, there is no guarantee that the United States will recover sufficiently in the short to medium term to provide the region with the financial support that is needed to redress the devastation brought by COVID-19. Moreover, Anthony Bryan has warned that Biden's long-term strategic plan for renewable energy will be detrimental to the economic fortunes of some countries (e.g., Trinidad and Tobago) which depend on fossil fuel (Bryan 2020) – at least in the short term.

Historically, the economic relations of CARICOM and its member states with traditional partners – the European Union, United States, and Canada – were conducted on a preferential basis, but these relations are changing to reflect the neoliberal currents of the global economy. Through the Lomé Conventions, the European Union provided trade preferences and aid to the ACP group (now the OACP). The 2000 Cotonou Agreement, which replaced the Lomé framework, envisaged the transition to a reciprocal trade regime. The European Union signed a reciprocal trade agreement – an Economic Partnership Agreement (EPA) – with CARIFORUM in 2008.[8] Following BREXIT, the CARIFORUM – UK Economic Agreement was signed in 2019.

While the aid provisions remain intact, the European Union's new policy, which seeks to graduate countries from middle- and high-income categories from grant-based aid, threatens EU aid to the Caribbean (Keijzer et al. 2012). The fears that the European Development Fund (EDF) would not continue in the post-Cotonou framework has become a self-fulfilling prophecy. In the European Union's new budget for 2021 to 2027, they have introduced a new instrument to deliver development assistance – the Neighborhood Development and International Cooperation Instrument which will absorb the EDF. This instrument has been regionalized; neighborhood countries,

---

[7] Bahamas, Dominican Republic, Haiti, Jamaica, and Saint Lucia.
[8] The United States and Canada have sought, unsuccessfully to date, to replace their non-reciprocal arrangements (The Caribbean Basin Initiative and Caribbean Canada Trade Agreement, respectively, with reciprocal economic relationships).

Sub-Saharan Africa, Asia, and the Americas and the Caribbean. This means that the region will be competing for development funds with Latin American countries, including big ones such as Mexico, Brazil, and Chile (Ambassador Patrick Gomes, email communication, November 13, 2020).

The European Union has been promoting and engaging with CARICOM and CARIFORUM as separate entities and within the Latin American and Caribbean framework – through the EU-Latin American and Caribbean (LAC) Strategic Partnership. The Joint Caribbean–EU Strategy, endorsed in 2012, serves to consolidate the political aspects of the relationship and complement the trade and development elements (European Commission 2013). Although the European Union funds regional integration, Girvan has stated that the European Union's economic policies hinder regional integration efforts and constrain policy space for designing development policy (Girvan 2017). CARIFORUM signed an EPA with the European Union in 2008 in the hope of gaining increased access to the EU market, accelerating regional economic integration, diversifying its exports, and developing trade capacity via EU development assistance (Caribbean Regional Negotiating Machinery 2018). However, CARIFORUM faces several challenges with the EPA, including revenue loss from tariff cuts, competition from EU exports, and adjustment and implementation costs (Meyn et al. 2009). The European Union's decision to unilaterally negotiate EPAs with six regions in the ACP broke more than three decades of solidarity among the ACP regions, weakened the leverage of the CARIFORUM in the EPA negotiations with the European Union, and soured EU relations with the Caribbean (Girvan and Montoute 2017).

The relationship between CARICOM and the United Kingdom needs special mention not least for the latter's long-standing historical ties with the majority of CARICOM member states but also because of the implications of its exit from the European Union for the region. Historically, UK–Caribbean relations had been conducted in the context of the wider EU framework and on a bilateral basis. For the former, this was actioned via the Lomé and Cotonou frameworks with the ACP group since 1975 and 2000, respectively, and the EPA with CARIFORUM since 2008. Considering the United Kingdom's exit from the European Union, the United Kingdom and CARIFORUM states signed an EPA in March 2019 which took effect in January 2021. The EPA contains various mechanisms for consultation between the parties. The Caribbean–UK Ministerial Forum also provides a space for UK engagement with CARICOM.

Both sides have pledged to deepen their bilateral relationship in the post–BREXIT era but the Windrush Generation controversy has placed a damper on these possibilities. To compound the challenges, the United Kingdom announced in 2020 that it will be cutting overseas aid in 2021 by £5 billion –

down to 0.5 percent of gross national income (GNI) from 0.7 percent of GNI (Gulland and Rigby 2020).

Nontraditional Partners

Not only are CARICOM and its member states grappling with reciprocal trade relationships with traditional partners, but the number of partners with whom they are engaging has also increased. CARICOM has pursued bilateral relations with nontraditional partners such as Spain, Austria, Italy, Turkey, UAE, and India for cooperation in disaster relief, climate change, sustainable energy and energy security, trade investment, tourism, entrepreneurial, scientific, technological, and personnel exchanges among other areas.

Parties have pledged to cooperate in international processes in areas of mutual interest: in the fight for a just economic order, climate change and other global challenges, and to mutually support each other's candidacy to key positions in international organizations (see for example CARICOM 2014a, 2014b, 2015 and Applewhaite 2011). New relationships that are more functional and supportive take precedence, as in the case of Spain and, to a lesser extent, Turkey. Relations with nontraditional partners do not have as long a history and are therefore not as deep, stable, and familiar – and they can change abruptly and radically, which occurred with a change of administration in Australia in 2013 (Colin Granderson, email interview, December 1, 2014).

Relations between the Anglophone Caribbean and Latin American countries increased dramatically in the 1990s. One of the signs of CARICOM's attention toward the wider Caribbean Basin was the push for the ACS, established in 1994. Subsequently, CARICOM signed several bilateral trade agreements with Latin American countries. CARICOM and some of its member states participate in Latin American arrangements that go beyond trade.

Guyana and Suriname are members of the Union of South American Nations (UNASUR) and are associate members of the Common Market of the South (MERCOSUR); Belize joined the Central American Integration System (SICA); and four countries have become members of the Bolivarian Alliance for the Peoples of Our America (ALBA).[9] CARICOM States (except Trinidad and Tobago and Barbados) are members of Petrocaribe, launched in 2005, and

---

[9] ALBA members are Venezuela, Cuba, Nicaragua, Dominica, Grenada, St Kitts, Antigua, St Vincent, St Lucia, and Suriname. Haiti, Syria, and Iran are observers.

CARICOM states are founding members of the Community of Latin American and Caribbean States (CELAC), established in 2010.

ALBA countries have received funding from Venezuela for social and economic development projects (Girvan 2011b). Petrocaribe participants[10] had been recipients of oil from Venezuela on a preferential basis, funding for oil infrastructure projects and development programs (Girvan 2011a). However, since 2018, the Petrocaribe initiative had been suspended due to Venezuela's declining crude oil production, US pressure on Venezuela and Petrocaribe beneficiaries, and the global fall in oil and gas prices. At the XVII ALBA Summit in December 2019, President Maduro promised to revive the initiative in 2020 (Caribbean Council n.d.).

Guyana's and Suriname's membership in UNASUR and MERCOSUR stems from their desire to be further integrated into the South American family of nations (see, for example, Ramoutar 2013 and Jagdeo 2010). Guyana envisages several benefits from participating in UNASUR, including transport and energy infrastructure integration, support for fighting drugs and crime, social development, and being represented by the two UNASUR countries in the G20 and in multilateral fora: Brazil and Argentina (Jagdeo 2010).

In addition, CARICOM engages with subgroupings and individual countries – SICA, Brazil, Mexico, Chile, and Cuba – in order to coordinate positions in international fora and to get support for education, health, statistics, entrepreneurial innovation, disaster management, agriculture, fisheries, transport, trade and investment, tourism, climate change, trade negotiations, small and medium enterprise development, food security, cultural industries, financing regional institutions, security, energy, intra-CARICOM cooperation, Spanish language, and diplomatic training (see, for example, CARICOM 2010, 2011, 2012, 2013 and Larocque 2014b). CARICOM's engagement with Latin America – through CELAC, for example – allows Latin American countries to better understand CARICOM's priorities, concerns, and peculiarities (Colin Granderson, email interview, December 1, 2014).

New interactions were also developed with the BRICS group, notably, China, India, and Brazil. First, these developments arose from the opportunities they provided for development assistance, investment and trade, alternative development models, diversification of economic relations, and reducing reliance on traditional partners.

---

[10] All CARICOM countries participate except Trinidad and Tobago and Barbados.

Second, the BRICS are potentially powerful allies in international fora on issues of interest to CARICOM. These issues include reforming the global economic order to take account of CARICOM member states' specific needs as small and vulnerable economies, as well as supporting CARICOM's interest in alleviating high debt and reversing the policy of graduation out of concessionary financing based on the current GDP-based criteria (see, for example, LaRocque 2014c).

One the one hand, India and Brazil have arrangements, albeit loose ones, for engaging with CARICOM: the Standing Joint Commission on Consultation, Cooperation and Coordination, and the CARICOM-Brazil Summit,[11] respectively. On the other hand, countries that had diplomatic relations with Taiwan[12] did not participate in the China–Caribbean Economic and Trade Cooperation Forum.[13]

China's largely bilateral approach toward CARICOM encourages competition rather than cooperation among member states. India designed the FOCUS LAC Programme in 1997 to engage with the Caribbean within the broader Latin American framework. Since 2015, China has been engaging with the region in the China–CELAC Economic and Trade Cooperation Forum and the China-LAC Business Summit.

The COVID-19 Pandemic, External Partnerships, South–South Cooperation, and Regional Cooperation

The COVID-19 pandemic has placed the importance of regional integration, South–South cooperation, and development cooperation into sharper focus. Regional integration can be a useful tool for enabling countries to effectively coordinate and implement joint policies for addressing emergency situations and successfully resolving crises. Regional cooperation is even more important where challenges are transnational in nature, such as climate change, crime, and health crises. In such cases, the security of one is linked to the security of others.

A CARICOM approach has been instrumental in mitigating the adverse effects of the pandemic on its member states through the following: coordinating the responses and pooling of the resources of member states, and presenting the

---

[11] No subsequent summits have been held since the inaugural summit in 2010.
[12] Belize, St. Kitts and Nevis, St. Lucia, and St. Vincent and the Grenadines.
[13] There have been three such fora to date: 2005, 2011.

region's needs to partners in global and regional fora. CARICOM's efforts have been supported by several regional agencies including: the Caribbean Public Health Agency (CARPHA); Caribbean Disaster Emergency Management Agency (CDEMA); Caribbean Agricultural Research and Development Institute (CARDI); Caribbean Development Bank (CDB); The University of the West Indies (UWI); Organization of Eastern Caribbean States (OECS) Commission; Eastern Caribbean Central Bank; and the Regional Security System (Byron et al. 2021).

The COVID-19 pandemic raised the age-old question of the necessity of deepening the regional integration project. In 2020, CARICOM Chair, Prime Minister Mia Mottley, reflected on whether this was the moment where the promise of CARICOM – the notion of a single domestic space and a single market – could be truly realized while balancing member states' sovereignty (Mottley 2020).

A major part of CARICOM's response has been via CARPHA – the single regional public health agency of CARICOM. The CARPHA is the region's collective response to effectively address the changing nature of public health challenges. The agency brings several Regional Health Institutes together under one public health umbrella to address issues requiring a regional response. Among the many objectives of CARPHA is "to support the Caribbean Community in preparing for and responding to public health emergencies and threats" (CARPHA, n.d., para. 5).

In keeping with this objective, CARPHA has been collaborating with member states and Caribbean coordinating partners and mechanisms to respond to the threat and to prevent transmission from imported cases. The key actions CARPHA has taken to date are as follows: activated its Incident Management Team and is coordinating the regional response; issued situation reports to CARPHA member states and other regional stakeholders (this includes member states' prevention measures and reopening plans); developed travelers' guidelines and shared with stakeholders; disseminated air and seaport guidelines; issued press releases and shared with the media and other regional stakeholders; activated the Security Cluster for the tracking of passengers from China through the CARICOM Implementing Agency for Crime and Security (IMPACS); provided COVID-19 testing and regular laboratory updates; conducted COVID-related research and data collection; engaged in public awareness campaigns/information dissemination on various aspects of the virus and the pandemic; and provided training and capacity building of relevant personnel and stakeholders (Cruickshank-Taylor 2020a).

Regional cooperation efforts were supported by international partnerships – countries and multilateral institutions. Some examples include: the

African Union, India, Cuba, China, the United Arab Emirates, Canada, Venezuela, the European Union, the United States, and the United Kingdom. Various forms of assistance also came from multilateral agencies such as the World Health Organization (WHO), the Pan-American Health Organization (PAHO), the Inter-American Development Bank (IADB), the World Food Programme, the Caribbean Development Bank (CDB), among others. Donations were delivered to CARICOM or its regional agencies. Others provided support at the national level, one example being UNAIDS in Jamaica (CDEMA 2021;Jamaica Observer 2021; Nurse 2020; PAHO 2020; Singh 2020; Telesur 2020)

The region faces two main challenges in relation to vaccines: access and hesitancy. In the case of access to vaccines, this is so despite their participation in the WHO COVAX scheme (Stabroek News 2021b). CARICOM has expressed concerns about equitable access to the vaccine with Prime Minister Andrew Holness of Jamaica lamenting that big countries are "hoarding" the vaccine through surplus buying (Scott 2021). Regional cooperation has been an important tool to overcome these obstacles. CARICOM has called for a global summit in the context of the WHO ACT – A Facilitation Council to address issues of equitable access (Stabroek News 2021a). In April 2021, the OECS Commission, in collaboration with several international organizations, convened a meeting to address vaccine hesitancy and inequitable access which exists mainly in Africa and the Caribbean (St. Lucia Times 2021) (see table 14.2 for vaccination rates in CARICOM countries).

Conclusion

CARICOM's diverse partnerships pose both challenges and opportunities. Diversified relationships allow CARICOM greater flexibility to maneuver in international relations and to provide enhanced opportunities for overcoming challenges and achieving its development objectives. Importantly, these relationships provide avenues for technology transfer, development of science and innovation, and sharing best practices for development strategies as well as allowing CARICOM to share its successes with its partners in a formalized framework.

By coordinating positions with more powerful states and providing mutual support for candidates to top positions in international organizations, CARICOM's interests gain traction on the international stage. Also, CARICOM's relations with new European and other partners who are seeking global recognition offer huge potential for both sides. For partners such as Turkey and Austria, for example, the Caribbean is an attractive partner because they need only to make small investments to have a significant impact and to

Table 14.2 Number of COVID-19 vaccination doses per 100 population administered in CARICOM countries as of February 25, 2022

CARICOM Country	Number vaccinated per 100 thousand
Antigua and Barbuda	126.06
Barbados	107.35
Belize	112.49
St. Kitts and Nevis	112.69
Trinidad and Tobago	108.35
Guyana	101.49
Suriname	84.62
Dominica	85.11
Bahamas	82.06
Grenada	75.63
St. Lucia	59.4
St. Vincent and the Grenadines	59.89
Jamaica	45.53
Haiti	2.01

Source: Mendoza (2021).

yield returns since CARICOM countries are small in size but large in numbers and, by extension, so are the number of votes they carry in the UN. CARICOM stands to gain much by pursuing friendships with "new and emerging kids on the block" who may not be as wealthy as others but who are eager to make a name for themselves on the global stage.

The relations of CARICOM and its member states with emerging economies and other countries in the "South," as well as with nontraditional partners, could support regional integration and bring sustainable development outcomes in the long term, if properly managed. These relations could complement, and in some cases serve as alternatives to, traditional sources of development cooperation. Development cooperation with emerging economies will become increasingly important as concessional funding from traditional sources shrinks. Additional alternative sources of development funding will become necessary as the Caribbean potentially faces competition within the wider LAC framework for traditional grant-based funding from the European Union.

"South–South" development cooperation could address shortcomings of cooperation with traditional partners. In the case of China, for example, the processing of funding is quicker, more efficient, and less cumbersome compared to the European Union (Girvan 2011c). The relationship between Caribbean and "Southern" partners is seen as more equal than between the

Caribbean and the United States and the European Union; not only are China, India, and Brazil fellow "developing" countries, but importantly, there is no history of a dominant or colonial relationship with CARICOM, as is the case of the United States and the European Union. This makes cooperation with new partners attractive to CARICOM.

On the other hand, CARICOM's "spaghetti bowl" of relationships poses the danger of overlapping and straining limited human and financial resources. Also, CARICOM's interests could be compromised as it attempts to coordinate and leverage such many players with competing interests. In that regard, CARICOM allocates greater resources to relations that are based on development and technical assistance than those of a purely political nature.

Individual member states are also engaging with several partners, which adds to the web of relationships. CARICOM has encouraged these relationships by calling on member states to "pursue and explore all opportunities available to them for their social and economic development, recognizing at all times their obligations under the Revised Treaty of Chaguaramas" (CARICOM 2008, para. 11). In this regard, Girvan has warned that:

> In the absence of coordination, CARICOM's external trade policy will continue to be a series of ad hoc bilateral responses to opportunities afforded by global and hemispheric reconfiguration, lacking a coherent strategic dimension [. . .] There is also a danger of regional fragmentation associated with the fall-out from external trade policy to domestic policy. The Community could, in effect, be pulled in several different directions at the same time. (Girvan 2011a, 16)

However, according to Colin Granderson, although "membership of diverse processes can create dissonance on occasion, [. . .] member states tend in general to give priority to the CARICOM position" (Colin Granderson, email interview, December 1, 2014).

While member states may genuinely wish to preserve the unity of CARICOM, there are indications that national interest and the quest for national development will supersede the preservation of the regional integration project. Regional integration was not intended to be an end in itself; it was a tool to help achieve the development objectives of member states and was necessary for their survival as small states (see, for example, Bishop et al. 2011, 13). Today, member states have been seeking alternative avenues in pursuit of their development objectives; bilateral relations with emerging economies such as China have been one such avenue. The stalling of the CSME is partly because member states' development needs are being met outside of the CARICOM framework, making its completion less urgent.

Notwithstanding the benefits of "South–South" relationships, they are not inherently altruistic; they are to be properly managed for positive development outcomes. For example, China's engagement with the Caribbean is said to be displaying neo-colonial characteristics and reinforcing the region's dependency (Gonzalez-Vicente and Montoute 2020). China's export of manufactured goods and import of raw materials (Girvan 2011c), the huge trade imbalance, lack of technology transfer, and unwritten conditionalities could be damaging to CARICOM countries, albeit different from the conditionalities of traditional partners. The One China Policy undermines Caribbean regional integration (Montoute, 2013). If left unchecked, this could potentially perpetuate the underdevelopment of the region.

The COVID-19 pandemic has further highlighted the importance of regional integration, CARICOM as an entity more specifically, and the value of its external partnerships. CARICOM has managed the pandemic mainly through its regional institutions and, arguably, the degree of success it has had can be attributed to the strength of regional cooperation. This led Allan Chastanet, former prime minister of St. Lucia, to say in the early stages of the pandemic, "You [CARICOM] had Saint Lucia's back and we thank you. This is what being part of CARICOM is about" (Dunkley-Malcolm 2020c, para. 3). CARICOM's response has therefore reinforced the importance of regional integration.

While the region is seeing the benefits of regional integration, the crisis has also shown the challenges. One example relates to the CARICOM Travel Bubble.[14] Countries opted out of the Bubble as COVID-19 cases began to rise in other participating countries. This exposed the limits of regional integration, in which case, national interest was the overriding concern. In this instance, some of the drivers for collective action proposed by Sandler (2010) were not present to preserve the CARICOM Travel Bubble: mutual net gains for all participating nations, equitable distribution of net gains from collective action, and the promise of commercial gains from the effort.

Support from external partners (traditional and nontraditional) has been vital to CARICOM's response. CARICOM as a regional entity has been able to leverage its collective strength to lobby and garner external support. This

---

[14] An arrangement made in September 2020 between "low-risk" CARICOM countries in which travellers from participating countries would be exempted from PCR testing prior to arrival and quarantine restrictions in the destination country if they had not travelled to a country outside of the Bubble for at least fourteen days prior to the date of travel. The countries in the Bubble were Antigua and Barbuda, Barbados, Dominica, Grenada, Montserrat, St. Kitts and Nevis, Saint Lucia, and St. Vincent and the Grenadines.

assistance has been predominantly channeled through the relevant associate regional bodies. External partnerships in the COVID-19 scenario have therefore supported and reinforced regional cooperation. South–South cooperation has been critical for managing the pandemic in the Caribbean. Notably, Cuba's provision of medical personnel, India's donation of vaccines, and the African Unions' solidarity with the Caribbean for the purchase of vaccines have contributed significantly to addressing the challenges of the pandemic.

In closing, I make three observations: (i) the pandemic has further vindicated CARICOM and the regional integration project, yet regionalism continues to be tested by the model of inter-governmentalism, national interest, and the assertion of state sovereignty (Grenade 2011); (ii) the pandemic illustrates the value of external relationships and multilateral cooperation in a moment of crisis. External support was key to the region's management of the pandemic; (iii) the significance of south–south cooperation is underestimated relative to north–south cooperation; the potential of this strategy for overcoming development challenges is huge; and (iii) COVID-19 highlighted the need to expand the use of external partnerships for investments in health, education, and other areas of human development in a post-COVID-19 setting.

References

Applewhaite, Lolita. 2011. "Remarks by Ambassador Lolita Applewhaite, Secretary-General (Ag), Caribbean Community (CARICOM), on the Occasion of the Presentation of Credentials by His Excellency Paolo Serpi, Plenipotentiary Representative of Italy to the Caribbean Community." *CARICOM Secretariat*, 7 April. http://www.caricom.org/jsp/pressreleases/press_releases_2011/pres128_11.jsp?null&prnf=1.

Bishop, Matthew Louis, Norman Girvan, Timothy M. Shawn, Solange Mike Raymond, Mark Kirton, Michelle Scobie, Debbie Mohammed, and Marlon Anatol. 2011. "Caribbean Regional Integration: A Report of the UWI Institute of International Relations." University of the West Indies, April. https://sta.uwi.edu/iir/documents/IIR_Research_Documents/IIRRegionalIntegrationReportFINAL.pdf.

Bryan, Anthony. 2020. "Tough Times Ahead for T&T as Biden Takes Charge in the USA." *Trinidad and Tobago Guardian*, 29 November. https://www.guardian.co.tt/news/tough-times-ahead-for-tt-as-biden-takes-charge--in-the-usa-6.2.1250198.a9fb3d795c.

Byron, Jessica, Jacqueline Laguardia- Martinez, Annita Montoute, and Keron Niles. 2021. "Impacts of COVID-19 in the Commonwealth Caribbean: Key Lessons." *The Round Table - The Commonwealth Journal of International Affairs*, 110 (1): 99–119. https://doi.org/10.1080/00358533.2021.1875694.

Caribbean Council. n.d. "Maduro Says PetroCaribe to be Revived this Year." https://www.caribbean-council.org/maduro-says-petrocaribe-to-be-revived-this-year/.

CRNM (Caribbean Regional Negotiating Machinery). 2018. "What Europe is Offering Africa: The Pros and Cons of EPAs: CRNM Note on CARIFORUM Economic Partnership Agreement." *Caribbean Regional Negotiating Machinery*, April 2008.

CARICOM. 2008. "Communiqué Issued at the Conclusion of the Eleventh Meeting of the Council for Foreign and Community Relations (COFCOR), 7–9 May 2008, Bolans Village, Antigua and Barbuda." *CARICOM Secretariat*, 10 May. http://www.caricom.org/jsp/pressreleases/pres125_08.jsp.

———. 2010. "Brasilia Declaration Issued by the First CARICOM-Brazil Summit, Brasilia, Brazil." *CARICOM Secretariat*, 16 April. http://www.caricom.org/jsp/communications/meetings_statements/brasilia_declaration.jsp.

———. 2011. "Joint Declaration Following the Third CARICOM-SICA Summit of Heads of State and Government, San Salvador, El Salvador, 19 August 2011." *CARICOM Secretariat*, 19 August. http://www.caricom.org/jsp/pressreleases/press_releases_2011/pres323_11.jsp.

———. 2012. "Second Meeting of the CARICOM-Chile Joint Commission, Santiago, Chile, 3 - 4 February 2012: Final Act." *CARICOM Secretariat*, 3 February. http://www.caricom.org/jsp/pressreleases/final_act_caricom_chile_joint_comm_feb_12.pdf.

———. 2013. "Final Declaration, Fourth Meeting of Minister of Foreign Affairs of CARICOM and the Republic of Cuba." *CARICOM Secretariat*, 6 September. http://www.caricom.org/jsp/pressreleases/press_releases_2013/pres189_13.jsp.

———. 2014a. "CARICOM and Turkey to Strengthen Relations: Issues Declaration on a New Era of Cooperation and Consultation." *CARICOM Secretariat*, 28 July. http://www.caricom.org/jsp/pressreleases/press_releases_2014/pres19514.jsp.

———. 2014b. "CARICOM, Spain Strengthen Diplomatic Relations." *CARICOM Secretariat*, 25 April. http://www.caricom.org/jsp/pressreleases/press_releases_2014/pres89_14.jsp.

———. 2014c. "Strategic Plan for the Caribbean Community, 2015 - 2019: Repositioning CARICOM, Vol. 1 – The Executive Plan." *CARICOM Secretariat*, 3 July. https://caricom.org/wp-content/uploads/STRATEGIC-PLAN-2016_opt.pdf.

———. 2015. "CARICOM, Austria Strengthen Diplomatic Ties." *CARICOM Secretariat*, 28 January. http://www.caricom.org/jsp/pressreleases/press_releases_2015/pres14_15.jsp.

———. n.d. "International Development Partners." *CARICOM Secretariat*. https://caricom.org/international-development-partners/.

CARPHA. n.d. "About the Caribbean Public Health Agency." https://carpha.org/Who-We-Are/About.

CDEMA. 2021. "CDEMA hosts Exercise SYNERGY 2021." *CDEMA*, 29 July. https://www.cdema.org/news-centre/press-releases?start=5.

Cruickshank-Taylor, Victoria. 2020a. "CARPHA COVID-19 Response." *CARPHA*, 14 October. https://carpha.org/More/Media/Articles/ArticleID/366/CARPHA-COVID-19-Response.

———. 2020b. "IDB Contributes US$750K to Support CARPHA's Coordinated COVID-19 Response in the Caribbean." *CARPHA*, 22 June. https://www.carpha

.org/More/Media/Articles/ArticleID/336/IDB-Contributes-US-750K-to-Support
-CARPHA%E2%80%99s-Coordinated-COVID-19-Response-in-the-Caribbean.

Dunkley-Malcolm, Jascene. 2020a. "CARPHA Partners with PAHO to Ensure
Caribbean States' Equitable Access to COVID-19 Vaccine." *CARICOM Today*,
21 October. https://today.caricom.org/2020/10/16/carpha-partners-with-paho-to
-ensure-caribbean-states-equitable-access-to-covid-19-vaccine/.

———. 2020b. "CARPHA Receives Medical Supplies from the People's Republic of
China." *CARICOM Today*, 24 July. https://today.caricom.org/2020/07/22/carpha
-receives-medical-supplies-from-the-peoples-republic-of-china/.

———. 2020c. "Regional Response to the Novel Corona Virus is 'Regionalism
Working' – Prime Minister Chastanet." *CARICOM Today*, 20 April. https://today
.caricom.org/2020/02/19/regional-response-to-novel-corona-virus-is-regionalism
-working-prime-minister-chastanet/.

European Commission. 2013. "EU Relations with the Caribbean: European
Commission Memo 13/798." *European Commission*, 18 September. https://ec.europa
.eu/commission/presscorner/detail/fr/MEMO_13_798.

Ferguson, Tyron, 2012. "Shiprider Revisited: Security and Transnational Crime in the
Caribbean." *Caribbean Dialogue*, 8 (4): 29–48.

Girvan, Norman. 2001. "Reinterpreting the Caribbean." In *New Caribbean Thought:
A Reader*, edited by Folke Lindahl and Brian Meeks, 3–23. Kingston, Jamaica:
University of the West Indies Press.

———. 2011a. "ALBA, Petrocaribe, and CARICOM: Issues in a New Dynamic." In
Venezuela's Petro-Diplomacy: Hugo Chavez's Foreign Policy, edited by Ralph Clem,
Anthony Maingot, and Cristina Eguizábal, 116–34.Gainesville: University Press of
Florida.

———. 2011b. "Is ALBA a New Model of Integration? Reflections on the CARICOM
Experience." *International Journal of Cuban Studies*, 3, no. 2/3 (Summer/Autumn):
157–80.

———. 2011c. "Global and Regional Reconfigurations of Power: Implications
for Caribbean EU Relations." Presentation, the Joint Caribbean-EU Strategy:
Reflections and Analysis Workshop, Institute of International Relations, UWI.

———. 2013. "Re-inventing the CSME - Edited Text of Address to The Caribbean
Association of Judicial Officers 3rd Biennial Conference," 27 September. http://www
.normangirvan.info/wp-content/uploads/2013/09/CAJO-ADDRESS-By-Girvan.pdf.

———. 2017. "The Implications of the Economic Partnership Agreement (EPA) for the
CSME." *Social and Economic Studies*, 58 (2): 91–127.

———. and Annita Montoute. 2017. "The EU and the Caribbean: The Necessity of
Unity." In *The ACP Group and the EU Development Partnership: Beyond the North-
South Debate*, edited by Annita Montoute and Kudrat Virk, 79–110. Cham: Palgrave
Macmillan.

Gonzalez-Vicente, Ruben and Annita Montoute. 2021. "A Caribbean
Perspective on China–Caribbean Relations: Global IR, Dependency and
the Postcolonial Condition." *Third World Quarterly*, 42 (2): 219–38. doi:
10.1080/01436597.2020.1834841.

Granderson, Colin. 2012. "CARICOM Foreign Policy in the Changing Global Environment," 20 August.

Grenade, Wendy. 2011. "Regionalism and Sub-Regionalism in the Caribbean: Challenges and Prospects: Any Insights from Europe?" *Jean Monnet/Robert Schuman Paper Series*, 11 (4): 2–25.

Gulland, Anne and Jennifer Rigby. 2020. "Foreign Office Minister Baroness Sugg Resigns after Aid Budget Slashed by £5bn in Spending Review." *The Telegraph*, 25 November. https://www.telegraph.co.uk/global-health/climate-and-people/foreign-aid-budget-slashed-5bn-sunaks-spending-review/.

IDB (Inter-American Development Bank). 2005. "CARICOM Report No. 2." *IDB*, August. http://ctrc.sice.oas.org/trc/Articles/CARICOM_Report_2.pdf.

———. 2020. "CARPHA Receiving Additional Support to Fight COVID-19." *IDB*, 15 May. https://www.iadb.org/en/news/carpha-receiving-additional-support-fight-covid-19.

Jagdeo, Bharrat. 2010. "Speech given at the Opening Ceremony of the Fourth Summit of the Union of South American Nations." http://minfor.gov.gy/docs/otherspeeches/opening_ceremony_unasur.pdf..

Jamaica Observer. 2021. "CARICOM could Source COVID-19 vaCcines through Africa." *Jamaica Observer*, 15 January. http://www.jamaicaobserver.com/latestnews/Caricom_could_source_COVID-19_vaccines_through_Africa?profile=1467.

Jessop, David. 2020. "US and the Caribbean: Time to Seize the Moment." *Dominican Today*, 13 November. https://dominicantoday.com/dr/opinion/2020/11/13/the-us-and-the-caribbean-time-to-seize-the-moment/.

Keijzer, Niels, Jeske van Seters, Brecht Lein, Florian Krätke, and Annita Montoute. 2012. "Differentiation in ACP-EU Cooperation: Implications of the EU's Agenda for Change for the 11th EDF and beyond: Discussion Paper 134." *European Centre for Development Policy Management*, October. https://ecdpm.org/publications/differentiation-acp-eu-cooperation/.

LaRocque, Irwin. 2014a. "Opening Remarks by Ambassador Irwin LaRocque, Secretary-General Caribbean Community Speech at the 17th Meeting of the COFCOR, Georgetown, Guyana, May 20-21, 2014." *CARICOM Secretariat*, 20 May. https://caricom.org/opening-remarks-by-ambassador-irwin-larocque-secretary-general-caribbean-community-at-the-seventeenth-meeting-of-the-council-for-foreign-and-community-relations-cofcor-georgetown-gu/.

———. 2014b. "Remarks by the Secretary-General of the Caribbean Community (CARICOM) Ambassador Irwin LaRocque at the Opening Ceremony of the Third CARICOM-Mexico Summit, Merida, Yucatan, Mexico, 29 April 2014." *CARICOM Secretariat*, 30 April. http://www.caricom.org/jsp/pressreleases/press_releases_2014/pres94_14.jsp.

———. 2014c. "Remarks by the Secretary-General of the Caribbean Community Ambassador Irwin LaRocque on the Occasion of the Presentation of Credentials by Her Excellency Maureen Isabella Modiselle, Plenipotentiary Representative (Designate) of The Republic of South Africa to the Caribbean Community." *CARICOM Secretariat*, 18 February. http://caricom.org/jsp/pressreleases/press_releases_2014/pres28_14.jsp.

Mendoza, J. 2021. "COVID-19 Vaccination Rate in Latin America 2021, by Country." *Statista*, 17 December. https://www.statista.com/statistics/1194813/latin-america -covid-19-vaccination-rate-country/.

Meyn, Mareike, Christopher Stevens, Jane Kennan, Nick Highton, Sanoussi Bilal, Corinna Braun-Munzinger, Dan Lui, Jeske van Seters, Collette Campbell, and John Rapley. 2009. "The CARIFORUM-EU Economic Partnership Agreement (EPA): The Development Component." *European Parliament Directorate General for External Policies of the Union*, 31 March. http://www.odi.org/sites/odi.org.uk/files/odiassets/ publications-opinion-files/4205.pdf.

Montoute, Annita. 2013. "Caribbean-China Economic Relations: What Are the Implications?" *Caribbean Journal of International Relations and Diplomacy*, 1 (1): 110–26.

Mottley, Mia. 2020. "Special CARICOM Heads of Government Meeting on Wednesday 15th April 2020." YouTube Video. 1:19, 12 April. https://www.youtube.com/watch?v= _LG-O2FAcLE.

Nichols, Alicia. 2019. "CARICOM Foreign Policy Coordination: Priority or Pipe Dream?" *Caribbean Trade Law and Development*, 3 February. https:// caribbeantradelaw.com/2019/02/03/caricom-foreign-policy-coordination-priority -or-pipe-dream/.

Nurse, Michelle. 2020. "Statement by the Organization of Eastern Caribbean States on Cuban Medical Brigades." *CARICOM Today*, 29 June. https://today.caricom.org /2020/06/23/statement-by-the-organisation-of-eastern-caribbean-states-on-cuban -medical-brigades/.

———. 2021. "First CARICOM-Africa Summit to be held 7 September." *CARICOM Today*, 20 September. https://today.caricom.org/2021/09/03/first-caricom-africa -summit-to-be-held-7-september/.

PAHO. 2020. "The United Kingdom Contributes $3.8m for COVID-19 Response in the Caribbean." *PAHO*, 22 May. https://www.paho.org/en/news/22-5-2020-united -kingdom-contributes-38m-covid-19-response-caribbean.

Ramoutar, Donald. 2013. "Remarks by Ramoutar at the XLV MERCOSUR Summit." *Caribseek News*, 12 July. http://news.caribseek.com/index.php/caribbean-islands -news/guyana-news/item/54323-remarks-by-ramotar-at-the-xlv-mercosur-summit.

Sandler, Todd. 2010. "Overcoming Global and Regional Collective Action Impediments." *Global Policy*, 1 (1): 40–50.

Scott, Romario. 2021. "Holness Slams Vaccine Grab – PM Says Rich Countries under False Sense of Security Hoarding COVID Cure." *The Jamaica Gleaner*, 9 January. https://jamaica-gleaner.com/article/lead-stories/20210109/holness-slams-vaccine -grab-pm-says-rich-countries-under-false-sense.

Singh, Priti. 2020. "Continuing Cooperation between Caribbean Community (CARICOM) and India during the COVID-19 Pandemic." *Extraordinary and Plenipotentiary Diplomatist*, 4 August. https://diplomatist.com/2020/08/04/ continuing-cooperation-between-caribbean-community-caricom-and-india-during -the-covid-19-pandemic/.

Stabroek News. 2021a. "CARICOM 'Deeply Concerned' at Inequitable Access to COVID vaccines." *Stabroek News*, 13 January. https://www.stabroeknews.com/2021

/01/13/news/guyana/caricom-deeply-concerned-at-inequitable-access-to-covid
-vaccines/.

———. 2021b. "Jamaica PM Says Rich Countries Hoarding COVID-19 Cure." *Stabroek News*, 9 January. https://www.stabroeknews.com/2021/01/09/news/regional/jamaica/jamaica-pm-says-rich-countries-hoarding-covid-19-cure/.

St. Lucia Times. 2021. "OECS, African Union Partner to Overcome Vaccine Challenges." *St. Lucia Times*, 17 April. https://stluciatimes.com/oecs-african-union
-partner-to-overcome-vaccine-challenges/.

Telesur. 2020. "Venezuela Donates COVID-19 Tests to Caribbean Countries." *Telesur*, 10 April.

15

Resetting and Reinventing the Association of Caribbean States

JUNE SOOMER

Introduction: Context and Conceptualization

The creation of the Association of Caribbean States (ACS) represented a strategic opportunity to develop new forms of regional cooperation based on the notion of widening rather than deepening integration. It is now more than two and a half decades since visionary leaders from around the Caribbean Sea sat together in Cartagena de Índias, Colombia, to make decisions to bring the peoples of our countries together to form the ACS (The Convention Establishing the Association of Caribbean States 1994). This organization consists of twenty-five independent member states and eleven associates. It has been making strides to enhance cooperation among the states, countries, and territories to contribute to the future cultural, economic, and social development of their peoples, transcending their separateness of the past. This deepening cooperation is also supported by now twenty-eight observers throughout the world.

The conceptualization of the Greater Caribbean as a region for the deepening and broadening of regional integration was imagined by a decolonization movement which enunciated administrative, political, economic, and social autonomy in the English-speaking Caribbean and also throughout the Caribbean littoral. The dismantling of colonial empires in the Caribbean meant that there was a purposeful autonomy that girded a desire to forge new ties and linkages with new nations in their search for sustainability, and new opportunities for development for countries that were, at independence, abandoned for their audacity. From the onset, territoriality in the form of regional integration thus became entrenched in the advancement toward self-sufficiency and the search for global recognition. It is out of this discourse that the equality of the struggle for independence emboldened and dared these small island developing states to seek partnership and cooperation on an equal footing with neighbors scattered around the Caribbean Sea. Norman Girvan, citing various books by anticolonial and anti-imperial scholars, writes that "as early as the 1930s and

1940s the seeds of a broader pan-Caribbean consciousness were being planted in a series of books" (Girvan 2006, 3) and that this would be fleshed out later by future authors and leaders.

While the idea of a pan-Caribbean regionalism had been evolving since the early labor unrest in the Caribbean, at the political level, it was Dr. Eric Williams, the first Prime Minister of Trinidad and Tobago, who often expressed his resolve on an extended Caribbean Community embracing everybody – Anglophone, Dutch, Hispanophone, and Francophone countries. This notion would much later be articulated and augmented by Errol Barrow's statement in 1986 that the Caribbean was indeed a civilization. The sophistication of these sentiments was the recognition that this diverse region had all the human, social, cultural, and emotional attributes to advance the notion of regional integration based on south–south cooperation in an early postcolonial world. This confidence cannot be lost on us as we explore the makings of the Greater Caribbean. Sir Shridath Ramphal, one of the architects of the *Time for Action* Report, remarks in his Memoir on the courage displayed by the early Caribbean leaders which he notes must not go unnoticed as it constitutes the product of their strong political will and commitment to regional integration.

In the recent past, Ralph Gonsalves, Prime Minister of St. Vincent and the Grenadines, has channeled Errol Barrow by expounding on the definition of that Caribbean civilization – a distant civilization that has evolved geographically and historically – and identifies eight characteristics of this region. He proposed that "the islands of the Caribbean and the countries washed by the Caribbean Sea, constitute, geographically, the physical base of the civilisation" (Gonsalves 2014, 17). If we already have a tangible and historical basis, how do we build on this to consolidate that civilization? That enhancement must be entrenched within the broadening of that concept to the Greater Caribbean.

Another imperative of the conceptualization of the ACS is the inherent resistance which underpins decolonization. Patsy Lewis et al. in Pan-Caribbean Integration: Beyond CARICOM note that by drawing on a pan-Caribbean regionalism that transcends language and culture, the concept was constructed in an identity of resistance (Lewis et al. 2018, 7). While that statement directly referred to Haiti and CARICOM in 2002, it should be recalled that this country officially had already become a member of the ACS in 1994. The widening of regionalism was, therefore, emboldened by a defiance that was a contrast to the gradualism that would later hinder the early potential of that expansion.

The expression of this grandiose conceptualization in the manifestation of an ACS was nonetheless limited by the initial fear to imagine the Greater Caribbean as a space that could embrace a more complex regional integration. The underlying and ongoing fears included the fragility and vulnerability of the island states, the imagined limitations, and distrust of the obvious size, languages, and political diversity of the region would encumber promise. The strengths therefore become the weakness, which ensured the emergence of a fragile organization not recognizable in the initial boldness of the postulations.

Anthony Payne writes that "the ACS was envisaged as 'being active in an integration sense' and a wide set of possible areas of co-operation was listed, including the negotiation of special trading terms, the widening of communication links, joint activities in tourism and health matters, the management of the resources of the Caribbean Sea and the curbing of drug trafficking" (Payne 2007, 268). He supports the view that the ensuing institutional framework to execute the implementation of these mandates was inadequate. He posited that the ACS Secretariat was set up on a weak footing, and it has to be said that it has so far failed to develop a significant profile in any key aspect of the international economic and security agendas that have lately faced the Caribbean Basin as a whole. Nevertheless, it exists, and this remains a potential vehicle for forging greater unity in the Basin (Payne 2007, 269).

The indictment that even at the time of the signing of the Convention in 1994, there was nothing much expected from the ACS in its early years speaks to the great divisions in the region at the time and which remain, and may have widened because of the sustained assault on regional integration and on multilateralism from within and outside of the Greater Caribbean. Yet these opinions were expressed in 2006 and approximately fourteen years after its utterance, the question may be asked: What is the justification for the continued existence of the ACS into its twenty-six years?

It was the July 1986 Heads of Government Meeting that called for a general prospective study on the development prospects of the Caribbean Region in the context of the fundamental and apparently irreversible structural changes that were taking place in the global environment (Hall and Chuck-A Sang 2007, 8). It is therefore no coincidence that in November 1986 Errol Barrow made his speech on Caribbean civilization. It would be eight years before the ACS would be established, and Norman Girvan points to the length of time it took for commencement in July 1994. By this time the weakening of multilateralism had already commenced with the establishment of the World Trade Organization (WTO). Despite this occurrence, there remained consensus among CARICOM states that they could still influence international decision-making and "leverage through working with allies and benefiting from the support of friendly countries and institutions" (Hall and Chuck-A Sang 2007, 8). This cooperation would remain the hallmark of the ACS throughout its existence.

Edwin Laurent stated that "The push for economic integration throughout the Americas to include North, Central and South America and the Caribbean, was motivated by both economic and political consensus" (Laurent 2007, 25). However, there were key issues such as the exclusion of Cuba from the December 1994 Summit of Heads of Government of the Western Hemisphere convened by Bill Clinton, which undermined solidarity. The primary decision at that meeting was the creation of the Fair Trade Area of the Americas (FTAA), and this arrangement would be the beginning of a series of bilateral trade arrangements between CARICOM and individual states in the Greater Caribbean. At this juncture it was clear, these countries imagined that bilateralism and multilateralism were not mutually exclusive and that they envisioned the ACS adopting a multilateral approach to the FTAA as well as the formation of the WTO in January 1995.

The emergence of the ACS would be further hindered by the "banana dispute" (Laurent 2007, 46) among the membership which had commenced in 1993. This dispute would occupy the region along with the challenges to sugar in the European Union. The relationship therefore commenced on the battlefield of international trade, and it is a small wonder that the role assigned to the ACS Secretariat was trade facilitation without the resources necessary to participate in the emerging global trade infrastructure of the following two decades.

Can the ACS be considered an "integration" movement? Have we gone through the process of creating that regionalism? Anthony Payne had similar questions and saw it "as a method of international cooperation that enables the advantages of decision-making at a regional level to be reconciled with the preservation of the institutions of the nation state" (Payne 2007, 284). These questions continue to be a conundrum for the region. Yet the Greater Caribbean has been decisive on critical consensus matters such as the region as a zone of peace and on its consistent advocacy against the transshipment of nuclear waste through the Caribbean Sea.

While the ACS was created on a fragile footing, one so weak that its disappearance had been predicted, the question which should be asked is why it has survived for so long. Perhaps the answer lies in the response to the survivability of CARICOM as proposed by Norman Girvan who posited that CARICOM's survival will depend on both ideological and economic convergence as well as on its ability to reinvent itself (Girvan 2001, 189). The ACS will also have to reinvent itself; this will be explored below along with its remarkable ability to survive the formation of the FTAA, the WTO, and other such challenges.

The Purpose and the Architecture

The proposal to establish the ACS was espoused in Time for Action – The Report of the West Indian Commission. The decision to establish the ACS as a broad framework for the adoption of common positions among the states, countries, and territories of the Caribbean was, therefore, a manifestation of a vision espoused in the framing of a decolonized region.

No other mechanism for cooperation in the wider Caribbean envisioned such an expansive call. From the beginning, four regional groups were distinguished: CARICOM, the Group of Three (Colombia, Mexico, and the Bolivarian Republic of Venezuela), Central America, and the Non-Grouped (Cuba, Dominican Republic, and Panama) (Report of the West India Commission 1993, 21). The Overseas Territories were included as associate members. The creation of the ACS represented a strategic opportunity to develop new forms of regional cooperation and, to a large extent, this is at the core of its survival.

The recommendations of the Report cannot be isolated from each other as together they set up the blueprint for the transformation of the small island developing states of CARICOM. The widening of the integration movement along with its purposes and architecture must therefore be viewed along all the foundational pillars of nation building. The Report ensured that "the process of deepening CARICOM integration and the process of widening regional partnership were not irreconcilable strategies" (Report of the West India Commission 1993, 21). Henry Gill in 1995 referred to it as a "quantum leap in Caribbean regionalism," and Jessica Byron on the celebration of its twenty-fifth anniversary stated that "it sought to transcend all of the long-standing differences and disjunctures across El Gran Caribe... and it formulated innovative approaches to membership and to administering the cooperation that was envisaged. It is still a very special regional organization" (Byron 2020, 1).

The purpose of the Greater Caribbean was also shaped by the question of transforming "geographical proximity into economic networking in spite of difficulties in trade and economic cooperation in the past" (Report of the West India Commission 1993, 432). It was recognized that this issue was complicated by the myriad of relationships with the countries on the rim of the Caribbean Sea and the resources that would be needed to consolidate some of those relationships. It was expressed that "we have to be confident of both our identity and capacities, and be ready to take a lead in the creation of a real community of the entire Caribbean" (Report of the West India Commission 1993, 444). This hesitant confidence would ensure that the CARICOM countries would enter into an arrangement where they wanted to consolidate their survival. Consequently, in 1994, the largest democracy in the region, Mexico, would find itself in an arrangement with the smallest democracy, St. Kitts and Nevis, based on advantages and cooperation among all and for all.

One of the primary mandates of the organization would become trade and external economic relations, as Venezuela and the Dominican Republic commenced their overtures with regard to free trade with the CARICOM region. There was also the hope expressed that Central America would become a possible partner as they were moving toward the recognition of Belize.

The widening of integration was also premised on the defining and consolidation of the identity of the West Indies, while recognizing that the Greater Caribbean region was also in the process of refining its identity. The Report made it clear that even in this state of refinement, "it in no way precludes us venturing upon a larger enterprise, not only in our search for additional protection against the storms of change, but also in order to realise what is a natural regional bonding arising out of common historical roots" (Report of the West India Commission 1993, 26). That both national and regional identities were at the heart of the philosophy of the widening project is undeniable. That identity supported by the concept of a Greater Caribbean around the Caribbean Sea was optimistic.

Education was expected to support this widening experiment – part of the transformation of marginalized small states – and a pillar of nation building. This education would focus on technological change, investment, and engagement with new partners to ensure that the needs and concerns of these countries would move toward the center away from the periphery. Consequently, another foreseen purpose for the widening was diplomacy and the way in which the dual track would enhance the negotiating capability of the transformation. As noted in the Report, diplomacy was important in the widening of regional cooperation as the "larger the regional presence the major players confront in negotiations the more ready will they be to pay attention . . . (to) the construction of special regional and hemispheric joint diplomacy" (Report of the West India Commission 1993, 68).

The architecture has also included the Summit of Heads of State and Government which issued expressions of political will through political directions. To date, there have been eight such summits and twenty-five Regular Meetings of the Council of Ministers. It is at these meetings that consensus is reached, and objectives and direction are refined at the highest level. The SELA Report on the evolution of the ACS makes it clear that "the term 'Greater Caribbean' has become, therefore, a political concept that has led to the collective spirit and unity among the various member countries of the Association, since it not only defines the vast area bordering the Caribbean Sea, but also takes into account the common historical, social and cultural characteristics of its members" (The Permanent Secretariat of SELA 2015, 8).

While the literature and analysis point to purposes, it is clear that this is not a relationship defined strictly by collaboration on technical and developmental projects. Though these have been very successful, they are only a manifestation of a much deeper connection. It is a bond that was never encumbered by the ideological underpinnings of the Cold War, the threat of reprisal, the language difference, or the distance. Multilateralism was part of the redefining of the region and part of the evolution of a more global identity for the Caribbean man and Caribbean woman. That this identity was framed around the Caribbean Sea has proven prognostic and speaks to the vision of the framers who have named the Caribbean Sea as a zone of peace and cooperation and who from the onset have put on the agenda the need for this sea to be a considered a special area for sustainable development.

That semi-enclosed sea, 90 percent of which is bordered by continental or island landmasses, represents 1 percent of Global Ocean Area. It is a global biodiversity hotspot with more than twelve thousand Marine Species. It has the second-largest barrier reef in the world. It also constitutes 14–27 percent of the Global Ocean Economy because of fishing, mining, and tourism. That complex sea around which more than 115 million people live is both the history and the future of the ACS.

The advocacy by the ACS at the level of the United Nations to have this sea named a special area in the context of sustainable development has been unrelenting. The Caribbean Sea is the opportunity for the reinvention of the ACS. Yet the consolidated regional political pugnacity needed is lacking the consistent leadership architecture.

Resetting for Survival, Relevance, and Resilience

In the context of a dynamic global environment, it is increasingly essential for countries and regions to reach beyond their traditional spheres of relations and to build partnerships to address shared development challenges. The Greater Caribbean, like most parts of the world, is engaged in a constant exercise of optimizing opportunities and mitigating risks, including those posed by climate change. Recognizing the interdependence and the enhanced possibility for development through leveraging that interdependence, Caribbean leaders created the ACS over two decades ago. Today the Association can attest to the fact that, through coordination, cooperation and concerted action, it has better identified regional development needs, transferred capacities, and navigated shared challenges. The largest and smallest ACS members pool their resources to advance the region, demonstrating the success of south–south cooperation as a model for development. The membership and its ever-growing group of committed partners have shown incredible solidarity through their technical and financial support.

The Greater Caribbean as a region has no choice but to mobilize and rationalize all the resources at its disposal to counter the negative impact of a myriad of challenges on the people, on the environmental sanctity, on the critical tourism, trade and transport industries, and on socioeconomic growth and stability.

Indeed, the Secretariat has been restructured recently to more coherently, synergistically, and creatively address these threats. Thus, trade, sustainable tourism, and transport are addressed individually and collectively by the Directorate for Trade and Sustainable Development. Efforts to protect and preserve the Caribbean Sea, to safeguard the land and marine environment while garnering efforts to address all facets of disasters are coordinated by the Directorate for Disaster Risk Reduction, the Environment and the Caribbean Sea. Additionally, in response to the repeated call by membership for more resolute pursuit and management of the partnerships and resources necessary for better coordination and cooperation, a new Directorate for Cooperation and Resource Mobilization has been established and operationalized (ACS Agreement No. 22/18, 2018). This was part of the reinvention of the association, a revitalized Secretariat better fit for purpose, in preparation for its twenty-fifth anniversary.

As part of its reimagination the organization has been engaging concretely with its twenty-eight[1] observers in strategic partnerships. In 2016, it introduced an annual Cooperation Conference, similar to a donor's conference, where projects were presented for financing and implementation. The restructuring also ensured a focus on a myriad of projects in its portfolio ready for investment. In 2019, the organization was charged with raising one hundred million US$ for the next triennium (The 2019–2021 ACS Plan of Action 2019, 8).

Financial resources are managed by the Special Fund within the Directorate of Cooperation and Resource Mobilization based on guidelines in the ACS Cooperation Resource Mobilization Strategy. Winston Dookeran asserts that the mandate of the ACS to increase both trade and investment has not received the consensus that would lead to the necessary convergence in these area, and he recommends that development financing must be at the heart of strengthening integration (Dookeran 2017, 159). The Ministerial Council of the ACS has recognized the need for this convergence and that this regional configuration was best placed to consolidate this promise.

---

[1]   The twenty-eight observers of the ACS are Argentina, Belarus, Bolivia, Brazil, Canada, Chile, Ecuador, Egypt, Finland, India, Italy, Japan, Kazakhstan, The Kingdom of the Netherlands, Korea, Morocco, Palestine, Peru, Russia, Serbia, Slovenia, Spain, Saudi Arabia, Turkey, United Arab Emirates, Ukraine, United Kingdom, and Uruguay.

Resilience must also be reemphasized as part of the reinvention of the ACS region. Leadership is the key, and the leaders of the Greater Caribbean cannot afford to vacillate, falter, or procrastinate on the dreams and aspirations of those who have been subjugated and encumbered by years of domination. While Errol Barrow proffered that the region has not loitered on colonial premises after closing time, we have nevertheless lingered in the halls of fear and dependency for too long.

The ACS also has the advantage of partnerships across other multilateral organizations, and this provides an opportunity for convergence on a wide range of issues.[2] This has created a natural bridge for linkage and exchange between the subregional integration and cooperation schemes in which its member states participate, as well as a point of convergence of the States and Territories grouped around the Greater Caribbean Basin. It also has great potential to become a unifying mechanism in the future for coordination and convergence of integration and cooperation. Unity is not achieved by decree; it is constructed little by little. It understands shared principles, shared values and precise objectives, and forcibly demands a commitment to obtain concrete milestones. As the principal intergovernmental organizations of the region, with mandates to promote robust environmental, economic and social development, tailored to the unique reality of the region, the Secretariat convened the seventh inter-secretariat meeting in January 2020.[3] This was designed to deliver a coherent results-oriented, work program that optimized limited resources. Membership must bring their varying strengths to the south–south cooperation table so that there is removal of the malaise for which regional organizations are accused.

The relevance of the ACS moving forward must be assessed in the revamping and repurposing of the organization for the future. The 2019–2021 Plan of Action has ensured that key issues such as climate change and its related concerns and risks are systematically taken into consideration; youth and gender are more comprehensively mainstreamed into activities; fourteen of the seventeen SDGs

---

[2] The ACS members are all member states of SICA; it comprises fourteen of the fifteen member states of CARICOM, nine of the eleven member states of ALBA-TCP11, and the eighteen member states of PETROCARIBE; The Economic Commission for Latin America and the Caribbean (ECLAC) has all twenty-five of the member states and seven associates in common.

[3] The Founding Observer Organization of the ACS are the CARICOM Secretariat, Latin American Economic System (SELA), Central American Integration System (SICA), Permanent Secretariat of the General Agreement on Central American Economic Integration (SIECA), United Nations Economic Commission for Latin America and the Caribbean (ECLAC), and the Caribbean Tourism Organization (CTO).

are mainstreamed into the work program; associate members are increasingly involved in activities from conceptualization to evaluation; capacity building within the organization is strategic; concrete projects and tangible resources are applied to issues that the leaders have identified as priorities – not least culture and education, which are so fundamental to the very identity of this coastal civilization. This is how the ACS will continue to make a difference and retain relevance. It has created a shared space for the honest exchange of common and divergent experiences, to learn from each other, to nourish existing relationships, and to pioneer new avenues for cooperation.

Endangered but Empowered: COVID-19 and New Challenges

The ACS currently has image, reach, influence, and impact and thus must continue to be the organization that rode the wave of inertia and moved toward development. Being a relatively new regional organization, there have been successes and significant strides in addressing the underpinning issues that contribute to the vulnerability of the region. This was stressed at the 2016 Summit of Heads of Government under the theme "Together to confront the challenges of sustainable development, climate change and peace in the Caribbean," which was aimed at strengthening the organization as a mechanism of coordination, cooperation, and concerted action, in accordance with its founding principles (Rapporteur's Report: Cuban Summit Seventh Summit of The Association of Caribbean States. (Havana, Cuba, 4th 2016, 1).

In other words, the heads of government were going back to their establishment principles in order to move forward. These principles included unity, sustainable development, and the creation of a zone of peace, multilateralism, and decolonization.

Additionally, the ACS has ample potential and capacity to generate authentic transformations. Even though the region faces great challenges, namely economic and financial vulnerabilities, the grave and unique challenge of climate change, and the fragile sovereignty constructs, this organism provides the window of opportunity to share common experiences from different perspectives. Enhancing and reaffirming initiatives in early alert systems, inclusion and strategic intelligence, as well as the strengthening of interregional and global relations are all essential for the full progress of nations to be achieved. The new regional paradigm has as its main focus convergence and solidarity, consolidated by regional resources and international financing in priority areas. The heads of government have offered and stressed that this was a most befitting offering of sustainability to their citizens.

The first extraordinary meeting of ministers of foreign affairs and ministers of health of the ACS on COVID-19 was held in March 2020. Since that event, the ACS Secretariat has coordinated the actions of membership in the face of the pandemic, with the aim of identifying best practices and lessons learned through a series of regional meetings with membership and founding observers to address the impact of the pandemic in the Greater Caribbean. This has resulted in two strategic documents that have provided the framework for cooperation on the pandemic.[4] The focus on vulnerable groups reflected the emphasis placed on the importance of democratic societies that "promote gender equality, are family centred, respectful of human rights and aware of the difficulties faced by persons in vulnerable situations" (Declaration of Managua issued by the 8th Summit of the ACS. Managua: Nicaragua, 2019, paragraph 24).

It also reflected the people-centered approach to regional integration that has been stressed since 2016. The ACS Secretariat also created a Greater Caribbean COVID-19 Dashboard to provide regional decision-makers and the wider public with live statistics that trace the evolution of the spread and control of the coronavirus in the Greater Caribbean. It remains the only tool dedicated to only the Greater Caribbean.

It is clear that while the ACS is moving away from the gradualism that has been a plague upon colonized people and has made major steps forward, it can still revert to fear and uncertainty. Since 2016, it has been ensuring a reinvention that is commencing to yield synergies and convergence. While it is a region under threat, it is also a region with great potential. Reimagining the space has brought it back to its original vision. It is in this vision that it will fulfill its potential.

References

Association of Caribbean States. 2018, 16 March. *Agreement No. 22/18, 2018. Agreement to Approve the Recommendations for the Restructuring of the Secretariat of the Association of Caribbean States. 23rd Ordinary Meeting of the Ministerial Council.* Margarita Island, Bolivarian Republic of Venezuela.

Association of Caribbean States. 2019, 29 March. *The 2019 – 2021 ACS Plan of Action. 8th Summit of Heads of State and/ or Government of the ACS.* Managua: Nicaragua.

---

[4] The two documents are: An ACS Draft Strategy for Managing COVID-19 in the Region and Towards the Creation of a Humanitarian Corridor in the ACS Membership: Addressing the Inequality of Vulnerable Groups during Disasters and Crises.

Association of Caribbean States. 2016. *Rapporteur's Report: Cuban Summit Seventh Summit of The Association of Caribbean States.* Havana, Cuba.

Association of Caribbean States. 2019. *Declaration of Managua. 8th Summit of the ACS.* Managua, Nicaragua.

Association of Caribbean States. 1994. *The Convention Establishing the Association of Caribbean States (ACS).*

Byron, Jessica. 2020. *Opening Remarks Joint ACS-IIR Symposium.* Trinidad: University of the West Indies.

Dookeran, Winston. 2017. *Crisis and Promise in the Caribbean: Politics and Convergence.* London: Routledge.

Girvan. Norman. 2017. *Cooperation in the Greater Caribbean.* Kingston, Jamaica: Ian Randal Publishers.

Girvan, Norman. 2001. "Reinventing CARICOM: A Question of Survival." *Social and Economic Studies,* 50 (2): 189–94.

Gonsalves, Ralph. 2014. *Our Caribbean Civilization and Its Political Prospects.* Kingstown: Strategy Forum Inc Kingstown St Vincent and the Grenadines.

Hall, Kenneth and Myrtle Chuck-A. Sang (eds.). 2007. *CARICOM Single Market and Economy: Challenges, Benefits, Prospects.* The Integrationist. Kingston, Jamaica: Ian Randle Publishers.

Lewis, Patsy, Terri-Ann Gilbert-Roberts, and Jessica Byron. 2018. *Pan-Caribbean Integration: Beyond CARICOM.* London: Routledge.

Laurent, Edwin. 2007. *Understanding International Trade: A CARICOM Perspective.* The Integrationist. Kingston, Jamaica: Ian Randle Publishers.

Payne, Anthony. 2007. *The Political History of CARICOM.* Kingston, Jamaica: Ian Randle Publishers.

Report of the West Indian Commission. 1993. *Time for Action.* Kingston, Jamaica: The Press.

SELA. 2015. Evolution *of the Association of Caribbean States* (ACS). Caracas: The Permanent Secretariat of SELA.

16

Geopolitical Shifts and Health Diplomacy

VIJAY KUMAR CHATTU

> *"The coming years will be a vital period to save the planet and to achieve sustainable, inclusive human development."*
>
> Anthony Guterres, Secretary-General of the United Nations

Background

The COVID-19 pandemic has exposed the prospect that the gains made over the past decades to address poverty, hunger, good health, and well-being may face numerous setbacks unless the global community unites to address the challenges collectively to enable humanity to survive and thrive. As of May 31, 2023, globally, there have been 767.3 million confirmed cases and 6.9 million deaths reported to the World Health Organization (WHO 2023). There are over 2.75 million cases in the 35 countries of the Caribbean region, with 30,096 deaths recorded as of January 10, 2022 (CARPIIA 2022). The International Labour Organization (ILO 2020) estimates that the pandemic wiped out the equivalent of approximately 305 million jobs globally in lost work hours in the second quarter of 2020. According to the Sustainable Development Goals (SDGs) report 2020, the COVID-19 pandemic disrupted SDGs' progress where the most vulnerable were affected the most. The leaders of the Group of Seven (G-7) have emphasized that there is a strong need for a coordinated international approach that is evidence based, consistent with democratic values, and utilizes the expertise of the private sector to address the challenges of the pandemic (EC 2020). The Caribbean is part of the small island developing states (SIDS) afflicted by economic difficulties and has unique vulnerabilities and characteristics (UNCSD 2012).

Geopolitical Shifts and Global Forces

According to the August 2020 issue of Foreign Affairs, "The pandemic has been a global political stress test," which highlights that capable states with good leadership who embrace reforms become stronger and more resilient, while those with weak state capacity – political and economic – will be in trouble and set for stagnation (Fukuyama 2020). Accordingly, a shifting order of things is taking place. The World Economic Forum's January 2021 summit has set the theme as The Great Reset – "the Covid-19 crisis could reverse global human development – measured in terms of education, health, and living standards. Small island developing states are particularly vulnerable and will have an inordinate amount of difficulty of recovering, without sufficient development finance" (WEF 2020).

Weakening of World Hegemons and Shifts in the Structure of World Power

This pandemic has witnessed the collapse of the liberal world order because the leading patron, the United States, has given up its responsibility to support the WHO at this time of crisis. Although the United States has an impressive track record of epidemic/pandemic crisis management from previous epidemics, the leadership blocked the state from functioning effectively, leading to a gradual decline of its influence. This, in turn, could lead to a resurgence of fascism with an increase in nationalism, isolationism, xenophobia, and attacks on the liberal world order (Fukuyama 2020). The rise of nationalism among countries will worsen the chances of failure of international cooperation, leading to conflicts. According to Kickbusch, the notion of countries such as the United States or the United Kingdom showing leadership is the old model of multilateralism. As a pathway for the new notion of multilateralism, countries like Germany and France have created an alliance with regional organizations such as the African Union, Asian groupings, and so on. In this new scenario of a post-pandemic era, the regional organizations have a bigger voice and key role in global health, which also indicate stronger WHO regional offices (HPW 2020). The Caribbean Community (CARICOM) and the Caribbean Public Health Agency (CARPHA) should take a proactive role and explore the various options to get global attention on the Caribbean region and secure sustainable financing mechanisms to implement regional and global policies to address the bottlenecks. They should also aim to achieve the goals of the SDGs.

Emerging Revolution of Digitalization Globally

Digital technologies will continue to disrupt and transform the global economy at an accelerating phase. The pandemic has brought various technologies into the market that facilitate people to work from home and seek medical advice, counseling services, and prescription through telemedicine and telehealth services. The impact of this digitalization globally will cascade down across all sectors and industries, redefining consumers' expectations and business models. The current model of "work from home" has become a new normal over the past two years, and it has affected all the countries of all income levels in some form in their daily life, including work, leisure, and communication. According to the forecasts by the new Cisco Annual Internet report, with the emergence of 5G technology, the performance capabilities will improve to deliver dynamic mobile infrastructures for Artificial Intelligence (AI) and Internet of Things (IoT) applications, including autonomous cars, smart cities, connected health, immersive video, and more. The key projections by 2023 are summarized below (Box 16.1) (CISCO 2020).

BOX 16.1 KEY FINDINGS FROM THE CISCO ANNUAL REPORT FORECASTS BY 2023

5 G will support more than 10% of the world's mobile connections.

The average 5G speed is 575 megabits per second or 13 times faster than the average mobile network

A majority of 66% (5.3 billion) of global citizens will have access to the internet\

There will be over 30 billion devices/connections, of which 45% are mobile

Average broadband speed will rise from 46 Mbps to 110 Mbps

Wi-Fi6 hotspots will grow 13-fold from 2020 to 2023 and will be 11% of all public Wi-Fi hotspots

Source: prepared from Cisco Annual Report, 2020.

A Changing Order in the Politics of Multilateral Diplomacy

During this pandemic, the US administration has resisted the international health cooperation efforts and withdrew its support from the WHO. In the case of China, though it has halted the epidemic within its domestic borders and started to help countries with its "mask diplomacy" and some financial assistance to some parts of Asia, its role in covering up the epidemic during the initial phase raised doubts among nations. Further, an independent investigation was initiated against China by the WHO, which was supported by over one hundred countries. Thus, due to the absence of credible leadership for international cooperation from the United States and China, the "middle powers" (nations with little dominance in defense power but from the top twenty economies with good multilateral affairs) such as France, Canada, the Netherlands, Sweden, Germany, and the United Kingdom were trying to fill the gaps in the international leadership through their energetic role in multilateral diplomacy. They have shown their commitment and dedication by raising over US$ 14 billion for providing free vaccines through Vaccine Alliance to the countries that cannot afford them (Jones 2020).

A Loss of Legitimacy in Regional and Global Political Alliances

Legitimacy is central for any international organization to make a difference in world politics. Though legitimacy dynamics are critical in global governance, they are often insufficiently recognized and conceptualized in standard accounts for international cooperation (Tallberg and Zürn 2019). The May 2020 issue of *The Economist*, specifically on the geopolitics of the pandemic, suggests three areas to observe for change: the shift in the balance of power from the West to the East, changes in the future of Europe, and China's relations with the developing world (Dookeran 2020). This pandemic is a great example of showcasing the importance of global health globally as the rapid spread of COVID-19 infections in this interconnected world needs billions of dollars in vaccine investments to break the chain of COVID-19.

Reorganization of World Political Order amid COVID-19

The Emergence of a New Political Order

Is the world political order of the Bretton Woods vintage now on its knees? Academics have argued that the world order has moved from hegemons to multipolar and even to a multiplex world. Now, the world's political order may better be described as "flat" in today's situation – no hegemons, no multipolar, and no multiplex – Amitav Acharya (Dookeran 2020). Global security alliances out of the Cold War are now faced with new global challenges in cyber and information technologies and populist politics at home. In this setting of transactional and real politic, different configurations of power relations are emerging, and we are beginning to see the following trends that may shape the future political order. The renewed focus should be on regionalism – resiliency vs. efficiency – as a driver of the global economy. A changing direction in the flow of funds and shifts in the supply chain have been observed. The liberal democracies are less liberal and in fact have more authoritarian tendencies but are adhering to the fundamentals of democratic systems. Amid these geopolitical shifts and in the race to form a new global order, the small and island nations will not have an automatic place. Hedging will lead to "floating coalitions" based on interest and realpolitik and not so much on power and ideology (Dookeran 2020).

The Growing Divide in Inequality among and within Nations

The post-COVID-19 recovery can be made better if these efforts and principles are based on the SDGs. According to the UN Under-Secretary-General for Economic and Social Affairs, "The continued pursuit of these universal Goals will keep Governments focused on growth, but also inclusion, equity, and sustainability. Our collective response to the pandemic can serve as a 'warm-up' for our preparedness in preventing an even larger crisis – that is, global climate change, whose effects are already becoming all too familiar" (UN 2020). Even the United Nations (UN) Secretary-General stressed that COVID-19 was not affecting everyone in the same way, as it has exposed and exacerbated existing inequalities and injustices. The poorest and most vulnerable, including children, older persons, persons with disabilities, migrants, and refugees, are being hit the hardest by the pandemic, and women are bearing the heaviest brunt of the impact (UN 2020).

Observations of Some Liberal Democracies and Authoritarian Regimes during the Pandemic

The European Union (EU) is one of the regional blocs that suffered the most from the epidemic. Recently, with the rise of the radical right in Europe, identity politics has gained considerable momentum, and far-right parties have become partners in power, either directly or indirectly. The fact that each country makes its own health issue a priority eliminates the political-economic integrity and solidarity that are the most important engine of the EU (Balci and Tuncay 2020). On the one hand, Iran, which has a theocratic form of government, initially lied to its citizens after getting engaged in identity politics, paving the way for a major epidemic. On the other hand, China used its authoritarianism as a means of settlement politics during the epidemic and prevented further spread to other provinces with strict and rapid on-the-spot measures. With its democratic ideology, the United States failed to display its leadership on the global platform and, at the same time, could not control the growing pandemic and the deaths due to COVID-19 infections. It has shown its hegemony by not easing the Iranian embargoes during the crisis and also in ignoring the desperate calls for help from Italy during this global health crisis. For the first time, the United States entered into a new nationalist foreign policy with the motto of sharing costs with its allies, and it preferred to close its borders and supplies to its allies. The enormous number of cases and deaths at home has greatly undermined its ability and legitimacy to be a superpower, with ongoing competition and trade disputes with China (Balci and Tuncay 2020).

Tackling Global Challenges through Renewed Global Order and Global Cooperation

The US–China Rivalry and Emergence of "Middle Power"

Lee Hsien Loong, the prime minister of Singapore, in a June 4, 2020, article in Foreign Affairs titled "*The Endangered Asian Century: America, China and the Perils of Confrontation*," concluded with great hope, noting that: "The strategic choices that the United States and China make will shape the contours of the emerging global order. It is natural for big powers to compete. But it is their capacity for cooperation that is the true test of statecraft, and it will determine whether humanity makes progress on global problems such as climate change, nuclear proliferation, and the spread of infectious diseases" (Loong 2020).

The WHO had to face severe funding gaps as the United States decided to withdraw its support of US$ 35 billion during the COVID-19 crisis. The organization has a global membership of 194 countries, but it is mostly three or four major economies that direct WHO as per their terms; this scenario needs to be changed. In this era of globalization, we need different kinds of partnership – those that are sustainable, based on multilateralism, and promoting health as common goods to run the WHO – rather than those dominating three or four countries that dictate what everyone has to do.

During this crisis, the middle powers stepped in to finance the public health response to support the WHO by raising US$ 8 billion, followed by the Netherlands, Sweden, and the United Kingdom through the World Bank to raise another US$ 14 billion in surge financing to support the developing countries which were severely affected by the COVID-19 pandemic. Therefore, there is a great scope for newer partnerships from the middle powers such as Germany, France, Switzerland, the United Kingdom, and Canada along with the European Union to get more actively involved to restore the credibility of the existing multilateral system and support the global work of WHO without being driven by two or three major economies which contribute a major share (Jones 2020).

The Challenging and Critical Role of WHO

The WHO, though facing financial challenges, has been playing a crucial role in the pandemic by leading a global response through its 150 country offices in the following ways (UN News 2020):

- Helping countries to prepare and respond
- Providing accurate information, clearing the misinformation, and busting dangerous myths

- Ensuring vital supplies reach frontline health workers
- Training and mobilizing health workers
- The search for an effective vaccine – launched a global "Solidarity Trial"

The WHO and its partners such as GAVI and Coalition for Epidemic Preparedness Innovations (CEPI), together called COVAX, are supporting the building of manufacturing capabilities and had been buying supplies well in advance so that by the end of 2021, they could have ensured a fair distribution of two billion doses globally. The role of COVAX is to ensure equitable access and distribution to protect people in all countries by prioritizing the people most at risk. Through the Advance Market Commitment, which is a financing instrument, the COVAX supports the participation of ninety-two lower-middle and low-income economies and secured the investment of US$ 2 billion from sovereign donors, philanthropies, and the private sector (COVAX 2020). Currently, there are fifty COVID-19 vaccine candidates in various phases of trials. As of date, few vaccines have been approved, namely Pfizer/BioNTech vaccine, which received emergency validation from WHO, Moderna vaccine manufactured by Moderna Therapeutics, and Oxford-AstraZeneca COVID-19 vaccine. The WHO has a critical role in ensuring equity and fairer distribution to everyone irrespective of the rich and poor status of the countries. The role of health diplomacy is pivotal in this context where the countries, especially SIDS, can gain access to these essential vaccines by negotiating through regional bodies and strengthening collaborations and partnerships with the international community and global stakeholders.

Critical Role of G20 in the Global Governance

The G20 is a forum of nineteen nation-states, the European Union, and a range of other invited nation-states and intergovernmental organizations. One of the Think-20 reports suggests that: "To revitalize the multilateral system of global cooperation for everyone's benefit, the G20 should critically reflect upon and revamp its partnerships with non-state actors like CSOs and private companies" (Scheler and Dobson 2020, 5). The report also suggests that the G20 should take the consultative processes seriously by engaging with non-state actors, providing them with supporting structures, and promoting multi-stakeholder cooperation. The multi-stakeholder governance assumes that effective governance of the global commons like climate, digitalization, and global health requires cooperation among various groups of stakeholders constituting state and non-state actors. Unlike multilateralism, which considers governments to be the exclusive governors, multi-stakeholderism makes stakeholders the central actors (Glekman 2018).

The G20 leadership would augment cooperation between international organizations, member states, and stakeholders, including non-state actors and public–private global health partnerships such as GAVI – the Vaccine Alliance – in the global governance of COVID-19 and future pandemics. The T20 group suggested that new trade agreements should be developed, especially concerning medical supplies and goods. These could echo aspects of the G20's anti-protectionist pledges in response to the global financial crisis, including standstill agreements against introducing new tariff measures. The group also emphasized that the G20 should implement new practices for assessing countries' resilience and rapid-response mechanisms in the face of the interlinked economic, social, health, and environmental shocks from pandemics (T20-Task Force 11, 2020).

The BRICS and its Global Influence

Under the Russian Chairmanship in 2020 with the theme of *"Partnership for Global Stability, Common Security and Innovation Growth,"* the BRICS (Brazil, Russia, India, China, and South Africa) block aimed to ensure a sustainable and fair world in the interest of all the countries of the planet. The theme for the twelfth BRICS Academic Forum and BRICS Think Tank Council meeting in Moscow on October 22–24, 2020, was *"BRICS New Vision for a Better World."* The BRICS academic community provided the policy proposals: (1) to strengthen the cooperation within the grouping and (2) to increase its further role in the global governance system. These efforts of BRICS to make globalization work for all are going to be tested by the pressures of isolationism and increasing imbalances between globally integrating markets and still fragmented policymaking. Therefore, the new geopolitical and economic realities require BRICS to recommit to their founding mission and enhance the "strategic partnership for the benefit of our people through the promotion of peace, a fairer international order, sustainable development, and inclusive growth" (BRICS 2020).

As mentioned, this COVID-19 pandemic turned on the "test mode" for the global governance institutions to respond to crises through international cooperation. Despite the commitment of the international community to tackle the novel coronavirus, the global governance system experienced multiple challenges in meeting the needs of the COVID-19 reality as a result of a failed leadership, as discussed in the previous sections. The healthcare crisis increased political turbulence, caused a new wave of protectionist measures, and undermined efforts to build a more resilient world with a common goal of sustainable development for all.

Strengthening Regional and Global Partnerships

According to the United Nations, "partnerships are voluntary and collaborative relationships between various parties, both public and non-public, in which all participants agree to work together to achieve a common purpose or undertake a specific task and, as mutually agreed, to share risks and responsibilities, resources and benefits" (UNDESA 2015). CARICOM must strengthen ties with all stakeholders and partners involved in the region's development agenda, ensuring the participation of all members. Recognizing and comprehending the historical significance of the CARICOM region's cultural, economic, and political components is vital, especially as initiatives to protect and promote regional health and development are devised (Chattu and Chami 2020).

Further, Goal 17 of the UN Sustainable Development Goals (SDGs) recognizes multi-stakeholder partnerships as important vehicles for mobilizing and sharing knowledge, expertise, technologies, and financial resources to achieve these goals in all countries, particularly developing countries. The goal also seeks to develop and support effective public, private, and civil society partnerships by building on partnership experience and resourcing strategies.

The region needs to see beyond the existing traditional partnerships with the Americas, the United Kingdom, and Europe in this context. During this COVID-19 pandemic, the region suffered greatly in trade, tourism, and economic loss apart from deaths. As of December 31, 2021, only six CARICOM countries had 40 percent or more of their populations fully vaccinated, ranging from 61 percent to 40.2 percent. As a result, CARICOM still has a long way to go in adequately vaccinating its populations (CARICOM Today 2022). India was the first country to provide COVID-19 vaccines to small Caribbean nations in 2021. Many nations in the region have kick-started their immunization campaigns with assistance from India's Vaccine Maitri Initiative, which gave vaccines to low-income countries such as Dominica, St Kitts, and Nevis, St. Lucia, Guyana, Barbados, Grenada, and Suriname (*The Economic Times* 2021). Further, the Indian Health Minister Mansukh Mandaviya indicated that "there is a strong potential to deepen our partnership in various areas especially in healthcare and pharmaceuticals" and further tweeted, "India would be happy to export COVID-19 vaccines and share its digital health interventions" (*The Economic Times* 2021). As a result, India's vaccine diplomacy resulted in breakthroughs and alliances for the region, and CARICOM should take advantage of the move.

Similarly, China has a significant influence in the region by exporting cheap products and, more recently, with the COVID-19 vaccines. The Chinese supplied a million doses to the Dominican Republic, and the first supply of the global COVAX effort, in which the European Union played a key role, reached the Caribbean. For example, it has delivered 1 million doses to the Dominican Republic, 14,000 vaccination shots to Jamaica, and a promise of 20,000 Sinopharm vaccines to Guyana (Hoffmann B 2021).

The fifteen states of the CARICOM have more voting power at the United Nations than the whole of South America. The majority of the people of Afro-Caribbean descent mainly have African ancestry with strong historical and cultural links between the two regions. Besides, the African region and the CARICOM, with its 1.4 billion population, comprise sixty-nine votes at the United Nations and World Trade Organization. The first landmark summit of the African Union and CARICOM on September 7, 2021, is significant, highlighting its global negotiating power. This new cooperation will open the doors for more economic activity, direct trade and investment, and cultural exchanges. Besides, the cooperation between the regions has grown over time, as indicated by participation in the Organization of African, Caribbean, and Pacific States (OACP) and recent initiatives by African governments to make COVID-19 vaccinations available to CARICOM via the African Medical Supplies Platform (AMSP) (Richardson C 2021).

The CARICOM needs to explore and establish new relationships with other nontraditional partners to counter the region's challenges and find effective solutions for emergencies such as natural disasters, rise in sea level, climate change, and others.

Caribbean Region and Its Preparation for Geopolitical Shifts

Caribbean Community (CARICOM)

The Caribbean Community (CARICOM) is a grouping of twenty countries: fifteen member states and five associate members. CARICOM came into being on July 4, 1973, with signing of the Treaty of Chaguaramas by prime ministers of Barbados, Guyana, Jamaica, and Trinidad and Tobago. The Treaty was later revised in 2002 to allow for a single market and a single economy. CARICOM rests on four main pillars: economic integration, foreign policy coordination, human and social development, and security (see figure 16.1) (CARICOM, n.d).

The Caribbean region has the highest burden of non-communicable diseases (NCDs) in the Americas. In light of this, the Caribbean Cooperation in Health Initiative, approved by health ministers in 1986, made NCDs a priority concern. In their 2001 Nassau Declaration, the CARICOM heads of government identified the human immunodeficiency virus (HIV) infection, NCDs, and mental health problems as regional priorities. They called for strategies for preventing and treating NCDs and articulated principles and processes to preserve and enhance

PILLARS OF REGIONAL INTEGRATION

| ECONOMIC INTEGRATION | FOREIGN POLICY COORDINATION | HUMAN AND SOCIAL DEVELOPMENT | SECURITY |

Figure 16.1 The four pillars of the Caribbean Community.
Source: Caribbean Community (CARICOM, n.d).

"the health of the Region which is the wealth of the Region" (CARICOM 2016, 12). In 2005, the Caribbean Commission on Health and Development reported that the number of deaths from diabetes, hypertension, and heart disease combined was ten times higher than the number of deaths from acquired immunodeficiency syndrome (AIDS) and declared NCDs a "super-priority." At the CARICOM Summit in July 2006, leaders received a report on "the macro-economic implications of non-communicable diseases." Trinidad and Tobago agreed to host a special regional consultation on compliance with specific tobacco, diet, and physical activity recommendations.

Critical Role of CARICOM in the Americas and the Need for External Assistance

CARICOM directly and indirectly contributes to global economic governance, international security, and energy policies. The Caribbean has also been the highest per capita recipient of Canadian development assistance since 1963. Due to the strategic location, vulnerabilities due to climate and natural disasters, and epidemics of infectious, vector-borne, and chronic diseases, these small island nations are faced with annual natural disasters of various kinds, including storms, hurricanes, and floods, among others. There is a great need for support from the developed nations to create sustainable growth and improve the technology and development of these small states. There is evidence of progress in the commitments made in the past, especially in health and social development. The progress is often not as projected due to the natural disasters, financial crisis, and harsh climate changes impacting human lives.

In the quest for a stable and peaceful international order while preserving strategic autonomy, small states will constantly search for strategic opportunities. Perhaps the strategic logic of our times will see the advent of "floating coalitions," in response to countries hedging in this fluid geopolitical climate. Countries like ours in the Caribbean cannot afford to be bystanders but must engage constructively in the present order of things. The Caribbean will face strategic choices in the practice of diplomacy, and concrete actions will depend on an assessment of the following (Dookeran 2020):

1. Focus on regional pandemic surveillance and public health coordination
2. Select bridges for communications with major economies and adopt new protocols for decision-making
3. Negotiate an economic platform within international financial institutions in both a short and long-term perspective
4. Workout flexible engagements – in health diplomacy and development finance – and be partners in floating coalitions of the present

Strengthening Regional Health Systems and Emergency Preparedness

The region has frequent epidemics of various infectious agents (vector-borne or zoonotic), and some of them are endemic in certain states such as Dengue, Chikungunya, and the Zika virus. To improve the health indicators in the region, overall public health should be improved, which would pave the way to achieve health-related SDGs. The region should focus on building appropriate systems and improving the infrastructure for detection, surveillance, prevention, control, and response to emerging epidemics of infectious diseases, including COVID-19. By ensuring robust surveillance systems, health security can be improved, and the member states will be equipped to respond to future outbreaks in the region. The Regional Health Security should be prioritized and addressed in all the regional forums. It should ensure proper coordinating mechanisms are in place and build the institutional capacities of CARPHA to support the region by responding to the health threats/emergencies. The application of block-chain technology for real-time surveillance shows a very promising scope for strengthening disease surveillance systems and improving health security in the region (Chattu et al. 2019). The recent support of US$750,000 from the Inter-American Development Bank (IDB) to support CARPHA for the enhancement of Laboratory Response Capacity and the strengthening of real-time disease surveillance and response through the CARPHA Regional

Travellers' Health Program (THP) for all its members will be a big boost (Scott 2020). The Japan Special Fund is financing this grant. It will support CARPHA's work with Barbados, Belize, Guyana, Jamaica, and Trinidad and Tobago to enhance COVID-19 detection abilities, mobilize surge response capacity, and strengthen real-time disease surveillance and response (IDB 2020).

Health Diplomacy and Caribbean Regional Security

Health Diplomacy and Impact of CARICOM Summits

CARICOM leaders actively encouraged a broader range of countries and organizations to take action toward the control of NCDs. A hypothetical scenario of a pandemic/crisis and the role of health diplomacy for multisectoral coordination are shown in figure 16.2. In the context of CARICOM, the following are some of the recent and specific regional policies addressing NCDs.

BOX 16.2 REGIONAL POLICIES OF THE CARIBBEAN RELATED TO NCDS

Regional Policies and Plans

1. Plan of Action for the Prevention and Control of Non-Communicable Diseases in the Americas 2013–2019
2. Port of Spain Declaration "Uniting to Stop the Epidemic of NCDs"
3. Caribbean Cooperation in Health Phase IV 2016–2025
4. Caribbean Cooperation in Health Phase III 2010–2015
5. Six Point Policy (To prevent childhood obesity through improved food and nutrition security) 2017.

Port of Spain Summit Declaration, 2007

The CARICOM Summit on Chronic Non-Communicable Diseases – the first government summit ever devoted to non-communicable diseases (NCDs) – was convened by the CARICOM in Trinidad and Tobago in September 2007. Leaders in attendance issued the Declaration of Port of Spain, a call to prevent and control four major NCDs and their risk factors. An accountability instrument for monitoring compliance with summit commitments was developed for CARICOM by the University of the West Indies in 2008 and revised in 2010. The instrument – a one-page color-coded grid with twenty-six

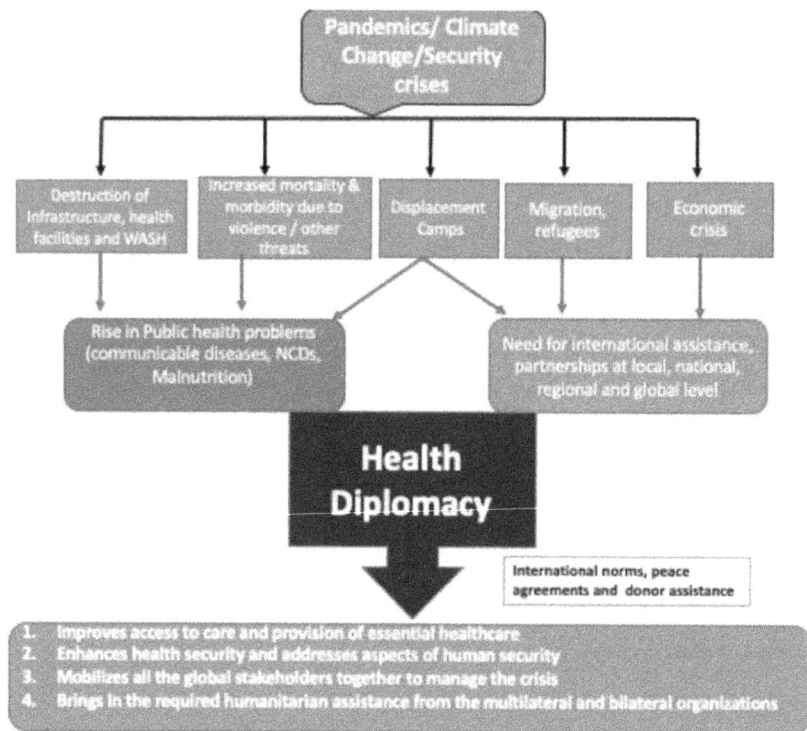

Figure 16.2 A hypothetical scenario of a pandemic crisis and the role of health diplomacy for multisectoral coordination in the geopolitical environment.

Source: Prepared by the author.

progress indicators – is updated annually by focal points in Caribbean health ministries, verified by each country's chief medical officer, and presented to the annual Caucus of Caribbean Community Ministers of Health. In this study, the G8 Research Group's methods for assessing compliance were applied to the 2009 reporting grid to assess each country's performance. Given the success of the CARICOM Summit, a United Nations high-level meeting of the General Assembly on the prevention and control of NCDs was held in September 2011. In May 2013, the World Health Assembly adopted nine global targets and twenty-five indicators to measure progress in NCD control.

CARICOM and PAHO, as the joint secretariat for the Caribbean Cooperation in Health Initiative, were responsible for monitoring and evaluating compliance with the commitments acquired under the Declaration of Port of Spain. These activities were central to advancing the NCD agenda. Before recommending a global summit on NCDs, CARICOM leaders needed to demonstrate that their regional summit had made a difference in their countries. In 2008, Guyana's

Health Minister and World Health Assembly president Dr. Leslie Ramsammy advocated for NCDs to be given a more prominent place on the global public health agenda and made the subject of an additional MDG. In July 2010, at the Thirty-first Regular Meeting of the Conference of Heads of Government of the Caribbean Community, UN Secretary-General Ban Ki-moon pledged his full support for the high-level meeting and commended CARICOM for raising the critical issue of NCDs.

The CARICOM Summit was successful in several ways. It was the first summit of heads of government to focus on the problem of NCDs, and it resulted in multiple collective, multilateral commitments for the implementation of policies and actions of NCD control. Although there is room for improvement, countries fulfilled some important commitments acquired at the Summit. The CARICOM Summit sparked interest in a global summit on NCDs and resulted in the UN high-level meeting on NCDs. An accountability mechanism based on annual reporting is critical for monitoring progress and highlighting areas that need correction.

Addressing Major Regional Challenges

CARICOM's top priority issues are those related to climate change, human health, and social development to create opportunities for its citizens and ensure security. The pandemic has exposed many weaknesses in our systems. It has served as a reminder that various stakeholders such as governments, the private sector, civil society, and individuals need to share responsibilities and act responsibly to achieve the environmental goals and the health-related SDGs.

There is a great need to protect the ecosystems on land and in water, along with combatting global warming in the region due to its geographic landscape and location (UNEP 2020). The closed borders, availability of commodities, and confinement at home due to the lockdowns and other public health regulatory measures have forced behavioral changes among people in the region and worldwide. According to the UNEP, there is a great need to ensure sustainable Food and Agriculture systems and healthy lifestyle choices by choosing responsible consumption and production, which will be the fundamental building blocks for sustainable development goals.

The incidence of zoonoses, such as COVID-19, will continue to rise when human activity destroys wild habitats. There is a vital need for the governments, the private sector, and civil society to build and support sustainable pathways for farming, mining, and housing to manage and build resilience for future threats of all kinds of sources. The governments should develop and strengthen the biosafety and biosecurity policies, and regulatory measures to detect, prevent, control, and manage zoonotic infections. The SDG 2020 report highlights that "Disruption to health and vaccination services and limited access to diet and nutrition services have the potential to cause hundreds of thousands of additional under-5 deaths and tens of thousands of additional maternal deaths in 2020" (UN, 2020). Even the Caribbean Cooperation in Health Phase IV 2016–2025 (figure 16.3) emphasized multisectoral action and regional public goods (RPGs) to address common challenges in areas where a regional approach holds the best potential to add value to national efforts (CARICOM 2016).

Promoting Technology and Digital Health Interventions

Digital health is rapidly emerging as one of the most defining trends of this decade, with far-reaching implications for geopolitical and socioeconomic realities in the future (Ranganathan 2020). Telemedicine and digital technologies demonstrate exceptional potential in improving access and delivery in remote settings (WHO 2018). According to WHO, the concept of telemedicine includes "the delivery of healthcare services, where distance is a critical factor, by all healthcare professionals using information and communications technologies for the exchange of valid information for the diagnosis, treatment, and

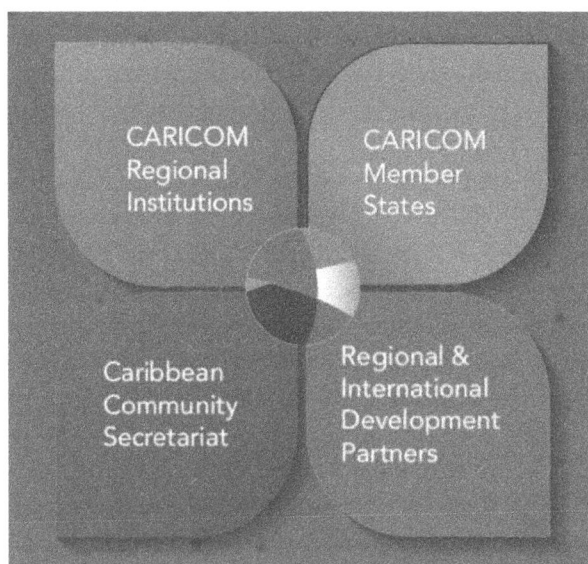

Figure 16.3 Partnerships and Governance Arrangements for the Caribbean Cooperation in Health Phase IV.

Source: Caribbean Cooperation in Health Phase IV (CARICOM, 2016).

prevention of disease and injuries, research and evaluation, and the continuing education of healthcare workers, to advance the health of individuals and communities" (WHO 2010, 9).

In the Caribbean, telehealth and telemedicine are still in their infancy, with a lack of cohesive telehealth strategies and policies that must be enhanced to improve access to all citizens, particularly during the COVID-19 pandemic. Telemedicine would be essential in developing futuristic and resilient health systems supporting SIDS amid pandemics. Technological innovations such as artificial intelligence and robotics will have a long-term impact on future medicine to respond to future pandemics beyond the current pandemic (Chattu and Chami 2020). Therefore, a telemedicine initiative, particularly one aimed at containing a pandemic, should be built on accessibility, equity, and fairness principles.

As with any new program, monitoring and evaluation are required to guarantee acceptability, effectiveness, and cost-effectiveness. Such monitoring is best carried out by the local authorities, specifically the Ministry of Health, with cooperation from academics and other research institutions (Chattu et al. 2020). Bhaskar et al. have highlighted that though some pilot projects in telemedicine were conducted in the Bahamas and Jamaica, ongoing work is required to provide telehealth solutions to the broader population, especially those in remote locations (Bhaskar et al. 2020). Thus, the region needs to adapt much faster and make digital transformation a driving force for change.

Transforming Education and Economy

Latin America and the Caribbean have had the world's longest school closures to date (Turkewitz 2021). As per the report of the Economic Commission for Latin America and the Caribbean (ECLAC), due to the COVID-19 pandemic, the countries in the region have, on average, gone more than an academic year (forty weeks) with no in-person classes or with long periods of interruption which have affected 167 million students at all education levels. The report further proposes the following seven strategies for coping with the current challenges to transform education in the region (ECLAC 2021):

1. Rethink hybrid teaching and flexible education modalities
2. Stimulate the development of socioemotional skills
3. Emphasize integral education
4. Facilitate access to, and use of, technology through digital training programs
5. Support, promote, and protect the mental health of the students and teachers

6. Strengthen collaboration between family members and teachers
7. Strengthen cooperation among countries to face the education crisis.

According to the United Nations, research has linked education to economic growth because education improves production (which in theory should lead to higher income and economic performance). Furthermore, the socioeconomic factors in economic progress cannot be overlooked. Higher education thus integrates workforce development and economic growth by tailoring instructional programs to a country's needs. Nadine has highlighted that government and industry partners must collaborate to identify specific requirements and, as a result, provide work-based learning opportunities such as apprenticeships in domains identified as driving economic development. She further emphasized that education is the main driver of sustainable economic growth and development (Nadine 2013). Thus, the region needs to transform its talent to enhance lagging labor productivity which is the main drag on low/ sluggish economic growth in the region.

Strengthening Health Security through Health Diplomacy

The pandemic caused a lot of devastation and profound impacts on every nation's economic and social consequences, especially the small island developing nations. According to the UNEP, the current global warming rate is linked to an increased likelihood of pandemics, extreme weather events (recent bushfires in Australia, California, droughts, floods), destabilization of global food, and derailment of economic and security systems, ultimately impacting human health. Therefore, to prevent further pandemic outbreaks, the policymakers and the heads of the states should prioritize and get engaged in delivering meaningful, sustainable solutions, and strengthening the multisectoral partnerships.

The role of health diplomacy is very critical at this juncture, as health has taken a predominant role globally amid the COVID-19 pandemic. Apart from health, the various thematic areas such as water, climate, oceans, urbanization, transport, science, technology, and energy aimed to achieve SDGs need cohesive and synergistic efforts. Health diplomacy has great potential to strengthen the global health partnerships to ensure robust health systems and health security (see figure 16.4).

For example, recently, the UNEP joined the international community by mobilizing resources for emergency health, economic, and security responses. It initiated a new collaboration with the Secretariat of the Convention of the Biological Diversity to support national governments to handle the threats

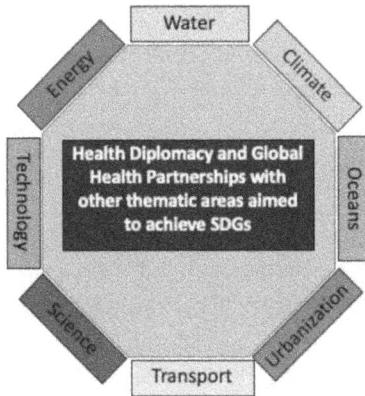

Figure 16.4 Thematic areas of sustainable development goals and health diplomacy in action through global health partnerships.

Source: Prepared by the author.

posed by zoonotic pathogens (UNEP 2020). The health diplomats can get engaged with intersectoral negotiations to further the domain of health and security. The concept of "One Health" is an excellent strategy that could be applied, and through health diplomacy, all the crosscutting areas of health, security, climate change, and sustainable development can be addressed, thereby promoting all the dimensions of human security (Chattu et al. 2019).

Recommendations

The CARICOM should be proactive, select bridges for communications with major countries, and adopt new protocols for decision-making and sustainable development. Also, given the various challenges of economic crisis, geopolitical shifts, and through diplomacy, it should negotiate an economic platform within international financial institutions from both a short- and long-term perspective.

There is a great need to work out flexible engagements – in health diplomacy and development finance – and be partners in floating coalitions of the present. The region must focus on promoting and advancing health diplomacy in the Caribbean and investing more to develop "centers of excellence" in collaboration with national/regional agencies. The specialized centers in the region such as the Centre for Biosecurity in Barbados and the Diplomatic Academy of the Caribbean at the St. Augustine campus of the University of the West Indies can be further strengthened with more involvement of global leaders and technical experts to upgrade them as centers of excellence for training in health diplomacy. The region should build a multidisciplinary team at national levels to foresee the emergencies/disasters/epidemics and ensure health security through proper coordinating mechanisms.

Conclusions

The pandemic has shaken up the foundations of the world of public policy – in finance, politics, health, and other areas. If it is treated as temporary, we would have lost forever the opportunities for making public policy changes that are critical to our times. In this sense, notwithstanding its huge "life and livelihood" costs across the globe, the pandemic may well be a catalyst for geopolitical shifts in the world order of things. Protecting humanity from future, global threats requires strong global partnerships for health, nature, and biodiversity, sound management of medical and chemical waste, and protecting our environment by addressing planetary health challenges with priority.

With growing differences among big nations and the Cold War between major powers, it is quite possible that small nations and island nations will not have an automatic place. The region needs to explore new partnerships, strengthen its infrastructure, and improve its citizens' health, which is more critical at this juncture. The region has shown its success in health diplomacy. This should be further promoted by establishing centers of excellence and actively engaging with the regional and global institutions to ensure funding and knowledge transfer and address the critical future challenges of health security and climate change.

Acknowledgment

The author thanks Prof. Winston Dookeran (Institute of International Relations, the University of the West Indies, St. Augustine, and Secretary-General of EUCLID University) for his valuable inputs and critical feedback that were helpful in improving the quality of this chapter.

References

Balci, Ali, and Kardas Tuncay. 2020. "Analysis -COVID-19 Pandemic as a Global Political Crisis," 24 March. Accessed 19 October 2020. https://www.aa.com.tr/en/analysis/analysis-covid-19-pandemic-as-global-political-crisis/1777581.

Bhaskar, S., S. Bradley, V.K. Chattu, A. Adisesh, A. Nurtazina, S. Kyrykbayeva, S. Sakhamuri, S. Yaya, T. Sunil, P. Thomas, and V. Mucci. 2020. "Telemedicine across the Globe-Position Paper from the COVID-19 Pandemic Health System Resilience

PROGRAM (REPROGRAM) international consortium (Part 1)." *Frontiers in Public Health*, 8: 644.

BRICS. 2020. BRICS Academic Forum "BRICS New Vision for a Better World." National Committee on BRICS Research, Moscow, 22–24 October. Accessed 19 October 2020. https://mcusercontent.com/b8f92f57a9c052e81e58a68af/files/50683987-0e01-4a31-a5f6-24fceeb8f3bf/BRICS_Academic_Forum_Concept_note_and_program_online.pdf.

CARICOM. Caribbean Community. "Who We Are." Accessed 2 October 2020. https://caricom.org/our-community/who-we-are/.

CARICOM. 2016. "Regional Public Goods for Sustainable Health Development." Summary of the Regional Health Framework 2016–2025. Caribbean Cooperation in Health Phase IV. Accessed 12 October 2020. https://www.paho.org/en/documents/caribbean-cooperation-health-phase-iv-cch-iv-0.

CARICOM Today. 2022. "CARICOM, COVID and the 2022 Foreign Trade Policy Agenda." Accessed 20 January 2022. https://today.caricom.org/2022/01/05/caricom-covid-and-the-2022-foreign-trade-policy-agenda/.

CARPHA. 2022. "Coronavirus Disease (COVID-19) Pandemic." Caribbean Public Health Agency (CARPHA) Situation Report No. 212, 17 January. Available at https://www.carpha.org/Portals/0/Documents/COVID%20Situation%20Reports/Situation%20Report%20212%20-%20January%2017%202022.pdf.

Chattu, V.K., and G. Chami. 2020. "Global Health Diplomacy Amid the COVID-19 Pandemic: A Strategic Opportunity for Improving Health, Peace, and Well-Being in the CARICOM Region—A Systematic Review." *Social Sciences*, 9 (5): 88.

Chattu, V.K., R. Khan, S.K. Chattu, M. Taywade, and R.P. Patil. 2020. "Telemedicine and Telehealth Applications for the Post-COVID-19 Pandemic Future." In *Economics of Covid-19 Digital Health Education & Psychology*, edited by B.S. Lal and N. Patel, 269–93. New Delhi: Adhyayan Publishers & Distributors.

Chattu, V.K., A. Knight, K.S. Reddy, and O. Aginam. 2019. "Global Health Diplomacy Fingerprints on Human Security." *International Journal of Preventive Medicine*, 10 (1): 204.

CISCO. 2020. "The Network. New Cisco Annual Internet Report." Accessed 19 October 2020. https://newsroom.cisco.com/press-release-content?type=webcontent&articleId=2055169.

COVAX. 2020. "COVID Vaccine Facility and COVID-19 Vaccines." Accessed 4 January 2021. https://www.who.int/emergencies/diseases/novel-coronavirus-2019/covid-19-vaccines.

Dookeran, W. 2020. "Geopolitical Shifts in the Pandemic World Order," 24 June. Accessed 2 October 2020. https://thecaribbeancamera.com/geopolitical-shifts-in-the-pandemic-world-order/.

EC. 2020. "G7 Leaders' Statement on COVID-19." European Council. Accessed 18 October 2020. https://www.consilium.europa.eu/en/press/press-releases/2020/03/16/g7-leaders-statement-on-covid-19/.

ECLAC (Economic Commission for Latin America and the Caribbean). 2021. "Challenges and Opportunities for Secondary Education in Latin America and the Caribbean during and after the Pandemic," 10 December. Accessed 22 January 2022. https://www.cepal.org/en/insights/challenges-and-opportunities-secondary -education-latin-america-and-caribbean-during-and.

Fukuyama, F. 2020. "The Pandemic and Political Order." *Foreign Affairs*, July/August. Accessed 18 October 2020. https://www.foreignaffairs.com/articles/world/2020-06 -09/pandemic-and-political-order.

Glekman, H. 2018. *Multistakeholder Governance and Democracy: A Global Challenge*. London and New York: Routledge.

Hoffmann, B. 2021. "The Caribbean's Skilful Vaccine Diplomacy." *International Politics & Society, Foreign and Security Policy*, 31 March. Accessed 15 January 2022. https:// www.ips-journal.eu/topics/foreign-and-security-policy/the-caribbeans-skilful -vaccine-diplomacy-5084/.

HPW (Health Policy Watch). 2020. "WHO, The Pandemic and Europe's New Global Health Leadership Role," 29 September, accessed 19 October 2020. https:// healthpolicy-watch.news/77167-2/.

IDB (Inter American Development Bank). 2020. "CARPHA Receiving Additional Support to Fight COVID-19," 15 May. Accessed 19 October 2020. https://www.iadb .org/en/news/carpha-receiving-additional-support-fight-covid-19.

ILO. 2020. "ILO Monitor: COVID-19 and the World of Work. Third Edition: Updated Estimates and Analysis." Accessed 19 October 2020. https://www.ilo.org/wcmsp5/ groups/public/---dgreports/---dcomm/documents/briefingnote/wcms_743146.pdf.

Jones, B. 2020. "Can Middle Powers Lead the World Out of the Pandemic?" *Foreign Policy*, June. Accessed 18 October 2020. https://reader.foreignaffairs.com/2020/06/18 /can-middle-powers-lead-the-world-out-of-the-pandemic/content.html.

Loong, Lee Hsien. 2020. "The Endangered Asian Century: America, China, and the Perils of Confrontation," July/August. Accessed 19 October 2020. https://www .foreignaffairs.com/articles/asia/2020-06-04/lee-hsien-loong-endangered-asian -century.

Nadine, K. Stewart. 2013. "Education and Economic Transformation." The University of the West Indies, Mona Campus, 23 July. Accessed 15 January 2022. https://www .mona.uwi.edu/cop/news/education-and-economic-transformation.

Ranganathan, S. 2020. "Towards a Holistic Digital Health Ecosystem in India." ORF Issue Brief No. 351, April, Observer Research Foundation. Accessed 15 January 2022. https://www.orfonline.org/research/towards-aholistic-digital-health-ecosystem-in -india-63993/ .

Richardson, C. 2021. "Africa and Caribbean together Seek Global Bargaining Power." The Lowy Institute, 23 September. Accessed 15 January 2022. https://www .lowyinstitute.org/the-interpreter/africa-and-caribbean-together-seek-global -bargaining-power.

Scheler, R., and H. Dobson. 2020. "Joining Forces: Reviving Multilateralism through Multi-stakeholder Cooperation." Task Force 5: The Future of Multilateralism and Global Governance. Accessed 19 October 2020. https://t20saudiarabia.github.io/ PolicyBriefs/T20_TF5_PB2.pdf.

Scott, Josimar. 2020. "IDB Grant to Enhance CARPHA's COVID-19 Response," 22 May. Accessed 19 October 2020. https://caribbeanbusinessreport.com/news/idb-grant-to -enhance-carphas-covid-19-response/.

T20. 2002. COVID - 19: Multidisciplinary Approaches to Complex Problems. Transversal G20 Response to COVID-19: Global Governance for Economic, Social, Health and Environmental Resilience. Accessed 19 October 2020. https://t20saudiarabia.org.sa/en/briefs/Pages/Policy-Brief.aspx?pb=TF11_PB14.

Tallberg, J., and M. Zürn. 2019. "The Legitimacy and Legitimation of International Organizations: Introduction and Framework." *Review of International Organizations*, 14: 581–606. https://doi.org/10.1007/s11558-018-9330-7.

The Economic Times. 2021. "India May Export Covishield, Covaxin to South American and Caribbean Nations." Accessed 12 January 2022. https://economictimes.indiatimes.com/industry/healthcare/biotech/pharmaceuticals/india-may-export-covishield-covaxin-to-south-american-caribbean-nations/articleshow/87994071.cms.

Turkewitz, J. 2021. "Latin America Confronts a Pandemic Education Crisis." *The New York Times*, June. https://www.nytimes.com/2021/06/26/world/americas/latin-america-pandemic-education.html.

UNCSD. 2012. "The Future We Want." The United Nations Conference on Sustainable Development, 12 June, Rio de Janeiro, Brazil. Accessed 18 October 2020. https://sustainabledevelopment.un.org/topics/sids.

UNDESA (United Nations Department of Economic and Social Affairs). 2015. "Sustainable Development Goals: Sustainable Development Knowledge Platform." Accessed 6 August 2020. https://sdgs.un.org/goals.

UN. 2020. "United Nations Sustainable Development Goals Report 2020." Accessed 18 October 2020. https://www.un.org/development/desa/publications/publication/sustainable-development-goals-report-2020.

UNEP. 2020. "COVID-19: Four Sustainable Development Goals that Help Futureproof Global Recovery." *Ecosystems and Biodiversity*, 26 May. Accessed 18 October 2020. https://www.unenvironment.org/news-and-stories/story/covid-19-four-sustainable-development-goals-help-future-proof-global.

UN News. 2020. "5 Reasons the World Needs WHO, to Fight the COVID-19 Pandemic," 9 April. Accessed 18 October 2020. https://news.un.org/en/story/2020/04/1061412.

WEF. 2020. "World Economic Forum." The Great Reset. Accessed 18 October 2020. https://www.weforum.org/great-reset.

WHO. 2010. *Telemedicine: Opportunities and Developments in the Member States – report on the Second Global Survey on eHealth*. Global Observatory for eHealth Series – Volume 2. Geneva: World Health Organization. Accessed 28 July 2021. http://www.who.int/goe/publications/goe_telemedicine2010.pdf.

WHO. 2018. "Artificial Intelligence for Good Global Summit." Director Generals' address on 15 May 2018. Accessed 12 April 2020. https://www.who.int/dg/speeches/2018/artificialintelligence-summit/en/..

WHO. 2023. "Coronavirus Disease (COVID-19) Dashboard." World Health Organization, 31 May. Accessed 1 June 2023. https://covid19.who.int/.

17

Complexity Theory in International Relations Studies

Small States Behavior and the COVID-19 Crisis

FAIES JAFAR

Introduction

After almost a century since its emergence, the study of International Relations (IR) continues to attract different methods and theories to analyze, explain, and understand associated phenomena. Constantly evolving and dynamic international politics has persuaded scholars in past decades to search for new and more compelling approaches, including the possible engagement of complexity science. The associated terms differ in the literature and among scholars; complexity, complexity theory, complex system, and complex science are employed interchangeably. In some instances, scholars have argued that there is "neither a single science of complexity nor a single complexity theory exists yet" (Mitchell 2009, 14) and have favored using the terms "complexity" and "complexity thinking"; others have cast doubts "about the contribution complexity theory could or could not make to theory and practice" (Eppel and Rhodes 2018, 949). Despite the varied positions, the literature features considerable publications on CT and its applications in many different disciplines.

Studies have focused mainly on substantive areas and in some instances have looked at special cases of CT and attempted to apply it to IR to establish a generalized conclusion. The broadness of the theory necessitates answering epistemic questions regarding the way and the extent to which it can be engaged effectively. This challenge, as explained in this chapter, no doubt maintained a gap in the body of the knowledge on how complexity can be used to add invaluable insights if/when it is included in the analysis.

In attempting to fill this gap, the chapter proposes a novel approach on how to introduce CT into IR studies by dividing it into three sections. The first section establishes an epistemic framework for understanding complexity by giving attention to areas perceived as most relevant to IR. The second section provides a critique of the existing associated literature with a focus on where and how IR literature has considered complexity. In the third section, CT was applied to several small Caribbean states including Dominica, Grenada, Bahamas, St. Kitts, and Nevis in terms of challenges and response (mainly adaptation) to the COVID-19 crisis.

The chapter also included several challenges facing the engagement of the theory in IR studies.

A Framework for Understanding the Complexity Theory

The ontology and epistemology of CT are centered on the observations and the study of dynamic systems. Such systems are characterized by their sensitivity to initial conditions and their constant evolution and emergence, resulting in the formation of nonlinear structures (Black 2000, 521). Nonlinear interactions of the components of a complex system delimit, if not eliminate, the possibility of prediction on which realists (rationalists) center their scholarship (Bousquet and Curtis 2011, 51).

Initial conditions are those variables that existed at the time when the dynamic system moved from one status into the other, for example, the change of world order, shifts in the balance of power, and governing regime change. In dynamic systems, initial conditions do not exist independently but emerge from the constant evolution of each system. During this process, conditions act as independent variables at the initial stage, and their interaction/engagement with different system components results in adjustments until the system enters a new equilibrium. Differences in the quality/values (or both) of the initial conditions play a vital role in determining the future of the newly emerging properties of the system (Kavalski 2007, 441).

The change of the initial conditions in the dynamic structures is not like those seen in the static systems. In static system, no matter how many times x is applied, the function values (y) can be known and a representing graph of the relation can be drawn. In other words, for a particular x, a particular y is available, and it is, therefore, predictable. In the dynamic system, this is not the case, since governing initial conditions will change, and there is no guarantee that for a particular x, the corresponding y will have a particular value. The emergence of new conditions forms additional boundaries and results in new patterns of relations, hence shifting the system into a different order (Knoespel 1991, 116). In such a case, the nature of the nonlinearity will leave almost no option for prediction.

With unique collective behaviors and properties, a complex system moves into a new state called emergence. This explains the change of state and the nature of the current system as compared to the previous one (Batterman 2010, 1031). The associated process is called evolution, which highlights the ability of the system to adapt to the surrounding environment. For a system to survive, it must undergo constant changes, allowing for a semi-cyclic adaptation to take place (Geyer and Rihani 2010, 43). It is "semi" because during constant interactions between the system components and the surrounding sphere, new inputs infiltrate, resulting in offsetting/changing the initial conditions. Therefore, new inputs become new outputs; neither one is like the previous one. The process continues until the system enters a new level of equilibrium where a new wave of cyclic changes begins.

Understanding these concepts mandates the expansion of the scope of studies by including different disciplines such as biology, environmental studies, sociology, management, mathematics, and chemistry, among many others (Burnes 2005, 74). Additionally, fundamentals of complexity suggest that CT can provide a framework that bridges different disciplines and thus can be regarded as a theoretically informing interdisciplinary platform. IR is an interdisciplinary area of study that is naturally linked to different discourses in order to analyze, explain, and understand events and the associated phenomena.

Among CT's fundamental concepts is the nature of the complex system. The existence of the complexity is neither incidental nor accidental. Objective evolution of the system is in isolation to the human conscience, although humans, as rationally thinking agents, are not isolated from the system itself. The evolution of the system, which is influenced by the surrounding factors, may bring the system to the verge of disorder or chaos (Doll 2008, 184). In the language of CT, chaos is not the status of disorder, randomness, or confusion understood in conventional way, but rather an "orderly disorder characteristic of the systems" (Hayles 1991, 1) and describes different types of order that rely on the previous status of the system (Knoespel 1991, 116).

In a complex system, newly emerging characteristics are not necessarily contrary to previous ones; they can be integral and compatible, even if they are different. There is no perfect reincarnation of the previous structures, relations, or entities that highlights the differences between the quality of the new and the previous status of the system. The system components and their interdependence relations have non-localizable connections; the produced differences, however, are subject to the system's tendency to interiorization (the amalgamation of processes constantly responding to the environment) by known and unknown factors (Deleuze 1994, 183 and 256), and since the system is constantly subjected to the influences of the external conditions, reproduction and repetition of the same components and relations are less possible (Deleuze 1994, 256).

The tendency to interiorization helps the system to reorganize itself, particularly when it is on the verge of chaos. This major property features a self-organizing, self-regulating, or self-governing process. It modulates spontaneous order and events, and the quality is reflected in the ability of the system to respond to unpredictability and to provide a "counter-order" to potential chaos (Smith and Jenks 2006, 253). The latter emerges from the interaction of the system's entities, whereby its ontological changes (Kavalski 2007, 439) render a combination of pure natural process, outcomes of human actions/choices, role of institutions, governance, and many other known and even unknown entities (Barry 1982, 3). The unknown entities might be problematic, as they add ambiguity to any theoretical or conceptual framework that considers the concept of self-organizing in their analytical model. This ambiguity has encouraged some scholars to critique the self-governing phenomenon, describing it as the Gaia hypothesis. They have based their critique on the consistency of teleological patterns that promote the ends as proof of its existence without presenting concrete causality logics (Lenton 2001, 494). Another critique is based on the notion that social realities, which form an important part of the political realm, consist of a substantial level of control by humans and institutional agencies exhibiting organizational properties in addition to the self-organization ones. Hence, in politics, evolution and emergence are not purely objective or spontaneous phenomena. This adds complexity to the theorization of the complex system (Wight 2016, 65).

The ability of a complex system to adapt and adjust reinforces its self-organizing capacity (Kavalski 2007, 440). Adaptation and evolution enjoy a circular relationship as both are exposed to and influenced by the environment (Morçöl 2012, 43). Adaptation causes different interdependent entities to move from one status into another and opens the way for the selection of conditions and attributes to maintain the system's state or move into a unique one that maintains its stability.

Adaptation is an important component of what is called Complex Adaptive Systems (CAS). It is a model or type of regime characterized by its ability to constantly adapt to external factors and newly emerging conditions. Although it is exposed to a wide sphere of the whole complex system, CAS is a special case of it. Constant evolution and adaptation are limited to the quantity and quality of information fed into and conditions influencing the system, apart from the length of the time associated with this process (Rihani 2002, 8). CAS is also a special case because it is an agent-based model. Examples of agents in the context of IR include powerful leaders, influential groups, lobbies, and certain institutions involved in the state's foreign affairs.

Beside CAS, CT recognizes the importance of other subsystems or regimes such as chaotic, orderly, and other organized patterns. What makes CAS special for this chapter is its association with political phenomena in areas such as policymaking and related decisions, the emergence of domestic and international governance, and the attempt by groups of states to design and implement integration projects, among many other issues. In addition, an advantage of engaging CAS in IR studies is that the model can help us reconfigure the role of the agency that is in constant interaction with the structure. It diagnoses its relations with the structure by identifying the role of rationality and cognition in the whole system through feedback loops, for instance. It, therefore, opens the way to integrate macro to micro levels of analysis by reducing the compatibility problems among different levels (Buckley 1998, 79). CAS is included in broader discussions in this chapter in the next section.

CT can offer a framework that challenges conventional thinking. Its ability to include many disciplines that seem remote from each other can help expand research epistemology and reasoning about the phenomenon. This, however, is not without challenges since, for scholars, the engagement of many disciplines may seem unrelated to their area of knowledge and, by extension, their comfort zone.

Where and How Complexity Theory Is Positioned in IR Literature

Engaging CT in IR studies is relatively new. In the last two decades, there have been a few attempts to include it in the list of theories in this discipline. The main synthesis among a discernible ratio of these studies is their focus on the nature of the international system and the attempt to reconfigure its complexity by disproving reductionism as being sufficient to explain its behavior; importantly, they emphasize the system level in their analysis (see, e.g., Clemens 2013, 205; Cudworth and Hobden 2010, 400; Jervis 1997, 12; Scartozzi 2018, 129). In addition, some studies have envisioned the international system as a CAS and upon this ontological and epistemological assumption, analytical and theoretical frameworks have been constructed (Holloman 2008, 288; Scartozzi 2018, 109–30). Other studies have introduced complexity and described it as a main path toward the "fifth debate" in IR, a paradigm that challenges the dominant rationalism and linear thinking in favor of nonlinearity. This paradigm also emphasizes the interdependence of different agencies and their surroundings (Kavalski 2007, 445).

In line with the above, this section focuses on two areas extracted from the literature. The first is ontological, which looks at the nature of the international system in the context of CT. The second critiques the literature associated with IR studies and CAS.

Reconfiguring the International System Beyond Anarchism

The emphasis on the nature of the international system in the context of the CT may have gained the most attention by scholars who have attempted to use it in their IR analysis. The overarching approach contrasts and compares the anarchism of the international system governing relations among nations with system complexity (Kissane 2014, 203). Beyond the conceptual and introductory levels, the content of the comparison, however, is problematic, since the ontology of CT considers complexity as all-inclusive. Therefore, anarchy, like many other properties, is merely part of it and at best is a subsystem that includes a set of attributes that assist us in understanding a specific area of study: in this case, international politics (Açikalin and Bölücek 2014, 33). Such ontology, however, is advantageous in the sense that it helps us develop insights, suggesting that anarchism itself is not rejected by the complexity approach. Rather, it is included in it, and in some cases, international anarchism is reconfigured through it, although from a different stance than those common in the literature on realism.

Cesare Scartozzi's (2018, 129) analysis, for example, established the self-governing property as another ontology of the anarchic complex international system and in this way added such "ontology" to the balance of power concept, whereby the main character explains the driver of the anarchic system envisioned by neorealism (Waltz 1979, 103). Self-governing is active in a world where there is no central government in charge of its affairs; however, the available literature thus far has not made a reference to the nature of the relation between such phenomenon and the balance of power. The main challenge facing such an approach is the lack of material proof; hence, it leads to reliance on observation of the results of the patterns of relations among states before drawing a theory based on the outcomes of relations. This may open the door for criticism because it emphasizes teleology in the analysis (Wight 2016, 65).

Beyond anarchism, the literature on CT offers many other systems, such as rhizome, constant evolutions, composite, and non-state actors' (NSA) interest-based regimes, among many other known and unknown systems. CT includes all these without claiming that it is an agglomeration of all; rather, it includes them among many others that may not yet been known to scholars. Such inclusion reinforces a complexity approach to IR by converting it into a highly interdisciplinary area of study and by extension leaves no space for reductionism. In such a reality, therefore, it is expected that IR studies will have noticeable shifts, not only in terms of the studies' ontology and epistemology, but also in relation to their methodologies.

A rhizoidal system, for example, introduces a unique perspective to IR. The international sphere is analogous to a rhizome, an entity characterized as having no start, no end, and unclear boundaries and consisting of many sub-entities that might be connected at any point and at any time. New connections are constantly emerging leading to the formation of unique entities and allowing the diffusion of the impact of the emerging phenomenon in all directions and at any time. Such emergence can be vertical+- or horizontal and its dimensions are possibly determined only at a particular point in time since it will change at other times, leading to the formation of many layers of plateaus and branches (Deleuze and Guattari 2004, 23). Applying this concept implies that the rhizoidal nature of the international system maintains its openness and constant interaction. The variants in dimension may not necessarily imply the generation of parts like the previous, as some aspects of the system are self-similar, while others are not (Mandelbrot 2013, 146–48).

In the composite system, the picture seems clearer. Entities of this system are neither scalars nor vectors; the sum of their effects is not equal to the whole, and it can be more or even less depending on the direction of their effects and the surrounding conditions. If entities are modeled in terms of vectors, the immediate consequence is the adoption of the superposition principle (Arrighi and Dowek 2013, 130), which is a linear Newtonian notion that explains the sum of the magnitude of entities that are not necessarily interacting with each other. Static linearity and the lack of interactions are rejected by a complex system.

Rejecting reductionism by CT particularly when defining the international system might seem attractive in the sense that it promotes the adoption of holistic approaches. However, such an assumption may face tremendous challenges in several areas important to IR studies, mainly at the methodological level. A rhizoidal system's layers, for example, are not only hierarchical, which has vertical patterns, but also consist of horizontal layers, which may include government, charismatic individuals, and NSAs, such as civil societies and NGOs, in addition to other state players (Harrison and Singer 2006, 26). The attempt to engage CT, therefore, becomes a taxonomic impediment, which ultimately makes it difficult to capture the most appropriate units and variables necessary for the analysis.

The International System as a CAS

Some studies (see, e.g., Alker 2008, 327; Cudworth and Hobden 2010; Hobden 2016, 177; Kavalski 2007; Scartozzi 2018) have attempted to model the international system and its interacting factors as a CAS. The international system includes material power, state actions, and behavior, human and other agencies' roles, domestic to external structure relations, and global governance, among others. The studies' main ontological and epistemological assumptions are centered on the world being a CAS, in which there are constant evolutions and interactions among its different components. At the state level, the evolution that highlights a neo-Darwinian approach to IR may depend on objective and subjective factors. The first may include state material limitations, such as an abundance of natural resources, military power, geographical location, populations, and so on while subjective factors comprise mainly the quality and levels of available competency of state institutions and individual agencies.

Envisioning the international system as a CAS implies that this system's environment is part of a larger environment (Olssen 2016, 153). This is because CAS functions on two levels of interactions: inter and intra. The first signifies the quality and quantity of repeated cycles of interactions between CAS and its surroundings. Such exposure updates and helps evolve the system constantly, for instance, by feeding it with information, new events, new policies, impacts of other systems, and so on. The intra-level is a localized fluid of CAS energy. More specifically, it consists of all attributes and actions taken within the CAS's boundaries and depends on the quality of functioning agents and institutions within the system's environment (Buckley 1998, 78).

The antithesis to this suggests that envisioning/modeling the international system as CAS might be problematic. This is because CAS' interaction with the adjacent environment suggests that it is a smaller part of a surrounding environment, yet not every complex behavior can be labeled as CAS. In other words, CAS is a special case of a complex system (Chen and Wang 2009, 188–89), and since the international system is a complex structure, a methodological question arises as to how CAS helps us understand international political phenomena.

Not only methodological but also ontological questions emerge. CAS is well known in areas of agent-based modeling studies (Kavalski 2007, 447). In the language of social and political interactions, CAS may reduce the debate to the agent-structure level and, by doing so, influence the outcomes of analysis by the inclusion of ontological reductions. Such "tendency would be highly contentious within the broader confines of CT" (Cudworth and Hobden 2016, 172; Olssen 2016, 140). An example is when a state's Foreign Policy (FP) sensitivity to global changes is frequently observed. If the FP is highly self-adjusting and actively responding, then CAS can act as a theoretical framework for such FP analysis.

Small States Behavior and the COVID-19 Crisis

Reviewing the complexity, IR literature helped to develop an important observation of the absence of enough applications and examples, including examples that could simplify the engagement of CT in IR analysis. Examples and applications of CT to IR in published studies suggest a common trend characterized by emphasizing a particular aspect of CT and then attempting to apply it to an international event or vice versa, that is, IR to CT (see, e.g., Bousquet and Curtis 2011, 56; De Roo 2015, 360; Hobbs 2015, 252; Kavalski 2016; Shine 2015, 172). The dense language of complexity may have encouraged scholars to adopt conceptual metaphors in explaining and applying CT (Bousquet and Curtis 2011, 56). Although this might be advantageous in the sense that it clarifies CT's concepts and their applications, it is possible that it undermines its authenticity. It raises an epistemic concern about the extent to which CT can be helpful in offering different and distinct insights to those introduced by other theories.

In this section, CT is applied to the case of small states' behavior in the context of the COVID-19 crisis. The aim is to broaden the application of CT-IR and to expand the knowledge of scholars and IR students by aiding them in establishing epistemic frameworks that consist of CT in IR studies.

In his study on IR of small states, James N. Rosenau (1983, 22–26) generated a theoretical perspective that foreign policies of small states are responsive and adaptive in nature due to their limited capabilities. Rosenau concluded that the size of small states is a variable that portrays the causal factors influencing the state's policy behavior. The evidence presented in his study centered on the observation that leaders involved in policymaking in small states seek to formulate policies that promote integration among the nearest or internal group of states. Additionally, leaders tend to coordinate certain policies that enable them to respond to emerging events and strengthen the autonomy of the state's foreign policies by following strategies of constant adaptation of international issues.

Rosenau, among a few other scholars (see, e.g., Beyer 2006, 306; Coaty 2019, 42; Goetschel 1998, 23), brought the adaptation of small states as an important methodology for the state's survival. This behavior lies at the heart of CT. In a complex system, small states are sensitive interdependent entities with the external environment. Their interdependence moves them from one status into the other as a direct result of acute new inputs from the adjutant environment. These inputs may include security threats, natural disasters, and managing globally transmitted challenges such as epidemics and others.

A small state is a relatively confined unit in comparison to big states. Its macro actions are micro in relation to big states. However, and against the background of CAS explained in this chapter, the smallness of the state as ontology is problematic when it comes to investigating the distinctions between its interactions internationally from those at the domestic level. The separation between environmental and internal loops, for instance, becomes complicated as a direct consequence of the confinement.

An active IR of a small state may help the investigation determine whether its behavior can be modeled as a CAS. A state government is the action unit; its adaptation to external reality helps mitigate its impact and allows it to capture opportunities. The example of this is seen in the early response of the Republic of Trinidad and Tobago in March 2020 when the government adopted a one-shot decision to close the border in response to the spread of the COVID-19 worldwide (Nanton 2020). During the early months of 2020, this small state recorded minimal positive cases (Worldmeter 2020) as compared to many countries in the world. This type of policy decision is taken when minimal information is available and when the state's foreign policymakers are risk-averse. Filtering and using information may be necessary since the scale of demand is low, and the information that finds its way to policymaking ultimately leads to a change of behavior.

In 1963, Edward Lorenz introduced his butterfly hypothesis. He stated, "a butterfly flaps its wing and sets molecules of air in motion, which would move other molecules of air, in turn moving more molecules of air eventually capable of a starting a hurricane on the other side of the planet" (Andrews 2010, 6). Replacing the butterfly flaps with the transmission of COVID-19, scholars and intellectuals can then understand coronavirus/COVID-19's incredible diffusion worldwide in a particular way. CT has a specific place for the butterfly phenomenon and as elucidated previously, the theory explains that the world ontology is characterized by a system or a set of known and unknown numbers of systems and other components and that constant evolution of the system emerges into new initial conditions. The butterfly effect depends on these conditions, which then takes different turns and changes its quantitative impact and the quality of the system behavior.

In crisis studies, chaos theory (Hayles 1991, 1) presents itself as an important platform for analysis of the complex system. Chaos Theory explains the system that is on the verge of entering a disorder status. The spreading of COVID-19 together with the generated crisis worldwide materializes such an example.

The diffusion and impact of the COVID-19 crisis materialize this point and provide a clear example of how to apply CT to an international crisis. The virus emerged in Wuhan (initial condition), the capital city of the Hubei province (Campbel and Gunia 2020) and was traced to a seafood market (another initial condition). The next initial condition can be the subjective choice of a particular animal (for eating purpose) by individuals: this is a micro-level behavior. Such a choice caused, in isolation of the consciousness of individuals, the transfer of the virus from an animal to human. Therefore, the emergence of the virus in Wuhan led to the death of a significant number of people throughout the world, and this is exactly what Edward Lorenz was telling us.

The extensive spread of the virus worldwide, which then became a fact, respected no borders. Figures published by the Chinese government in January and February 2020 of the scale of new cases of infections and deaths put the world mainly in a "stay tuned" position until governments-initiated action when cases arrived on their doorstep. Weeks later, the virus that is suspected to have emerged in China evolved into a worldwide crisis that countries such as Italy, Spain, and then the United States recorded non-comparable figures of casualties (Worldmeter 2020) to those announced by Chinese authorities.

Worldwide, countries began sharing information about the upcoming tsunami of the COVID-19. Political analysts and politicians asked many questions and received less answers. Discourses then took another turn with the heated exchange and accusations of the source, the cause, and the spread of the virus. For instance, the American intelligence community concluded that Beijing obscured the "extent of the coronavirus outbreak in its country" (Bloomberg 2020a) while China framed its disagreement with such allegations by clarifying that their country was "open and transparent" (Bloomberg 2020b).

These are new initial conditions setting a new equilibrium. Figures of rapid spread of the virus in Western countries brought the world to the edge of chaos. This is evident by frequent announcements by many state leaders exploring the possibilities of the diffusion and the losses beyond their states' abilities, announcements of shortage in medical supplies, slowing in the economic cycle, and closure of airports among many other actions.

Approaching the verge of the chaos generated waves of new IR. China engaged in health diplomacy by sending medical supplies and staff to many countries. The World Health Organization became the compass of the mainstream and the social media. News of potential vaccines/treatments are received in a hopeful manner. Even protocols of handshaking among leaders took on different forms. Unique tensions among countries emerged. Germany accused the United States of "seizing thousands of protective face masks that Berlin authorities have already paid for" (Deutsche Welle 2020), and a similar war for masks erupted between France and Turkey (Lister, Shukla, and Bobille 2020).

To bring the world crisis under control, complexity's self-organization property can draw a normative view of the ability of the international system to self-restore. In the context of the COVID-19 pandemic, self-organizing emerges from a set of mechanisms developed subjectively such as actions taken by individuals, institutions, governments, known and unknown agencies, and states to develop vaccines, enhance awareness, impose certain measures and policies, and share information internationally. The mechanism is also objectively formed via environmental feedback, informal actions, coincident, group effects of known and unknown agencies, and unknown historical reasons. Complex interdependence and interactions among the system's parts develop into a spontaneous emergence of order which plays the main role in bringing the status into an orderly fashion: a new equilibrium.

Scholars are more concerned about subjected factors in restoring the semi-chaotic status. This is because it might be possible to evaluate the impacts of measures taken by powerful agencies, for instance, policy responses and the ability to study qualitative changes such as public opinion. Therefore, subjective factors influencing self-organizing mechanisms evolve into politics. There is no guarantee that particular actions taken by one state will not be in conflict with the interest of other states. In some cases, actions may require the cooperation as one state (alone) may not be able to implement their policy. Both possibilities fall at the heart of IR studies.

For small states, policy response coordination became an inescapable choice. For instance, in 2020 Ambassador Colin Granderson, the Assistant Secretary-General of the Caribbean Community (CARICOM) Secretariat (CARICOM 2020), called for the necessity to have collective efforts and share information among member states regarding COVID-19 challenges.

Such calls, at an early stage of the pandemic, can better be described as normative since available information is very limited. CT adds that in such a realm, having positive feedback loops is impossible due to a lack of information. Besides, drawing analogies and conducting time history analysis may be problematic due to the uniqueness of the entire situation and is a challenge facing both large and small states. However, for the latter, it is expected that the scale of impact and the need for creative response is higher and thus, the constraint is greater. For example, reports suggest that starting from spring 2020, the tourism sector in Jamaica witnessed around 75 percent layoff in the workforce and the ratio in Belize stands around 30 percent (Mohammed and Rei 2020, 9). These countries, among many others in the Caribbean, are highly dependent on tourism for employment and foreign exchange.

Groups of small Caribbean states made decisions to either restrict as was the case in Barbados or close their borders, for instance Dominica, Grenada, Bahamas, Dominican Republic, St. Kitts, and Nevis during the non-hurricane season (Turner 2020). The CAS model explains that in such a realm, states that depend significantly on tourism will suffer two negative feedback loops. The external (environmental loop) is due to state of self-isolation from the rest of the world, and the internal loop is related to the domestic social and economic structure. Furthermore, and due to inherited vulnerabilities in small states, their ability to self-organize will take long until they return to equilibrium, which might not be the case in most large states.

Large countries such as the United States, United Kingdom, and Germany implemented measures (KPMG 2020a) such as tax-related liquidity assistance, employment support, and suspension of certain finance obligations by citizens. These are not typical actions taken by small states. Even with some attempts at COVID-19 response measures provided by states such as Trinidad and Tobago (KPMG 2020b) to people and companies, the aid per capita remained low.

Although the response of small Caribbean states to COVID-19 may support the neorealists notion in terms of state material power (available resources) versus its ability to respond, CT brings a unique perspective. The success of the response of the small state depends on its leaders and institutions to read and scan available information and hence craft the most appropriate policies. CAS models can diagnose the state's level of engagement and the quality of its interactions with the world and the state's behavior reflects its sensitivity to an international environment. Ultimately, CAS's important component of listing the lessons learned helps the state if well documented and managed to look at options and make policy decisions; otherwise, it will be merely a normative project.

Actions taken by these states today form initial conditions for tomorrow and the post-COVID-19 era. Although nonlinearity associated with CT may leave no place for predictions, as stated previously, it is up to the leaders' competencies of small states to filter the most effective information for policy action and seeking opportunities for their states. Vaccine diplomacy conducted by prime minister of Barbados, Mia Mottley, with India in early 2021 (Mint 2021) is another example of creating conditions for further relations.

2020 was a year of pandemic politics such as the US blaming China for the pandemic and medical equipment disputes. The year 2021 is shaping up to be a year of vaccines diplomacy/battle in terms of acquiring the vaccines through cooperation, competition, and even conflicts. The turning point between both stages highlights the "emergence" property of CT and the move from one equilibrium into the other. Since small states such as those in the Caribbean are known as impact receivers, Rosenau's invitation for adaptation seems inevitable. Reactions observed in these states suggest their attempt to adapt and the absence of having a pre-adaptation mechanism, which is problematic. Almost after half a century of existence, CARICOM needs to invest in developing platforms for more effective communication and policy orchestration. These are among many other non-escapable subjective conditions to move toward having an active and functional intuitive complex adaptive system in place.

Conclusion

In this chapter, I have identified and explained the compatibility of CT in the IR field. More specifically, I aimed to clarify where, when, and mainly how to engage CT in IR analysis and at different levels. The review of the associated literature highlighted a major observation that published papers have focused on substantive areas of CT; however, an epistemic confine was generated by not exploring important aspects of CT. The reviewed published papers missed a few fundamentals of CT. This is highly important, as it may have ontological and epistemological consequences in favor of limiting engagement with CT. Furthermore, this chapter made it explicit that the theory includes many concepts that are unfamiliar to IR. CT mandates an engagement of the interdisciplinarity of multiple levels and methods of analysis, which no doubt requires extra effort and skills to tackle and include in constructing any theoretical framework.

A complex international sphere is not an external structure to the state; it includes domestic, external, and in-between structures. The immediate consequence of this is a noticeable advantage to the IR literature since it eliminates dividing lines between domains, the so-called levels of analysis. It enriches IR studies by allowing many causal variables in the analysis, even though this complicates the analysis and opens the way for further over-determination. CT rejects the trade-off of highly sophisticated analysis for the express purpose of introducing simplified approaches to understand phenomena.

The application of the theory in the case of the COVID-19 pandemic and the response by small states demonstrated how complexity can reconfigure international phenomena in unique ways. It is a new language for IR scholars. Crisis is a certain stage of the butterfly effect; adaptation plays an important role in emergence which suggests that CT can continue to explain changes in the world structure. In such a realm, the small state is a confined unit of the complex world seeking to find its way to minimize the potential impact of a global challenge that may force their policymakers to offset their conventional normative views when they make their policy decisions. In this regard, CT brings a unique lens to small states' behavior and a different epistemology of their IR.

Author's Note

Formal permissions were granted to reproduce a modified form of each of the following articles that are integrated into one chapter.

Article title: *Integrating Complexity Theory in IR Studies* (doi: 10.18278) Journal: Journal on Policy and Complex Systems Journal website: https://www .ipsonet.org/publications/open-access/policy-and-complex-systems Publisher: Original publication courtesy Policy Studies Organization and a grant from the American Public University System Publisher website: http://www.ipsonet.org/ Year published 2020

Article title: *Applying Complexity Theory to the Coronavirus Crisis* Journal: E-International Relations Website: https://www.e-ir.info/ Year published 2020 Link to publication: https://www.e-ir.info/2020/04/18/applying-compl exity-theory-to-the-coronavirus-crisis/

References

Açikalin, Şuay Nilhan, and Cemal Alpgiray Bölücek. 2014. "Understanding of Arab Spring with Chaos Theory – Uprising or Revolution." In *Chaos Theory in Politics*, edited by Santo Banerjee, Şefika Şule Erçetin, and Ali Tekin, 29–47. New York: Springer.

Alker, Hayward R. 2008. "Ontological Reflections on Peace and War." In *Intelligent Complex Adaptive Systems*, edited by Ang Yang and Yin Shan, 300–30. New York: IGI Publishing.

Andrews, Andy. 2010. *The Butterfly Effect: How Your Life Matters*. Tennessee: Thomas Nelson.

Arrighi, Pablo, and Gilles Dowek. 2013. "Fundamental Physics." In *Irreducibility and Computational Equivalence: 10 Years after Wolfram's. A New Kind of Science*, edited by Hector Zenil, 127–34. New York: Springer.

Barry, Norman. 1982. "The Tradition of Spontaneous Order." *Literature of Liberty: A Review of Contemporary Liberal Thought*, 5 (7): 1–47.

Batterman, Robert W. 2010. "Emergence, Singularities, and Symmetry Breaking." *Foundations of Physics*, 41 (6): 1031–50.

Beyer, Jessica. 2006. "Annotated Bibliography." In *Small States in International Relations*, edited by Christine Ingebritsen, Iver Neumann, and Sieglinde Gstöhl, 293–318. Seattle: University of Washington Press.

Black, Janice A. 2000. "Fermenting Change - Capitalizing on the Inherent Change Found in Dynamic Non-linear (or complex) Systems." *Journal of Organizational Change Management*, 13 (6): 520–25.

Bloomberg. 2020a. "China Concealed Extent of Virus Outbreak, U.S. Intelligence Says." Accessed 9 April 2020. https://www.bloomberg.com/news/articles/2020-04-01/china-concealed-extent-of-virus-outbreak-u-s-intelligence-says.

———. 2020b. "China Rejects U.S. Intelligence Claim It Hid Virus Numbers." Accessed 6 April 2020. https://www.bloomberg.com/news/articles/2020-04-02/china-accuses-u-s-of-shifting-virus-blame-after-intel-report.

Bousquet, Antoine, and Simon Curtis. 2011. "Beyond Models and Metaphors: Complexity Theory, Systems Thinking and International Relations." *Cambridge Review of International Affairs*, 24 (1): 43–62.

Buckley, Walter. 1998. *Society - A Complex Adaptive System: Essays in Social Theory.* Australia: Gordon & Breach Publishers.

Burnes, Bernard. 2005. "Complexity Theories and Organizational Change." *International Journal of Management Reviews*, 7 (2): 73–90.

Campbel, Charlie, and Amy Gunia. 2020. "China Says It's Beating Coronavirus. But Can We Believe Its Numbers?" Accessed 9 April 2020. https://time.com/5813628/china-coronavirus-statistics-wuhan/.

CARICOM. 2020. "CARICOM Foreign Ministers Meet to Coordinate Foreign Policy amid COVID-19 Pandemic." CARICOM. Accessed 1 December 2020. https://caricom.org/caricom-foreign-ministers-meet-to-coordinate-foreign-policy-amid-covid-19-pandemic/.

Chen, Kai, and Hengshan Wang. 2009. "Research on Web 2.0 System Design Based on CAS Theory." In *Complex Sciences: First International Conference, Complex 2009, Shanghai, China, February 2009*, edited by Jie Zhou, Revised Paper, Part 1, 188–95. Berlin and Heidelberg: Springer Verlag.

Clemens, Jr. Walter, 2013. *Complexity Science and World Affairs.* New York: State University of New York Press.

Coaty, Patrick, C. 2019. *Small State Behavior in Strategic and Intelligence Studies: David's Sling.* Costa Mesa: Palgrave Macmillan.

Cudworth, Erika, and Stephen Hobden. 2010. "Anarchy and Anarchism: Towards a Theory of Complex International Systems." *Millennium: Journal of International Studies*, 39 (2): 399–426.

———. 2016. "Complexifying International Relations for a Posthumanist World." In *World Politics at the Edge of Chaos: Reflections on Complexity and Global Life*, edited by Emilian Kavalski, 169–88. New York: State University of New York Press.

Deleuze, Gilles. 1994. *Difference and Repetition.* New York: Columbia University.

Deleuze, Gilles, and Félix Guattari. 2004. *EPZ Thousand Plateaus.* New York: Continuum.

De Roo, Gert. 2015. "Going for Plan B – Conditioning Adaptive Planning: About Urban Planning and Institutional Design in a Non-linear, Complex World." In *Handbook on Complexity and Public Policy*, edited by Robert Geyer and Paul Cairney, 349–68. Maryland: Edward Elgar Publisher.

Deutsche, Welle. 2020. "US Accused of Seizing Face Mask Shipments Bound for Europe, Canada." Accessed 9 April 2020. https://www.dw.com/en/us-accused-of-seizing-face-mask-shipments-bound-for-europe-canada/a-53010923.

Doll, William. 2008. "Complexity and the Culture of Curriculum." In *Complexity Theory and the Philosophy of Education*, edited by Mark Mason, 181–203. West Sussex: John Wiley & Sons.

Eppel, Elizabeth Anne, and Mary Lee Rhodes. 2018. "Complexity Theory and Public Management: A 'becoming' Field." *Public Management Review*, 20 (7): 949–59.

Geyer, Robert, and Samir Rihani. 2010. *Complexity and Public Policy: A New Approach to 21st Century Politics*. London: Routledge.

Goetschel, Laurent. 1998. "The Foreign Security Policy Interests of Small States in Today's Europe." In *Small States Inside and Outside the European Union: Interests and Policies*, edited by Laurent Goetschel, 13–32. London: Kluwer Academic Publisher.

Harrison, Neil E., and J David Singer. 2006. "Complexity Is More than System Theory." In *Complexity in World Politics: Concepts and Methods of a New Paradigm*, edited by Neil E. Harrison, 25–42. New York: State University of New York Press.

Hayles, N. Katherine. 1991. "Introduction: Complex Dynamics in Literature and Science." In *Chaos and Order: Complex Dynamics in Literature and Science*, edited by N. Katherine Hayles, 1–36. Chicago: University of Chicago Press.

Hobbs, Catherine. 2015. "Local Government Service Design Skills through the Appreciation of Complexity." In *Handbook on Complexity and Public Policy*, edited by Robert Geyer and Paul Cairney, 245–60. Maryland: Edward Elgar Publisher.

Hobden, Stephen. 2016. "Nature as an Actor in International Politics." In *Encounters with World Affairs: An Introduction to International Relations*, edited by Emilian Kavalski, 167–86. London: Routledge.

Holloman, Kimberly. 2008. "Complex Adaptive Systems Theory and Military Transformation." In *Applications of Complex Adaptive Systems*, edited by Yin Shan and Ang Yang, 287–305. New York: IGI Publishing.

Jervis, Robert. 1997. *System Effects: Complexity in Political and Social Life*. Princeton: Princeton University Press.

Kavalski, Emilian . 2007. "The Fifth Debate and the Emergence of Complex International Relations Theory: Notes on the Application of Complexity Theory to the Study of International Life." *Cambridge Review of International Affairs*, 20 (3): 435–54.

———. 2016. "Inside/Outside and Around: Observing the Complexity of Global Life." In *World Politics at the Edge of Chaos: Reflections on Complexity and Global Life*, edited by Emilian Kavalski, 1–27. New York: State University of New York Press.

Kissane, Dylan. 2014. *Beyond Anarchy: The Complex and Chaotic Dynamics of International Politics*. Germany: Ibidem Press.

Knoespel, Kenneth J. 1991. "The Employment of Chaos: Instability and Narrative Order." In *Chaos and Order: Complex Dynamics in Literature and Science*, edited by N. Katherine Hayles, 100–22. Chicago: University of Chicago Press.

KPMG. 2020a. "Germany: Government and Institution Measures in Response to COVID-19." *General Information*. Accessed 2 January 2021. https://home.kpmg/xx/en/home/insights/2020/04/germany-government-and-institution-measures-in-response-to-covid.html.

———. 2020b. "Trinidad and Tobago: Government and Institution Measures in Response to COVID-19." *General Information*. Accessed 2 January 2021. https://home.kpmg/xx/en/home/insights/2020/04/trinidad-and-tobago-tax-developments-in-response-to-covid-19.html.

Lenton, Timothy. 2001. "Gaia Hypothesis." In *Encyclopaedia of Global Change: Environmental Change and Human Society*, edited by Andrew Goudie and David J. Cuff, 491–95. Oxford: Oxford University Press.

Lister, Tim Sebastian Shukla, and Fanny Bobille. 2020. "Coronavirus Sparks a 'war for masks' in Desperate Global Scramble for Protection." Accessed 4 April 2020. https://edition.cnn.com/2020/04/04/europe/coronavirus-masks-war-intl/index.html.

Mandelbrot, Benoit B. 2013. *Fractals and Scaling in Finance: Discontinuity, Concentration, Risk. Selecta in finance*. Connecticut: Springer.

Mint. 2021. "India's Vaccine Diplomacy: Barbados PM Thanks Modi for Covid Jabs." *Mint*. Accessed 5 February 2021. https://www.livemint.com/news/india/indias-vaccine-diplomacy-barbados-pm-thanks-modi-for-covid-jabs-11612495080548.html.

Mitchell, Melanie. 2009. *Complexity: A Guided Tour*. Oxford: Oxford University Press.

Mohammed, Nadimah, and Diego Rei. 2020. "Tourism Sector in the English- and Dutch Speaking Caribbean: An Overview and the Impact of COVID-19 on Growth and Employment." ILO. Accessed 2 December 2020. http://www.ilo.org/wcmsp5/groups/public/---americas/---ro-lima/---sro-port_of_spain/documents/publication/wcms_753077.pdf.

Morçöl, Göktuğ. 2012. *A Complexity Theory for Public Policy*. New York: Routledge.

Nanton, Sampson. 2020. "T&T Shuts Down Borders, Bars to be Closed." *Trinidad and Tobago Guardian*. Accessed 1 December 2020. https://www.guardian.co.tt/news/tt-shuts-down-borders-bars-to-be-closed-6.2.1080079.6b07bec899.

Olssen, Mark. 2016. "Ascertaining the Normative Implications of Complexity Thinking for Politics beyond Agent-Based Modeling." In *World Politics at the Edge of Chaos: Reflections on Complexity and Global Life*, edited by Emilian Kavalski, 139–66. New York: State University of New York Press.

Rihani, Samir. 2002. *Complex Systems Theory and Development Practice: Understanding Non-linear Realities*. New York: Zed Books.

Rosenau, James N. 1983. "The Adaptation of Small States." In *Issues in Caribbean International Relations*, edited by Basil A. Ince, A.T. Bryan, H. Addo, and R. Ramsaran, 3–28. New York: University Press of America.

Scartozzi, Cesare M. 2018. "A New Taxonomy for International Relations: Rethinking the International System as a Complex Adaptive System." *Journal on Policy and Complex Systems*, 4 (1): 109–33.

Shine, Kasey Treadwell. 2015. "Policymaking as Complex Cartography? Mapping and Achieving Probable Futures Sing Complex Concepts and Tools." In *Handbook on Complexity and Public Policy*, edited by Robert Geyer and Paul Cairney , 171–89. Maryland: Edward Elgar Publisher.

Smith, John, and Chris Jenks. 2006. *Qualitative Complexity: Ecology, Cognitive Processes and the Re-emergence of Structures in Post-humanist Social Theory*. London: Routledge.

Turner, Matt. 2020. "Caribbean Border Closures, Travel Restrictions and Total Cases." Travel Agent Central. Accessed 2 November 2020. https://www.travelagentcentral.com/caribbean/caribbean-border-closures-travel-restrictions-and-total-cases.

Waltz, Kenneth N. 1979. *Theory of International Politics*. USA: Addison-Wesley Publishing Company.

Wight, Colin. 2016. "Theorizing International Relations: Emergence, Organized Complexity, and Integrative Pluralism." In *World Politics at the Edge of Chaos: Reflections on Complexity and Global Life*, edited by Emilian Kavalski, 53–77. New York: State University of New York Press.

Worldmeter. 2020. "Coronavirus Cases." Accessed 9 April 2020. https://www .worldometers.info/coronavirus/.

18

Small States Diplomacy

COVID-19 and the Geostrategic Change

WINSTON DOOKERAN

Introduction

Colgan and Keohane (2017) titled their early analytical challenge to the Trump presidency as "The Liberal Order Is Rigged: Fix It Now or Watch It Wither." They argued that "the Brexit and Trump phenomenon reflect a breakdown in the social contract at the core of liberal democracy" (Colgan and Keohane 2017, 38) and attributed this to populism as defined by "a faith in strong leaders and a dislike on limits of sovereignty and of powerful institutions" (Colgan and Keohane 2017, 36), and concluded that to stave off complete defeat, political ideas must be rebranded and substantive policies must be developed to make globalization serve the interests of middle and working-class citizens. If this is not done, the global liberal order will wither away (Colgan and Keohane 2017, 40).

Acharya (2017, 271) in reply to the "outpouring of anxiety over the future of the liberal order" quietly claimed that "Trump's ascent to power is a consequence – not a cause – of the decline of the liberal order" (Acharya 2017, 272) and that "the myths, limitations, and decline of this order have been anticipated and forewarned for some time" (Archarya 2017, 271). In any event, the liberal order, however defined, was "centered on the Atlantic littoral" (Acharya 2017, 271) and "the crisis of the liberal order has deeper roots, owing to long-term and structural changes in the global economy and politics" (Acharya 2017, 272).

According to Ikenberry (2020, 133), "the next global era is that of great-power competition and this fractured world, the thinking goes, will offer little space or multilateralism and cooperation." He adds that instead "the U.S. grand strategy will be defined by what international relations theorists call "the problems of anarchy" hegemonic struggles, power transitions competition for security, spheres of influence and reactionary nationalism" (Ikenberry 2020, 133). He points out that "internationalism, was not about tearing down borders and globalising the world but instead managing the complexities of economic and security interdependence in the pursuit of national well-being" (Ikenberry 2020, 134). A key insight of this argument was "what is unique about the post-war liberal order is its capacity for self-correction" (Ikenberry 2020, 135).

Are We in a Post-Hegemonic Cycle in International Politics?

Maybe it was this very insight that led Andy Knight to suggest that the "world seems to be crying out for an alternative ... which will depend on the convergence of interests and attitudes of the existing preponderant power and emerging powers, as well as on the willingness of the United States to accept a new role in a post-hegemonic world order" (Knight 2014, 301). It may be reasonably asked, would the evolving world order focus on "ideas and ideology" and could that be decoupled from the military, economic, and technological sources of power? This, in my view, is the dialectics necessary to sort out the contradictory processes working simultaneously in understanding the *realpolitik* in today's practice of statecraft and diplomacy.

The Dialectics of *Realpolitik* in Small States Diplomacy

In the practice of diplomacy, there are three ideas that I would raise, notably: the advent of a multiplex world order, regionalism in the evolving world order, and the small states' rise to prominence in that order. In doing so, I am mindful of John Bew's insights that "ideas were important in politics – increasingly so, in the democratic age – but their importance was to be judged by their political force rather than their purity or elegance" (Bew 2016, 6). He elaborates that in the conduct of international relations, we may be witnessing a reassertion of the genesis of *realpolitik*, exercised in a world of extreme uncertainty or rapid transformation, and an attitude of cynicism and cold calculation. Bew (2016, 303) concludes that "What matters was the political power of an idea rather than its rationality." Is this an ideological moment that attempts to reconcile idealism with the pursuit of national interests?

In the search for a new vocabulary of international relations, Acharya (2017, 283) urged scholars to remain "open to new concepts and theories [...] and new possibilities of a world order that have no precedents in history." His journey into a multiplex world order is a lucid and a logical response in a period of, extreme uncertainty, and points to a changing framework but cannot claim to define a new order of things, simply by "cross-cutting globalism" (Archarya

2017, 277) as the new order will remain in flux in this cycle of hegemonic decline. In transitions from one world order to the next, there is always a lag, as certain resilient elements of the old order give way to the new one. The transformation is usually never abrupt.

The dominance of the global economic and security order that has engaged world leadership in this era has overshadowed the key role of regionalism in the emerging world order. Estevadeordal and Goodman (2017) in their publication on Regional Public Goods, Global Governance, and Sustainable Development, carefully showed how regional leadership, alliances, and networks fit together in the new frontiers of twenty-first-century cooperation. Acharya (2017, 52), in a penetrating chapter, focuses on an alternative conceptualization of regionalism – hegemonic, integrationist, and multiplex – and concludes that old regional mechanisms are evolving toward wider and more complex functions, and new mechanisms are emerging. Regionalism will be confronted by the new balance of power situations, and so will be forced to seek more leverage room for itself and for relations with non-regional actors.

Will this lead to less-structured integration and more spontaneous convergence among countries? The study of convergence spaces, rather than integration models, may become more relevant. Will the lines of distinction between the private and public sectors become more blurred, where risk sharing takes on a more critical place in the analytical calculus of development paradigms? These and other questions give credence to the insight that in regionalism, new mechanisms are emerging. One of the mechanisms that might be emerging in the new regionalisms is subsidiarity – a social organization where political issues should be dealt with for resolution at the most immediate level (Knight and Persaud 2001).

Increasingly, countries on the periphery have been searching for more wiggle room in the international order, and as Keohane (1969, 291) observed several years ago, "one of the most striking features of contemporary international politics has been the conspicuousness of small states . . . who through diplomatic innovation have risen to prominence, if not to power." The underlying premise of this observation has been based on the pillars of the liberal order, free trade, multilateral diplomacy, the growth of democracies, and values in institutions of governance. The erosion of these pillars may pose a risk to the prominence of small states that have gained from accepting policies rooted in the neoliberal order. The vulnerabilities of small states will extend beyond issues of geography, economics, and ecology and now include policy shifts, resource flows, and the existential threats of natural disasters, as they crucially affect the survival of these states. The world of small states, unique as it is in its problems and its solutions, will now search for more inviting alliances that could secure its sustainable development.

A Challenge for New Thinking in Latin America and the Caribbean

At the Development Bank of Latin America (CAF) conference in 2017, Susana Malcorra urged new thinking on "a renaissance of the global system" as she addressed the new global dynamic in Latin America (quoted in Dookeran 2018, 85). Noting that the unipolar order has been gradually eroded, she added that the pressures of modernity and globalization are bringing business and political leadership together in almost every country of Latin America (quoted in Dookeran 2018, 85–86). This goes beyond the traditional private-public partnership and focuses on the catalytic role of the state in forging new enterprises. A new dialogue on Latin America in world affairs has started, where lines of distinction between an Atlantic and Pacific Latin America are now blurred, and the international roadmap remains unclear (quoted in Dookeran 2018, 86).

At the first-ever United Nations Security Council meeting to invite small states, held under the presidency of New Zealand in 2015, the theme that global challenges demand collective responsibility was pervasive, and no doubt predicated on the notion of multilateralism, a key pillar to the liberal thought and order. Alicia Bárcena had called for revitalizing multilateralism to promote the 2030 Agenda and suggested that it is at the cornerstone of small states' voice and influence in accepting collective responsibility for global challenges (quoted in Dookeran 2018, 86). In these circumstances, platforms for multilateral diplomacy for articulating small states' interests and their commitment to global responsibility will be redefined to reflect more willing advocates in the council of nations. This will be a tall challenge for small states in today's world of diplomacy.

At the high-level symposium in Argentina, Alicia Bárcena emphasized that cooperation must be promoted and expanded on a multilateral bases, a theme she had raised earlier among leaders in Europe at the European Union-ECLAC Forum. She had described the current global context as "marked by the weakening of multilateralism and the return of protectionism" (quoted in Dookeran 2018, 86) and called for more dialogue space in the new context for sustainable development, as outlined in the UN 2017 World Economic and Social Survey.

Historically, Caribbean countries have been faithful to the prescriptions of the Washington Consensus, as they agreed that the gains of globalization will allow them a better insertion into the global economy. Rather than lament that the landscape of that order is now closing doors, a new diplomatic engagement to open doors will of necessity occur. This too signals the need for more inviting alliances and poses a huge challenge to the conduct of international relations, at a time when global institutions are themselves engaged in responding to the realities of a flux in power relations.

The challenge to the liberal order is not really a challenge to the values underpinning that order, as much as it is a correction to the excesses of that order and the consequential shift in the structure of global power. Will this be a transient phenomenon, or will it have an ideological reach and thus alter in a more far-reaching way the value premises of democratic societies and also add new momentum to a post-hegemonic cycle in world politics?

Norman (2020) in revisiting John Rawls' political philosophy that underpins liberal thought observed that COVID-19 marks an inflection point at which we must ask, collectively, what principles we regard as fundamental to an undermined faith in the present liberal order as people have prioritized health over freedom; it is not clear how useful it is to define justice in terms of fairness; and what freedom is and what institutions are needed to sustain it. In this discourse, Norman (2020) adds that the real question may not be whether the liberal project can be revived, but whether some post-liberal political philosophy – a philosophy that better acknowledges the facts and experiences of particular societies and particular identities – may not do more to elucidate and enlighten human life and human possibility. The COVID-19 experience may have unwittingly started a discourse on the philosophical basis of a post-liberal order.

Reflections on the COVID-19 Pandemic and the Caribbean

In 2005, the Presidents of China and the United States prepared and signed a Pandemic Response Protocol, later to be subscribed to by 88 countries. It enumerated ten core principles. At the World Economic Forum (WEF) annual meeting in 2017, the Coalition for Epidemic Preparedness Innovations was launched to accelerate the development of vaccines against emerging infectious diseases. The COVID-19 outbreak was declared a pandemic by the World Health Organization (WHO) on March 11, 2020. In making the announcement, the director general of WHO said "we have rung the alarm bell loud and clear . . . this is not just a public health crisis. It is a crisis that will touch every sector, so every sector and every individual must be involved in the fight" (quoted in Dookeran 2020).

In fighting this public health crisis, steps at suppressing the spread, enhancing the health system, seeking resources for immediate treatment, and pursuing the protocol for discovering a vaccine have engaged societies and governments widely. But what is most telling is the economic fallout of this effort. Global economic activity will drop dramatically in an uncertain policy environment. Awareness of the full implications of this "falling off the edge" is growing as the impact becomes multifaceted in several spheres.

As the economy enters into a "loop-type" cycle of shocks – between demand and supply – old policy prescriptions for recessionary times may no longer work. The coronavirus crisis has induced a supply shock – reducing wages and production that, in turn, fuel a demand shock – a fall in purchasing power. This becomes a "loop-type" cycle of shocks in growth models and shock absorbers to mitigate the effects on growth (Dookeran 2020).

But buffers and shock absorbers are weak in the Caribbean economy. Shocks are absorbed through adjustments in labor and austerity. That will work, depending on the magnitude of the shocks. Already, it is argued that to prevent an immediate collapse, the size of the fiscal injection must be equivalent to the fall in the gross domestic product. It is a tall order in any circumstances but has dire complications to debt, credit, incomes, and poverty levels. This is above the cost implication of financing modes used and the prospect of recovery in a "loop-like" cycle. We are in unchartered waters, and the choice between lives and livelihood is already a harsh reality (Dookeran 2020).

Measures currently being adopted by powerful and small countries are dubbed as stimulus packages. This may not be an appropriate description, as it implies a sustained growth element when its focus is more on survival than sustainability. For small countries, rapid economic growth requires a new look at the role of the state in economic development and a shift toward a catalytic role of the state, where the state will act primarily as a catalyst for economic development. There are examples where the state has been the major catalyst to sustained development, notwithstanding the obstacles to the growth process that lie in undue reliance on the outdated controls and systems of state-centric development.

The market forces themselves will not suffice to protect the public good, exposing the myth that the private sector could be the driver of economic growth. Perhaps, at this time we should embrace the notion of a catalytic role of the state in economic development, as a role that causes change while adopting measures of sustainability. This will open a new calculus in the orthodox distinction between the private and public sectors.

Dookeran (2020) notes that credible analytical leadership is required, and universities must become truly rigorous and entrepreneurial. Changes in research priorities and teaching methods initiated in this non-normal period will likely remain permanent as the economic metrics change. This will call for new systems and a switch to the digital world. The international mobility of students, as the middle class gets hit, will put at risk the outreach programs for higher education's reach into the global marketplace. These and other changes will spur entrepreneurial outcomes within the university system.

On the wider front, Dookeran (2020) points out that new drivers of industry change may arise – more use of digital transaction, innovations in public hygiene, changes in the way the travel and the tourism sectors operate, security of production of food and medicine, wider corporate goals and a truly entrepreneurial university could be the changing imperatives of our times. New research agenda, priorities for institutional progress, infrastructure for teaching and learning, and governance systems will all shape the curve ahead of us. This will speak to the relevance of the university to society and the revitalization of development.

The COVID-19 pandemic cannot be solved by internal efforts alone. Global coordination and diplomacy are needed to add new resources – technical, business, and financial – to the solution matrix. The G20 countries began to talk, but much more is required to get a coordinated global economic response to the uphill tasks ahead. The Working Group of the Caribbean established as a doorway to the G20 could be revived to provide a Caribbean voice to the global financial demands. In addition, the special drawing rights window of the International Monetary Fund (IMF) must be redesigned for "fair share" in the application of the immediate balance-of-payment resources. These and other initiatives also require an entrepreneurial approach to diplomacy (Dookeran 2020).

The *Foreign Affairs Review*, in its March 31, 2020, issue wrote that the United Nations Security Council must act and declare COVID-19 a threat to international security. While admitting that the WHO was the technical focal point for a pandemic response within the United Nations, it lacked the authority to cut through political obstacles that will hasten international cooperation and allow the United Nations to "manage engagement with the World Bank and the IMF as well as informal bodies like the G7 and G20" (Malley and Malley 2020). In such a declaration, the Caribbean will be able to find some diplomatic leverage, in the complex geopolitics that small nations face today.

Strategic Shifts in the Pandemic World Order

As expressed by Fukuyama (2020, 31), the pandemic has been a global political stress test where capable states with good leadership who embraced reforms became stronger and more resilient, while those with weak state capacity – (political and economic) – will be in trouble and set for stagnation. Accordingly, a shifting order of things is taking place. The WEF's January 2021 summit has set the theme as "The Great Reset." Schwab and Malleret (2020, 103) state that the COVID-19 crisis could reverse global human development – measured in terms of education, health, and living standards. Small Island Developing States (SIDS) are particularly vulnerable and will have an inordinate amount of difficulty in recovering, without sufficient development finance.

The Caribbean Is Undergoing a Political Stress Test?

In reading the "Political Stress Test" and "The Great Reset" I ask four questions:

a) What Are the Global Forces That Underline the Geostrategic Shifts?

- Another hit on globalization.
- The driver of globalization's next chapter will be digitalization.
- A changing order in the politics of multilateral diplomacy.
- A weakening of world hegemons and shifts in the structure of world power.
- A loss of legitimacy in regional and global political alliances.

The EIU ViewsWire (2020) issue, specifically on the geopolitics of the pandemic, suggested three areas to watch for change: the shift in the balance of power from West to East, changes in the future of Europe, and China's relations with the developing world. The *Economist* asked the questions without an answer: Would US global leadership diminish? And how will emerging powers capitalize on these shifts?

b) Is the World Political Order of the Bretton Woods Vintage Now on Its Knees?

Academics have argued that the world order has moved from hegemons to multipolar and even to a multiplex world. Now, the world's political order may be better described as "flat" in today's situation, not G20, not G7, but rather a "Go Order" – no hegemons, no multipolar, and no multiplex – a la Amitav Acharya. Global security alliances that emerged out of the Cold War are now faced with new global challenges in cyber and information technologies and populist politics at home. In this setting of transactional and *realpolitik*, different configurations of power relations are emerging, and we are beginning to see the following trends that may shape the future political order.

- The renewed focus on regionalism – resiliency vs efficiency – drives the global economy.
- The growing divide in inequality among and within nations.
- A changing direction in the flow of funds and shifts in the supply chain.
- Liberal democracies that are less liberal, with more authoritarian tendencies, but adhering to the fundamental of democratic systems.
- A global order in which small nations and island nations will not have an automatic place.
- Hedging will lead to "floating coalitions," based on interest and *realpolitik*, not so much on power and ideology.

c)   How Will These Trends Affect Global Cooperation?

Lee Hsien Loong, Prime Minister of Singapore, in an article in *Foreign Affairs* on June 4, 2020, titled "The Endangered Asian Century: America, China and the Perils of Confrontation," concluded with a fervent hope. Loong (2020, 56) noted that the strategic choices that the United States and China make will shape the contours of the emerging global order. It is natural for big powers to compete. But it is their capacity for cooperation that is the true test of statecraft, and it will determine whether humanity makes progress on global problems such as climate change, nuclear proliferation, and the spread of infectious diseases. This call has been echoed in several quarters, and the recent T20 policy brief, referred to later, articulated specific recommendations to "make it happen."

d)   Will the Caribbean Region Be Ready for the Geostrategic Shifts?

In the quest for a stable and peaceful international order, while preserving our strategic autonomy, small states will be on a constant search for strategic opportunities. Perhaps the strategic logic of our time will see the advent of "floating coalitions," in response to countries hedging in this fluid geopolitical climate. Countries like ours in the Caribbean cannot afford to be bystanders but must engage constructively in the present order of things. The Caribbean will face strategic choices in the practice of diplomacy, and concrete actions will depend on an assessment of the following:

- Focusing on regional pandemic surveillance and public health coordination.
- Selecting bridges for communications with major countries and adopting new protocols for decision-making.
- Negotiating an economic platform within international financial institutions in both a short- and long-term perspective.

- Working out flexible engagements – in health diplomacy and development finance – and being partners in floating coalitions of the present.
- Securing access to the benefits of global research in medical science.

The pandemic has shaken up the foundations of the world of public policy – in finance, in politics, in health, and in other spheres – and if it is treated as temporary, we would have lost forever the opportunities for making public policy changes that are critical to our times. In this sense, notwithstanding its huge life and livelihood costs across the globe, the pandemic may well be a catalyst for geopolitical shifts in the world order of things.

Challenges in the Practices of Diplomacy for Small States

Small states are often viewed as inconsequential to world politics, thus requiring innovative approaches in the practice of diplomacy. Godfrey Baldacchino and Anders Wivel in a compelling and articulate book on the subject summed up the challenge as follows: "small states today remain restrained by limited capacity and capabilities in pursuing their domestic and international ambitions and are stuck as weak actors in asymmetric relationships, creating dependency and threatening their values and interests. However, they also benefit from being weak, since this allows them a bigger action space and success in pursuing coping strategies" (Baldacchino and Wivel 2020, 14–15). Coping strategies in diplomacy for small states will indeed be tested in this era of geopolitical reset and the quest for global solidarity, a period of tired paradigms and starting over again, and in a time of changing geostrategic shifts.

Schwab and Malleret (2020, 103) linked the pandemic with the geopolitics by calling for a geopolitical reset: "the coronavirus is spreading globally and sparing no one, while simultaneously the geopolitical fault lines that divide societies spur many leaders to focus on national responses, a situation that constrains collective effectiveness and reduces the ability to eradicate the pandemic." The pandemic is accelerating geopolitical trends that were in existence before the crisis, like the shifts at the end of multilateralism, the vacuum of global governance, and the rise of various forms of nationalism. As such, we are entering a world of entropy, summed up by the noted Swiss economist Jean-Pierre Lehmann in the following way, "there is no new global order, just a chaotic transition to uncertainty" (Klaus and Malleret, 2020). Increasingly, countries cannot rely on hegemons to provide global public goods and "will now have to tend their own backyards themselves."

The T20 policy brief by Thomas et al. (2020) reaffirmed the need for global solidarity and the significance of global public goods in the post-COVID-19 era and outlined multidisciplinary approaches to the complex problems facing the world today. It sets the stage, noting that "we must act together and build the strength and global reach of our multilateral institutions because it makes a compelling case for global solidarity and because until every country is disease free, no country will be disease free" (Thomas et al. 2020, 8). The policy brief, among several recommendations, calls for the closing of access gaps between the Global North and the Global South with particular reference to the health sector and equitable access to vaccines, therapeutics, and diagnostics (Thomas et al. 2020, 11).

The WEF in pioneering "The Great Reset" initiative established a COVID-19 Action Platform. It is centered on multi-stakeholder cooperation, listing three focus priorities as outlined below:

- Galvanize the business community for collective action.
- Protect people's livelihoods and facilitate business continuity.
- Mobilize cooperation and business support for the COVID-19 response.

It calls for coordinated action by governments, businesses, civil society, and individuals combined with global multi-stakeholder cooperation acting with an unprecedented scale and speed to arrest this unprecedented crisis.

Klaus Schwab, the executive chairman of the WEF, in a call for a new capitalism, urged that "the great reset should seek to lend a voice to those who have been left behind, so that everyone who is willing to "co-shape" the future can do so . . . some of the pillars of the global system will need to be replaced, and others repaired or strengthened" (Schwab and Malleret 2020, 103). Others, like the *Economist* (2020, 16) in calling for a rethink in macroeconomics in the post-COVID-19 era, succinctly quipped that "what is clear is that [the] old economic paradigm is looking tired." Still others like Thomas et al. (2020) are exploring global collective action and equitable approaches to COVID-19 as expressed in the T20 Task Force 11 entitled "COVID-19: Multidisciplinary Approaches Complex Problems."

These initiatives pose challenges to small states in forging a platform that is unique and will mitigate risks and mobilize resources in a global policy setting. Small nations will find their wiggle space restricted, adding complex challenges in the practice of diplomacy in a world order of ever-changing geostrategic shifts.

Andy Knight, in an email communication with the author offered some insights into his forthcoming book. Knight (2022) refers to the late Robert Cox prediction that "we may be moving towards a post-hegemonic era in which no major power is able or even willing to take on the challenge of global leadership." He calls this "a new world disorder," characterized by turbulence, in-equilibrium instability, and flux. Referring to Arnold Toynbee's "interregnum" where there is the diffusion of power due to the phenomenon of globalization, it is unlikely that any state will be in a position to take on the mantle of a global hegemon. Knight (2022) concludes that in such a scenario, in a multiplex and multi-centric world, regional actors and subaltern actors may find space in which they can normatively help to shape the new world order.

References

Acharya, Amitav. 2017. "After Liberal Hegemony: The Advent of a Multiplex World Order." *Ethics & International Affairs*, 31 (3): 271–85. https://doi.org/10.1017/S089267941700020X.

Baldacchino, Godfrey, and Anders Wivel. 2020. *Handbook on the Politics of Small States*. Cheltenham: Edward Elgar Publishing.

Bew, John. 2016. *Realpolitik: A History*. New York: Oxford University Press.

Colgan, Jeff D., and Robert O. Keohane. 2017. "The Liberal Order Is Rigged: Fix It Now or Watch It Wither." *Foreign Affairs*, 96 (3): 36–44. https://www.proquest.com/docview/1909733994?OpenUrlRefId=info:xri/sid:primo&accountid=45039.

Dookeran, Winston. 2018. *The Caribbean on the Edge: An Anthology of Ideas and Writings*. Washington, DC: ECLAC. https://repositorio.cepal.org/bitstream/handle/11362/43984/1/S1800820_en.pdf.

———. 2020. "Reflections on the COVID-19 Pandemic and the Caribbean." *Elucid Global Health* (blog), 30 March. https://globalhealth.euclid.int/reflections-on-the-covid-19-pandemic-and-the-caribbean/.

EIU ViewsWire. 2020. "World Politics - Geopolitics after Covid-19: Is the Pandemic a Turning Point?" *EIU ViewsWire*, 1 April. https://www.proquest.com/wire-feeds/world-politics-geopolitics-after-covid-19-is/docview/2385081583/se-2?accountid=45039.

Estevadeordal, Antoni, and Louis W. Goodman, eds. 2017. *21st Century Cooperation: Regional Public Goods, Global Governance, and Sustainable Development*. Abington, Oxon: Routledge.

Fukuyama, Francis. 2020. "The Pandemic and Political Order." *Foreign Affairs*, 99 (4): 26–32. https://www.proquest.com/magazines/pandemic-political-order/docview/2415032046/se-2?accountid=45039.

Ikenberry, G. John. 2020. "The Next Liberal Order: The Age of Contagion Demands More Internationalism, Not Less." *Foreign Affairs*, 99 (4): 133–42. https://www-proquest-com.ezproxygateway.sastudents.uwi.tt/magazines/next-liberal-order/docview/2415031641/se-2?accountid=45039.

Keohane, Robert O. 1969. "Review: Lilliputians' Dilemmas: Small States in International Politics." *International Organization*, 23 (2): 291–310. https://www.jstor.org/stable/2706027.

Knight, Andy W. (Professor, Department of Political Science, University of Alberta, Canada). 2022. E-mail message to author, 25 January.

Knight, W. Andy. 2014. "US Hegemony." In *International Organization and Global Governance*, edited by Thomas G. Weiss and Rorden Wilkinson, 292–308. Abingdon: Routledge.

Knight, W. Andy, and Randolph B. Persaud. 2001. "Subsidiarity, Regional Governance, and Caribbean Security." *Latin American Politics and Society*, 43 (1): 29–56. doi: 10.1111/j.1548-2456.2001.tb00169.x.

Loong, Lee Hsien. 2020. "The Endangered Asian Century: America, China and the Perils of Confrontation." *Foreign Affairs*, 99 (4): 52–8. https://www-proquestcom .ezproxygateway.sastudents.uwi.tt/docview/2415031962/AE64B0BF6C7B49AFPQ/1 ?accountid=45039.

Malley, Robert, and Richard Malley. 2020. "When the Pandemic Hits the Most Vulnerable: Developing Countries Are Hurtling Toward Coronavirus Catastrophe." *Foreign Affairs*, 31 March 2020. https://www.foreignaffairs.com/articles/africa/2020 -03-31/ when-pandemic-hits-most-vulnerable.

Norman, Jessie. 2020. "Revisiting John Rawls's A Theory of Justice." *Prospect*, 7 October 2020. https://www.prospectmagazine.co.uk/magazine/liberalism-john-rawls-jesse -norman-katrina-forrester-theory-of-justice-andrius-galisanka.

Schwab, Klaus, and Therry Malleret. 2020. *Covid19: The Great Reset*. Geneva, Switzerland: World Economic Forum.

The Economist. 2020. "Starting Over Again." *Economist*, 436 (9204): 13–16. https://www -proquest-com.ezproxygateway.sastudents.uwi.tt/magazines/starting-over-again/ docview/2426764469/se-2?accountid=45039.

Thomas, Yonette Felicity, Obijiofor Aginam, Sainath Banerjee, Alex Ezeh, Sandro Galea, Franz Gatsweiler, Blessing Mberu, et al. 2020. "T20 Saudi Arabia Group Policy Brief –Reaffirming the Significance of Global Public Goods for Health: Global Solidarity in Response to Covid-19 and Future Shocks - Task Force 11 Covid-19: Multidisciplinary Approaches to Complex Problems." https://www.g20-insights .org/wp-content/uploads/2020/11/T20_TF11_PB1.pdf.

19

Frontiers of the Global Pandemic

A Look at the New Chapters Ahead

WINSTON DOOKERAN AND MANFRED JANTZEN

The Pandemic in a One-World-Information-Space

Shannon (1948) in a landmark article popularized as "The Mathematical Theory of Communication" laid the foundation for digital circuits and information theory. This is credited as the beginning of the information age where access to and the control of information are the defining characteristic of this current era of human civilization. This may well be the origin of the digital age, now in full flow in the aftermath of the COVID-19 pandemic. This context is referred to as the One-World-Information-Space in a planetary symbiotic convergence model where the current global pandemic has become a flashpoint in bringing to light long-simmering, perturbing issues not addressed by societies and their sovereign nation-states in their development journey (Dookeran 2012, 15). The pandemic may well be the tipping point event that heralds in a new global frontier calling for a resetting, reconceptualizing, and redirecting of societal and global priorities with paradigm-shifting impact. This may require research-based contextualization of future societal and global development.

Questioning the Traditional Social Contract

Predominantly in Western societies, the global pandemic is questioning the societal value system and endangering the painfully accumulated and always fragile trust bond between the nation-state and its citizens. The pandemic event is testing the validity, legitimacy, and effectiveness of the social contract between the nation-state and its citizenry. It does so in the following ways:

- It simultaneously delivers an external and internal shock to established societal performance systems in a chaotic environment.
- It exposes external and internal societal vulnerabilities of its essential infrastructure by having been "open" to the rest of the world without appropriately protecting the quality of life of its citizens.

- It brings to light society's external and internal resilience, its survival capability to withstand adversity through flexibility, and agility drawing on its accumulated knowledge, and experience deposited in its accumulated layers of culture.
- It severely tests the societal governance and the political systems, at all levels of the state, to deliver the promises of the social contract.

In traditional democratic Western societies, the social contract is deeply rooted and embedded in culture. The global pandemic reveals long-festering societal issues that require a contextualization of the social contract in a One-World-Information-Space. While the core principles of the social contract need a revitalization, they also point the way forward to an overarching cyber-social contract which will:

- Ensure national security with overriding individual safety.
- Enforce national law with guaranteed individual justice.
- Provide national governance with participatory individual politics.
- Promote national wealth with achievable individual opportunity.

In the last century, these core guiding principles of the social contract, with their profoundly entrenched cultural value system, created the necessary social and political stability for improving the quality of life in global societies. These guiding principles of the social contract provided fertile grounds for:

- Breakthroughs in science and technology, including the eventual paradigm-shifting global information-communication network.
- Developing agricultural capabilities for feeding a vastly increased global population.
- Providing conditions for a dramatic increase in life expectancy with advancement in healthcare.
- Allowing for the maturing of democratic-participatory political systems, particularly former colonies achieving independence.
- Developing a powerful wealth-producing global market economy that allows nation-states to become powerful engines of economic development.

The global pandemic, while uncovering serious weaknesses of the nation-state and its social contract with its citizens, also opened new frontiers to create and claim economic, social, and political space in an emerging global cyber civilization. Shafik (2021) makes the case for a new social contract – choosing different ways to pool risks and share resources, striking different balances between individual and collective responsibility – brought about by the new pressures of aging, artificial intelligence, and climate change that now comes to the fore in the aftermath of the 2020 pandemic. In her words "we owe each other more. A more generous and inclusive social contract would recognize our interdependencies, provide minimum protection for all, share some risks collectively and ask everyone to contribute as much as they can for as long as they can" (Shafik 2021, 188).

An Emerging Frontier Paradigm

Since the 1950s, technological innovations powered an information and communications technology platform that allowed information to flow as the dominant resource near the speed of light – in cyberspace and accessible in every place. The power of this information flow is seen today on the internet. This has created a frontier world that has dangerously opened a gap between our social systems and our technological platforms. In this gap, it also increases the potential for increases in disruptive systemic change, political stress, and shifts in global power relations. It is a chaotic frontier world where the past, the present, and the future collide violently in tectonic change that is nonlinear, disruptive, and unclear as to its outcome on global power relations.

Rewriting Integration and Convergence in the Space Ahead

As global power relations shift, so do economic boundaries. Economic integration models designed in the past century are under great stress amid the fluidity of the political setting. Other forces at work have also created a quest to look beyond orthodox models of integration, in a new phase of regionalism in globalized markets. As nations muddle a way forward, economic convergence has returned to the drafting board, partly due to a new convergence in technology and supply chains. Figure 19.1 depicts a frame for the interaction between culture, politics, and economics that leads to a symbiotic convergence process.

In the aftermath of the COVID-19 pandemic, these processes are impacted by the current ripples in the liberal order, as it questions the old orthodoxies of private sector/public sector dichotomies in regionalism, populism, and development. It raises new possibilities for the world order in this cycle of hegemonic decline emerging out of historical forces and populist politics of today.

The question may be asked: Is this a change in public values in the practice of *realpolitik* or is it merely a correction of excesses? Regardless, the changing

An Emerging Planetary Infrastructure
A Symbiotic Convergence Framework

We are experiencing an emergence of a symbiotic converging global economic, political and cultural infrastructure in the frontiers of human progress on spaceship earth. The historical and current development progress provides the foundation for tomorrows planetary solar civilization.

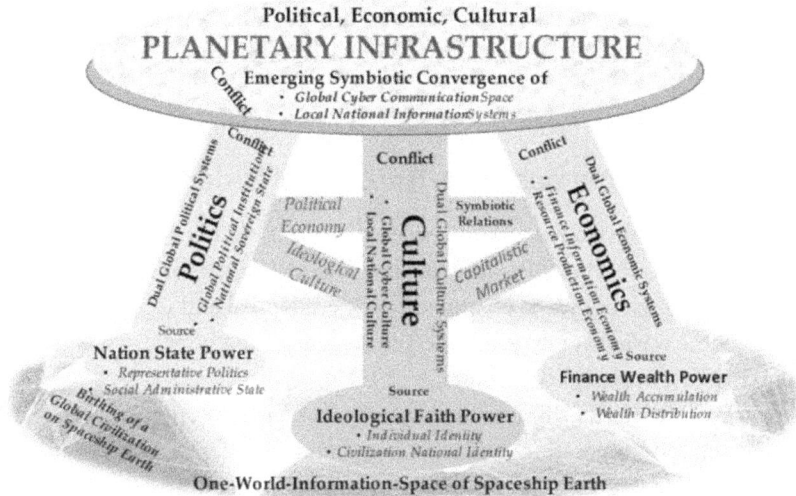

Political, Economic, Cultural

PLANETARY INFRASTRUCTURE
Emerging Symbiotic Convergence of
- *Global Cyber Communication Space*
- *Local National Information Systems*

Conflict

Conflict

Conflict

Politics

Dual Global Political Systems
Global Political Institutions
National Sovereign State

Political Economy

Ideological Culture

Dual Global Culture Systems
Global Cyber Culture
Local National Culture

Culture

Symbiotic Relations

Capitalistic Market

Economics

Finance Information Economy
Resource Production Economy
Dual Global Economic Systems

Source

Nation State Power
- *Representative Politics*
- *Social Administrative State*

Birthing of a Global Civilization on Spaceship Earth

Source

Ideological Faith Power
- *Individual Identity*
- *Civilization National Identity*

Source

Finance Wealth Power
- *Wealth Accumulation*
- *Wealth Distribution*

One-World-Information-Space of Spaceship Earth

Figure 19.1 Symbiotic convergence model.
Source: Developed by Manfred Jantzen, author.

balance of power situations will see a new networking of regionalism and influence in the wiggle room for small states in the conduct of foreign relations. In the Caribbean, it echoes the call for a brand-new paradigm in the alignment of power and in politics and performance, and it places a high priority on new approaches to public diplomacy.

A publication from the Inter-American Development Bank similarly stated the following:

> The quest for regional integration has been the centerpiece of the development strategy for Latin America and the Caribbean...the regulatory architecture does not necessarily provide the nimbleness required to compete in the global economy of the twenty-first century . . . it is in the region's best interest to go beyond the current mosaic of small agreements and move gradually towards a unified regional market. By connecting these dots policy makers can upgrade their integration software by moving the competitiveness needle and mustering the gravitational pull by taking an aggressive approach to convergence and picking different routes to convergence, depending on their political circumstances. (Inter-American Development Bank 2018, 7)

Latin America and the Caribbean (LAC) regional integration initiatives suffer from an original sin, that is, fragmentation. LAC has not been able to capitalize on the recent surge in global value chains through which goods that were previously produced in one country are sliced up and co-produced in many parts of the world. Overall, the results suggest the move toward convergence, which may have significant and positive impacts on the formation of regional supply chains.

Small State Diplomacy in a Transitional Order

The transformation from one world order to the next will not be an abrupt, easy transition. The prominent global economic and security order has allowed for fundamental regionalism to be neglected. Estevadeordal and Goodman (2017) highlight the ways that regional leadership, alliances, and networks will coexist in twenty-first-century cooperation.

However, it merits discussion that this new global order can result in less-structured integration and more spontaneous convergence between countries. This will include snowball effects, such as the blurring of the lines separating private and public sectors. In regionalism, subsidiarity may also be a potential emergent mechanism. Furthermore, small states on the periphery have been seeking more scope for negotiation and operation in the global order. Keohane (1969) observed that "one of the most striking features of contemporary international politics has been the conspicuousness of small states," which, through diplomatic innovation, "have risen to prominence, if not to power" (291).

The underlying premise of this observation was based on the pillars of the liberal order, free trade, multilateral diplomacy, the growth of democracies, and values in institutions of governance. The erosion of these pillars may pose a risk to the prominence of small states that have gained from accepting policies rooted in the neoliberal order. The vulnerabilities of small states will extend beyond issues of geography, economics, and ecology and will now include policy shifts, resource flows, and the existential threats of natural disasters as they affect the survival of these states. The world of small states, unique as it is in its problems and its solutions, will now search for more inviting alliances that could secure its sustainable development.

The Next Shift in Globalization

Clearly, there have been major shifts in thinking on the nature of regionalism and the structural shifts in globalization. In the Caribbean, historical structuralism – reflected in production patterns and social structures – is rooted in vulnerabilities, fragilities, and resilience, and predicated by development strategies. It underlined the difficulties in advancing sustainable growth paths and global competitiveness.

As such, scholars like Lino Briguglio contributed significantly by constructing matrices for measuring resilience and showing how external shocks impact economic fundamentals and macro outcomes. International institutions like the International Monetary Fund and the World Bank have, in their analysis of Caribbean countries, often viewed external shocks risks as a temporary phenomenon that can be mitigated through financial flows. Bustillo et al. (2018) illustrated the link between the flow of funds and the resilience and effectiveness of accessing funds from the global financial markets for Caribbean countries.

Today, several structural shifts are happening in the global markets that alter the roadmap for the insertion of small economies in the global space. A recent report by Lund et al. (2019, 1) concluded that:

> Our findings reveal that globalization is in the midst of a transformation. Yet the public debate about trade is often about recapturing the past rather than looking towards the future. The mix of countries, companies and workers that stand to gain in the next era is changing. Understanding how the landscape is shifting will help policy makers and business leaders prepare for globalization's next chapter and the opportunities and challenges it will present.

Ulgen et al. (2022, 9) in a tantalizing title Rewiring Globalization, wrote that "the political salience of anti-globalization sentiment . . . will depend on the extent to which post-pandemic social contracts re-embed markets in social values. For centrist politicians, the challenge will be to convince electorates that they can deliver the necessary transformation in policy thinking to ease the sense of unfairness felt by those left behind and overcome their distrust of the elites who helped shaped the system they oppose."

The Frontier World in Transition

We live in a frontier world, in a chaotic time. It is a time of turbulence, turmoil, and violence, but within those lenses, there is an embryonic and emerging new model, creating a transition in shifting paradigms. A tension has emerged between the centrifugal forces of fracture and fragment of the old and the centripetal forces of information and cyberspace are creating a new synergistic core.

There is tension in this transition, as depicted in Figure 19.2. The old paradigm power embedded in the culture and institutions of the industrialization age clashes with the new paradigm power of Big Data and digital transformation. The clash is tectonic in impact, as local and global structures and relations adjust in the One-World-Information-Space. Out of this chaotic time, a logical flow for sustainable progress must be discovered.

Disruptive Transformation

While the current academic literature seemingly agrees with the collapsing of the liberal order and the consequent challenges that arise, many researchers fail to address the forces underpinning these new global challenges. It is reasonable to question the causes behind the disruptions of the old hegemonic order. The lack of clarification regarding the elements of assumptions that sustained the so-called liberal order may have led to a misreading of the dynamics of the past five decades. As such, the proposed solutions are not all grounded in the emerging global realities. The search is on for a renewed understanding of the dynamics of this emerging world order, a search that is crucial for the rebuilding of a political and economic framework.

It is indisputable that the dawn of this new age requires not only fixes of the old but disruptive transformation of the entire sociopolitical and economic

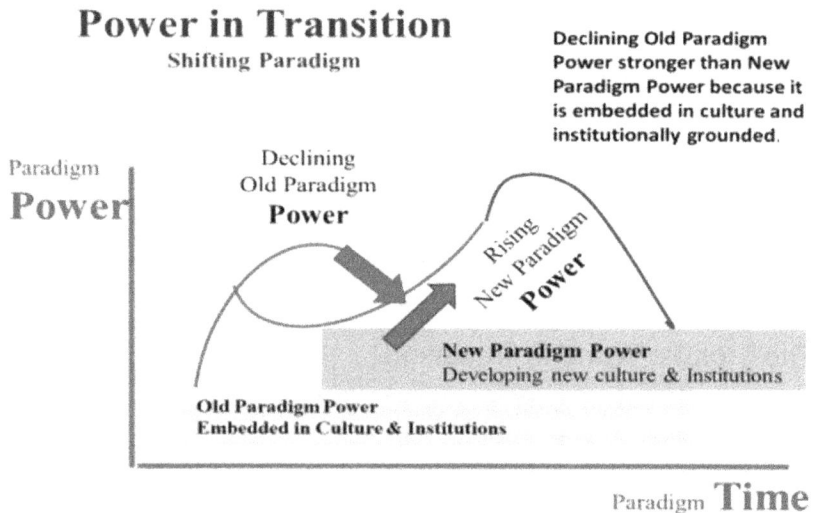

Figure 19.2 Shifting paradigm power.

Source: Developed by Manfred Jantzen, author.

systems on both a local and global scale. Unfortunately, the fragmentation of the failing old order and the disarray of its former powerful institution are all that many of us recognize. What we do not appreciate and what we refuse to accept is a fait accompli that the new order is already here.

Any new approach to the politics within nation-states and their political systems, as well as nation-states and their diplomacy, must be grounded in the dynamics of the new global cyber information reality. This reality is generated and sustained by the commanding forces unleashed from an information-communication-technology platform that has created a One-World-Information-Space. There is a shifting paradigm of tectonic proportion from the familiar and traditional place-location-centered world, with its powerful centripetal force vying to maintain supremacy, to a new frontier world with its centrifugal forces spreading its controlling distributive network planet-wide, creating a One-World-Information-Space.

Several questions may be asked of this fractured shifting paradigm of the global environment, notably: What is good government? What is the appropriate political system and leadership? What is the role of the state? Is there a need for a new social contract between the state, government, leadership, and the citizens? Scanning the real world provides the context, but it is in understanding the knowledge, the concepts are formulated, and as such a conceptual framework to answer these critical questions follows.

The Paradigm Power of Global Business

The Impact of Global Business on Politics and Sovereignty of Nation-States

Already large private enterprises with a global reach have successfully laid claim to the emergent One-World-Information-Space. Some of these business entities are functioning in all nation-states of the world and can thus administer and manage their global ownership in a highly competitive world market. Their business priorities, policies, strategies, and execution capabilities, and their approach to delivering products and services to their local, regional, and global customers may well serve as an insightful framework for the embattled nation-states and their societal agenda to improve the quality of life of their citizens. Figure 19.3 depicts a schematic picture of how business is linked in an adaptive framework in the One-World-Information-Space.

These powerful enterprises are so successful at competing in a capitalist global market due to this business approach, with a central focus on satisfying customer and shareholder expectations to improve their quality of life.

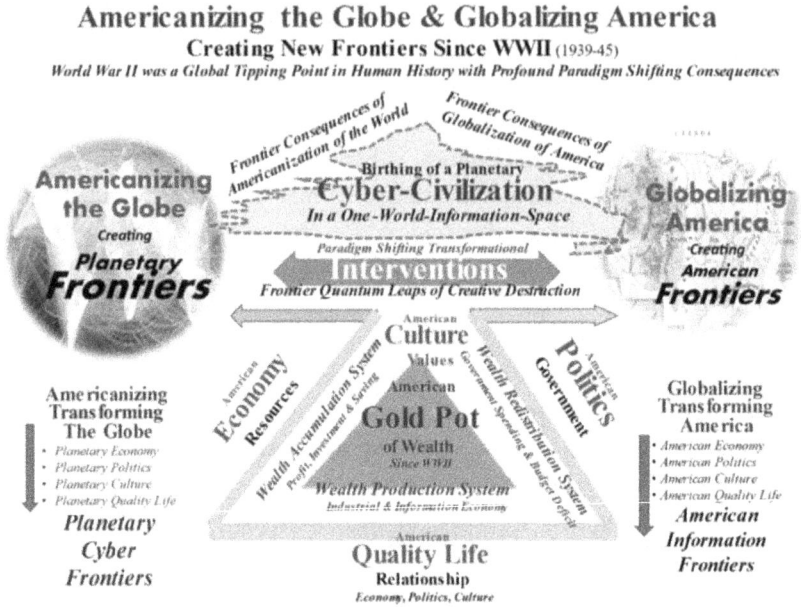

Figure 19.3 A global business approach to government in a new world order, a knowledge service enterprise in a One-World-Information-Space.

Source: Developed by Manfred Jantzen, author.

Yet is this not also the goal of good government? Surely, both the business approach and the traditional political approach reside in a complex societal and cultural framework that shapes their successful execution. Nevertheless, the current global business enterprises both dominate the world market and wield influence over local and national governmental direction and policies, including international relations and policies of global institutions.

It is therefore evident that the business approach guided by the political agenda of the government can be demonstrative of an emerging model for the nation-state and its societal priorities of improving the quality of life for all its citizens. While customer expectations drive the business model, citizen expectations drive the political model. The rise in global populism may well have its roots and sustainable power in business enterprises, as there appears to be a global customer expectation revolution that has spread to the political systems. In this One-World-Information-Space, national power defines national borders and political boundaries, and as such the power of the nation-state, sovereignty, and border control will be the most unresolved critical political issues in this emerging period of a global world disorder (Knight 2022).

Frontier Disruptive Leadership
Knowledge Service Center
In a One-World-Information-Space

Frontier Disruptive Leadership

In Economic, Political & Cultural Context
Opportunities, Risks & Limitations

Disruptive Frontier Leadership views:
- *The National State* (Frontier Administration).
- *International Institutions* (Frontier Diplomacy).
- *Business Enterprises* (Frontier Management)
  - ➤ *as an interconnected, interactive, interrelated and integrated global information space and*

  - ➤ *functioning as complex adaptive systems in a global frontier environment (System Thinking).*

The Frontier Leadership Challenge is to explore and exploit the opportunities, vulnerabilities and risks of
- **Limitless** Information Communication Technology Space
- **Borderless** Global Information Market Economy
- **Reality of Political Borders** of Sovereign States
- **Existence** of **Local Societal Cultures** with deeply embedded value and performance systems.

Knowledge Service Center (KSC)

in a One-World-Information Space
Core Professional (CP's) as Leaders and Managers

- *Core professionals(CPs) lead and manage the KSC as a network of relationships, a community of interests and stakeholders (Customers, Citizens, Shareholders)*

- *KSC operates a sophisticated Information Communication Technology (ICT) infrastructure including Artificial Intelligence (AI) Capabilities*

- *KSC scans, collects, analyses (Big Data) for changes in the global & national environment.*

- *KSC distributes external and internal information for critical decision making.*

- *KSC provides intelligence to frontier leadership for formulation and execution of strategies and evaluation of solutions.*

Figure 19.4 Creating new frontiers since WWII, Americanizing the globe, globalizing America.

Source: Developed by Manfred Jantzen, author.

A striking feature of the global world disorder is schematically reflected in Figure 19.4 which shows the underlying forces that have created a global tension between Americanizing the globe and globalizing America. This tension is at the source of the globalization debate and depicts the frontiers that are evolving after World War II, now being confronted by the continuous power shifts in the aftermath of the COVID-19 pandemic.

The new global *realpolitik* and the emerging populism demand a voice for its customer-citizens. Although the global business enterprises thrive in a One-World-Information-Space supported by a global information-communication-technology platform, they do not operate in a societal vacuum. Many international societies and civilizations have become willingly or unwillingly Americanized. This is inclusive of the spread of the liberal order. As such, the dominant American businesses with advances in the information-community-technology platform have subtly transferred their business practices grounded in American culture to other nations. Their political agenda of democratizing a global civilization poses a danger to political systems and the sovereignty of nations, especially small nation-states. These powerful business enterprises therefore appear to have an excess of influence on global politics.

Leadership Challenges for Business Leaders

As a new breed of business leaders rush to lay claim to this new global frontier space, typically without the formal consent of the existing political system, they threaten political leadership and the power of global institutions. At present, only a handful of elite business enterprises are more powerful than even the most powerful nation-states in wielding influence over the behavior and thinking of their customers around the world. The unintended consequence of the rise of these few elite businesses is that they impose their own political agenda on the rest of the world and face no consequences. This privilege is demonstrative of the failing political systems of the dominant state, their government, and their political leadership. Global business leaders may be flourishing, but they are also out of the control of the political system of the nation-state and its deeply embedded societal culture and value systems.

The search for growth models in this frontier world should therefore start with an understanding of the formulation and execution of the successful business growth strategy in a One-World-Information-Space. A fundamental difference between the traditional and frequently linear growth models, which were predominantly advocated by an academic elite, and the business growth strategy in a turbulent global environment, is that the business growth is based on a bottom-up approach to customer satisfaction whereas the government's strategy is based on a top-down approach to improving the citizens' quality of life.

According to Lund et al. (2021, vi), the future of work after COVID-19 will witness massive disruption to the workforce and generate large-scale workforce transition which accelerates many of the work imperatives that were already clear before COVID-19. They argue that the impact of the pandemic on work will see workers facing unprecedented transitions requiring wholly new skills which will continue to its shape and direction in the years to come (Lund et al. 2021, 21). The trends in remote work, digitization, and automation will see shifts in labor demands across occupations, as occupational transitions may increase by as much as 15 percent by 2030 (Lund et al. 2021, 14). This, as Lund et al. (2021, vii) note will require business leaders and policymakers (to) build out digital infrastructure, enable faster reskilling, and innovate new worker benefits and support mechanisms.

Regionalism – Sleepwalking into a Crisis?

According to the Global Risks Report 2019, the world is facing a growing number of complex and interconnected challenges – from slowing growth and persistent economic inequality to climate change, geopolitical tensions, and accelerating the pace of the fourth industrial revolution. In isolation, these are daunting challenges; faced simultaneously, we will struggle if we do not work together in a collaborative and multi-stakeholder approach to shared global problems (World Economic Forum 2019, 5).

Is the world sleepwalking into a crisis? The idea of "taking back control" – whether domestically from political rivals or externally from multilateral or supranational organizations – resonates across many countries. Although we are increasingly subject to global problems and the risks continue to intensify, the collective will to tackle them appears to be lacking. Five areas of concern are thereby highlighted: economic vulnerabilities, geopolitical tensions, societal and political strains, environmental fragilities, and technological instabilities.

Political Stress of Frontier Leadership?

The interplay of global economic forces would suggest that regionalism is once again in the offering, but the old models are not aligned to the emerging power structure, or indeed to the demands of economic development. The old orthodoxies of customs unions are facing political stress, as seen in the BREXIT dilemma; closed models of integration as evident in Latin and Central America are bursting at the seams. Open regionalism clashed with the global rules of international trade regimes embedded in the World Trade Organization. Furthermore, in finance, market power far outstrips regulatory controls. Even the political legitimacy of integration models is now being questioned. In this economic terrain, it is useful to determine whether economic convergence-integration without borders will be a new frontier in integration models (Dookeran 2013, 18; Malaki 2013, 87). This is but a call for frontier disruptive leadership in a One-World-Information-Space, as depicted in Figure 19.5. It shows the dichotomy between disruptive leadership and knowledge systems.

Questions about the Role of the State in the Caribbean

In the Caribbean, these shifts and tensions were succinctly expressed by the Prime Minister of Jamaica (1994–2008), P.J. Patterson as follows:

Everywhere, there is a growing acceptance that the old and traditional style of governance is obsolete. But even though the old order is no longer extant, that new order for which we yearn has yet to be established as a result of constant and cataclysmic changes virtually with each passing day. Consequently, there is still an ongoing search to create a brand-new paradigm for the exercise of political power and the management of national economies. To pass the final litmus test, any replacement must be accountable, responsible, inclusive, open, and transparent or it will not survive. (Patterson 2012, xi–xii)

Figure 19.5 Frontier disruptive leadership leading a knowledge service center in a One-World-Information-Space.

Source: Jantzen (2016).

This idea was articulated by Dookeran (2012, xvii) in an opening statement: "The partnership approach to distributing power, and entrenching good governance and development in small states, is rooted in political philosophy." This raises two questions: By what right or need do people form states? and What is the best form of the state? In answer, a consensus eventually emerged that the state would refer to a set of enduring institutions through which power is distributed and its use justified; the government would refer to those who manage state institutions and create the laws by which the people, including the governors, would be bounded according to the social compact.

As such, new questions have come to the core. How is digital transformation fueled? What are the implications for economic strategy in a data-driven economy? What policy choices will drive innovation in an age of transition? How will cyber security be integrated into strategic agendas? There are many questions concerning how. It is irrefutable that the changing political calculus will usher in new stress tests in decision-making, and periods of extreme uncertainty. Increasing emphasis will now be placed on the role of the state.

Turning around an economy often requires a shift from the step-by-step process of conventional models toward new approaches based on capturing strategic options. The conditions for such a shift are more likely to emerge during crises, such as riots, natural disasters, and pandemics. The role of the state in economic development has been a central question for leaders, as they always seek a balance between ideology and strategy. It has always been about a political equilibrium, although at times through the optics of economic development.

Relying on a state-centric model for development or an unbridled market system were the extremes of policy choices, creating a false dichotomy between the private sector and the public sector. The new incarnation of this dichotomy is private–public partnership. None of this will endure, but we need to know where we are, if only to shift gears in a time of crisis. How must we shift gears at this time?

Rapid economic growth requires a new look at the role of the state in economic development, a shift toward a role where the state acts primarily as a catalyst for economic development. There are past instances of this scenario. The obstacles to the growth process lie in the undue reliance on the state and its outdated controls and systems. Major economic costs are incurred. Yet, market forces themselves will not suffice to protect the public good. Perhaps we should embrace the notion of a catalytic role for the state in economic development. This notion is strategic and was employed by Singapore Prime Minister Lee Quan Yew in promoting state investment at the time into global ventures in shipping, finance, air and sea travel. The circumstances are different today, but the logic of a catalytic role of the state could change the calculus of state economic activities.

Pandemic as Global Political Stress Test

In the years ahead, undoubtedly, there will be new seating arrangements at the table of global affairs in which the sphere of influence cannot be taken for granted. We refer to this age of contagion as the One Health Strategy of which the jarring pandemic of today testifies, accompanied by shifting alignments of political forces. Some have postulated that these unprecedented times have threatened the breakdown of global order. Undeniably, the world will face a global political stress test in the years ahead (Dookeran 2020). In what way will that manifest?

The BREXIT dilemma and Trump's presidency are both indicative of the deep political stress affecting liberal democracy. There are conflicting views on this assertion. For instance, Colgan and Keohane (2017, 36) ascribe this to "populism . . . defined by a faith in strong leaders and a dislike of limits on sovereignty and powerful institutions," while Acharya (2017, 272) refers to Trump's power as a consequence of the collapse and not a cause. In spite of the polarity in opinions, the core of the matter is the uncertainty surrounding the emerging world as well as the vital need for an alternative beyond the hegemonic, politically unstable global order.

Survival and Sustainability in a New Order of Things

Measures at recovery from the devastation of the pandemic have already seen changes in the logic of economic management, as the alarm once held by deficit financing has given way to the need for it. This highlights the antiquity of the old paradigm. Health security is on the daily radar screen, and the risks continue to rise just as new risks surface. Consequently, the alignment of world power is shifting in uncertain directions.

The void in global leadership emerging from the pandemic and the global recovery efforts is likely to spill over into a new order of things. In a recent article entitled "A New Crisis Playbook for an Uncertain World," the authors offer rules to guide leaders during these challenging times – the first rule asserts that "leaders must gain the trust of all the stakeholders in the communities where they operate" (Katsos and Miklian 2021, 7). Already, there are signals from various states and bodies that action is required. For example, there are those who are re-evaluating the outdated orthodoxy of recovery economics which is under stress; there are those who are calling for an emergency G20 gathering to fill the void in leadership; and there are wealthier nations who are advancing priority claims to the vaccine while low-income countries face exposure for several more years. These issues are certainly trigger points in the stress tests, but they demonstrate something much more telling: a lack of coherency on how the politics will respond on the global scale. This disruption will spill over into regional and national arenas.

What are the trends in thinking about the perspectives in the near future? First, political postures will not be the sole preserve of the wealthier, more powerful countries. The world will bear witness to new assertions from other nations regarding global affairs. For instance, in Europe, there is the advance of a pathway to a strategic autonomy in a more resilient political terrain; in the Far East, there is the quest to build immunity to global political rivalries; in Africa, there is the intensifying call to promote greater continental diplomatic leverage; in Latin America, there is the refusal to be neglected in the upcoming global re-shift; and the small island nations of the Caribbean and the Pacific vie for survival and sustainability.

For small countries, the following global perspectives on governance and security agenda must be addressed. There are issues regarding health security, such as the effectiveness of regional pandemic surveillance and coordination of health security measures, and the adoption of sustainable self-financing instruments to provide universal health coverage for the society, including the poor. Furthermore, the matter of democratizing access to global research and products in medical science – such as the COVID-19 Vaccines Global Access Facility – will require a revitalization and reform of the World Health Organization (WHO).

In regard to governance, the resetting of the platform of financial flows is imperative to the reworking of the international financial institutions and the global marketplace. Additionally, there is a need for a diplomatic initiative to establish channels of communication with the centers of global power, as well as a renewed focus on the technical issues such as the universal vulnerabilities index and the subject of ocean governance and security for small island developing states.

Rethinking Reform of the World Health Organization

In the wake of the COVID-19 pandemic, there have been several calls from experts and politicians for reform of the WHO, to rethink the governance of the WHO, make it more independent and less politicized, and renew its worldwide mandate to promote health, set international health standards, keep the world safe, and serve the vulnerable (Kelland and Mason 2021). The WHO has a broad mandate as a coordinating authority on international health issues but faces challenges in inflexible funding, bureaucratic complexity, gaps in its access to quality essential health services, and its capacity to respond better to future pandemics (KFF 2021).

Having dealt with successive waves of various health challenges being declared as Public Health Emergencies of International Concern (PHEIC) within the twenty-first century alone, many scholars and health experts have called for greater enforcing mechanisms within the body, as all the resolutions and counsel given by the WHO are non-binding on member states. Alas, the time of reckoning has come due to COVID-19 where states are now faced with the realities of dealing with a pandemic. In today's era of globalization, with the mass movement of people and goods, the incidence of further PHEICs and pandemics are increased (Abraham 2022).

For the post-pandemic age, it is expected that the WHO through the International Health Regulations will give the institution some teeth to match its bark. Given the devastation of the pandemic, it is expected that calls to be heralded by members of the international community that some resolutions and conventions agreed upon by the World Health Assembly are binding on states with consequences for states that are judged to be ignoring their global commitments and duties. This raises issues of the trade-off and conflicts between national compliance and sovereign rights in a wider interconnected world. As such, the WHO is expected to increase its technical assistance mechanisms to help developing states improve their data collection and reporting facilities as a key part of preparing/circumventing another PHEIC or pandemic situation (Abraham 2022).

Shifting to a Cyber-Social Contract

The social state is metamorphosing into the cyber state. The role of the social state must change from control and ownership to facilitator catalyst and partnership. The dual economy of America can prosper, as the economics of capitalism can live with the economics of the social state. There is a clash of global civilization, between cultures and between the dual economy of China with a state-centric ideology and the dual economy of America with its market-centered ideology. This dual economy model is not sustainable, and there is an urgent need for a new convergence model under the emerging cyber state. In the digital ecosystem, Inglis and Krejsa (2022) call for a "new social contract for the digital age," a cyber-social contract to build thrust. This, they argue will require a high level of collaboration between government and industry that will reap untold social, economic, and geopolitical benefits.

In the frontiers ahead, a widening gap between theory and practice will emerge. Policy directions will remain unclear, as both theoretical constructs and policy action are in a period of upheaval and cataclysm. At the core of the analytics are the convergence of dual economies within and across countries, globalization as a process to strengthen regionalism, and the emergence of multi-track as opposed to multilateralism in the practice of diplomacy. The old pedagogical distinction between developed and developing countries may no longer serve as a useful hypothesis. Thus, in a paradoxical sense, the boundaries of scholarship are opening to new possibilities, new frontiers, in the cyberspace, and social contracts of tomorrow's world.

References

Abraham Ryan. 2022. "The Practice of Global Health Diplomacy during Public Health Emergences of International Concern (PHEIC) with an Added Highlight on Caribbean Diplomacy." Paper presented at SALISES, The University of the West Indies, St. Augustine.

Acharya, Amitav. 2017. "After Liberal Hegemony: The Advent of a Multiplex World Order." *Ethics & International Affairs*, 31 (3): 271–85. https://doi.org/10.1017/S089267941700020X.

Bustillo, Ines, Helvia Velloso, Winston Dookeran, and Daniel E. Perrotti. 2018. *Resilience and Capital Flows in the Caribbean*. Washington, DC: Economic Commission for Latin America and the Caribbean.

Colgan, Jeff D., and Robert O. Keohane. 2017. "The Liberal Order Is Rigged: Fix It Now or Watch It Wither." *Foreign Affairs*, 96 (3): 36–44.

Dookeran, Winston. 2012. *Power, Politics and Performance: A Partnership Approach to Development*. Kingston, Jamaica: Ian Randle Publishers.

———. 2013. "A New Frontier for Caribbean Convergence." *Caribbean Journal of International Relations and Diplomacy*, 1 (2): 5–20.

———. 2020. "Pandemics as Global Political Stress Tests." Paper presented at The Year Ahead Virtual Conference Carlton University, Ottawa, Canada, 4 December.

———. 2022. *The Caribbean on the Edge: The Political Stress of Stability, Equality, and Diplomacy*. Toronto: University of Toronto Press.

Estevadeordal, Antoni, and Louis Goodman (eds.). 2017. *21st Century Cooperation: Regional Public Goods, Global Governance, and Sustainable Development*. Abington, Oxon: Routledge.

Inglis, Chris, and Harry Krejsa. 2022. "The Cyber Social Contract: How to Rebuild Trust in a Digital World." https://www.foreignaffairs.com/articles/united-states/2022-02-21/cyber-social-contract.

Inter-American Development Bank. 2018. *Connecting the Dots: A Road Map for Better Integration in Latin America and the Caribbean*. Washington, DC: Inter-American Development Bank.

Jantzen, Manfred. 2016. *Solution Leadership in Borderless Developing States*. Port of Spain, Trinidad and Tobago: Foundation for Leadership and Governance.

Katsos, John E., and Jason Miklian. 2021. "A New Crisis Playbook for an Uncertain World." *Harvard Business Review Digital Articles* (November 17): 1–14. https://search-ebscohost-com.ezproxygateway.sastudents.uwi.tt/login.aspx?direct=true&db=bth&AN=153917814&site=ehost-live.

Kelland, Kate, and Josephine Mason. 2021. "WHO Reform needed in the Wake of Pandemic, Public Experts Say." https://www.reuters.com/article/us-health-coronavirus-crisis-idUSKBN29I210.

Keohane, Robert. 1969. "Review: Lilliputians' Dilemmas: Small States in International Politics." *International Organization*, 23 (3): 291–310.

KFF (Kaiser Family Foundation). 2021. "The US Government and the World Health Organization." https://www.kff.org/coronavirus-covid-19/fact-ssheet/the-u-s-government-and-the-world-health-organization/.

Knight, Andy (Professor, Department of Political Science, University of Alberta, Canada). 2022. E-mail message to author, 25 January.

Lund, Susan, Anu Madgavkar, James Manyika, Sven Smit, Kweilin Ellingrud, and Olivia Robinson. 2021. *The Future of Work after Co-Vid 19*. New York: McKinsey Global Institute. https://www.mckinsey.com/featured-insights/future-of-work/the-future-of-work-after-covid-19.

Lund, Susan, James Manyika, Jonathan Woetzel, Jacques Bughin, Mekala Krishnan, Jeongmin Seong, and Mac Muir. 2019. *Globalization in Transition: The Future of Trade and Value Chains*. New York: McKinsey Global Institute. https://www .mckinsey.com/featured-insights/innovation-and-growth/globalization-in -transition-the-future-of-trade-and-value-chains.

Malaki, Akhil. 2013. "A Partnership Approach to Caribbean Convergence." *Caribbean Journal of International Relations and Diplomacy*, 1 (3): 83–94.

Patterson, P.J. 2012. *Foreword to Power, Politics and Performance: A Partnership Approach to Development*, by Winston Dookeran. Kingston, Jamaica: Ian Randle Publishers.

Shafik, Minouche. 2021. *What We Owe Each Other: A New Social Contract*. New York City: Penguin, Random House.

Shannon, C.E. 1948. "A Mathematical Theory of Communication." *Bell Technical Journal*, 27 (3): 379–423. doi: 10.1002/j.1538-7305.1948.tb01338.x.

Ulgen, Sinan, Anirudh Burman, Ding Yifan, Rozlyn C. Engel, Tobin Hansen, Wei He, Ceylan Inan, et al. 2022. *Rewiring Globalization*. Washington, DC: Carnegie Endowment for International Peace. https://carnegieendowment.org/files/Rewirin gGlobalization_final_Revised1.pdf.

World Economic Forum. 2019. *The Global Risks Report 2019*. Geneva: World Economic Forum. https://www.weforum.org/reports/the-global-risks-report-2019.

Afterword

KAREN SANDERSON COLE

One ought never to turn one's back on a threatened danger and try to run away from it. If you do that, you will double the danger. But if you meet it promptly and without flinching, you will reduce the danger by half

– Winston Churchill

Every new age is led by visionaries, and nowhere are visionaries more unquestionably needed than in a crisis. As it relates to economics, "No previous infectious disease outbreak, including the Spanish Flu, has impacted the stock market as forcefully as the COVID-19 pandemic" (Baker et al. 2020). Countries, economies too, must employ crucial shifts in thinking to create new research and policies. The current climate requires a "Reset or Perish" because "every sector, industry, company, startup and indeed every individual must adapt to survive" (Ramchandani 2020).

Disruptions in the economy of First World nations spell even greater economic disaster for developing countries. The prime minister of Barbados, Mia Mottley, called for measures that "must consider not only the strong but also the most vulnerable." She pointed to the grave debt within the Caribbean region – estimated at about 8.8 billion dollars for 2020–2021 (Amanpour 2020). Many of these economies depend on tourism, which has experienced a great loss in projected revenue.

Tourism is not the only casualty. Jimenez and Daniel (2020) quantify the impact through the realities of weaker health systems, inadequate social protection systems, and limited space to provide a fiscal response. This is a concern shared by leaders in the region. Prime Minister Andrew Holness of Jamaica has said, "I don't see a trade-off between health and economy. I don't see the two things as mutually exclusive: You need healthy people to make the economy work and a working economy gives you healthy people" (*Jamaica Observer* 2020).

This rapidly changing world context is one of the reasons why this volume is timely and appropriate. Here, the focus is on answering these questions and more by analyzing the connection between theory and practice, examining economic flows, and offering for serious consideration a framework for a reset agenda. The Caribbean needs to be specific, focused on the frontiers that loom large before it. Our attitude to change matters.

In a world where developed countries are themselves grappling with internal issues and problems, the Caribbean can no longer sit still and await handouts, guidance, or leadership. Research and policy need to move beyond a traditional pattern that is based on a static concept of the world, for it is not business as usual. Our new objectives must be clearly articulated, measurable, and realistic – cognizant of the process, people, and resources needed. Progress has to be seen as a community responsibility. There must be a national and regional commitment by all political parties while still allowing for variation and fresh ideas in how the vision is accomplished.

It is evident that current Caribbean research and policy need to be replaced with new objectives. This has been the focus that has been argued so eloquently in this collection. The contributors to this volume have demonstrated ably and innovatively practical ways in which theory can be reconceptualized and applied to challenges that the region faces in traditional areas of health, governance, economies, and diplomacy – impacted with renewed force by the COVID-19 pandemic. The text is also significant in continuing to provide evidence of the challenge that the University of the West Indies had set in 1948 to be that light rising from the West (Oriens Ex Occidente Lux), distinguishing itself not only in the areas of innovation in medicine and the arts but also in the area of economics.

Economies have taken a hard hit, making it evident that new ways of thinking and doing things are paramount. The current pandemic has seen big countries with trillion-dollar budgets humbled to the same extent or more than small countries with few resources. In fact, the new prominence of previously little-known technology companies has also made it clear that the time is right for anyone with the right vision to offer well-timed solutions for burgeoning problems.

This collection is elegantly poised to present for serious consideration a framework for a reset agenda, pointing to sources – some traditionally overlooked, others new – as avenues through which sustainable development and economic resilience can be enhanced. It reminds us that there are new opportunities before us, and we need those, as represented here, who can insightfully see into the future, grasp the potential of the present, and strategize for survival.

References

Amanpour, Christiane. 2020. "CNNi's Amanpour (April 29) Featuring Barbados Prime Minister Mia Amor Mottley," 29 April. News Video, 10:59. https://youtu.be/awL3tKAFiU8.

Baker, Scott et al. 2020. "The Unprecedented Stock Market Reaction to COVID-19," 19 June. https://bfi.chicago.edu/working-paper/the-unprecedented-stock-market -reaction-to-covid-19/.

Jamaica Observer. 2020. "Tourism Industry Has to Prepare for Post-Covid-19." https:// www.jamaicaobserver.com/latestnews/Tourism_industry_has_to_prepare_for_post _COVID19_?

Jimenez, Miguel, and Egas Daniel. 2020. "Mozambique's Response to COVID-19: Challenges and Questions." *IGC*, 8 July. https://www.theigc.org/blogmozambiques -response-to-covid-19-challenges-and-questions/.

Ramchandani, Nisha. 2020. "Reset or Perish: A Guide to Adaptive Leadership." *Eller Executive Education*, 18 June. https://executive.eller.arizona.edu/news/2020/06/reset -or-perish-guide-adaptive-leadership.

About the Contributors

David Anyanwu graduated with a Ph.D. in International Relations from the Institute of International Relations of the University of the West Indies, St. Augustine, in 2013. His research interests cover convergence, regionalism, competitiveness, trade barriers, and public security. He leads Federal Government Relations for Cargill Limited in Canada.

Vaalmikki Arjoon is a lecturer in Finance at the University of the West Indies. Dr. Arjoon previously held faculty positions at the University of Nottingham (the United Kingdom and China campuses). He also works very closely with several local and international business chambers and is a notable media commentator on economic and financial issues.

Miriam L. Campanella was a senior fellow at the European Centre for International Political Economy (ECIPE) and the Jean Monnet Professor at the University of Turin, Italy. Professor Campanella conducted research at MIT on general systems theories and the economics of complex systems and has written extensively on the subject.

Vijay Kumar Chattu is a medical doctor specialized in global health and international relations based at the University of Toronto. He is also Adjunct Professor at the University of Alberta and Visiting Research Fellow at the United Nations University-CRIS, Belgium. He co-authored over 350 publications and is listed among the world's top two percent Scientists in Public Health by Stanford Rankings.

Winston Dookeran is Professor of Practice at the University of the West Indies. He is the author of several books, among them *The Caribbean on the Edge* (University of Toronto Press, 2022). He is a graduate of the London School of Economics and Political Science (UK) and of the University of Manitoba (Canada) which also conferred him with an Honorary Doctor of Laws (*honoris causa*) degree. Professor Dookeran held appointments at Harvard University, the University of Toronto, the United Nations University (Helsinki), and at the UN Economic Commission for Latin America and the Caribbean (Washington). He also served as governor of the Central Bank and as Minister of Finance in

Trinidad and Tobago. Winston Dookeran received numerous awards including Trinidad and Tobago's highest honor, the Order of the Republic of Trinidad and Tobago (ORTT) in Economics, and India's prestigious overseas award, the Pravasi Bharatiya Samman (PBSA) for meritorious achievements in public service.

Wendy C. Grenade holds a Ph.D. and Master's degree in international studies from the University of Miami, with concentrations in comparative politics and international relations. Currently, Dr. Grenade is Professor in the Department of Humanities and Social Sciences at St. George's University, Grenada. She previously taught in the Department of Government at the University of the West Indies, Barbados.

M. Raymond Izarali is a philosopher and Associate Professor in the Department of Criminology at Wilfrid Laurier University, Canada. Dr. Izarali's research interests include globalization, global terrorism and security, human rights theory, Africa, the Caribbean, and South Asia. He has published numerous edited books, among them *Terrorism, Security and Development in South Asia: National, Regional and Global Implications* (Routledge, 2021). Dr. Izarali also published peer-reviewed articles in the *Global Studies Journal, International Journal of Social Inquiry, Critical Criminology, Africa Review, Perspectives on Terrorism, and The Round Table Journal.* He is a former director of the Tshepo Institute for the Study of Contemporary Africa at Wilfrid Laurier University.

Faies Jafar holds a Ph.D. in international relations and a Master's degree in civil engineering from the UWI. His research focus includes small states behavior, foreign policy analysis, Middle East politics, and IR theories. He is a senior instructor at the University of Trinidad and Tobago, Project Management and Civil Infrastructure Systems Group.

Manfred Jantzen is former director of the doctoral (DBA) programme at the Arthur Lok Jack Global Business School, UWI, Trinidad. He received his Ph.D. from the University of Wisconsin. Dr. Jantzen is the author of *Solution Leadership in Developing Countries: Organizational Interventions in a One-World-Information-Space* and a pioneer in "frontier studies."

Preeya Mohan is Senior Fellow at the Sir Arthur Lewis Institute of Social and Economic Studies, University of the West Indies, St. Augustine. Dr. Mohan has conducted research on, and is widely published on, Caribbean economic policy and sustainable development, and is an applied economist skilled in the use of econometric methods and data analysis.

Annita Montoute is Lecturer in international organization, global governance and multilateralism at UWI, Trinidad. Dr. Montoute's research interests include civil society, security, and the Caribbean's external relations. Her books include *Changing Cuba-U.S. Relations. Implications for CARICOM States* (2020) and *The ACP Group and the EU Development Partnership: Beyond the North-South Debate* (2017).

Shane Justin Pantin is a judicial research counsel at the Judiciary of Trinidad and Tobago. He obtained a BA (history) and LLB from the University of the West Indies, Trinidad, and a Legal Education Certificate (LEC) from the Hugh Wooding Law School. His areas of interest include world and Caribbean history, and international law.

Khushbu Rai is a senior economist at the Ministry of Commerce, Trade, Tourism and Transport in Fiji. She has worked as a young professional at the World Trade Organization representing the South Pacific. Ms. Rai obtained her Master's in Development Economics with Honours from the University of the South Pacific (USP) as well as her Postgraduate Certificate in Tertiary Teaching.

Karen Sanderson Cole is Lecturer in the Faculty of Humanities and Education, the University of the West Indies (UWI), St. Augustine. Dr. Cole holds a Ph.D. in languages and linguistics from the UWI and has an interest in the study of biographies of Caribbean personalities.

June Soomer holds a Ph.D. in history from the University of the West Indies. She lectured at the UWI and universities in the United States, and worked at the Eastern Caribbean Central Bank from 1996 to 2006. She was Saint Lucia's ambassador to the OECS and CARICOM from 2008 to 2016 and the secretary-general of the Association of Caribbean States from 2016 to 2020.

Helvia Velloso is Economic Affairs Officer at UN-ECLAC in Washington DC, focusing on financial flows to Latin America and the Caribbean with emphasis on development and green financing, and macro-policy analysis of the US economy. She was trained in economics at the University of California at Berkeley and the Federal University of Rio de Janeiro.

Index

www.ingramcontent.com/pod-product-compliance
Lightning Source LLC
Chambersburg PA
CBHW021806270326
41932CB00007B/81